# Human Agency at Work

Michael Goller

# Human Agency at Work

## An Active Approach towards Expertise Development

With a foreword by Prof. Dr. Christian Harteis

Springer VS

Michael Goller
Paderborn, Germany

Dissertation submitted and accepted at the University of Paderborn (Original title: "Agency at work: A quantitative study on the professional development of geriatric care nurses"), Germany, 2017

OnlinePlus material to this book can be available on
http://www.springer.com/978-3-658-18286-1

ISBN 978-3-658-18285-4 ISBN 978-3-658-18286-1 (eBook)
DOI 10.1007/978-3-658-18286-1

Library of Congress Control Number: 2017941051

Springer VS


Printed on acid-free paper

This Springer VS imprint is published by Springer Nature
The registered company is Springer Fachmedien Wiesbaden GmbH
The registered company address is: Abraham-Lincoln-Str. 46, 65189 Wiesbaden, Germany

*For Elisabeth*

# Foreword

It is an important educational task to prepare subsequent generations for responding to societal tasks and requirements and to enable them to contribute to societal welfare through gainful employment. The paradigm of permanently changing work conditions raised the main claim of European educational policy: Lifelong learning. How well and how far individuals can contribute to societal working tasks substantially depends on the development of their competences and capabilities. These have to be permanently refreshed and reshaped in the context of daily work. Hence, workplace learning became an important issue for organising work as well as for educational research.

Individuals differ in their success in workplace learning. Even though there is evidence that occupational status is a crucial factor influencing learning opportunities at work, workplace learning occurs at all levels of employment: blue-collar jobs, white-collar jobs, common labour, service workers, or managers. Educational researchers have established the concept of agency which is an attempt to describe and understand stakeholders' achievements regarding the aforementioned economic and social goals. The concept describes individuals' capacity to make intentional choices and to act on these choices in ways that make a difference in their professional lives. Agency comprises skills, attitudes, and beliefs which support individuals to act independently in order to transform workplace practices. Maintaining agency implies strategies of advancing and renewing skills and competencies. This requires individuals' participating in cultures of knowledge creation and the exchange of knowledge. The hallmarks of such participation are raising crucial questions about work, identifying opportunities, and engaging in learning activities. Hence, agency makes a difference in the success of subsequent workplace learning and the development of professional expertise.

In his comprehensive study, Michael Goller examines the construct of work agency, which is prominently used and discussed in research publications on workplace learning. The construct emerges in international discourse mainly in contexts that follow a sociocultural paradigm. Their focus is mainly on qualitative and reconstructive research approaches that aim at understanding specific interaction processes. They neither intend to generalise impact interrelations nor do they lead to precise differentiations of the construct, which would be understood as operationalisation in quantitative research approaches. Michael Goller criticises the abstract nature of the research discourse on agency and intends to further develop the construct and the research discourse by developing and empirically examining a model of impact relationships.

Therefore, Michael Goller analyses agency in the context of daily working life. He applies the prevalent understanding of agency and interprets employees as active agents in the context of their work environments, who can shape their work circumstances through active participation, (partly) independent decision-making and (partly) autonomous behaviour and acting. From an educational perspective, agency can be considered as a precondition for workplace learning and professional development.

Michael Goller conducts a comprehensive literature review of educational, psychological, and social sciences research on workplace learning and develops an operationalisable construct of agency by considering human agency, on the one hand, as the capability and the tendency towards intentional decisions and, on the other hand, identified activities aiming at influencing the work environment. Hence, agency is considered as an antecedent of agentic behaviour. Individuals act, decide, and behave differently. Theoretically, each concrete individual behaviour at the workplace can be located on a continuum between the extreme points of completely agentic behaviour and completely non-agentic behaviour. Michael Goller works out empirical evidence that agentic behaviour at work depends on three influences: (a) agentic competence (i. e., the capability to set goals and to decide), (b) agency belief (i. e., the belief to bear agency competence), and (c) agency personality as a trait.

As a theoretical framework for professional development, Michael Goller refers to research on expertise which considers the improvement of performance through learning from experience, learning in social interactions at work, and by the exploration of artefacts and resources at the workplace. Observing agentic behaviour related to professional development, he focuses on self-initiated (a) creation of relevant experiences, (b) help seeking and feedback seeking, and (c) participation in formal learning opportunities at work. Additionally, he considers autonomy, social support, and time pressure at work as environmental influences on the probability of agentic behaviour at work.

On the basis of his theoretical analyses, Michael Goller raises his research question on how human agency explains workplace learning and professional development. He specifies three context-specific sub-questions, which aim at clarifying (a) agency's influence on agent behaviour in the workplace, (b) the influence of agentic behaviour on the development of professional expertise, and (c) the influence of context factors on agentic behaviour in the workplace. To answer these questions, Michael Goller chooses the domain of elderly care nursing and conducts three subsequent empirical studies.

Firstly, an interview study with nine experienced senior nurses in management positions clarifies the relevance and appropriateness of the theoretically derived constructs for the practice of elderly care nursing. Such a clarification study was necessary because there are no such studies on agency in elderly care nursing. The interviews focus on the behaviour and professional development of elderly care workers and organisational conditions at nursing homes. In essence, the interviews confirm the relevance and appropriateness of the selected constructs for the domain of elderly care nursing, and they contribute to further clarifications of the theoretical framework regarding contextual influences at the workplace. On this basis, Michael Goller develops a comprehensive research model that maps impact relations between agency, agentic behaviour, and professional expertise – including the consideration of context factors of workplaces.

Secondly, a pilot study in a selected nursing home examines the research design and the selected scales and measurements. Large parts of the design, scales, and measurements can be confirmed. However, it turns out that the planned use of social network analyses for the measurement of expertise does not achieve sufficient acceptance in the field. Hence, Michael Goller uses self-report scales for the measurement of expertise in the main study.

Thirdly, 909 elderly caregivers from 32 nursing homes participated in the main study, of which 879 persons could be included in the analyses. Michael Goller decided to use a cross-validation approach and divided the data set randomly into a calibration ($n_k = 432$) and a validation ($n_v = 447$) sample. He conducted explorative and confirmatory factor analyses with the calibration sample, in order to modify or exclude items and scales wherever necessary. Michael Goller estimates his theoretical model on the basis of PLS-structural equation modelling with the calibration sample first, and then with the validation sample. As assumed, the results confirmed that agency can predict agentic behaviour. In both samples, there is a consistent impact of agentic behaviour on professional expertise through job enrichment and participation in formal learning at work. However, the context factors considered in the model revealed limited importance. On the basis of the theoretical model, 23% of the variance in professional expertise can be explained in the calibration sample, whereas in the validation sample, 31% of that variance can be explained. Hence, the explanatory power of the model is satisfactory. It provides the following answers to the sub-questions identified above: (a) Agency proves to be a predictor of agentic behaviour, (b) two of four facets of agentic behaviour predict the development of professional expertise, however (c) the context factors are of limited importance.

Both the theoretical as well as the empirical analyses of this study are of outstanding quality. Theoretically, Michael Goller succeeds in reviewing the literature on workplace learning research and in specifying the widely used but quite abstract understanding of agency. He comprehensively analyses the discourse about agency and he critically looks into the arguments on influences, features, and impacts of agency. Thus, these theoretical analyses make an important contribution to the systematisation of the discourse on agency. As Michael Goller also succeeds in providing empirical evidence for the impact of agency on the development of expertise, he also reveals the relevance of the construct of agency for educational research as well as for educational practice and human resource development.

Probably, the most important contribution to the research discourse is to format an understanding of agency that can be used for quantitative research and testing of hypotheses. Whereas researchers dealing with the construct of agency usually remain within the areas of their own research paradigms, Michael Goller acknowledges the research conducted within sociocultural frameworks; he transforms their insights and also merges insight from neighbouring disciplines (i. e., psychology, social sciences) in a way that allows him a precise operationalisation of the construct of agency. Hence, he is treading new paths of research. Empirically, his study confirms, based on a bigger data set, what qualitative research on agency revealed based on case studies. Even though there will be colleagues who may tend to oppose the use of a quantitative research approach for investigating agency, I am sure that this study will receive high acknowledgement in the field.

Paderborn, February 2017

Christian Harteis

# Acknowledgements

Although there is only one name printed on the cover of this book I want to acknowledge that other people strongly contributed to this PhD thesis. It is only at the first glance that the reading, the conceptualisation, the data analyses, as well as the writing appear to have been done by me alone. A second—much closer—look soon reveals that many individuals supported me during all these different phases of my PhD. The most important of these supporters shall be mentioned here.

First of all, I want to thank Christian Harteis for his supervision, for a very successful introduction into the relevant scientific community, for all the fruitful discussions about agency and research in general, as well as for his critical but ever-constructive criticism of my work. Christian, I am grateful for the extensive support you have provided over the years. I hope I have proved to be a similarly valuable staff member for you.

Hans Gruber has earned my thanks due to his work as second referee. I thank him for his early feedback on some of my ideas, for his willingness to review this thesis in such a short period of time, as well as for the faith he had in my scholarly competences.

Furthermore, I am very grateful to all my colleagues and friends who constantly involved me in critical discussions about agency, workplace learning, empirical research, data analysis, and academic life in general. Some of you even read, reviewed, and criticised parts of this thesis. Many thanks for all the academic support you provided me with over the years: Stephen Billett, Carla Bohndick, Kathrin Brünner, Peter Burgold, Anna Liza Daunert, Anneli Eteläpelto, Dagmar Festner, Christoph Fischer, Frederic Hilkenmeier, Päivi Hökkä, Thilo Klein, Viola Klotz, Eva Kyndt, Susanna Paloniemi, Katja Vähäsantanen, Mario Vennemann, Katrin Wienold, and Sabrina Wiescholek. In addition, I especially want to thank you for all the pleasant time we spent together that was not directly related to this PhD or other facets of work. It helped greatly to recharge my batteries and to—in a certain sense—keep my sanity.

I also want to thank all the student assistants who supported me with such tedious tasks as interview transcription, interview coding, survey preparations, data entry, data validation, and final manuscript checks: Joanna Aistermann, Annika Erlenkötter, Marina Uthoff, Franziska Wehrhahn, and Philipp Weyer. In the same sense I would like to thank Christiane Müller for all the administrative work she took off my hands over the years. Elizabeth Stevens deserves my gratitude for copy editing the final version of this manuscript.

A special thanks goes to all the participants of the three empirical studies that are the core of this thesis. I also want to thank all the CEOs of the participating nursing homes, the head nurses working in the wards of these nursing homes, as well as all the staff at IN VIA Akademie Paderborn (especially CEO Birgit Marx and Susanne Klein). Without your willingness to act as gate keepers, to allow me to acquire study participants, and to discuss the survey instruments, I would not have been able to gather any data.

Last but certainly not least I want to thank my family. Over the years, you all provided strong emotional and material support. You never lost faith in my abilities even when I did. A special thanks is due to my wife, Elisabeth. You not only supported me in any possible way (including many discussions about agency and professional development, as well as critically proofreading the whole manuscript); you also constantly helped me to push my own limits. It is no exaggeration to say that you are the one who made this project feasible. I just cannot express how grateful I am.

Without all of you this long-lasting and sometimes very exhausting endeavour would not have been possible.[*] I am deeply indebted to you. Thank you!

Paderborn, November 2016

Michael Goller

[*] Essentially all parts of this thesis were developed using free software (free like in free speech, not like in free beer). I would therefore also like to thank all the developers of wonderful applications like Inkscape, Kile, LaTeX, LibreOffice, ownCloud, R (including all the packages employed), RStudio, Ubuntu Linux, and Zotero. Your efforts make my academic (and my private) life much more convenient!

# Contents

# List of Symbols and Abbreviations

| | |
|---|---|
| $\Delta\chi^2$ | Difference between two $\chi^2$ test statistics |
| *AVE* | Average variance explained |
| *CFI* | Comparitive fit index |
| *CI* | Confidence interval |
| *df* | Degrees of freedom |
| *GoF* | Goodness of fit index |
| *Max* | Maximum |
| *MIC* | Mean item correlation |
| *Min* | Minimum |
| *MSA* | Measure of sampling adequacy |
| *ns* | Not significant |
| *PoA* | Percentage of agreement |
| *RMSEA* | Root mean square of error approximation |
| *SD* | Standard deviation |
| *SRMR* | Standardised root mean square residual |
| *VIF* | Variance inflation factor |
| $\alpha$ | Standardised Cronbach's $\alpha$ |
| $\alpha^k$ | Krippendorff's $\alpha$ |
| $\beta$ | Standardised regression coefficient |
| $\chi^2$ | $\chi^2$ test statistic |
| $\gamma$ | Standardised path coefficient in a latent change score model |
| $\lambda$ | Factor loading |
| $\omega$ | Construct reliability |
| $\rho$ | Corrected correlation in meta-analyses |
| *b* | Unstandardised regression coefficient |
| *d* | Effect size Cohen's *d* |

| | |
|---|---|
| $f^2$ | Cohen's $f^2$ effect size |
| $ICC$ | Intra-class correlation coefficient |
| $k$ | Number of studies included in a meta-analysis |
| $M$ | Mean |
| $N$ | Population size |
| $n$ | Sample size |
| $n_A$ | Sample size of calibration sample |
| $n_B$ | Sample size of validation sample |
| $p$ | $p$ value |
| $r$ | Correlation coefficient |
| $R^2$ | Coefficient of determination |
| $t$ | $t$ test statistic |
| $V$ | Cramer's $V$ |
| $W$ | Wilcoxon rank-sum test statistic |
| $w$ | Effect size Cohen's $w$ |
| ADF | Asymptotic distribution free |
| CEO | Chief executive officer |
| CFA | Confirmatory factor analysis |
| DBFK | Deutscher Berufsverband für Pflegeberufe [German association for care professions] |
| e | Measurement error |
| EFA | Exploratory factor analysis |
| EM | Expectation maximisation |
| FA | Factor |
| IQ | Intelligence quotient |
| ISTA | Inventory for stress-related task analyses |
| MAP | Minimum average partical |
| ML | Maximum likelihood |
| NCS | Nurse competence scale |
| no. | Number |
| OCB | Organisational citizenship behaviour |
| p. | Page |
| PE fit | Person-environment fit |
| PFA | Principal factor analysis |
| PLS | Partial least square |

| | |
|---|---|
| RQ | Research question |
| SDT | Self-determination theory |
| SEM | Structural equation modelling |
| SES | Socio-economic status |
| SNA | Social network analyses |
| U. K. | United Kingdome |
| U. S. | United States |
| VET | Vocational education and training |
| vs. | versus |
| WPL | Workplace learning |

# List of Figures

# List of Tables

# 1 Introduction

## 1.1 Problem Statement

Within recent discourses on workplace learning the concept of human agency has gained more and more attention. The idea of human agency is seen as essential to explain employees' professional learning and development. Because a range of scholars regularly use human agency within their writings, some authors argue that the concept plays a key role within the workplace learning (WPL) literature (e. g., Tynjälä, 2013).

In very general terms, the concept of agency refers to the idea that something or somebody has the capacity to cause something else (Schlosser, 2015; Shanahan & Hood, 2000).[1] This something or somebody is commonly denoted as the agent. The concept of human agency therefore describes how human beings are agents of influence and power who are able to cause things and to bring about change (Bunnin & Yu, 2004; Eteläpelto, Vähäsantanen, Hökkä, & Paloniemi, 2013; Hornsby, 1995; Shanahan & Hood, 2000; Wehmeyer, 2004). In this sense, notions of human agency are usually explicitly or implicitly associated with ideas that individuals make choices, take initiatives, and act proactively in order to exert control over their lives and their respective environments (Crockett, 2002; Emirbayer & Mische, 1998; Eteläpelto et al., 2013; Martin, 2004).[2]

1 It should be emphasised that the term agency has also been used academically to describe both an institution (department, government unit or company) that offers certain kinds of services for individuals or other institutions, and an institution or a person (an agent) that acts on the behalf (i. e., the interest) of somebody else. These two meanings are mainly used in political science and economics (especially for the latter meaning see e. g., Eisenhardt, 1989; Rees, 1985a, 1985b). Within the following chapters neither of these two conceptualisations will be further discussed.

2 Human agency can be conceptualised as an individual or a collective phenomenon. Individual agency describes the idea that single individuals exert control and take initiative. In

Within the WPL literature the concept of human agency is mainly used to express the way in which individuals are capable of exerting control over their learning in work-related contexts (e. g., Billett, 2011b; Eraut & Hirsh, 2007; Eteläpelto et al., 2013). Individuals are understood as agents who actively decide to what extent they engage or disengage with work-related activities like tasks, interactions or training opportunities (Billett, 2004b, 2011b). For instance, one individual might decide to engage deeply in a given problem at work while another completely ignores it. To give another example, one individual might energetically try to avoid participating in a provided training course at work where another tries deliberately to convince her supervisor to be released from work in order to take part in that very same seminar. It is therefore not only the affordances and constraints—that is, the sociocultural and physical characteristics of a workplace—that determine the learning and development at work but also the individual and their actions as such. In other words, the concept of human agency is used to account for individuals' influence on their own professional development in contrast to the effects of situational forces (e. g., Billett, 2011b; Hager, 2011).

Unfortunately, the whole discussion about the role of human agency in processes of learning and professional development has been quite abstract in nature. In many cases the concept is used without being explicitly defined (e. g., Billett, 2006; Eraut, 2007; Evans, Kersh, & Sakamoto, 2004; Skår, 2010). Even if a definition is presented, the nature of the concept often remains quite abstract and vague. At least four (partly overlapping) theoretical problems arise from this shortcoming. First, it is unclear whether the concept refers to an individual feature that allows individuals to make choices and to engage in actions, or the actions themselves. Both perspectives can be read into the literature (e. g., Harteis & Goller, 2014; Vähäsantanen, 2013). Second, some authors who use the concept to refer to human actions do not explicitly specify the particular actions that count as agency (e. g., Eteläpelto et al., 2013). Neither do they discuss

contrast, collective agency represents the idea that influence, control, and initiative have a more collective origin (for a possible conceptualisation of this phenomenon in the WPL literature see e. g., Edwards, 2005, 2009, 2010; Edwards & Mackenzie, 2005; for a discussion in the life-course research literature see e. g., Crockett, 2002; Hitlin & Long, 2009; Shanahan & Hood, 2000). Agency as a collective phenomenon will be excluded from any further discussion since the focus of this thesis is on the development of single individuals.

what kinds of actions are not part of the concept. A concept that subsumes all kind of human actions, however, is not meaningful and might be easily judged as redundant. Third, some authors do not sufficiently demarcate agency from other concepts frequently used in the WPL literature. For instance, Eteläpelto, Vähäsantanen, Hökkä, and Paloniemi (2014) discuss agency in relation to individuals' identity, yet both concepts—agency and identity—seem to be used in an overlapping and very indistinguishable way in their writings. Fourth, although agency has been discussed as being rather important for learning at and for work, the existing literature has not yet managed to derive testable hypotheses that explicitly describe how human agency is related to different antecedents and/or consequences.

The theoretical problems just stated might also be the reason why empirical research on the concept is still very scarce. The few existing studies employed mostly qualitative research methodologies such as interviews (e. g., Bryson, Pajo, Ward, & Mallon, 2006; A. Fox, Deaney, & Wilson, 2010; Vähäsantanen, Saarinen, & Eteläpelto, 2009), focus groups (Skår, 2010), or ethnographic approaches (e. g., Forsman, Collin, & Eteläpelto, 2014; Hökkä, Eteläpelto, & Rasku-Puttonen, 2012; R. Smith, 2006). Usually these studies stated that they indeed found evidence that individuals exercise agency at work and that such work agency was positively related to learning outcomes. The evidence presented in these studies was often characterised by detailed descriptions but also often by very unspecific accounts of a few single cases. A valid generalisation based on such findings is hardly possible.

Quantitative studies that employ hypothesis-testing methods to investigate the assumed relationship between agency and expertise development do not exist.[3] The lack of such quantitative studies might best be explained by the conceptual vagueness of the concept as well as the absence of testable hypotheses. However, studies that employ a set of quantitative empirical methods are actually required to test whether the theoretically claimed relationship of human agency and professional development really holds. From a very strict episte-

3 During the work on this thesis the PROAGENT group around Anneli Eteläpelto started to investigate human agency with quantitative methods (see Vähäsantanen, Paloniemi, Hökkä, Eteläpelto, & Räikkönen, 2016). However, this research is still in progress and was not available to the author till he finished his empirical study.

mological perspective one may even argue that the prominence of the concept within the WPL literature has to be questioned if such empirical evidence is persistently missing.

To conclude, the concept of human agency has been quite popular in recent discussions on workplace learning and professional development. Its notion is strongly related to the idea that individuals can exert control over their work-related learning and development processes. Although many authors use the term agency in their writings, surprisingly, they are often unclear about their meaning when referring to the concept (see Chapter 2 for a more detailed discussion on this argument). Apart from these conceptual problems, a lack of testable hypotheses as well as reliable empirical findings characterises the whole discussion around the concept of human agency.

## 1.2 Research Goal

The main research goal of this thesis is to provide a first attempt to *investigate empirically the role of human agency in work-related learning and professional development processes by using hypothesis-testing methods.* This main goal can be broken down into four separate sub-goals:

1. This thesis aims to give a structured overview of the current discussion of human agency within the WPL literature. Such a review intends to clarify how human agency is conceptually defined and how the concept is used to explain work-related learning and professional development.

2. Based on the literature an operational definition of human agency has to be derived. Such a definition does not yet exist but is strongly required to use the concept in empirical studies that employ hypothesis-testing methods. Whereas a conceptual definition explains what human agency is, the operational definition defines how the concept should be empirically assessed (Jaccard & Jacoby, 2010).

3. This thesis aims to develop a (causal) research model that allows testable hypotheses about the relationship of human agency and professional learning and development to be derived. This model seeks to incorporate hu-

man agency as the main independent variable and expertise as the main dependent variable. Expertise comprises all skills and knowledge that allow employees to respond proficiently to the requirements of their work. Such skills and knowledge can be understood as the ideal outcome of a long-lasting process of professional learning and development. The construction of the model has to be grounded in the relevant literature.

4. An empirical study has to be designed and conducted to test the theoretically-derived research model. The explicit aim of this study is to gather sufficient quantitative data to test whether the hypotheses about the relationship of human agency and work-related learning and development statistically hold or whether they have to be rejected. It is also aimed to investigate how well the concept explains the development of expertise in work contexts.

By achieving these goals, this thesis will significantly add to the current literature on WPL. In particular, this thesis closes the research gap identified in Section 1.1 by (a) deriving testable research hypotheses on the relationship of human agency and the development of expertise, as well as (b) conducting an empirical study that allows these hypotheses to be tested.

## 1.3 Outline of this Thesis

This thesis is structured in a theoretical and an empirical part. The theoretical part is composed of three chapters. Chapter 2 aims to provide conceptual clarity about the concept of human agency. For this purpose, discourses about human agency within the workplace learning literature as well as literature on social-cognitive psychology, life-course research, and organisational behaviour are reviewed and discussed. Within these writings two distinct perspectives of human agency can be identified: (a) as an individual feature (i. e., a capacity or a disposition; e. g., Bryson et al., 2006; Hitlin & Elder, 2007b), and (b) as something individuals do (e. g., Eteläpelto et al., 2013; Vähäsantanen, 2013). Both conceptualisations will be incorporated into a single conceptual framework in this thesis. The first perspective is integrated into the central concept of work agency, which will be defined as capacity and tendency to make intentional choices, to initiate actions based on these choices, and to exercise control over the self and environment in work-related contexts (for similar conceptualisations see Eteläpelto et al., 2013; Harteis & Goller, 2014). The second perspective is subsumed under the notion of agentic actions. Agentic actions are self-initiated behaviours that are based upon the choices of the acting individual. It is assumed that some individuals tend to be more capable and more inclined than others to take control over their lives and therefore engage more often in agentic actions. However, the decision to engage in certain behaviours does not only depend on individual characteristics. The conceptual framework derived in Chapter 2 therefore also incorporates sociocultural and material context factors. Context factors are understood to alter the a priori probability to engage in certain agentic actions.

Chapter 3 aims to explain how exactly individuals can agentically exert control over their own professional learning and development process and thereby contribute to becoming experts in their respective work domains. A main focus will be laid on the disclosure of agentic actions that are suited to take charge discretely of one's own expertise development. As will be seen, three such agentic actions can be identified: (a) deliberate efforts to craft new work-related experience, (b) deliberate efforts to seek information about work-related matters and feedback about one's own current work performance, and (c) all deliberate efforts to take part in institutionalised learning activities like training or seminars. In addition, this chapter also focuses on identifying work-related context factors that determine how and whether individuals engage in development and learning-related behaviours. In this sense, Chapter 3 concretises the conceptual framework derived in Chapter 2.

Chapter 4 brings together the discussions presented in Chapters 2 and 3. In a first step, this chapter introduces the research questions this thesis aims to answer empirically. The overarching research question is as follows: How does human agency relate to work-related learning and professional development? Based on the conceptual framework derived beforehand, this research question can be broken down to three separate research questions:

1. How does work agency as an individual-level feature explain employees' engagement in agentic actions?
2. How does the engagement in those agentic actions relate to the development of work-related expertise?
3. How do organisational context factors affect the engagement in agentic actions?

In a second step, the theoretical discussions presented in Chapters 2 and 3 are then used to derive hypotheses as preliminary answers to these questions. These hypotheses are then translated into a final research model. Chapter 4 also briefly introduces the empirical approach to test the derived research model. Altogether, three consecutive studies will be conducted in the domain of in-patient geriatric care nursing. A combination of qualitative and quantitative methods will be employed.

In-patient geriatric care nursing was chosen as a research domain for several reasons (see Chapter 4 for a more detailed explanation). First, because of several demographic and cultural reasons the demand for institutionalised care for elderly people has become more and more important in Germany in the last couple of decades. Second, at the same time Germany—similar to many other Western countries—faces a skill shortage of elderly care personnel. A common strategy is to employ staff who are not trained and not qualified as geriatric care nurses. The subsequent development of appropriate skills and knowledge is especially important for such employees. However, not all nursing homes equally support their staff in such an endeavour. It can therefore be assumed that agentic nurses are more prone to develop expertise than their less-agentic counterparts. Third, the domain of geriatric care nursing has experienced a range of crucial medical and technical advancements in recent years. Learning and development is therefore necessary also for already qualified personnel in order to keep up with these advancements. Since these advancements are not always automatically introduced and taught in all nursing homes, agentic nurses are more commonly expected to keep up than less-agentic nurses.

The empirical part of this thesis is composed of four chapters. Chapter 5 describes the first study. This qualitative interview study aimed to obtain initial insights into geriatric care nurses' agency at work. This was necessary because not much is known about how geriatric care nurses exercise their agency at work. Two concrete goals were pursued in this study: (a) investigate whether the proposed research model in its current form can be tested in the domain of geriatric care nursing, and (b) derive information on how to operationalise the concepts included in the model. As will be seen, based on the empirical insights of this study the underlying research model had to be slightly adapted. The derived adaptations make the research model simultaneously more concrete and more suitable for the domain of geriatric care nursing.

Chapter 6 describes the second study of this thesis, which aimed to develop and to pilot test the quantitative study design and the survey instrument to be used to answer the research questions posed in Chapter 4. Based on the insights of this pilot study, the general research design as well as the survey instrument was slightly adapted.

Chapter 7 describes the third and last study of this thesis. The main aim of this study was to empirically test the advanced research model derived in Chapters 4 and 5. This was done by employing a cross-sectional study design. Altogether, usable data of 879 geriatric care nurses working in German nursing homes were gathered. These data were analysed using structural equation modelling in combination with a cross-validation approach. This procedure allowed for robust testing of all hypotheses derived from the theoretical discussion of part one.

Chapter 8 presents a final discussion of all findings obtained in this thesis. The chapter aims to answer the research questions posed in Chapter 4. In addition, implications for practice as well as further research are derived.

# 2 Agency: An Abstract and Multifaceted Construct

The aim of this chapter is to provide clarity about the concept of human agency.[4] In a first step, the workplace learning (WPL) literature is reviewed to explain how agency is used, how it is conceptualised, and how it is theoretically related to other constructs (Section 2.1). Unfortunately, the discussion of agency within this literature is rather abstract in nature. The discussion allows neither derivation of an operational definition of the concept nor construction of a nomological network of relevant antecedents and consequences of agency in work contexts. It is therefore necessary to consult literature of other disciplines to overcome this shortcoming (Section 2.2). Research conducted in social-cognitive psychology, life-course research, and organisational behaviour theorisation on proactivity especially is suited to improve the conceptual understanding of agency and to derive a conceptual framework that links agency to both antecedents and outcomes. Both literature reviews are brought together in Sections 2.2.4 and 2.3. The latter section develops a working definition of agency as well as a first conceptual framework that is later used to empirically investigate the relationship of agency and expertise development. The chapter closes with a summary in Section 2.4.

4 From this point on the shorter term agency will be used to describe the notion of human agency. Ideas of non-human agency will be excluded from all further discussions.

## 2.1 Agency in the Workplace Learning Literature

Based on a larger review, Tynjälä (2013) suggested that the concept of agency has been used threefold within the WPL literature. First, agency has been described as an individual-level feature that affects how employees interpret learning and work situations as well as whether and how they engage in different learning activities. Second, agency has been employed to describe learning activities as such. Within this second category agency is understood as something employees do (see also Biesta & Tedder, 2007). Third, agency has been described as a consequence of learning processes. Agency is understood as something that changes due to learning experiences.

Unfortunately, Tynjälä (2013) cites only very few references for each of the three suggested categories (Billett, 2002, 2004a, 2011a; Hänninen & Eteläpelto, 2008; Vähäsantanen & Billett, 2008). In addition, she does not describe how agency is defined or conceptualised within the referenced writings.[5] It follows that a more comprehensive review is necessary to get a deeper understanding what agency is and how scholars interested in learning and professional development use the concept. The next sections therefore give a comprehensive overview of the WPL literature concerned with the concept of agency. The three derived categories of Tynjälä's review are used to structure and systematise this literature: Section 2.1.1 reviews literature that conceptualises agency as a prerequisite of learning in work contexts; Section 2.1.2 discusses all literature that understands agency as an activity—that is, as something individuals do; and Section 2.1.3 focuses on agency as an outcome of work-related learning. Each of these sections first describes the theoretical conceptualisation of agency and then reviews the empirical findings based on the particular theoretical ideas. Section 2.1.4 summarises the main findings and discusses potential limitations of the literature reviewed.

5 It should be noted that Tynjälä's review did not focus on agency alone. The review sought to give a systematic overview about research conducted on learning for and through work in general. Agency only emerged as one of the relevant concepts within these discussions.

### 2.1.1 Agency as a Prerequisite of Work-Related Learning

**This section discusses the two most prevalent theoretical models that incorporate the notion of agency as an important prerequisite of learning in work contexts. Within the underlying literature review of this thesis, Billett's co-participation model as well as Eraut's double-triangle model emerged as the two most often referenced theoretical frameworks that explicitly include such ideas of agency. Both models are genuinely concerned with questions of how individual agency and workplace characteristics interact and thereby explain employees' professional development processes.**

#### 2.1.1.1 Billett's Co-Participation Model

Billett's (2001c, 2004b, 2006, 2011a) co-participation model is one of the best elaborated and described theories concerning agency in the WPL literature. The model describes the interdependence of work practices (i. e., activities and interactions) and individuals' participation in those work practices to explain learning at work. It strongly emphasises that both workplace characteristics and the agency of employees determine how and what is learnt at work.

Billett's ideas are rooted in the sociocultural paradigm of learning (e. g., Lave, 1993; Rogoff, 1991, 1995; see also Hager, 2011). An important assumption of this school of thought is that learning is a process of participation within social goal-directed activities (Billett, 2004b, 2011a; Billett & Smith, 2006; Hager, 2011; Sfard, 1998). The development of work-related knowledge, skills, and abilities—within these accounts—is therefore inseparably connected to individuals' engagement and participation in work-related practices. It follows that the quality and quantity of learning processes at work are strongly determined by the kind of practices in which individuals are able to participate. Individuals with only limited access to work-related practices will have limited access to learning opportunities at work. Conversely, individuals with access to a wide range of such practices also have access to a wide range of learning opportunities at work.

The access to work activities and therefore learning opportunities is not necessarily equally distributed within organisations. Opportunities to engage in certain work practices are largely determined by the power structure and the interests of different stakeholders at work (Billett, 2001c, 2004b, 2011a). More concretely, the distribution of workplace affordances—the opportunities to participate in certain work practices (activities, interactions, guidance)—is based upon workplace hierarchies or the affiliation to different status groups. Managers, for instance, reserve crucial and prestigious activities and tasks to themselves, and full-time employees may restrict the access to workplace practices for their part-time counterparts. Workplace affordances are also distributed according to the personal characteristics of employees. For example, innovative and demanding tasks are more often delegated (i. e., afforded) to younger employees who are characterised as being more capable than their older counterparts (age-biased task discrimination; Bender, 2010).

Although the access to work practices is a crucial element in his co-participation model, Billett (2004b) argues that "situational factors alone are insufficient to understand workplaces as learning environments. What is required is an understanding of the way individuals' agentic action and intentionalities [...] shape how they participate in and learn through work" (p. 316). Consequently, Billett (2001c, 2004b, 2011a) introduces the concept of agency in his model to acknowledge that individuals are not fully subjugated by the social context and learning is not just a product of socially afforded or even enforced practices. On the one hand, the concept is used to explain that individuals do not just reactively and passively participate in work practices, but actively elect whether and to what extent they want to engage in affordances provided at work. On the other hand, agency is used to express that individuals also actively decide how to engage with constraints that are imposed by the workplace. For instance, an employee might actively try to bypass age-biased task discrimination by agentically asking her[6] employer for more innovative and demanding tasks. It therefore follows that, although important, workplace characteristics alone do not explain what and how individuals learn at work.

Billett (2004b, 2006, 2011a) describes the role of agency on an even more fundamental level. With reference to Valsiner (1998), he notes that individu-

6 Within this manuscript all generic individuals (i. e., no concrete persons like authors, or study participants) are referred to with the female form. This is thought to avoid lengthy formulations like "he or she" or "his or her". All female references automatically include the male form.

als have to be highly selective in what they react to and how, in the steady stream of social suggestions they encounter in daily (work) life. Agency determines how much attention is directed towards encountered social suggestions (e. g., work-related problems, new task assignments, etc.) and how individuals mentally and overtly engage with them. Individuals actively decide what is "judged worth of participation" (Billett, 2004b, p. 320). Under this perspective, individuals are able to choose actively from a range of responses between fully engaging in the activities that are suggested by the workplace to (almost) completely ignoring or rejecting them.

It follows that agency can also be exercised in situations that exert very high levels of social pressure to participate in certain social practices at work (e. g., because non-engagement could lead to dismissal). Individuals can, for instance, still choose to employ least-effort strategies in such situations. From an external perspective, the adoption of such a "good enough" (Jensen, 2007, p. 498) mentality might still sufficiently satisfy performance requirements. However, individuals adopting these kinds of strategies do not necessarily engage with afforded activities in a deep cognitive way (Billett, 2001c, 2004b).

Furthermore, employees are also able to fully deny engagement in work practices. Billett (2000, 2001c) gives the example of a young recruit who rejects the guidance offered by a mentor provided by his company. The recruit did not appreciate the mentor's help and was therefore highly reluctant to engage in any mentoring. In another study, Gustavsson (2007) reports on technical operators in a paper mill openly acknowledging that—based on their interest and motivation—they decide whether they want to participate in certain problem situations or whether they reject their participation. Resistance at work can therefore be seen as one particular manifestation of agency.

From a different perspective, employees are also able to create opportunities to participate in affordances that are not naturally provided by the workplace. The exercise of agency can therefore also directly foster learning in work contexts. Billett (2001b), for instance, reports about a worker who used any opportunity to get in touch with colleagues from a different department in which he wanted to work (see also Billett, Barker, & Hernon-Tinning, 2004). He followed colleagues' discussions on a two-way radio and also sat with them during lunch breaks in order to learn as much as possible about their work. This example illustrates how employees can overcome existing barriers to learning and developing by actively creating learning opportunities that were not available before.

Through exercising their agency individuals are therefore able to affect how and what they learn at work. Work-related learning outcomes are strongly related to how employees elect to engage in what is afforded to them. However, individuals must not be seen as completely independent from their social context; individuals are not fully free to act on their own behalf. Work-related learning has to be conceptualised as relational: it is related to both social practice and (personal) agency (Billett & Smith, 2006). Work-related learning simultaneously depends on what is afforded at work and on how individuals deal with the afforded opportunities.

This proposed interdependency is not important only for work-related learning. In his model, Billett (2006, 2008b, 2011a; Billett & Smith, 2006) also emphasises the interconnected role of activities and interactions afforded at work and the influence of agency in the remaking and transformation of social practice. Through the engagement in activities and interactions afforded at work individuals continually reproduce work-related practice. However, the remaking of work practices does not happen uniformly across all involved employees. As proposed before, individuals are not fully subjugated by social experience. They rather exercise agency by controlling both the kind of affordances they want to engage in and the intensity of that engagement. Consequently, individuals can either elect to remake or to transform social practice (Billett & Smith, 2006). Reproducing work practice requires employees to willingly—or at least uncritically—engage in activities provided by the workplace. Transformation of practices in contrast requires individuals to reshape and change afforded activities based on their own prospects and visions.

How and in what way agency is exercised at work is strongly related to individuals' identities, goals, interests, and beliefs that have developed through their particular personal life history (i. e., ontogeny; Billett, 2001c, 2004b, 2006, 2008b). Because individuals all make a unique set of work and non-work related experiences over their lifespan, there are no two humans alike. That is why individuals react differently to identical social suggestions and some engage qualitatively more in afforded workplace activities than others. So for example, some of the operators interviewed by Gustavsson (2007) might perceive the repairing of machines at work as interesting and, hence, might engage in this kind of activity. However, others might see fixing machines as not part of their work identity and therefore may avoid such kind of work. In another empirically derived example, R. Smith (2006) reports about newly employed fruit workers. Of the three observed workers, one had the goal to be a salesman. That is why this particular employee willingly took every chance to engage with activities seen as connected to a career in sales (i. e., answering the phone). Concerning the transformation of social practice, Billett et al. (2004) describe how a grief counsellor managed to transform his counselling practice in a way that allowed more engagement in face-to-face counselling. This particular kind of counselling overlapped more with this counsellor's interests and beliefs about what exactly characterises good counselling practice.

Although Billett uses agency as a central concept in his model he does not explicitly define it. However, two different implicit notions of agency could be extracted. In some of his writings (e. g., Billett, 2006), he uses agency to describe individuals' intentionality, subjectivity, and identity or their general interests and dispositions (Billett & Somerville, 2004) that are the foundation of goal-directed behaviours. However, in other publications he uses agency as a placeholder for intentional actions exercised by individuals in their daily (working) life (e. g., Billett, 2008a, 2008b). Those actions are termed manifestations of agency in still other publications (e. g., Billett, 2001c). It therefore seems that Billett uses agency—at the same time—as the cause of intentional actions and the actions themselves.

Figure 2.1 provides a graphical summary of the co-participation model. To sum up, the model describes the relational interdependence between social practice and agency in explaining both work-related learning and also the remaking and transformation of work practices. Learning at work "is shaped through interaction between social and individual contributions, yet with individuals playing a highly agentic role in those interactions" (Billett, 2006, p. 58). The concept of agency is used to explain how individuals deal with social suggestions at work. It is used to account for individuals' intentionalities—that is, "the focus and direction of engagement by individuals with what is experienced socially" (Billett & Smith, 2006, p. 151), as well as the degree of intensity

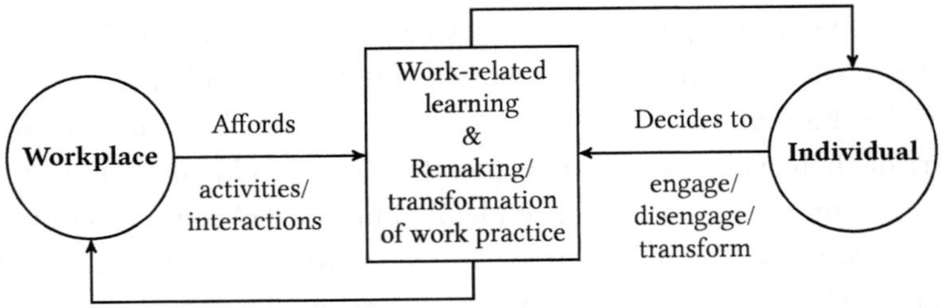


**Figure 2.1.** Co-participation model.

of this engagement—that is, the "priority and potency of the exercise of personal agency" (Billett & Smith, 2006, p. 151).

#### 2.1.1.2 Eraut's Double Triangle Model

Eraut's double-triangle model (see Figure 2.2) is another commonly cited theoretical framework that includes agency as a central presage component. The model was constructed based on a range of studies investigating employees' professional development processes in their early and mid-career phase (Eraut, 2007, 2010b, 2012; Eraut & Hirsh, 2007). Unfortunately, Eraut does not describe or discuss the single components of his model in great detail.

The upper part of the model depicted in Figure 2.2 focuses on context factors that are relevant to explain learning at work. The first set of context factors is concerned with the allocation and structuring of work. Eraut (2007) argues that work has to be sufficiently stimulating by being challenging but not overwhelming. Only workplaces that afford challenges that do not constantly diminish incumbents' confidence in their own abilities are described as being conducive to learning. However, workplaces that are constantly underchallenging also do not contribute to employees' professional development. The second set of context factors describes encounters and relationships with people at work. Work that provides opportunities to legitimately observe and work alongside more experienced employees allows individuals to progress developmentally. It is both the support that other employees provide during the engagement in new tasks as well as their feedback about current levels of performance that enable new incumbents to further develop their work-related

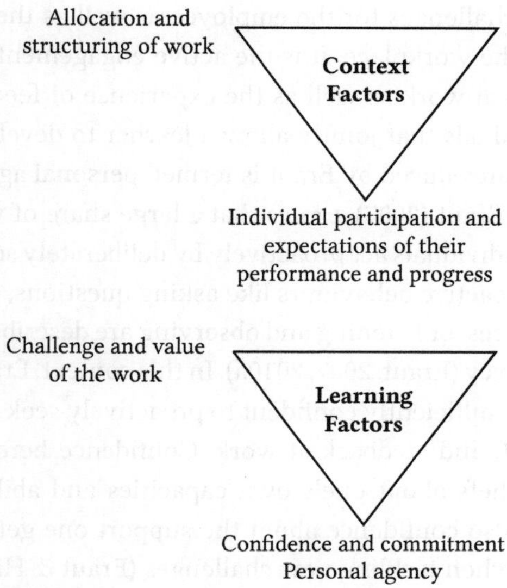


**Figure 2.2.** Double-triangle model. Reprinted and adapted from "Eraut, M. (2007). Learning from other people in the workplace. *Oxford Review of Education, 33*(4), 403–422, p. 418" with permission from Taylor & Francis.

skills, knowledge, and abilities. The last set of factors is labelled individual participation and expectations of their performance and progress. Here, Eraut (2007; Eraut & Hirsh, 2007) mainly refers to employers' implicit or explicit expectations about the performance of their employees and employees' gradual progress in mastering the particular practices of the workplace in question. In the best case, employees are well familiar with such expectations and the expectations are personally manageable for them. Unrealistic expectations might rapidly demotivate new employees to meet them in the first place. However, employees might also be less motivated to learn and develop if expectations are unknown or even non-existent.

The second part of the model (the lower triangle in Figure 2.2) focuses on the individual and the learning process as such. This triangle is thought to mirror the first part of the model. This is particularly obvious for both factors at the top of the triangle. As argued before, learning at work mainly depends on the provision of appropriate challenges for the employee as well as the feedback and support afforded by the workplace. It is the active engagement in appropriately challenging tasks at work as well as the experience of feedback and support from other individuals that jointly allow a learner to develop professionally. The third factor introduced by Eraut is termed personal agency, confidence and commitment. Eraut (2007) argues that a large share of workplace learning occurs because individuals act proactively by deliberately seeking out learning opportunities. Proactive behaviours like asking questions, getting information, locating resources, or listening and observing are described as manifestations of personal agency (Eraut, 2007, 2010a). In this context, Eraut argues that employees need to be sufficiently confident to proactively seek out appropriate challenges, support, and feedback at work. Confidence hereby means having both sufficient beliefs about one's own capacities and abilities (e. g., self-efficacy beliefs) and also confidence about the support one gets from co-workers and supervisors when tackling new challenges (Eraut & Hirsh, 2007).

Eraut therefore argues that workplace learning is partly based upon the initiative of the employee. First and foremost, the workplace is a context of work where learning opportunities are not necessarily provided to everybody in an automatic way (see also Goller & Billett, 2014). In certain circumstances development opportunities might only occur if the individual proactively seeks them out.

Again, Eraut does not give an explicit definition of agency in his writings. Agency is understood as an abstract capacity that is necessary to proactively take on new challenges at work. It is the requirement that individuals show initiative and deliberately engage in learning-related activities (Eraut, 2010b). It is not, however, clear whether confidence and commitment are a part of agency or more antecedents that enable individuals to exercise agency in the first place.

To sum up, Eraut (2007, 2010b; Eraut & Hirsh, 2007) argues that agency is central to all kinds of learning in work contexts. The learning of employees largely depends on their proactivity. They have to ask questions, seek out information or ask for guidance and support. Agency is used to describe the capacity and willingness to do so.

#### 2.1.1.3 Empirical Evidence

A few empirical studies used Billett's co-participation model as an explicit theoretical framework (e. g., Bryson et al., 2006; A. Fox et al., 2010; A. Fuller & Unwin, 2005). Probably one of the most comprehensive is the qualitative study conducted by Bryson et al. (2006), who interviewed 10 employees working in different hierarchical and functional positions at a vineyard. The main focus of this study was to investigate the interaction of workplace affordances and individual engagement as well as their role for competence and expertise development. Drawing on Billett's model, agency is seen as the foundation of individual engagement, whereby individual engagement was defined as the process where employees elect or refuse to participate in learning opportunities provided by the workplace (Bryson et al., 2006). Bryson and colleagues used the concept of proactivity, conceptualised as employees' active approach towards work in showing high levels of initiative in seeking information and creating favourable situations (see Section 2.2.3 for a further discussion of this concept), to explain individual differences between employees in their engagement in workplace affordances. It was assumed that individuals with a proactive personality should show more individual engagement.

Among other results, the study found evidence that proactive individuals did indeed "shape the nature of development affordances" (Bryson et al., 2006, p. 291) by taking initiative. Proactive employees could create learning opportunities even in rather hostile work environments where learning-relevant affordances were strongly restricted. Some employees proactively asked for and sought out both on-the-job learning affordances and institutionalised training opportunities which are usually not automatically provided to them. Others used their leisure time to deliberately engage in activities that provided positive spill overs to their daily work activities.

Fox and colleagues (A. Fox et al., 2010; A. Fox, Wilson, & Deaney, 2011; see also A. Fox & Wilson, 2015) employed both Billett's co-participation model and Eraut's ideas on self-initiated learning opportunities to investigate the workplace learning of beginning teachers. The authors conducted interviews with 17 novice teachers that mainly focussed on the teachers' perceptions of the learning support offered by their training schools. Another focus was laid on how the individuals engaged with the support offered by the school and how they dealt with more restrictive learning environments. Agency was conceptualised as the degree to which novice teachers attempt to take control over their work-related lives; agentic behaviour was defined as goal-directed, effortful, and proactive engagement in work practices (A. Fox et al., 2011).

The analysis of the interviews revealed that the existence of highly supportive working environments (e. g., environments that afforded strong opportunities to interact and exchange ideas with colleagues) did not automatically guarantee that beginning teachers used the support afforded. They still had to exercise agency in order to access the support provided to them. At the same time, a more restrictive learning environment did not automatically hinder workplace learning for all employees. Teachers who proactively engaged in networking activities could expand their professional support network far beyond the support structure initially afforded by their workplace. Fox and colleagues (2010) attribute the observed differences between teachers to different capacities and/or tendencies to exercise agency:

> Some individuals appear proactive in finding and using support from school and external sources. Some, while not being actively encouraged, make the best of support available. Still other BTs [beginning teachers] appear more passive or less willing to seek and use available sources of support. (p. 224)

Van Veldhuizen (2011; van Veldhuizen, Simons, & Ritzen, 2012) conducted a study that investigated the self-directed learning of teachers by also using Billett's model as the main theoretical framework. In this study, agency was operationalised via a measure of teachers' self-efficacy beliefs. Strong self-efficacy beliefs are believed to represent a strong sense of personal agency (again, similar to Eraut's ideas on agency). Furthermore, the study hypothesised that highly agentic individuals will engage more often in advanced learning activities that result in better learning outcomes. This effect should be especially strong in work contexts where job resources (e. g., variation and challenge, open and learning-oriented culture) outweigh job demands (e. g., pressure of work, job insecurity). In order to test these hypotheses van Veldhuizen (2011) gathered and analysed a rich dataset including competence tests of 15 teachers working in the Dutch education system as well as interviews with these teachers and their respective school leaders.

The analysis returned inconclusive results. At first glance, it seems that strong self-efficacy beliefs are indeed positively related to more desirable learning outcomes. At the same time, however, most teachers with high self-efficacy beliefs also experienced disproportionally more job resources than job demands. The positive learning outcomes can therefore be explicitly attributed neither to agency nor to context factors. Furthermore, the data did not allow confirmation of the hypothesis that a combination of strong self-efficacy beliefs and work contexts where job resources outweigh job demands leads to more elaborated learning outcomes.

All of the three reported studies conceptualised agency as an individual feature that predicted to what extent the study participants took control over their working life and to what extent they deliberately engaged in development-related activities at work. Both the studies of Bryson et al. (2006) and van Veldhuizen (2011) used proxy variables to explain why individuals engage qualitatively differently with their working environment. The concept of proactive personality was used in the first study and the concept of self-efficacy beliefs in the second. The study of A. Fox et al. (2011) did not theoretically conceptualise agency as a difference variable. However, in their data they found strong evidence that some novice teachers tend to take more control over their professional development than others. These differences were interpreted as differences in individuals' agency.

The studies of Bryson et al. (2006) and A. Fox et al. (2011) present evidence that directly speak in favour of both Billett's and Eraut's ideas. It seems that learning partly depends on how individuals agentically elect to engage in learning-relevant affordances provided by the workplace. The results of van Veldhuizen's (2011) study cannot be used as evidence for the influence of agency on professional development. However, his results do not speak against the models of Billett and Eraut.

### 2.1.2 Agency as Something Individuals Do

Some authors explicitly deny that agency is a property or some kind of feature of human beings (e. g., Biesta & Tedder, 2007; Lipponen & Kumpulainen, 2011). They rather conceptualise agency as something individuals do (Lipponen &

Kumpulainen, 2011). Agency is understood as decisions and goal-directed behaviours. There are a few theoretical and empirical articles that have adapted this view. Within the WPL community the working group around Anneli Eteläpelto has developed the most elaborated and best established theoretical account of this agency perspective. In a first step this subject-centred sociocultural perspective of agency is discussed in Section 2.1.2.1. Section 2.1.2.2 then presents empirical research that was based on this particular understanding of agency. Thereafter another set of studies that discuss and investigate agency as individuals' choices and actions is presented (Section 2.1.2.3). While they do not refer to the subject-centred sociocultural perspective, these studies still understand agency as certain kinds of activities initiated and exercised by the individual.

#### 2.1.2.1 Subject-Centred Sociocultural Perspective

In their influential review, Eteläpelto and colleagues (2013; see also Eteläpelto et al., 2014; Vähäsantanen, 2013) recognise the prominence of the concept of agency in the literature on learning in general and on workplace learning in particular. At the same time, the authors highlight that the concept lacks conceptual clarity because of "the absence of any explicit definition of its core meaning" (Eteläpelto et al., 2013, p. 46). One of their main aims therefore was to derive a precise definition of agency that can be used in discourses on learning in work contexts. They labelled their concept professional agency.

In order to derive this definition, Eteläpelto et al. (2013) analysed and reviewed an extensive body of literature on agency. The authors included literature from educational and social science as well as from psychology and gender studies in their review. Based on their analysis, four distinct lines of discussion could be identified: (a) social science discourses, (b) post-structural discussions, (c) sociocultural learning research, and (d) identity and life-course notions of agency.

Within social sciences, agency mainly comprises ideas of choice and goal-directed action initiated by an individual (e. g., Giddens, 1984). The concept is often implicitly or explicitly used as a notion of human freedom, individual volition, or power within a given social structure. An important part of the social science discourse is concerned with the questions of whether agency exists at all (e. g., Fuchs, 2001), how much agency individuals have (e. g., D. J. Campbell, 2000), and how agency and structure interrelate (e. g., Archer, 2000; Giddens, 1984). Post-structural discussions build upon the idea that language shapes and even constructs social reality. Radical post-structuralists therefore conceptualise agency almost exclusively as a discursive and collective phenomenon closely linked to language. Intermediate post-structural notions understand agency as "people's lived experience of their social relations and their capacity for self-reflection and action" (Eteläpelto et al., 2013, p. 60) within a socially constructed world. In sociocultural discourses individuals are perceived as agentic actors situated in a social world. Agency is related to and cannot be separated from individuals' subjectivities and professional identities (e. g., Holland, Lachicotte, Skinner, & Cain, 2003). Manifestations hereof might be found in decisions either to participate in afforded practices or to rebuff them (see also Billett, 2004b, as well as Section 2.1.1.1). Life-course notions of the concept mostly discuss agency as being related to choices and efforts that construct, influence, and shape individuals' life courses (i. e., biographies). However, agency is not understood to be exercised within a social vacuum. All kinds of agentic efforts are necessarily understood to be embedded in historical and social circumstances (e. g., Gecas, 2003; a more detailed discussion of theoretical discourses on agency within the life-course literature and especially the idea of bounded agency can be found in Section 2.2.2.3).

Informed by these four lines of theoretical discussion, Eteläpelto et al. (2013, 2014) developed a subject-centred sociocultural understanding of agency (see Figure 2.3 for a graphical depiction). This particular perspective is called "subject-centred" because it explicitly focuses on how subjects (i. e., a single subject or a group of subjects) (re-)negotiate their identities and how they construct their life courses over time. Both are understood as active learning processes. Consequently, learning and development are perceived to be inseparable from the notion of agency.

Eteläpelto et al. (2013) also agree with sociocultural accounts of thinking (see Section 2.1.1.1). Agency can only be understood as situationally and contextually bound. In other words, agency is—at the same time—facilitated and constrained by social and historic factors. Thus, an analysis of agency at work

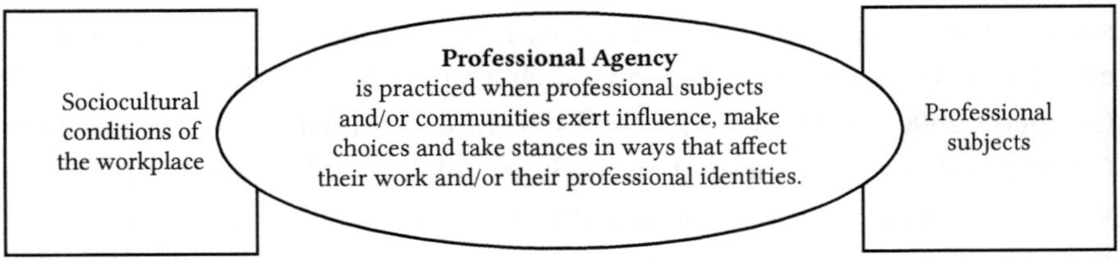


**Figure 2.3.** Subject-centred sociocultural understanding of agency. Reprinted and adapted from "Eteläpelto, A., Vähäsantanen, K., Hökkä, P., & Paloniemi, S. (2013). What is agency? Conceptualizing professional agency at work. *Educational Research Review, 10,* 45–65, p. 61" with permission from Elsevier.

has always to take into account material conditions, workplace culture, power relations or support structures (Eteläpelto et al., 2014). In accordance with this subject-centred sociocultural perspective, Eteläpelto et al. (2013) proposed the following definition of professional agency (i. e., agency exercised in relation to work contexts): "Professional agency is practiced when professional subjects and/or communities exert influence, make choices and take stances in ways that affect their work and/or their professional identities" (p. 61).

The subject-centred sociocultural understanding of agency is inseparably connected to the idea of professional identities (Eteläpelto et al., 2013, 2014; Vähäsantanen, 2013). Professional identities are defined as "subjects' conceptions of themselves as professional actors" (Eteläpelto et al., 2014, p. 650) which include subjects' individual sets of commitments, ideals, beliefs, interest, and values. It is argued that in order to successfully cope with constantly changing job market conditions as well as developments within their corresponding work domains, employees are required to regularly reflect and reconstruct their self-perception as professional actors within changing work contexts. This identity renegotiation is understood as a constructive learning process that takes place within the social context—the work culture, the material conditions of the workplace, as well as the relationships to colleagues or other work contacts. Individuals have to actively decide whether or to what extent they want to appropriate socially suggested identities.

Imagine a newly employed car mechanic who is mainly concerned with delivering high-quality service to her customers. However, her new employer does not appreciate quality as much and demands a more pragmatic way of work. One way to resolve this identity conflict would be that the mechanic tries to understand the reasons of her employer. Her preoccupation with high quality might cease soon as she understands that most customers do not value high-quality repairs on their old cars and are therefore not willing to pay for such services. This way, the mechanic would renegotiate and therefore eventually change her identity in a way that better fits her current workplace. However, another option is that the employee is not willing to adapt her identity. This may lead to less commitment towards her employer and even a job change later on. Yet another option would be that the employee tries to find ways to change the current practice such that simultaneously high-quality repairs are ensured and low-cost repairs are offered to the customers (for a similar example see Goller & Billett, 2014). All three options require the active engagement of the employee. She has to take decisions and act according to them. All three options also provide learning opportunities: (a) understanding of the idiosyncrasies of the new workplace, (b) reinforcement of one's own belief system, and (c) development of new working strategies that combine high-quality management and high-cost awareness.

At the same time, professional identities are perceived to affect the direction and manifestation of employees' agency at work. For instance, employees might deliberately engage in certain development activities because they aspire to become an expert in their field and because they are committed to their work. However, others may decide to disengage with certain parts of their job because they do not perceive them as worth pursuing or they are not really interested in them (e. g., Gustavsson, 2007).

It should be noted that this conceptualisation understands agency as something individuals do and not something individuals possess (in the sense of a disposition or a competence). Individuals' agency is expressed when they choose, prioritise, and eventually direct their behaviour towards self-set goals and aspirations over their (professional) life-course. Manifestations of work agency are, for instance, "suggestions for new or more productive work practices, inter-professional work strategies, or the reshaping of one's own work roles and identities" (Eteläpelto et al., 2014, p. 658). Nevertheless, the authors emphasise that agency also manifests itself when individuals actively reject suggestions by others. In fact, criticism and resistance is an important part of agency within the subject-centred sociocultural understanding of agency.

To sum up, the subject-centred perspective of agency is based upon a large body of literature and provides a first explicit definition of the concept. The proposed conceptualisation of professional agency is strongly intertwined with the idea that individuals are able to make choices and base their actions on these choices. This goal-directed behaviour can manifest itself as identity (re-)negotiation, deliberate learning efforts, efforts that are directed towards the transformation of the work environment or resistance against externally imposed reforms. Most importantly, it has therefore to be emphasised that subject-centred sociocultural perspectives understand agency as something individuals do.

Despite these positive aspects the subject-centred perspective of agency has still to be slightly criticised. First, it remains open whether the actions described as agency have to be initiated by the individual or can also be triggered by other agents. Such a broad conceptualisation, however, is not helpful to operationalise a phenomenon like agency. Second, a strong interrelation of agency and identity has been emphasised in several writings of Eteläpelto and her colleagues. However, their identity concept remains as abstract as the agency concept itself. Both concepts are occasionally used in a seemingly overlapping and indistinguishable way. Third, Eteläpelto and colleagues acknowledge the importance of the sociocultural context on professional agency. The material conditions of the workplace, the physical artefacts, the power relations, the work culture, as well as the support structure at work are seen as highly relevant factors that determine how individuals make choices and how they are able to act on these choices. Unfortunately, the authors do not explicitly explain how social context variables affect the exercise of agency at work. The notion of the importance of context factors therefore also remains quite abstract.

#### 2.1.2.2 Empirical Studies Directly Based on the Subject-Centred Sociocultural Perspective

Eteläpelto and her colleagues conducted a range of empirical studies that employed the subject-centred sociocultural understanding of agency (e. g., Eteläpelto & Saarinen, 2006; Forsman et al., 2014; Hökkä et al., 2012; Vähäsantanen, Hökkä, Eteläpelto, Rasku-Puttonen, & Littleton, 2008; Vähäsantanen et al., 2009). For instance, Vähäsantanen et al. (2009) interviewed 16 vocational teachers to investigate their agency during boundary-crossing episodes. The teachers were asked about their experience of workplace visits as a new part of their teaching job. During these visits their assignment usually comprised tasks like guidance and evaluation of students' workplace learning, support of the workplace trainers, as well as the provision of general information on the newly introduced workplace learning scheme. Based on their analysis the authors identified five distinct ways of exercising agency in this kind of situation. Teachers categorised as exercising restricted agency (first category) tried to fade into the background completely and did not want to disturb the working personnel. These teachers denied any critical stance against observed workplace behaviours that should have been judged as problematic or inappropriate from a professional perspective. In other words, they did not exercise any agency and felt quite restricted by the social context. In comparison, teachers categorised as exercising extensive agency (second category) used every opportunity to inform workplace personnel about the pedagogical idea of the students' workplace experience periods as well as about the correct conduct of their profession. It seemed as if these teachers were almost not affected by social suggestions (e. g., negative attitudes of the employees against the teachers) of their specific workplace contexts. Participants categorised as exercising multifaceted balancing agency (third category) are instead very aware of such context variables. However, because of this awareness they attempted to actively gain trust of the other employees in order to implement their own ideas. Teachers falling into the fourth category (situationally diverse agency) exercised agency in some situations but not in others. For instance, one teacher deliberately invested time to ensure the learning and development of the students he had to supervise. However, at the same time he was reluctant to initiate any efforts to influence work practices even if he could have done so. Teachers of the last category (relationally emergent agency) exercised agency only in such situations where they felt they already had a relationship of trust with the workplace personnel. If these teachers had to collaborate with unfamiliar workers they did not intervene in malpractice. However, after getting familiar with them and building up trust they often used opportunities to exercise agency by taking a critical stance against inappropriate work activities.

In conclusion, the study of Vähäsantanen et al. (2009) found that different teachers exercised distinctive forms of agency based on their sense of professional selves and their perceived professional function. Where some teachers exercised extensive agency by bringing in their own ideas and resisting social suggestions in the particular workplace setting, other teachers only exercised restricted agency by complying with given conditions. Those situations in which agency was extensively exercised created learning opportunities for students, the teacher, as well as the workplace personnel.

The study of Hökkä et al. (2012) investigated how Finnish teacher educators exercised their professional agency at work, how these teachers constructed and renegotiated their professional identity, and how different work contexts affected their identity construction. The two different contexts comprised their work as teachers and their duties as researchers within a teacher education department at a Finnish university. To answer the research questions empirically, the authors conducted qualitative interviews and collected ethnographic data in the form of diary records.

The most striking finding of this study was that the participating teacher educators described their opportunities for exercising agency and identity construction as very different between the two working contexts. During their teaching duties most teachers felt a strong sense of agency. They felt that they had "total ownership" (Hökkä et al., 2012, p. 90) over their own teaching practice which contributed largely to their construction of a strong teacher identity. This sense of agency or ownership was closely related to the high autonomy the participants experienced. In comparison, the teachers reported a strong feeling of being constrained and restricted in their work as researchers. The lack of resources especially (i. e., time, communication, and cooperation) led to an experience of agency deprivation in the university context. This was also perceived as the reason why most participants had not constructed an identity that interwove teaching and research. To sum up, social context factors like autonomy or time pressure seem to affect the sense and the exercise of agency in work contexts. Furthermore, a lack of agency might constrain the identity construction of employees.

Quite similar results were found by Vähäsantanen et al. (2008). The authors interviewed 24 teachers who belonged either to a vocational institution or teacher education department of a university. The work culture at the vocational institution was characterised as strongly controlling without much job discretion. On the contrary, the work culture at the university department could be described as less controlling and affording much more autonomy (see also Vähäsantanen, 2013). The interview data indicated that teachers in the vocational institution saw themselves as less agentic, especially when it came to relevant educational reforms. However, the same teachers experienced a strong sense of agency in their teaching work. Although the vocational institution was hierarchically organised and autonomy was low, teachers could still freely plan and implement their teaching. Teachers within the university department reported a strong sense of agency both in their daily work life as well as in regard to reforms.

#### 2.1.2.3 Further Empirical Evidence

Not all studies that are concerned with the idea of agency as something individuals do explicitly refer to Eteläpelto et al.'s (2013) subject-centred sociocultural understanding. Some of them loosely refer to Billett's ideas of agentic engagement or Eraut's notions of agency.[7] Others use the concept without explicitly referring to any theory. Nevertheless, all of these studies use agency as a placeholder to describe individuals' choices and self-initiated actions that are assumed to be linked to favourable learning outcomes. The next paragraphs aim at summarising and briefly discussing the theoretical groundings as well as the findings of those studies that conceptualise agency as something individ-

7 Some of the studies discussed in this section do refer to Billett's or Eraut's theoretical framework but do not discuss agency as an individual feature. That is why these studies are discussed in this section and not in Section 2.1.2.2.

uals do but do not explicitly adopt Eteläpelto and colleagues' subject-centred sociocultural understanding of agency.

Evans et al. (2004; see also Evans & Kersh, 2006) interviewed 60 individuals in order to investigate their relationship of life and work experiences, learning outcomes, and professional achievements. Similarly to the study of Bryson et al. (2006), the authors found evidence that workers engaging in agentic actions expand the learning opportunities of their workplace. The authors report upon interviewees referring to instances in which they proactively sought out further training courses by discussing and negotiating new learning and career options with their supervisor. However, in comparison to Bryson et al. (2006), they did not attribute this to a proactive personality but rather to a broad range of unspecific dispositions and attitudes. Although Evans and Kersh (2006) emphasise the constructive potential of individual agency they also argue that within the analysis of WPL the individual learner is always constrained by contextual factors and should not be perceived "as the prime determinant of learning" (p. 92; see also P. Hodkinson & Hodkinson, 2004).

In a different study, Skår (2010) investigates the learning experiences of Norwegian nurses in nursing homes and different hospital wards. The empirical material was derived from individual interviews with 11 nurses as well as two focus groups that employed data from the individual interviews as stimulus for further discussions. As a theoretical framework, amongst others, Billett's co-participation model was used. The data analysis revealed that an important part of work-related learning is a function of intentional efforts exercised by the nurses themselves—in other words, agency. For example, study participants reported actively seeking out colleagues for support who sometimes became role models or mentors. Furthermore, nurses proactively initiated discussions on work matters that helped them to gain new knowledge and skills. In other instances, nurses emphasised how they actively engage in knowledge-seeking efforts by consulting the internet, books or technical manuals.

Hoekstra, Korthagen, Brekelmans, Beijaard, and Imants (2009) studied experienced teachers' workplace learning as well as their perception of the work environment. Data were collected from 32 Dutch teachers using a multi-method approach including questionnaires and written reports about learning experiences. The authors also recorded some school lessons on video and conducted interviews after each lesson. Based on these data, two teachers were selected to represent the sample in the sense that they differed from each other the most. The first case (Miranda) represents a rather agentic teacher and the second one (Paul) a rather reactive one. Miranda actively engaged in introspection and reflection of her teaching activities, used the provided autonomy at work to learn from self-initiated experiments (e. g., trying out new teaching methods), and proactively sought out feedback from different sources. In comparison, Paul largely acted reactively. He did not actively try to reflect on work-related experiences. Furthermore, the provided work autonomy was perceived as stressful because it did not provide the guidance Paul would have liked. Similarly to the first case the school environment did not automatically provide much feedback. However, instead of proactively seeking out feedback (as Miranda did) Paul accepted this restriction.

In yet another study, the workplace learning of 24 sports coaches in New Zealand was investigated by Rynne, Mallett, and Tinning (2010). Theoretically, the study was—to some extent—based on Billett's ideas of agency. The authors were particularly interested in the relationship between learning opportunities afforded at work and agency exercised by the coaches. The work environment was described as competitive without offering much in the way of learning affordances. Interaction between coaches was rather limited because of a perceived competitiveness within the employing sport institute. At the same time, however, such interaction was highly valued by the coaches. The interviews revealed that coaches have to agentically foster interactions in order to regularly exchange information with colleagues. Without exercising agency, coaches remained largely isolated at work. Furthermore, Rynne et al. report that those coaches with a strong sense of control and security regarding their coaching practice as well as their employment status engaged more often in agentic actions.

To sum up, within this and the last section it has been presented that a few empirical studies have investigated the phenomenon of agency as individuals' choices and self-initiated actions. Some of the studies explicitly adopted the theoretical framework proposed by Eteläpelto et al. (2013) (see Section 2.1.2.1). Other studies used the notion of agency in a less confined way or referred either to Billett or Eraut (see Section 2.1.1). Either way, all of the presented studies conceptualised agency as something individuals do. Evidence could be presented that employees engage in a range of different agentic actions that are indeed related to learning outcomes. For instance, the studies report about individuals negotiating training opportunities and career options, actively seeking out colleagues to discuss work-related matters, or engaging in active reflection over incidents experienced at work. These studies also generated empirical evidence that some individuals tend to engage more often in agentic behaviours than others. These differences were most often traced back to differences in the particular social and physical work contexts. In particular, the lack of autonomy, time, and a culture of openness pose restrictions on personal agency.

### 2.1.3 Agency as an Outcome of Work-Related Learning

Only one study investigated the promotion and development of agency at work: Hänninen and Eteläpelto (2008) adapted an understanding of agency similar to the subject-centred sociocultural perspective. With regard to Holland et al. (2003) agency was defined as "human possibilities for actions that go beyond current constraints" (Hänninen & Eteläpelto, 2008, p. 100). The authors evaluated the outcome of an empowerment programme that aimed at fostering participants' agency in work contexts. The programme consisted of different workshops in which 19 hospital workers tried to further understand the relationship of their private and working life, their work-related social relationships, as well as the social dynamics of their organisation. Objects of this analysis were the work culture, the organisational philosophy, and the personal competencies of the participants. The explicit aim of the workshops was to foster self-awareness, self-respect, the capacity for interaction, and the experience of inner strength (i. e., self-efficacy). Six of the 19 participants were interviewed again 4 years after the completion of the 1-year programme. The focus of the interviews was directed towards the effects of the workshops on the participants' agency and their perceived well-being at work.

The interviews revealed that the workshop participants learnt to further understand the structure of their work organisation and especially their own role within this larger system. This made it much easier for the participants to find opportunities that allowed them to agentically translate their own interests and aspirations into goal-directed actions. This knowledge also helped them to realise impediments to such efforts. These insights allowed the participants to make choices concerning their work duties including their position within the organisation. For instance, some participants managed to deliberately enlarge their job profile by adding new and more demanding tasks to their job position. Others enrolled in further education courses to develop their work-related expertise. Other participants decided to resign from their former work or go into retirement.

In addition to the construction of new knowledge the workshops helped the participants to develop new tools to exercise agency at work. Maybe most importantly, the participants learnt new strategies to express their own opinions constructively. Due to the new tools as well as to new knowledge, participants developed a stronger sense of empowerment and more self-efficacy which made it easier for them to exercise agency even in rather contested situations. The interviews reported higher general satisfaction with the current work situation and this was attributed to the improved capacity to exercise agency at work.

A rather important conclusion of this study is that agency can be fostered as long as individuals are provided with opportunities to develop a stronger self-awareness and self-efficacy as well as the right tools and strategies that allow aspirations and decisions to be translated into feasible actions.

### 2.1.4 Recapitulation and Conclusion

It has been argued that the concept of agency has been used as a prerequisite of learning, as something individuals do, and as an outcome of work-related learning processes (Tynjälä, 2013). This early categorisation was used to identify and categorise both theoretical discussions of agency and empirical studies that are concerned with the phenomenon of agency. The majority of the theoretical and empirical contributions could be classified in the first two categories. Only one single study that used agency as an outcome variable was identified. Furthermore, this study used an understanding of agency that is largely overlapping with the subject-centred sociocultural perspective which has been predominant in the second category (agency as something individuals do.)

All literature covered in this review emphasises the relevance of agency in the context of learning at work. Similarly, the relevance of agency for the transformation of established (work) practices is a recurring element in the writings of many authors. It is surprising that an explicit definition of agency is missing in almost all of the contributions discussed here (except for Eteläpelto et al., 2013) despite the centrality of the concept. However, all discussions use agency as something related to actions that are based upon individuals' choices. Individuals are understood as active agents and are therefore conceptualised as the origin (or cause) of choices and actions.

The most striking difference between the conceptualisations of agency is that some authors (e. g., Bryson et al., 2006; Eraut & Hirsh, 2007) understand the concept more as an individual difference variable while others explicitly argue that agency can only be understood as an activity (e. g., Eteläpelto et al., 2013; Vähäsantanen, 2013). The latter perspective does not consider agency as an individual feature in the sense of a difference variable. Agency is rather conceptualised as something individuals do. Table 2.1 summarises both conceptualisations in an idealised form.

**Table 2.1.** Idealised conceptualisations of agency.

| Agency as an individual feature | Agency as something individuals do |
|---|---|
| • Antecedent of certan kind of actions<br>• Requirement to engage in agentic actions<br>• Relatively stable (pre-)disposition or tendency | • Goal-directed behaviour<br>• Certain kind of self-initiated actions<br>• Mainly situation specific |

However, some authors do not strictly restrict agency to one of the two perspectives. Both notions have been used in Billett's (2001c, 2004b, 2006, 2011a) co-participation model. Furthermore, although many studies privilege one of the two perspectives they also incorporate the other in their analysis. Eraut and Hirsh (2007), for example, speak about proactive individuals (proactive tendency as a difference variable) who initiate learning opportunities (e. g., proactively asking questions; i. e., a goal-directed and self-initiated action). Although researchers committed to the subject-centred sociocultural approach understand agency as something individuals do, one of their studies (Vähäsantanen et al., 2009) found that some of the study participants seem to exercise more agency than others. The intervention study of Hänninen and Eteläpelto (2008) even explicitly assumes that agency can be fostered. It follows that although these researchers do not understand agency as an individual feature they still acknowledge individual differences in the capacity or tendency to exercise agency.

Based on these insights it follows that Tynjälä's (2013) early suggestion for classifying the writings of some scholars as either being concerned with an understanding of agency as a prerequisite of work-related learning (e. g., Billett, 2004b, 2011a) or agency as a learning activity (e. g., Vähäsantanen & Billett, 2008) might better not be interpreted as a strict classification system. Although both of these idealised conceptualisations of agency can indeed be identified in the literature it is not always possible to unequivocally classify each conceptualisation into only one of the two categories. Apart from that, only one study was found that investigated agency as an outcome variable of learning and development processes (the third of Tynjälä's categories). At least at the moment this category seems to be less relevant in the WPL literature.

An important similarity between all theoretical accounts is that agency is always discussed in relation to the sociocultural and/or material context. It is acknowledged that individuals are not living in a social or material vacuum. All choices and actions are always—to a certain extent—influenced by social and material context factors. The exercise of agency depends on the affordances provided (e. g., social support, having sufficient autonomy; e. g., Lukic, Littlejohn, & Margaryan, 2012; Rynne et al., 2010) as well as on the constraints imposed by the workplace. However, apart from Billett's (2001c, 2004b, 2006, 2011a) discussion of the importance of workplace affordances and Eraut's (2007, 2010b, 2012; Eraut & Hirsh, 2007) enumeration of important workplace characteristics, the discourse on the relationship of sociocultural context factors and agency at work seems to be rather unsystematic. It is not possible to derive an empirically testable model that links context factors with agency based on the discussed literature.

In a similar vein, the relationship of individual level variables and the exercise of agency remains largely unaddressed in the WPL literature. The list of possible antecedents or drivers of agency comprises self-efficacy beliefs (van Veldhuizen, 2011), confidence and commitment (Eraut & Hirsh, 2007), proactive personality (Bryson et al., 2006), and interests (Billett & Somerville, 2004), as well as the rather abstract notion of identity (Billett & Somerville, 2004; Eteläpelto et al., 2013). The last one especially is used as an umbrella term to describe commitments, ideals, beliefs, interests, and values (Eteläpelto et al., 2013).

All empirical studies discussed in this chapter used qualitative methods. Not one of the reviewed studies used strict hypothesis-testing methods to investigate the relationship of work agency and other work-related phenomena (e. g., professional development, transformation of work practices). The striking absence of an operational definition of agency can be seen as the main reason behind this shortcoming. However, Eteläpelto et al. (2013) recently proposed a definition that might allow operationalisation of the concept in future studies. Another reason for the absence of quantitative empirical studies is the lack of a consistent set of hypotheses that describe the relationship of individual difference variables (e. g., self-efficacy), social context variables (e. g., autonomy at work), agentic behaviours (e. g., transformation of practices or seeking feedback at work), and certain learning outcomes (e. g., expertise level of individuals). Although such relationships are mentioned in the reviewed literature neither the direction nor the mechanism behind the relationship is discussed. At most, there is mutual consent that agency is positively related to professional development as well as to the transformation of work processes and structures. To sum up, there is presently nothing similar to a stringent and comprehensive theory suited to deriving a research model that can be tested with hypothesis-testing methods.

## 2.2 Agency in Other Research Traditions

This chapter gives an overview of the discussion on agency in other research disciplines that helps to overcome the shortcomings concluded in the last section. Eteläpelto et al. (2013) identified four distinct research traditions that discuss the concept: sociology, poststructural feminism, sociocultural approaches, and life-course research. Agency has also been central to discussions within welfare/development economics (e. g., Sen, 2001), philosophy (e. g., Ecclestone, 2007; Wisnewski, 2008), development psychology (e. g., Brandtstädter & Rothermund, 2002), social-cognitive psychology (e. g., Bandura, 2006b), and organisational behaviour research (e. g., Bindl & Parker, 2011). The latter two, as well as the literature on life-course research, discuss agency in relation to the development of individuals in general or to individuals' actions within work contexts; they have developed a nomological network of antecedents and outcomes of agency, and have already generated quantitative empirical research. Furthermore, they conceptualise agency in a way similar to the workplace learning literature. Hence, these research strands connect well to the research on agency discussed so far and will be the focus of the following literature review.

On the contrary, research on agency in development economics[8] and philosophy[9] either conceptualise agency in a way that is less compatible to the discussion outlined in Section 2.1 or do not empirically investigate the concept at all. It was therefore decided to exclude both of these research strands from the following overview. In addition, research on agency within development psychology is largely based on discussions originating in social-cognitive psychology as well as life-course research. In order to avoid repetition it was decided not to include development psychology writings in the overview given in this chapter. Excluded from this review also were sociological, poststructural fem-

8 Agency within the welfare/development literature is mostly discussed from a macro-political perspective. This thesis, however, is concerned with agency from a subject perspective.

9 Discussions of agency within philosophy are exclusively theoretical in nature. In addition, a range of philosophical ideas have already been included in discussions of agency within the literature on life-course research as well as the different research strands discussed in the review of Eteläpelto et al. (2013).

inism, and sociocultural discussions because they are already incorporated in the subject-centred sociocultural understanding of agency. Although life-course perspectives of agency are also already included in Eteläpelto and colleagues' (2013) agency conceptualisation (see Section 2.1.2.1) they are discussed here again because the empirical results of this research tradition were not fully addressed in their review.

This literature review is structured as follows: Section 2.2.1 discusses literature on social-cognitive psychology. Notions of agency within the life-course literature are then discussed in Section 2.2.2. A discussion of agency-related research within the organisational behaviour literature can be found in Section 2.2.3. Section 2.2.4 summarises and discusses the main findings of this literature review in respect to the findings presented in Section 2.1.

## 2.2.1 Social-Cognitive Psychology

Social-cognitive theory is a comprehensive psychological effort to explain human functioning and behaviour developed and promoted by Bandura (1982, 1986, 1989, 2012). The theory emphasises that human beings are inherently capable of shaping their own development and their life-course (Bandura, 2012). Individuals are understood as self-directed and agentic instead of just being reactive in nature. The aim of this theory is to explain the psychological mechanism behind the exercise of agency. The description "social-cognitive" was chosen to describe how the theory simultaneously accounts for the social origin of most human thought and action as well the relevance of different kinds of cognitive processes (Bandura, 1986, 2012).

The next two sections briefly describe and discuss the foundations of Bandura's social-cognitive theory (Section 2.2.1.1), his understanding of agency, as well as his theoretical ideas of how agency is related to desirable life outcomes (Section 2.2.1.2). It is followed by a review of studies that empirically investigated the main propositions put forward by Bandura (Section 2.2.1.3).

### 2.2.1.1 Triadic Recoprocity of Causality

At the core of social-cognitive theory lies the triadic reciprocity of causality. Bandura (1978, 1982, 1986) assumes that personal factors, behaviours, and environmental characteristics have to be understood as interactively related and therefore to reciprocally determine each other. The proposed relationship is depicted in Figure 2.4. Relationship (a) describes the interdependence between the person and their environment. For instance, a person might involuntarily activate environmental reactions just due to her social role, status or physical appearance. At the same time, the environmental reaction has the power to reinforce or mitigate the individual's self-perception as well as the individual's expectations about the environmental effects produced by her characteristics. The arrows marked as (b) represent the interaction between the person's behaviour and the environment. Situational characteristics—constraints and affordances—directly affect what behavioural options are at an individual's disposal in the first place. Contrarily, behaviour also alters the environment in ways which then determine the constraints and affordances the individual has to face in the future (this idea is also present in Billett's co-participation model; see Section 2.1.1.1). The last relationship, (c), concerns the reciprocal effects of behaviour and personal characteristics (especially cognitive processes). For example, individuals might only engage in behaviours which they expect to produce desired outcomes. Control beliefs are therefore thought to be important personal characteristics that predict behaviour (see Section 2.2.2.2 for a more detailed discussion of control beliefs). Such beliefs are then positively or negatively altered by the experience of success or failure that results from a particular behaviour.

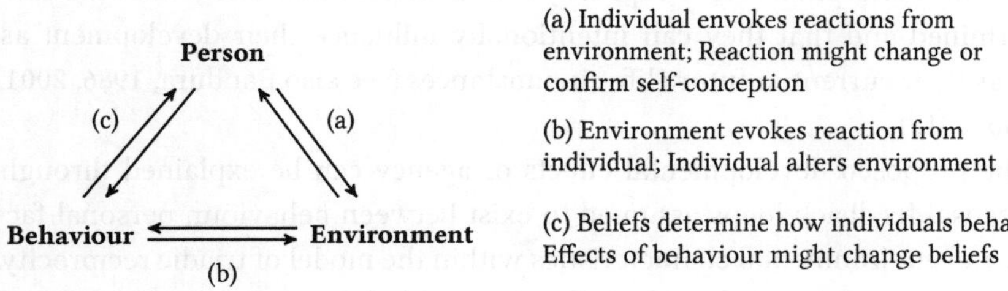


**Figure 2.4.** Triadic reciprocity of causality. Reprinted and adapted from "Bandura, A. (1978). The self system in reciprocal determinism. *American Psychologist*, *33*(4), 344–358, p. 345" with permission from APA.

The described reciprocal determinism is not thought to be a holistic theory where all the "classes of determinants act simultaneously as a fused whole" (Bandura, 2012, p. 359). The reciprocity is based on causal feedback loops between the three determinant classes which are assumed to unfold over time rather than simultaneously (Bandura, 1982).

#### 2.2.1.2 Human Agency within Social-Cognitive Theory

Bandura's (1982, 1986) understanding of agency is strongly based on the just introduced triadic reciprocity framework. He denies that individuals can be understood either as autonomous agents that are fully in control of their actions (autonomous agency) or as sole instruments of external influences that do not themselves have any self-directive abilities (mechanical agency) (Bandura, 1986, 1989). He argues that humans

> ...make causal contribution to their own motivation and action within a system of triadic reciprocal causation, action, cognitive, affective, and other personal factors, and environmental events all operate as interacting determinants. Any account of the determinants of human action must, therefore, include self-generated influences as a contributing factor. (Bandura, 1989, p. 1175)

Within social-cognitive theory agency is understood as an emergent interactive phenomenon (Bandura, 1986) that can be defined as the "capacity to exercise control over the nature and quality of one's life" (Bandura, 2001, p. 1). This conceptualisation explicitly acknowledges that individuals are self-determined and that they can intentionally influence their development as well as their current or future life circumstances (see also Bandura, 1986, 2001, 2006b, 2012).

The proposed developmental effects of agency can be explained through the causal feedback loops assumed to exist between behaviour, personal factors, and environmental characteristics within the model of triadic reciprocity. All behaviours—over time—affect the situational characteristics an individual has to face as well as personal factors like skills, knowledge, interests, beliefs, and so on. Although individuals are somehow determined by the environmental characteristics of their current situation as well as their present personal qualities, behaviour can be directed towards changing these features. Through intentional goal-directed behaviour—namely, agentic actions—individuals are able to change their life circumstances as well as their personal capacities. Any kind of environment an individual selects to be part of determines the individual's future scope of actions and the development of personal capacities (like skills and knowledge) as well as other personal characteristics (e. g., beliefs). It therefore follows that individuals are able, by exercising agency, to put themselves in more advantageous situations that are physically and socially less constrictive and that offer a range of options for personal development.

Consider a low-qualified individual in a marginalised occupational position that is in financial troubles. Career opportunities with better remuneration are not automatically offered. However, the employee agentically engages in training and career negotiation with her supervisor. This might then lead to offered training courses which enable the employee to secure a better job position in the future. This new job might then lead to even more training opportunities and new career options. A less agentic employee would not have negotiated any career advancements and would therefore still be working in her marginalised position.

Social-cognitive theory advocates that individuals are highly in control of their life trajectories. However, Bandura (2001, 2006b) also acknowledges that many aspects of human lives cannot be controlled directly and are rather products of fortuity. Social-cognitive theory is concerned with how individuals manage this fortuity. The central argument is that agentic individuals are able to pursue life courses that increase "the level and type of fortuitous encounters they will experience" (Bandura, 2001, p. 12) as well as to actively use the opportunities that are connected to unforeseen but promising events. In other words, agentic individuals select circumstances that are more likely to produce desired outcomes and are better equipped to recognise and use them. An employee, for instance, might be offered the opportunity to present at a business meeting because her supervisor is unable to attend on a short notice. This employee might then use this rather unforeseen opportunity to get herself introduced to the senior management and demonstrate her work-related skill set. This might lead to new career-related opportunities in the future.

To summarise, the notion of agency in social-cognitive theory is mainly related to the idea of how individuals exercise control over their life by engaging in goal-directed behaviour. Bandura (2001) describes "the power to originate actions for given purpose" as "the key feature of personal agency" (p. 6). Therefore, only intentional acts can be described as agentic. Reflexes or activities done by accident are not agentic in nature. Furthermore, it is important to separate the consequences of intentional actions from the action itself. Within social-cognitive theory the effect an intentional action brings about—whether it is intended or not—is not part of agency (see, for very similar ideas, Giddens, 1984).

Bandura (1982, 1986, 2001, 2006b) does not only describe the characteristics and possible effects of agency. His theory is also concerned with the psychological mechanism behind the exercise of agency. The following mechanisms explain how the formed intentions translate into agentic actions and also give initial insights into why some individuals might be able to exercise more agency than others:

1. *Forethought:* Intentions are understood as present commitments to realise future actions (Bandura, 2001; for a discussion on the effects of intentions on actions see Ajzen, 1991). To build up such commitments individuals set personal goals, anticipate potential outcomes of possible prospective actions, and select those that are most likely to produce the desired consequence. Individuals therefore create current motivators that help to direct and energise actions by cognitively representing future events. Through this mechanism individuals are able to bypass the dictate of current situations and therefore shape their own life trajectories. Bandura (2001, 2006b) calls this temporal extension of agency forethought. Without a goal to leave her current marginalised job position the low-qualified employee in the example above would not have engaged in any negotiation with her supervisor.

2. *Self-reactiveness:* After committing to certain goals individuals have to be able to translate and shape those commitments into action plans. More general and distal goals have to be broken down into a hierarchically structured goal system. In comparison to distal goals, proximal sub-goals allow individuals to sketch out much more detailed and motivating action plans. They help to "mobilize self-influences and direct what one does in the here and

now" (Bandura, 2001, p. 8). Based on these sub-goals, individuals can self-monitor their progress towards the general and more distal goal and correctively self-regulate their actions if necessary. The sole goal to improve her financial and social situation would not have been specific enough in the example described above. So it was necessary that the low-qualified employee broke down this distal aspiration into more achievable sub-goals like getting more work-related qualifications that enable her to progress within the organisation.

3. *Self-reflectiveness:* Social-cognitive theory assumes that humans are inherently capable of reflecting upon their capabilities to act and exercise control in the world (Bandura, 2001, 2006b). They are assumed to constantly self-examine whether they think they are capable of engaging in envisioned actions and whether there is at least a chance that the pursued actions will result in the desired outcomes (i. e., proximal or more distal goals). Self-reflectiveness is the most central mechanism behind agency. In social-cognitive theory it is not the actual capacities that determine whether an individual decides to engage in a certain goal-directed behaviour but judgements about whether these capacities suffice to do so (Bandura, 1982, 1986, 1989, 1997, 2001, 2006b). "Unless people believe they can produce desired results and forestall detrimental ones by their actions, they have little incentive to act or to persevere in the face of difficulties" (Bandura, 2001, p. 10). Judgements about one's own capacities to successfully execute a particular behaviour are subsumed under the concept of self-efficacy beliefs in Bandura's writings. Applied to the examples discussed before, one can see that neither would the low-qualified employee have engaged in the offered training opportunity nor would the other employee have agreed to present at the business meeting without being convinced that they could succeed in these actions. Individuals without self-efficacy beliefs would have probably declined the given opportunities.

With regard to the earlier sketched out triadic reciprocity one can now argue that the successful exercise of agency leads to a self-fulfilling prophecy. Individuals who successfully engage in goal-directed behaviours reinforce their self-efficacy beliefs giving them a strong incentive to set new—even higher—

goals and to engage in efforts that help them to succeed (Bandura, 1989, 2001). In a similar manner, individuals who manage to seize fortuitous opportunities might end up in life circumstances that offer even more fortuity in the future (Bandura, 2006b). Furthermore, Bandura (2001) argues that agency—that is, the capability to set goals, to translate those goals into action plans, and judgements that oneself is able to engage in the necessary actions—helps individuals to avoid detrimental paths that might be opened up by fortuitous events. For example, the self-set goal to pursue a professional degree combined with a feasible action plan based on more proximal goals as well as high beliefs in one's own capacity to master the study program might help an individual who lives in a very low socioeconomic status neighbourhood to resist the temptation of joining a criminal gang. The opportunities that result from the professional degree might then open up new development trajectories that would otherwise not have been accessible.

To sum up, Bandura explicitly defines agency as a capacity and therefore as an individual feature. Furthermore, social-cognitive theory of agency explains the psychological mechanism behind agentic actions and gives a rationale for why the exercise of agency should lead to positive effects for the agentic individual. Central aspects to his theory are self-efficacy beliefs which have also been exploited by life-course researchers (see Section 2.2.2). In Bandura's theory of agency, highly developed self-efficacy beliefs in combination with self-regulatory capabilities can be interpreted as requirements for all agentic actions. Such personal agency capacities help people to expand their freedom of action such that they are able to select, influence, and construct their life circumstances. Furthermore, they also help individuals to seize fortuitous opportunities they encounter (Bandura, 1986, 2001, 2006b). However, social-cognitive theory does not provide any rationale for why individuals should set certain development goals in the first place.

#### 2.2.1.3 Empirical Evidence

Bandura's social-cognitive theory and in particular his ideas about the centrality of self-efficacy beliefs gave rise to a large amount of empirical research in a range of different domains (e. g., work, education, health issues) that employed a great variety of different methods (e. g., experiments, questionnaire studies, cross-sectional and longitudinal studies). Over time, many reviews and meta-analyses aimed at summarising the results of this research. This section aims to give an overview of the findings generated by these studies. A particular focus will be laid on the relationship between self-efficacy beliefs and work-related actions as well as desirable outcomes variables.

Strong evidence could be found that self-efficacy beliefs are positively related to academic performance ($r = .38, p < .01, k = 38$, Multon, Brown, & Lent, 1991; $\beta = .08, p < .05$, based on longitudinal data, $k = 60$, Valentine, DuBois, & Cooper, 2004), performance in work settings ($r = .38, p < .01, k = 157$, Stajkovic & Luthans, 1998; $r = .23, p < .05, k = 12$, Judge & Bono, 2001; $\beta = .28, p < .05, k = 8$, S. D. Brown, Lent, Telander, & Tramayne, 2011), and specific task performance at work ($r = .32, p < .05, k = 123$, Judge, Jackson, Shaw, Scott, & Rich, 2007), and even performance in sport settings ($r = .38, p < .01, k = 84$, Moritz, Feltz, Fahrbach, & Mack, 2000). Furthermore, self-efficacy beliefs seem to be positively related to persistence in academic settings ($r = .34, p < .01, k = 18$, Multon et al., 1991), commitment of teachers to their profession ($r = .32, p < .001, k = 33$, Chesnut & Burley, 2015), job satisfaction ($r = .45, p < .05, k = 12$, Judge, Thoresen, Bono, & Patton, 2001), and the setting of higher goals at work ($\beta = .48, p < .05, k = 8$, S. D. Brown et al., 2011). Another meta-analysis found that high self-efficacy beliefs within a certain academic domain (e. g., math, English) is positively related to interest in this particular domain ($r = .59, p < .05, k = 53$, Rottinghaus, Larson, & Borgen, 2003). Furthermore, Shoji et al. (2015) just recently presented evidence that high self-efficacy beliefs might prevent burnout ($r = -.33, p < .05, k = 57$).

These meta-analyses speak much in favour of Bandura's claims that strong self-efficacy beliefs should be an important predictor of desired life outcomes. However, it has to be noted that most of the studies cited only took cross-sectional data into account. Although these studies usually speak of self-efficacy beliefs as a predictor of the criterion variables, a clear causal relationship cannot be established on such data sources. However, a few longitudinal studies did investigate the causal direction of the relationship of self-efficacy beliefs and other variables. For instance, Sitzmann and Yeo (2013) found evidence that self-efficacy beliefs are rather a product than a predictor of performance (see also Holzberger, Philipp, & Kunter, 2013). Nevertheless, Judge et al. (2007) based their meta-analyses on longitudinal data and could find evidence for the assumed causal relationship between self-efficacy beliefs and task performance. Furthermore, based on their longitudinal study, Caprara, Vecchione, Alessandri, Gerbino, and Barbaranelli (2011) found evidence that self-efficacy is a causal predictor of school grades in later years ($\beta = .20 - .31$, $p < .05$). In another recent study, Abele and Spurk (2009) could show that occupational self-efficacy at graduation positively predicts career satisfaction after 7 years of work experience ($\beta = .26$, $p < .001$), salary after both 3 and 7 years of work experience ($\beta = .10$, $p < .01$; $\beta = .08$, $p < .05$), and hierarchical status ($\beta = .09$, $p < .05$).

Another critical point that has to be emphasised is that the presented meta-analyses only investigated the direct relationship between self-efficacy beliefs and certain outcome variables. However, the social-cognitive theory of agency explicitly assumes that this relationship is mediated by agentic actions in which the individual is deliberately involved. At least three meta-analyses focussed on this mediation. Kanfer, Wanberg, and Kantrowitz (2001) could show that job search self-efficacy beliefs are significantly related to job search behaviour ($r = .27$, $p < .05$, $k = 28$) as well as to the unemployment period an individual has to face ($r = -.12$, $p < .05$, $k = 4$), the chance to find a job after a certain period ($r = .09$, $p < .05$, $k = 11$), and the number of job offers one gets after sending out applications ($r = .28$, $p < .05$, $k = 5$). Karsten, Mitra, and Schmidt (2012) investigated whether computer self-efficacy beliefs predict the use of computers. In their meta-analysis they found evidence that these task-specific self-efficacy beliefs are both positively related to the intention to use a computer ($r = .35$, $p < .05$, $k = 30$) as well as to the actual use of computers ($r = .34$, $p < .05$, $k = 32$). The early study of Sadri and Robertson (1993) analysed the relationship of self-efficacy beliefs and a range of work-related behaviours (e. g., career-related choices, propensity to change processes at work) and behavioural intentions (e. g., considering career options). Based on eight samples they found that self-efficacy beliefs positively predicted both actual choice and behavioural intentions ($r = .30$, $p < .05$). In a more qualitative literature review, Lent and Hackett (1987) also claim that there is much empirical support that self-efficacy beliefs are an important predictor of career-relevant behaviour like college major choices or utilising development-relevant situations.

A few other studies investigated the relationship of self-efficacy beliefs and agentic efforts that are either related to professional development or the transformation of work practices. Maurer, Weiss, and Barbeite (2003) investigated the antecedents of U. S. workers' participation in development activities. They could show that self-efficacy beliefs are positively related to participation in various development activities mediated via attitudes towards development and intentions to participate in development activities (indirect effect $\beta = .06$, $p < .001$). In an earlier study, Maurer and Tarulli (1994) found that strong self-efficacy beliefs positively predicted the voluntary participation in non-in-house learning and development activities of non-management employees (partial $r = .10$, $p < .01$, controlled for a range of other predictors) as well as the future participation in learning and development activities (partial $r = .11$, $p < .01$). Using regression analysis, Kyndt, Govaerts, Dochy, and Baert (2011) found evidence that self-efficacy beliefs are positively related to the learning intentions of low-qualified employees ($\beta = .31$, $p < .001$). However, using a hierarchical regression approach on a larger sample those results could not be replicated (Kyndt, Govaerts, Claes, De La Marche, & Dochy, 2013). On a similar account, Renkema (2006) found that self-efficacy beliefs positively predicted the intention to engage in formal learning activities (i. e., trainings) for both employees working in technical installation ($\beta = .23$, $p < .01$) and elderly care ($\beta = .21$, $p < .01$). In a study with teachers, van Daal, Donche, and De Maeyer (2014) reported that self-efficacy beliefs are positively related to certain workplace learning activities (experimentation at work: $\beta = .50$, $p < .001$ and informal interaction: $\beta = .24$, $p < .05$). Similar results were found by Oude Groote Beverborg, Sleegers, and van Veen (2015). In their study of VET teachers they found evidence that self-efficacy beliefs are positively related to information sharing and social reflection ($\beta = .31$, $p < .01$), self-reflection ($\beta = .32$, $p < .01$), experimentation ($\beta = .33$, $p < .01$), and keeping up-to-date by obtaining new information related to their professional field (e. g., reading professional literature; $\beta = .27$, $p < .01$). Hetzner, Heid, and Gruber (2015) found evidence that self-efficacy beliefs are an important predictor of reflection at work for employees working in banking ($\beta = .25, p < .05$).

Hirschi, Freund, and Herrmann (2014) investigated the relationship of self-efficacy beliefs and proactive career management behaviours (i. e., activities that are directed towards the development of one's own career). For both the student ($r = .33, p < .001$) and the working sample ($r = .21, p < .001$) the authors found a positive relationship between both concepts. Tims, Bakker, and Derks (2014) used data from a diary study of employees to test whether daily changes in workers' self-efficacy beliefs could predict daily job crafting efforts (i. e., efforts to proactively change the current work situation; see also Sections 2.2.3.1 and 3.3.1 for a discussion on this concept). Based on a multilevel structural equation modelling approach the authors found that self-efficacy positively predicts both the crafting of variety at work ($\beta = .23, p < .001$) and the crafting of development opportunities ($\beta = .22, p < .05$).

Most of the studies reported in this chapter used relatively short self-reporting scales to measure self-efficacy beliefs. Amongst others, scales exist that measure general self-efficacy beliefs (Schwarzer & Jerusalem, 1995; see also Chen, Gully, & Eden, 2001), teacher sense of efficacy (Tschannen-Moran & Hoy Woolfolk, 2001), job search self-efficacy (Caplan, Vinokur, Price, & Van Ryn, 1989), mathematics self-efficacy (Betz & Hackett, 1983), geriatric nursing self-efficacy (C. S. Mackenzie & Peragrine, 2003), and occupational self-efficacy (Rigotti, Schyns, & Mohr, 2008). Usually the scales exhibit relatively good psychometric properties.

However, it has to be noted that Bandura (1997, 2006a) explicitly emphasises that self-efficacy beliefs are highly domain specific. He argues that measures of self-efficacy beliefs will only predict individuals' engagement in certain actions if they are strongly targeted towards the behaviour of interest. Self-efficacy measures on a more general level (e. g., general self-efficacy beliefs) will lose predictive power of behaviours in specific domains (e. g., work-related behaviours). Evidence for this assumption could be shown through moderator analyses of some of the meta-analyses reported above (e. g., Chesnut & Burley, 2015; Moritz et al., 2000; Valentine et al., 2004; Chesnut & Burley, 2015; Moritz et al., 2000; Valentine et al., 2004; however, Shoji et al., 2015, could not find a moderating effect of the specificity of the measurement and job burnout).

To sum up, almost all empirical studies that used Bandura's social-cognitive theory focused on the hypothesised (central) relationship of self-efficacy beliefs and the engagement in certain kind of behaviours and/or desirable life-course outcomes (e. g., performance in different contexts, job satisfaction, income). The results of many studies speak much in favour of Bandura's hypothesis. Individuals' agency is related to their beliefs about their capacities to pursue certain actions that might result in desired outcomes. Strong self-efficacy beliefs are strongly related to the choice of more challenging goals, firmer commitment, and to the deliberate efforts individuals will invest to actually reach those goals even in the face of obstacles and failures. Furthermore, a range of short self-reporting scales exist that are developed to measure self-efficacy beliefs in a range of domains. Both the strong empirical evidence that speaks in favour of the important role of self-efficacy beliefs in the exercise of agency and the ready availability of suitable scales for questionnaire-based research might be the reason why many studies interested in the phenomenon of agency used self-efficacy beliefs as a proxy of the concept (e. g., van Veldhuizen, 2011; see also next section) or as an important antecedent of agentic actions (see Sections 2.2.3.2 and 2.2.3.3).

## 2.2.2 Life-Course Research

Life-course research studies the life trajectories of human beings (i. e., individuals or groups) over a substantial part of their life spans (Elder, 1998, 2003). It is not a solitary scientific discipline (George, 2003) but rather an interdisciplinary scientific community with members from anthropology, psychology, history, economics, and—mostly—sociology (Elder, 2003; Mayer, 2009). The shared interest of those scholars lies in the identification of a prototypical or even normative "pattern of age-graded events" (Elder, 2000, p. 1614) and the explanation of variations from such a pattern (Elder, 1998, 2000). In other words, life-course research sets out to explain the causes and/or effects of changes that occur within individuals' biographies.

One of the core assumptions within life-course research is that individuals actively construct their own life courses through the choices they make and the actions they take (Elder, 1998, 2003). Individuals are perceived to have the capacity to shape their own biographies by proactively formulating and persistently pursuing life plans. Individuals are thereby understood as the architects of their own life course (Gecas, 2003) or, put differently, as active agents who are able to actively orchestrate their life trajectories.

In a first step, the conceptualisation of agency from a life-course perspective will be shortly presented (Section 2.2.2.1). It is followed by a discussion on how life-course researchers explain the differences between individuals' agency (Section 2.2.2.2) and how socio-historic circumstances can both support and restrict the exercise of agency (Section 2.2.2.3). Empirical evidence of the positive effects of agency over the life course will be presented in Section 2.2.2.4.

#### 2.2.2.1 Conceptualising Agency from a Life-Course Perspective

Within the life-course literature, agency is the concept used to express the capacity of individuals to exert control over their own lives (Shanahan & Hood, 2000; see also Crockett, 2002; Hitlin & Elder, 2007b). Although agency is central to discourses on life-course research the concept is still contested. Hitlin and Elder (2007b) criticise the concept as very slippery because of definitional inconsistencies and a high level of abstractness of the existing definitions. In their influential publication they distinguish four types of agency that are used in the literature: (a) existential agency, (b) pragmatic agency, (c) identity agency, and (d) life-course agency. Existential agency describes the universal human potential to self-initiate actions and to exert some kind of free will in their daily life. Pragmatic agency is concerned with the deliberate direction of attention, time-critical choices, and actions based on those choices in situations where automatised responses fail (e. g., in situations that are novel for individuals). Identity agency refers to all kind of actions that are mainly based on social roles and social commitments. Hitlin and Elder (2007b) argue that agency—in the sense of identity agency—is also existent when individuals try to live up to social commitments or when they try to actively internalise them in the first place. The last type called life-course agency is concerned with the capacity to make choices and to engage in actions that help to meet self-set goals. Manifestations of agency in the life course are the selection and formulation of long-term plans (i. e., setting goals), the implementation of those plans via goal-directed behaviour, as well as perseverance in the face of problems and obstacles (e. g., Crockett, 2002; Hitlin & Elder, 2007b).

This typology is important to understand that agency is—at the same time—a universal capacity that all individuals exercise all the time and something in which individuals might strongly differ. Hitlin and Elder (2007b) argue as follows:

> We can differentiate between agency as a capacity that all individuals possess, like existential agency, and a variable capacity that some people utilize with greater facility. [...] We can analytically separate the pure capacity for life course decisions from the ability to successfully implement them. (p. 183)

Life-course research is mainly interested in individuals' differences of their ability to exercise agency in order to actively construct their biographies. The next paragraphs are concerned with psychological mechanisms that explain such differences.

#### 2.2.2.2 Explaining the Differences between Individuals' Agency

Differences in individuals' abilities to actively construct their life-courses are explained by two partly consecutive mechanisms (for a summary see Table 2.2). The first mechanism is based on Clausen's (1991) theory of planful competences. Clausen (1991) argues that individuals who are able to come up with advantageous and achievable life goals and who are able to translate these life goals into long-term plans are also able to make more "positive events happen" (p. 810) during their life course. He summarises these abilities in the concept of planful competence and assumes that some individuals are more competent than others. For Clausen, planful competence incorporates the ability to recognise and know one's own strengths (or weaknesses) as well as preferences. Put simply, competent individuals know themselves better than less competent ones. Furthermore, planful competence also encompasses the ability to figure out and choose goals that match these strengths and preferences. It is necessary that individuals are able to construct cognitive representations of possible and also reasonable future selves (see also S. Cross & Markus, 1991; Hitlin & Elder, 2007b). In other words, life-course agency requires that individuals have an idea what kind of person they want to be in the future. At the same time, the notion of planful competence also includes the idea that long-distance goals alone are not enough to motivate behaviour. Individuals need to be able to find, evaluate, and select courses of actions and social settings that permit them to meet the long-term goals in the best possible way (see also Shanahan & Elder, 2002). As can be seen, Clausen's ideas about planful competence partly match with Bandura's notion of forethought and self-reactiveness (see Section 2.2.1.2).

**Table 2.2.** Agency mechanism proposed in the life-course research literature.

| Planful competence | Control beliefs |
|---|---|
| Encompasses the ability to<br>• reflect about the abilities and preferences,<br>• come up with cognitive representations of future life states, and<br>• translates objectives into actions plans. | Beliefs about the extent of control an individual has about<br>• her capacity to cause certain means,<br>• the contingency between means and desired or undesired outcomes, and<br>• her capacity to affect life events. |

The second mechanism behind life-course agency is concerned with the effects of individuals' perceived control. Some life-course scholars (e. g., Gecas, 2003; Hitlin & Elder, 2007b) assume that strong beliefs about one's capacity to exert control over one's own life and to achieve certain goals are an important requirement for exercising agency (see also Section 2.2.1.2).[10] Only individuals who believe in themselves will decide to take actions to meet certain goals and persist during set-backs and the encounter of obstacles. Skinner (1995, 1996) distinguishes three types of control beliefs that have been employed in the life-course literature (see Kristiansen, 2014). A graphical representation of the proposed typology as the relationships between agents (i. e., the individual herself), means (i. e., certain kinds of goal-directed behaviours), and ends (i. e., possible outcomes of the behaviours in question) can be found in Figure 2.5.

10 It should be noted that Clausen (1991) also emphasises the importance of strong self-confidence—that is, the feeling of trust to be capable of dealing with current and future circumstances—within his writings (see also Shanahan & Elder, 2002).

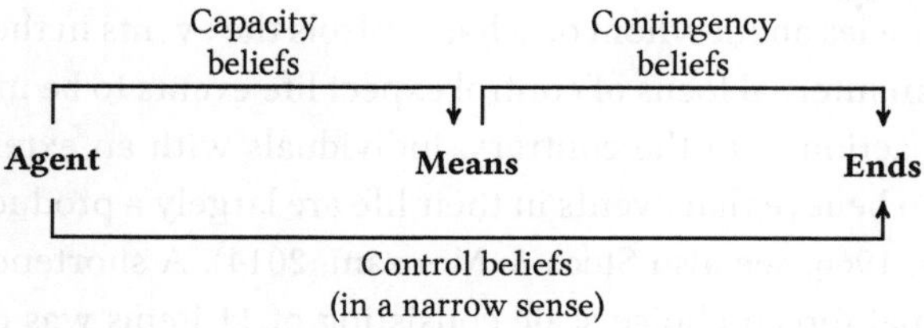


**Figure 2.5.** Typology of control beliefs. Reprinted and adapted from "Skinner, E. A., Chapman, M., & Baltes, P. B. (1988). Control, means-ends, and agency beliefs: A new conceptualization and its measurement during childhood. *Journal of Personality and Social Psychology, 54*(1), 117–133, p. 118" with permission from APA.

Capacity beliefs are concerned with an individual's perception about whether and how she has the capacity to cause certain means. Contingency beliefs "refer to generalized expectancies about the extent to which certain means or causes are sufficient conditions for the production of ends or outcomes" (Skinner, 1995, pp. 30–31). And finally, control beliefs in a narrow sense refer to expectancies about whether and how one can produce (or prevent) desired (or undesired) outcomes. Sometimes these three control beliefs are also summarised as an individual's general sense of agency (e. g., Bandura, 2006b; Hitlin & Elder, 2007a; Hitlin & Kirkpatrick Johnson, 2015; Hitlin & Long, 2009).

Within the life-course literature different potential empirical measures of agency have been discussed (Hitlin & Long, 2009; Kristiansen, 2014). The most important of these measures are concerned with the sense of agency and can therefore be classified in Skinner's (1995) proposed typology (see Kristiansen, 2014). The capacity to exercise agency in the life course has most often been related to individuals' self-efficacy beliefs (Gecas, 2003; Hitlin & Elder, 2007a, 2007b; Hitlin & Kirkpatrick Johnson, 2015; Hitlin & Long, 2009). Since self-efficacy beliefs are defined as "conviction that one can successfully execute [a] behavior required to produce [an] outcome" (Bandura, 1977, p. 193) they can be characterised as a measure of capacity beliefs (see Section 2.2.1.3 for different scales that try to capture self-efficacy beliefs).

As a measure of contingency beliefs the concept of locus of control has been introduced (e. g., Hitlin & Long, 2009). Locus of control refers to individuals' stable expectancies about whom or what controls the events in their lives. Individuals with an internal locus of control expect life events to be mainly caused by their own actions. On the contrary, individuals with an external locus of control tend to believe that events in their life are largely a product of external forces (Rotter, 1966; see also Steca & Monzani, 2014). A shortened version of Rotter's original forced-choice scale consisting of 11 items was developed by Valecha and Ostrom (1974). An overview about existing locus of control measures can be found elsewhere (Furnham & Steele, 1993; Steca & Monzani, 2014). In their meta-analysis, Ng, Sorensen, and Eby (2006) found evidence that an internal locus of control positively correlates with general well-being in life ($r$ = .33), job satisfaction ($r$ = .31), job commitment ($r$ = .17), job motivation ($r$ = .22), job performance ($r$ = .15), and career success ($r$ = .11; $p < .05$ for all correlations).

Three different constructs have been proposed to directly measure control beliefs in a narrow sense: (a) mastery, (b) personal control, and (c) dispositional optimism. Mastery and personal control are conceptually similar. Mastery has been defined as "the extent to which one regards one's life chances as being under one's own control in contrast to being fatalistically ruled" (Pearlin & Schooler, 1978, p. 4; see also Pearlin, Nguyen, Schieman, & Milkie, 2007). It could be empirically shown that a strong sense of mastery was positively related to health outcomes over the life course (Pearlin & Schooler, 1978; Pudrovska, Schieman, Paerlin, & Nguyen, 2005). Mastery as a latent personality trait can be measured using a short 7-item scale (Pearlin & Schooler, 1978). Personal control is defined as "a learned expectation that outcomes depend on one's own choices and actions" (Mirowsky & Ross, 1998, p. 419). It is assumed that individuals with a sense of personal control tend to seek much more information that helps them to take charge of their lives and to generate desired outcomes than individuals who do not feel in control over their lives (Mirowsky & Ross, 1998). Again, a strong sense of personal control has been found to be empirically related to markers of better health (Ross & Mirowsky, 2013). A short 8-item scale measuring personal control exists (Mirowsky & Ross, 1991).

The last construct, dispositional optimism, can be interpreted as a sense of agency that entails a long-term perspective (Hitlin & Elder, 2007a). Peterson

(2000) defines optimism by referring to the definition of Tiger (1979) as "a mood or attitude associated with an expectation about the social or material future—one which the evaluator regards as socially desirable, to his [or her] advantage, for his [or her] pleasure" (p. 44). The relatively stable tendency to display an optimistic attitude is called dispositional optimism (Zagorski, 2013). Hitlin and Elder (2007a) use optimism to refer to an individual's stable expectation about her ability to bring about desired outcomes or to prevent undesired ones. "The more optimistic a person is, the more they will have efficacious and positive influences on their lives and in their choices" (Hitlin & Elder, 2007a, p. 43). A 10-item scale that measures both optimism and pessimism has been proposed by Scheier, Carver, and Bridges (1994). In their review, Carver and Scheier (2014) argue that optimism is positively related to mental well-being and physical health. One possible explanation put forward by Carver and Scheier (2014) is that optimistic individuals adopt more often an agentic approach towards avoiding future health problems.

#### 2.2.2.3 Life-Course Agency and Socio-Historic Circumstances

The two proposed mechanisms behind the exercise of agency are both located at the level of the individual. However, at the same time, life-course scholars have explicitly recognised that agency cannot be fully disentangled from social and historical circumstances (Elder, 1998). Social and historical contexts always determine—to a certain extent—how individuals can shape and construct their own life courses. The work and family situation of an individual as well as the current political and social conditions might either constrain or permit the exercise of agency (Crockett, 2002; Elder, 1998; Elder & Shanahan, 2007). Consider a single mother of three who aspires to a higher education degree. This plan might only be feasible if she finds affordable day care for her children as well as a reliable source of income that allows her to pay for the tuition and the living costs during her study. In a society that offers low-interest student loans and provides special day care facilities for students such an endeavour might be more feasible than in a society that does not offer such opportunities. Furthermore, a general environment that supports the idea of women advancing on the educational track might also make it more probable that she will eventually do so. In comparison, a society where higher education is largely reserved for already well-educated males, like in the first half of the 20th century, might even prevent her from formulating the goal of a degree in the first place.

Thus, agency has always to be conceptualised as bounded (Shanahan & Hood, 2000; see also Evans, 2002, 2007)—but not fully dictated (Crockett, 2002)—by social and historical circumstances that manifest in constraints and opportunities to make choices and take actions within the life course (Elder, 1998; see also Mayer, 2009). Especially in such situations where certain options are not easily available, agency becomes more important (Shanahan & Hood, 2000). Reconsider the single mother from above. A social environment that generally supports (or even expects) women to enrol in higher education makes it easily possible that she will study because it is the normal thing to do. Strong agency is not necessarily required in such a situation. However, in less supportive social and/or historic situations she would have to expend much more effort to secure the goal of a higher education degree. Agency becomes more important to reach desired outcomes when individuals are situated in less supporting environments. Certain social conditions provide more options than others. However, some social-historic contexts tend to restrict options. Such contexts then are more likely to allocate individuals into certain predetermined life trajectories without much contribution from the individuals themselves. Within life-course discourses these ideas are summarised in the concept of bounded agency (Shanahan & Hood, 2000). In a certain sense this is very similar to Bandura's (1986, 2001, 2006b) notion of fortuity (see Section 2.2.1.2).

To sum up, agency is a central theoretical construct in life-course research. It is conceptualised on the level of the individual and life-course scholars explicitly acknowledge that individuals do indeed differ in their capacity to exercise agency. Within the life-course literature two main mechanisms that explain the differences between individuals' agency capacities are proposed. The first mechanism is concerned with the competence to reflect about one's own abilities and preferences, the ability to come up with cognitive representations of future selves (Hitlin & Elder, 2007b), and the ability to translate objectives into suitable action plans. The second mechanism is concerned with the effects of individuals' control beliefs and how these beliefs affect engagement in goal-directed behaviours. Several scales have been proposed to measure certain kinds of control beliefs. Although agency is understood as an individual difference variable, the life-course literature also strongly acknowledges that social and historical circumstance may always either constrain or foster the exercise of agency.

#### 2.2.2.4 Empirical Evidence

Agency is a central concept within life-course discourses. However, only a few empirical studies exist that have actually studied the phenomenon using the measures proposed above (Clausen, 1991; Hitlin & Elder, 2007a; Hitlin & Kirkpatrick Johnson, 2015; Shanahan & Elder, 2002). Three of these four studies used longitudinal data to investigate the effects of agency on several outcome measures. In comparison to cross-sectional studies this longitudinal approach generates much more reliable results. The findings of all four of these studies will be briefly sketched out below.

For his analysis, Clausen (1991) merged three samples of the Berkeley longitudinal studies (see also Eichorn, 1981). These studies first gathered different data from young children in the years 1928 to 1931 and did various follow ups years later (the remaining individuals were 53 to 62 years old in the last follow up). A subsample of 60–70 cases that contained all necessary information required was used for further analyses. Clausen found strong evidence that his operationalisation of planful competence positively predicts educational attainment before high-school graduation for males ($\beta = .54$, $p < .01$, $R^2 = .55$), controlling for parental socio-economic status (SES) and the IQ measured at age 17 to 18. Furthermore, another regression analysis revealed that planful competence measured during adolescence also predicts occupational status for male participants at the age of 53 to 62 ($\beta = .50$, $p < .01$, $R^2 = .54$) controlling for parental SES, IQ at age of 18, and educational attainment. It therefore seems that planful competence in younger years is—for males—strongly related to both educational and occupational outcomes during the life course. However, no such evidence could be found for females.

Shanahan and Elder (2002) used the rich data of the Stanford-Terman longitudinal study (see also Terman & Oden, 1959) for their analysis. For this study 856 males with an IQ of more than 135 born between 1904 and 1917 were studied in 12 waves over 69 years of their lives. The dataset includes data on work, marriage, achievement, ageing, and certain psychological trait measures. The original sample was divided in two subsamples (older cohort, $n = 448$; younger cohort, $n = 408$) and used to estimate different structural equation and regression models. The structural equation models assume that planful competence measured during adolescence should positively predict educational achievement in the year 1940 as well as occupational status in 1954 mediated by self-direction (including persistence, confidence, and purposefulness) measured during early adulthood controlling for family SES. The direct effect of planful competence on educational achievement and occupational status was also included in the model. The analyses revealed that planful competence positively predicted self-direction for both the older ($b = 0.14$, $p < .01$) and younger cohort ($b = 0.22$, $p < .001$).[11] Self-direction was, furthermore, positively related to educational achievement for the older cohort ($b = 0.37$, $p < .01$). In addition, the estimated model suggested that planfulness was also a direct predictor of educational achievement for the younger cohort ($b = 0.32$, $p < .001$). The second model revealed that planful competence was positively related to occupational status mediated by self-direction (indirect $b = 0.50$ for the older cohort; indirect $b = 0.80$ for the younger cohort; all direct paths are significant at the 1% level or below).

Hitlin and Elder (2007a) used cross-sectional data from a representative sample of 20 754 U. S. adolescents. The dataset included measures on health issues, social environment characteristics, family and relationship issues, as well as psychological features. The authors operationalised agency by using items that were argued to measure self-efficacy beliefs, optimism, and planful competences. Self-efficacy beliefs and optimism were used as effect indicators whereby planful competence was included as a causal indicator. The latent path analysis disclosed a positive relationship between agency and school cohesion ($\beta = .57$) and negative relationships between agency and school prob-

11 Only unstandardised path coefficients are reported in the study of Shanahan and Elder (2002).

lems ($\beta = -.58$), violent activity ($\beta = -.31$) and criminal activity ($\beta = -.29$) within the last 12 months ($p$ values for the path coefficients have not been included; however, the presented fit indices speak much in favour of all estimated models).

The last study (Hitlin & Kirkpatrick Johnson, 2015) used a panel dataset of 636 cases. The dataset included data measured in 1988 (SES of parents), 1991 (age 17–18, agency measures), and 2005 (age 31–32, outcome measures). Pearlin's (1978) mastery scale and the perceived life chances scale of Jessor, Donovan, and Costa (1988) were used as measures for agency. The latter can be understood as a mixture of optimism and the forethought aspect of Clausen's (1991; see also Bandura, 2001) planful competence. The regression analyses show that the perceived-life-chances measure was positively related to years of education ($\beta = .60$, $p < .001$), hourly earnings ($\beta = .17$, $p < .001$; only participants who were employed were included), and self-rated health ($\beta = .21$, $p < .001$). In addition, the perceived-life-chances measure was also negatively related to financial problems ($\beta = -.33$, $p < .05$) and depressive symptoms ($\beta = -.14$, $p < .05$). In contrast, the mastery measure was only significantly related to financial problems ($\beta = -.33$, $p < .05$) and depressive symptoms ($\beta = -.14$, $p < .05$). An additional analysis, however, showed that individuals who loaded low on both mastery and perceived life chances in their early years systematically scored worse on all outcome variables in the data measured at the age of about 30.

To sum up, empirical research on the effects of agency over the life course is still scarce, although three of the existing studies exploited longitudinal datasets with measurement points that expand over at least 18 years. The earliest and last measurement points of the Stanford-Terman longitudinal data are even 69 years apart. Although the study of Hitlin and Elder (2007a) was only cross-sectional in nature it still employed a representative sample with more than 20 000 individuals. Based on these sample characteristics the findings of these studies have to be assessed as highly robust and reliable. Interestingly, agency was operationalised very differently (mastery beliefs, optimism, self-efficacy beliefs, planful competences). However, each study found evidence that their agency measure significantly related to desirable life outcomes.

### 2.2.3 Organisational Behaviour Research on Proactivity

Organisational behaviour (OB) is the part of industrial and organisational psychology (Vinchur & Koppes, 2011) that is concerned with the study of human behaviours within organisational settings (Ivancevich & Matteson, 1993; Schermerhorn, Osborn, Uhl-Bien, & Hunt, 2000). Although it has a strong psychological orientation OB also draws heavily on the theories and empirical findings of other fields like sociology, business administration, and anthropology (Ivancevich & Matteson, 1993; Rollinson & Broadfield, 2002; Vinchur & Koppes, 2011).

Issues of agency have mainly been discussed within the OB community under the broader topic of proactivity at work. Proactivity describes all kinds of "self-starting, future-oriented behaviour that aims to bring about change in one's self or the situation" (Bindl & Parker, 2011, p. 567; for similar conceptualisations see Grant & Ashford, 2008; S. K. Parker & Collins, 2010; Tornau & Frese, 2013). At first glance this understanding of proactivity strongly overlaps with the agency conceptualisation put forward by Eteläpelto et al. (2013). Both focus on efforts initiated by the individual that aim to change either her own characteristics (e. g., knowledge) or the broader environment. However, OB scholars very seldom use the term agency within their discourses (see for occurrences: Grant & Ashford, 2008, p. 6, p. 9; Marinova, Peng, Lorinkova, Van Dyne, & Chiaburu, 2015, p. 105–115; S. K. Parker, Bindl, & Strauss, 2010, p. 829). The different terms in use might explain why scholars concerned with proactivity mostly neglected the theoretical accounts that were proposed in the workplace learning (see Section 2.1) and life-course discourses (see Section 2.2.2). Only Bandura's (1997, 2001, 2006b) social-cognitive theory and especially his ideas about the central role of self-efficacy beliefs have been strongly exploited in research on proactivity at work (e. g., Grant & Ashford, 2008). At the same time, research on proactivity has scarcely been taken into account by scholars interested in the phenomenon of agency. The only exceptions are the empirical study of Bryson et al. (2006) that operationalised agency as proactive actions, and the theoretical contribution by Harteis and Goller (2014) that firstly introduced the connection of both research strands (see also Goller & Billett, 2014). Although Eraut (2007, 2010b; Eraut & Hirsh, 2007) used the term proactivity in his double-triangle model (see Section 2.1.1.2) he did not refer to any of the relevant OB literature.

The following section (2.2.3.1) describes conceptual issues of agency within the OB literature. Section 2.2.3.2 then discusses several possible psychological mechanisms that explain individuals' engagement in proactive behaviour. Sections 2.2.3.3 and 2.2.3.4 are then concerned with individual and situational difference variables that predict proactive behaviour. Potential outcomes of proactive behaviour are discussed in Section 2.2.3.5. Empirical evidence that support the hypothesised relationships is reviewed within all three sections.

#### 2.2.3.1 Conceptual Issues

The discourse within the OB literature has been mostly phenomenon driven in the sense that—more or less independently from each other—different researchers noticed, conceptualised, and investigated particular behaviours that employees proactively engage in at work (Grant & Ashford, 2008; S. K. Parker & Collins, 2010). Amongst others, the phenomena of interest were: taking charge (employees voluntarily initiate constructive change at work; Morrison & Phelps, 1999), voice (employees make constructive suggestions for change at work; Van Dyne & LePine, 1998), issue selling (employees actively try to make other individuals aware of certain issues; Dutton & Ashford, 1993), feedback and information seeking (employees deliberately seek feedback about their work performance as well as information of how to deal with the requirements of their work; Ashford & Cummings, 1983; Morrison, 1993b), career initiative (employees actively attempt to take control over their career advancements by engaging in deliberate career planning or skill development; S. K. Parker & Collins, 2010; see also Seibert, Kraimer, & Crant, 2001; Tharenou & Terry, 1998), and job crafting (employees deliberately change the tasks and the relational boundaries that compose their job; Wrzesniewski & Dutton, 2001).

Only later these behavioural phenomena were summarised under the larger concept of proactive behaviour (e. g., Crant, 2000) and integrated into a wider nomological network (e. g., Bindl & Parker, 2011; S. K. Parker & Collins, 2010; Tornau & Frese, 2013). According to S. K. Parker et al. (2010) all proactive behaviours feature three unifying attributes: they are self-starting, change oriented, and future focused (see also Tornau & Frese, 2013). Self-starting refers to the idea that individuals might not only passively react to current circumstances but rather engage in discretionary efforts that try to proactively take control over situations that affect themselves. Change oriented means that proactive behaviours are aimed to change ill-fitting conditions in comparison to just accepting the status quo. And finally, future focused refers to the notion that proactive behaviours are not simply just-in-time reactions to current issues. They are rather anticipated responses that aim to bring about desired states in the future or to prevent undesired ones (see also Grant & Ashford, 2008).

Parker and Collins (2010; see also S. K. Parker et al., 2010) summarised the multiple proactive behaviour constructs in a larger higher-order category structure (see Table 2.3 for a summary). The first category was named proactive work behaviour and refers to all kinds of behaviours that "focus on taking control of, and bringing about change within, the internal organizational environment" (S. K. Parker & Collins, 2010, p. 636). Both taking charge and voice fall within this category. Behaviours within the second category are "concerned with taking control of, and causing change in, the broader organization's strategy" (p. 639). An example for this category is issue selling. The last category contains all deliberate efforts that aim to improve the individuals' fit with the organisational environment (person-environment fit, PE). This category contains concepts like feedback and information seeking, career initiative, and job crafting. The hypothesised higher order factor structure could be confirmed in an empirical study with 622 managers (S. K. Parker & Collins, 2010). The correlations between the three factors were all positive but differed in size (proactive work behaviour and proactive strategic behaviour: $r = .71$, proactive work behaviour and proactive PE fit behaviour: $r = .38$, proactive PE fit behaviour and proactive strategic behaviour: $r = .39$). These results can be used to argue that the different proactive behaviours proposed in the OB literature are conceptually and empirically different from each other. However, they are similar enough to group them into three different subsets. Each subset contains proactive behaviours that target similar domains of interest.

In general it seems that within the OB literature proactivity is conceptualised as a set of behaviours that relate to a range of outcomes that are desir-

**Table 2.3.** Categorisation of proactive behaviour.

| | Proactive work behaviour | Proactive strategic behaviour | Proactive PE fit behaviour |
|---|---|---|---|
| *Aim* | Aimed to bring about change in one's own work environment (or one's own workplace). | Aimed to bring about change in the broader organisation's strategy. | Aimed to improve the fit between one's own characteristics and the work environment. |
| *Focus* | Directed towards organisational processes or structures within one's own direct work environment. | Directed towards organisational processes or structures that are outside one's own direct work environment. | Either directed towards the individual or the organisation. |
| *Example* | Deliberately improving the customer handling. | Deliberately convincing managers to engage in more socially responsible practices. | Deliberately developing work-related competencies or changing the task structure of one's own job. |

able mainly from the organisation's perspective.[12] For instance, it is assumed that individuals initiate constructive change at work when they engage in taking charge efforts (Morrison & Phelps, 1999) and the voice concept has been explicitly conceptualised as constructive suggestions that lead to better per-

12 At this point it is also necessary to emphasise that proactivity is conceptually not the same as organisational citizenship behaviour (OCB) (see also Bindl & Parker, 2011). At the first glance OCB is similarly defined as proactivity. OCB contains all discretionary behaviours that aim at the effective functioning of the organization in question (Organ, 1988). However, Frese and Fay (2001) argue that OCB is more about compliance. In comparison, the exercise of proactivity at work often requires the violation of existing rules (i. e., the opposite of compliance). Furthermore, Frese and Fay (2001) maintain that OCB is more directed towards directly observable positive outcomes. Positive outcomes as the result of proactive behaviour might, however, only occur in the long run. Short-term effects of proactive behaviour might even be perceived as destructive in nature.

forming structures and processes at work (Van Dyne & LePine, 1998). Quite similarly, feedback and information seeking has been assumed to be related to individuals' work performance (Ashford & Black, 1996). In fact, a large amount of studies could back up these claims (see below). However, Tornau and Frese (2013) observe that counterproductive efforts—that is, behaviours that harm the organisation or the people belonging to the organisation (Spector & Fox, 2010)—might indeed also be self-started, change oriented, and future focused. To delineate behaviours that aim at destructive outcomes Tornau and Frese (2013) proposed the term destructive proactivity.

Apart from these behavioural phenomena, proactivity has also been discussed as a personality trait (e. g., Bateman & Crant, 1993; Fay & Frese, 2001; Frese, Fay, Hilburger, Leng, & Tag, 1997). This conceptualisation defines proactivity as a stable disposition that explains why some individuals engage more often in a range of proactive behaviours than others (Bindl & Parker, 2011; Tornau & Frese, 2013). A stronger proactive personality is hypothesised to positively predict individuals' proactivity (e. g., Crant, 2000; Frese & Fay, 2001; S. K. Parker et al., 2010; S. K. Parker & Collins, 2010; see also Section 2.2.3.3).

Historically, two different personality conceptualisations were developed: (a) proactive personality (Bateman & Crant, 1993) and (b) personal initiative personality (Fay & Frese, 2001; Frese et al., 1997). The former was originally described as "a personal disposition toward proactive behaviour, defined as relatively stable tendency to affect environmental change" (Bateman & Crant, 1993, p. 103). The latter was defined as "a behavior syndrome that results in an individual taking an active and self-starting approach to work goals and tasks and persisting in overcoming barriers and setbacks" (Fay & Frese, 2001, p. 97). Both concepts strongly overlap and have been treated as interchangeable. The strong conceptual overlap could also be shown empirically (Fay & Frese, 2001; Tornau & Frese, 2013). Short self-reporting scales with 10 and 7, respectively, items exist for both concepts (proactive personality: Seibert, Crant, & Kraimer, 1999;[13] personal initiative: Frese et al., 1997).

13 This is the short version of Bateman and Crant's (1993) 17-item scale. In addition, see also Schwarzer and Schmitz (1999) for a relatively similar scale that, however, is not based on the original scale developed by Bateman and Crant (1993).

A large number of OB scholars did not only discuss such conceptual issues but also tried to explain the psychological mechanisms behind proactivity as well the consequences of such behaviour. The next sections aim to summarise the current state of these attempts (see Figure 2.6 for a graphical depiction).

#### 2.2.3.2 Psychological Mechanism behind Proactive Behaviour

In his early review, Crant (2000) criticised that the proactivity literature was mainly concerned with conceptual issues as well as the identification of different antecedents that either foster or hinder individuals' proactivity (see also Grant & Ashford, 2008). In his opinion a theory of cognitive processes that actually explains whether and how individuals engage in proactive behaviour is largely missing. Such a theory would allow the question of why and how certain antecedents affect the propensity to engage in proactive behaviours to be resolved. Subsequently a few scholars tried to close this research gap.

Grant and Ashford (2008) argued that all proactive behaviours follow the same general cognitive process consisting of three phases that are directed towards changing future states: (a) anticipation, (b) planning, and (c) action. The anticipation phase requires the individual to discretely imagine possible and desirable futures that are different from the status quo. These possible futures can be related to oneself (e. g., a higher position at one's current organisation) or to the work environment (e. g., a less error-prone working process). Furthermore, the cognitive representation of possible futures might also allow mental trade-offs of the potential costs and benefits associated with each single considered future. If benefits are thought to exceed the costs of the behaviour a future state is considered to be attractive. The second phase is called planning. Within this phase individuals translate their goals (i. e., their envisioned and desired future states) into more detailed action plans. Action plans consist of "steps that link one's anticipations and future goals to concrete actions and outcomes" (Grant & Ashford, 2008, p. 10). Planning is therefore concerned with the consideration of feasible ways to implement the desired future state. Within the action phase the individual actually engages in a concrete behaviour that is directed towards materialising the desired future. Grant and Ashford define actions as the "physical manifestation[s] of anticipation and planning" (p. 11).

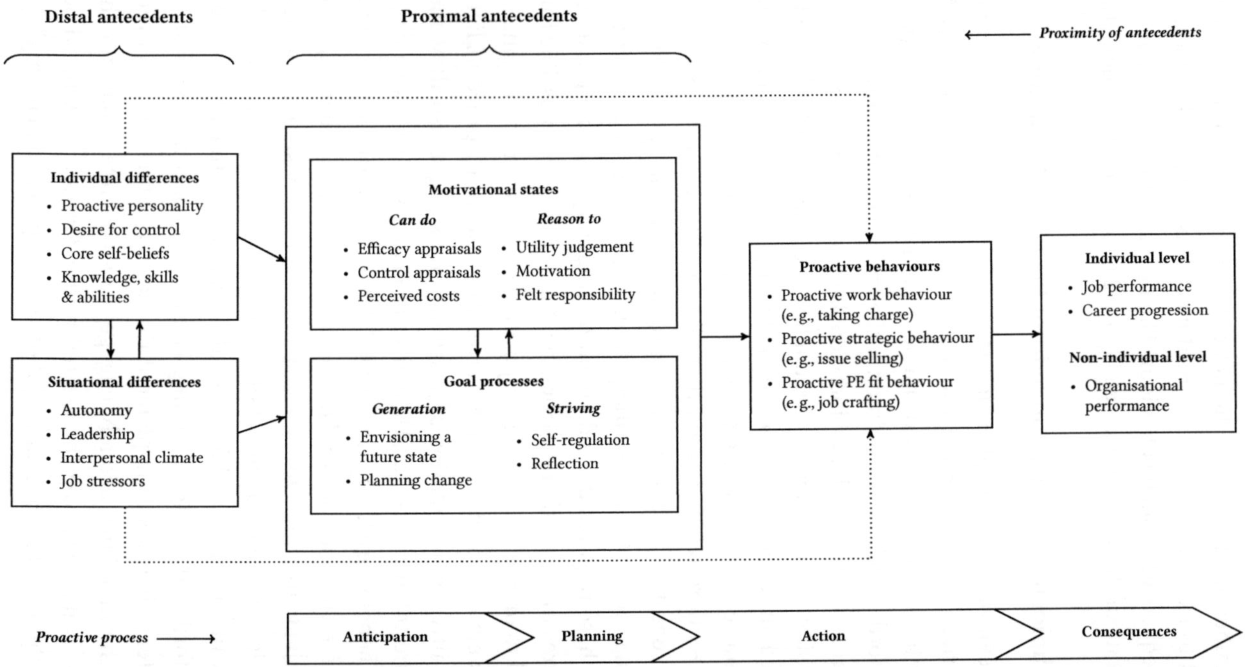


**Figure 2.6.** (Process) model of the antecedents and consequences of proactive behaviours (based on Bindl & Parker, 2011, p. 568; Grant & Ashford, 2008, p. 13; as well as S. K. Parker et al., 2010, p. 830).

Those actions might then result in some kind of consequences. Consequences can be either on the individual (e. g., higher job performance, career progression, increased well-being, changed work identity) or the organisational level (e. g., group effectiveness and performance, performance of the organisation because of transformations of work processes) (see also Griffin, Neal, & Parker, 2007). However, it has to be noted that the realised consequences might not always be intended ones. The realisation of desired future states is not necessarily in the realm of the individual.

S. K. Parker et al. (2010) also acknowledge the process character of proactivity. However, in their model they particularly focus on Grant and Ashford's (2008) anticipation and planning phase and specifically try to further explain the psychological mechanisms behind both phases. Similarly to Grant and Ashford they assume that proactive behaviour is a product of the mental representation of possible future states as well as the discretionary planning activities that help to bring about the desired future. These fundamental processes are referred to as goal generation.

Another important process is called goal striving. Goal striving subsumes both the actual engagement in behaviours as well as all supporting psychological mechanisms that aim to achieve the desired future state. The most important supporting mechanisms are self-regulation and reflection.

Self-regulation can be defined as the capability to alter one's own behaviour in order to meet goals or certain standards (Baumeister & Vohs, 2012). Probably the most important form of self-regulation is the resistance against momentary urges that are not in line with long-term goals. For instance, individuals might be distracted by other—at least on a short-term basis, apparently more enjoyable—tasks. Successful self-regulation in such cases includes either the postponement or the negligence of such urges. However, self-regulation is also needed when obstacles prevent individuals from directly reaching their initial goals. In such cases successful self-regulation allows individuals to either persist in the face of challenges or to find new strategies that help them to handle the encountered problems (see also Pintrich, 2005).

Strongly related to self-regulation is reflection. Within the model of S. K. Parker et al. (2010), reflection "consists of an individual's effort to understand the success, failure, or consequences of his or her proactive behaviour" (p. 833).

Reflection is necessary to gain information about one's own progress towards self-set goals as well as possible requirements to regulate one's action strategies.

In a next step, S. K. Parker et al. (2010) argue that a model of proactivity also needs to incorporate motivational states that explain whether an individual engages in proactive behaviour or not. On the one hand, these motivational states are strongly related to goal generation and goal-striving processes.[14] On the other hand, they allow for an explanation of how more distal antecedents affect proactive behaviour. Two often discussed motivational states are included in their model: "can do" states and "reason to" states (see also Bindl & Parker, 2011; J. B. Fuller, Marler, & Hester, 2012; S. K. Parker, Williams, & Turner, 2006).[15]

The first type of motivational state is related to the question of whether an individual is able to engage in a certain behaviour and whether the individual expects the behaviour to be linked to the desired outcome (can do). S. K. Parker et al. (2010) assume that proactive behaviour is always associated with certain risks (e. g., risk of failing, risk of meeting resistance from other people) or perceived costs (e. g., lost time or energy, resentment of coworkers). They therefore argue that an individual will only be proactive if she judges herself to be competent to engage in the proactive behaviour and if she is convinced of being able to deal with (possible) corresponding consequences. In the model depicted in Figure 2.6 such judgements are summarised as efficacy appraisals. In addition, Parker et al. suggest that individuals also need to be convinced that their self-initiated actions indeed lead to the desired outcomes. The concept of control appraisals is used to refer to the perceived link between certain actions and their consequences (see also Section 2.2.2.2).

The second type of motivational state is concerned with individuals' reasons to engage in proactive behaviour. S. K. Parker et al. (2010) argue that at

14 The authors suggest that motivational states drive goal processes in a unidirectional way. This, however, has not necessarily to be the case. Existing goals (or envisioned future states) might also affect an individual's motivational states. That is why the relationship between motivational states and goal processes is depicted as being interrelated in Figure 2.6.

15 These ideas are strongly related to expectancy-value theories (see e. g., Eccles & Wigfield, 2002).

least three broad categories of possible reasons exist. The first category of reasons is related to utility judgements. Utility judgements describe the degree to which an individual assumes that a certain behaviour will contribute to a current or future goal (e. g., career advancement). Individuals have a stronger incentive to engage in a behaviour they judge to be highly supportive for more distal goals. The second category of reasons is strongly related to the three basic needs postulated in the self-determination theory (SDT; Deci & Ryan, 1993, 2000; Ryan & Deci, 2000b). SDT assumes that all individuals are strongly inclined to engage in such actions that are self-determined and that allow both a feeling of competence and social relatedness. Individuals especially strive to engage in activities that are highly interesting and strongly enjoyable (intrinsic motivation). However, individuals are also highly motivated to engage in actions if they can strongly identify with the underlying values and corresponding goals of the behaviour (integrated motivation; e. g., changing the work processes in order to avoid mistakes in the future) as well as actions that are perceived to be personally important or highly valuable (identified motivation; similar to utility judgements if the more distal goal is highly relevant for oneself). The three types of motivation are sometimes summarised as autonomous motivation. The third category of reasons to states is concerned with individuals' feeling of responsibility (see also Crant, 2000). S. K. Parker et al. (2010) emphasise that individuals only perceive a reason to engage in proactive behaviour if they feel personally responsible for the accomplishment of a desired future state.

The effects of the just described proximal antecedents of proactivity can be summarised as follows: Proactivity requires the individual to envision a future state that is different from the current situation. This future state will be translated to concrete action plans if the individual has a reason to do so. For instance, the envisioned future might be judged to be instrumentally relevant for more distal goals or the future might be perceived to be highly compatible with the individual's own value system. Furthermore, the individual needs to feel personally responsible or accountable to create the future in question. If an individual has good reason to act proactively she still balances the perceived costs and benefits of the behaviour and considers whether she is capable of engaging in certain behaviours as well as the chances that the action actually result in the desired outcomes. Provided that all these considerations turn out positively the proactive behaviour in question will be started. Self-regulation processes and constant progress monitoring help to persist in the face of obstacles and setbacks.

#### 2.2.3.3 Individual Antecedents

A range of individual difference variables that explain variance in individuals' proactivity could be identified in a number of different studies. The most relevant ones are summarised in Figure 2.6 as individual distal antecedents. These difference variables are mainly assumed to affect proactive behaviours mediated by the proximal antecedents (motivational states, goal processes) described above (see continuous arrow in Figure 2.6). However, the model in Figure 2.6 also contains the direct, unmediated effect of these antecedent variables on proactive behaviours (dotted arrow). This is the case because an adequate explanation of how the distal and proximal antecedents interact to generate proactive behaviours is not presented for each single difference variable in the literature.

The most prominent individual difference variable discussed in the OB literature is proactive personality. A large number of studies included this stable personality trait as a direct predictor of proactive behaviour (e. g., Major, Turner, & Fletcher, 2006; S. K. Parker & Collins, 2010; S. K. Parker et al., 2006; Seibert et al., 2001; Thompson, 2005). Two recent meta-analyses found strong evidence that measures of proactive personality are indeed related to proactive behaviours. B. Fuller and Marler (2009) reported a medium-sized correlation ($r = .32$, $p < .05$, $k = 38$) between proactive personality and a range of different proactive behaviours (e. g., voice, taking charge, career initiative). In a similar vein, Tornau and Frese (2013) found correlations between different proactive personality measures (Bateman & Crant's self-reporting measurement; both a self-reporting and an interview measurement of personal initiative) and different proactive behaviours (taking charge and voice) between .28 and .50 (all $p < .05$, $k = 5–10$).

In other models, proactive personality is included as a predictor mediated by more proximal antecedents (namely cognitive-motivational states; e. g., Bindl

& Parker, 2011; Frese & Fay, 2001; S. K. Parker & Collins, 2010; S. K. Parker et al., 2006). Unfortunately, the scholars promoting these models do not theoretically explain how proactive personality is assumed to influence motivational states. However, a potential explanation might be that individuals with a strong proactive personality more often feel responsible to deliberately influence their own life and their environment. Furthermore, by definition individuals with a strong proactive personality strongly identify with the idea of deliberately taking charge of things. Based on the self-determination theory, such a strong identification with proactivity should lead to autonomous forms of motivation (see above). It therefore follows that proactive personality might be mainly related to "reason to" motivational states in the model proposed in Figure 2.6. Especially for the first explanation some empirical backup can be found. S. K. Parker and Collins (2010) found a positive correlation between proactive personality and the felt responsibility for change ($r = .30, p < .01$) in a sample of 622 managers. Furthermore, based on the same study they report correlations between felt responsibility for change and taking charge ($r = .55$, $p < .01$) as well as voice ($r = .41, p < .01$). In their meta-analysis, Tornau and Frese (2013) report medium-sized correlations between personal initiative measures and responsibility for change ($r = .31–.38$, all $p < .05$, $k = 3–5$). A correlation of $r = .61$ ($p < .05$, $k = 3–5$) was found between taking charge and responsibility for change.[16]

Desire for control is another trait variable that has been linked to proactive behaviour. Desire for control can be defined as a relatively stable inclination of a person to take control over events in her own life (Burger & Cooper, 1979).[17] The concept was first used by Ashford and Black (1996) to explain why newcomers in organisations engage in proactive socialising activities (see also Crant, 2000; S. K. Parker et al., 2010). Ashford and Black's (1996) theoretical argument was that job entry situations are always characterised as highly uncertain. Newcomers with a high desire for control should therefore proactively engage in a range of behaviours that help to reduce this uncertainty. In their

16 Correlations between responsibility for change and voice could not be reported because of an insufficient number of studies included in the meta-analysis ($k < 3$).

17 Theoretically related concepts are effectance motivation (R. W. White, 1959) and need for competence (Elliot, McGregor, & Thrash, 2002).

study, Ashford and Black found empirical evidence that desire for control is indeed related to activities like information seeking ($\beta = .30, p < .01$), general socialising ($\beta = .24, p < .05$), and active networking ($\beta = .29, p < .01$). Wrzesniewski and Dutton (2001) suggest that desire for control should also be a strong motive to engage in job crafting. Activities that change either the task structure or the relational boundaries of one's own job help to control what kind of events one experiences over the work day. Generally speaking, it therefore follows that individuals who are high in the desire for control should experience a strong "reason to" motivation to engage in all kind of behaviours that actually help to take control over all aspects of their life including their work.

Individuals' core self-beliefs are also hypothesised to affect whether employees engage in proactive behaviour or not (see Grant & Ashford, 2008; S. K. Parker et al., 2010). Core self-beliefs (or self-evaluations) are defined as "fundamental, subconscious conclusions individuals reach about themselves, other people, and the world" (Judge, Locke, Durham, & Kluger, 1998, p. 18). This psychological meta-trait is argued to represent a common factor that comprises individuals' self-concept, self-esteem, degree of neuroticism, locus of control, and self-efficacy beliefs (Judge, Erez, Bono, & Thoresen, 2002; Judge et al., 1998; Pajares & Schunk, 2002).[18] Within the OB literature on proactivity the last one especially has been repeatedly discussed and empirically studied. Strong self-efficacy beliefs are believed to enhance "can do" motivational states because individuals tend to be convinced that they are able to translate their goals into effective actions. Furthermore, individuals with strong self-efficacy beliefs tend to set higher goals and tend to persist more frequently in the face of challenges and obstacles (i. e., positive effects on goal processes; see also Bandura, 1977). Empirical research largely confirms these hypotheses (e. g., Bandura, 1978; Multon et al., 1991; Schunk, 1981; Taylor, Locke, Lee, & Gist, 1984; Wood & Bandura, 1989; see also Section 2.2.1.3). However, most studies

18 Although all of these concepts have been studied separately it is important to note that the meta-analysis of Judge et al. (2002) could show that the concepts self-esteem, neuroticism, self-efficacy beliefs, and locus of control highly correlate with each other and indeed strongly load on one common factor. In order to avoid multicollinearity problems further studies should therefore consider including only one of these scales in their analyses.

on proactivity included measures of self-efficacy beliefs as direct predictors of proactive behaviour without explicitly specifying the assumed underlying psychological mechanism (e. g., Frese, Garst, & Fay, 2007; J. B. Fuller et al., 2012; Morrison & Phelps, 1999; S. K. Parker & Collins, 2010; S. K. Parker et al., 2006; see also Sections 2.2.1 and 2.2.2.2 as well as the meta-analysis by Tornau & Frese, 2013). Nevertheless, self-efficacy proved to be a significant and important predictor of individuals' engagement in proactive behaviour in almost all of these studies.

The last individual factors considered here are knowledge, skills, and abilities. All three are assumed be important antecedents of proactive behaviour (Fay & Frese, 2001; Frese & Fay, 2001; Grant & Ashford, 2008; S. K. Parker et al., 2010; Tornau & Frese, 2013). At least three mechanisms have been suggested that explain how knowledge, skills, and abilities influence individuals' engagement in proactive behaviours. First, knowledge about work processes and the work environment in general allows individuals to better anticipate potential risks and benefits that are connected to a proactive behaviour in question (S. K. Parker et al., 2010). This should lead to sounder decisions whether to engage in proactive behaviour and therefore also to more mastery experiences. In the long run, mastery experiences should then increase self-efficacy beliefs (Frese & Fay, 2001) which have already been discussed as important predictors of proactive behaviour (see above). Second, individuals with thorough work-related knowledge should be more able to identify those work structures and processes that require improvement or change (Fay & Frese, 2001). Furthermore, thorough knowledge enables the individual to identify and choose the most appropriate and effective set of proactive actions to meet certain goals both in the beginning and in the case of setbacks or problems (Grant & Ashford, 2008; Tornau & Frese, 2013). More knowledgeable individuals should therefore be able more often to envision desirable future states, to translate their goals more effectively into actions plans, and to self-regulate their behaviour in a better way than their less knowledgeable counterparts. Third, highly routinised skills (i. e., proceduralised knowledge; J. R. Anderson, 1982) help individuals to free cognitive resources through the automaticity of familiar tasks (Palmeri, 2006). Those freed cognitive resources can then be invested in the identification of possible future states and translation of goals into action plans (goal generation) as well as in self-regulation and reflection processes (goal striving) (see also Norman, Eva, Brooks, & Hamstra, 2006; Ohly, Sonnentag, & Pluntke, 2006).

Only a few studies have investigated the relationship of proactive behaviour and measures of knowledge, skills, and abilities. Unfortunately, these studies used measures of individuals' qualification level or obtained education as proxies for knowledge, skills, and abilities. Whether these measures are valid proxies remains open to debate. Fay and Frese (2001) reported that job qualification correlates moderately positively with personal initiative behaviours for both a sample of East German participants ($r = .31–.48$, $ps < .01$) and West German participants ($r = .24–.46$, $ps < .01$). In contrast, a non-significant correlation between general education and taking charge behaviour ($r = .19$) was found by J. B. Fuller et al. (2012). Tornau and Frese (2013) used meta-analytical procedures to summarise all relevant studies. They reported average correlations of $r = .12$ ($p < .05$, $k = 10–15$) between personal initiative behaviour and educational level as well as average correlations of $r = .18$ ($p < .05$, $k = 3–5$) between personal initiative behaviour and general mental ability.

To sum up, many studies on proactivity investigated a range of individual difference variables. Both proactive personality and different core self-beliefs were included most often. Much empirical evidence speaks in favour that these antecedents are indeed positively related to proactive behaviour. Desire for control is another trait-like measure that has been proposed as a predictor of proactive behaviour. Only a few studies have investigated this relationship. However, those studies found a positive relationship between both constructs. It has also been theorised that knowledge, skills, and abilities are important antecedents of proactive behaviour. Unfortunately, the empirical studies that investigated this relationship came to a rather inconclusive result.

#### 2.2.3.4 Situational Antecedents

Similarly to the investigation of individual characteristics much effort has been invested in identifying situational antecedents of proactive behaviours. In the next paragraphs the ones that are most commonly included in empirical models are described and discussed. Again, the situational antecedents are assumed to affect proactive behaviour either directly (by a dotted arrow) or mediated by the more proximal psychological antecedents described above (see Figure 2.6).

Autonomy at work is assumed to strongly predict the occurrence of proactive work behaviours. Job autonomy (or job control) is defined as the "degree to which the job provides substantial freedom, independence, and discretion to the employee in scheduling the work and in determining the procedures to be used in carrying it out" (Hackman & Oldham, 1975, p. 162). In the literature, three mechanisms have been discussed that explain how job autonomy relates to proactive behaviour via motivational states. First, high levels of job autonomy should increase individuals' efficacy and control appraisals. In jobs that provide much discretion and control individuals can (relatively) freely decide how to tackle tasks and problems. Such situations signal to employees that they have the general option to engage in proactive behaviours that do not fully comply with familiar ways of practice. These signals should enhance judgements of efficacy in the sense that one is allowed and able to be proactive (Grant & Ashford, 2008). Furthermore, job autonomy directly affects how controllable a situation is for an individual (S. K. Parker et al., 2006) and therefore also increases employees' control appraisals which, in turn, are also related to proactive behaviours (Frese & Fay, 2001). Second, high levels of job autonomy should allow individuals to make mastery experiences in regard to self-started behaviours and therefore strengthen their respective self-efficacy beliefs in the long run (Frese & Fay, 2001; S. K. Parker et al., 2006). On the contrary, jobs that are tightly defined and do not provide much autonomy do not provide employees with any opportunities to make mastery experience. In such jobs, individuals learn to be reactive rather than proactive (Seligman, 1972, 1992). Third, Tornau and Frese (2013) suggested that individuals who experience high job control also feel more responsible for a wider range of issues connected to their work (see also S. K. Parker & Turner, 2002). This perceived responsibility might then motivate individuals to proactively engage in problem-solving activities they would otherwise just not have cared about.

Two recent meta-analyses summarised the empirical studies that investigated the relationship between job autonomy and proactive behaviour. Tornau and Frese (2013) report a medium-sized correlation between job control and personal initiative behaviour ($r = .30, p < .05, k = 6–9$), taking charge ($r = .33,$

$p < .05$, no information given about the number of $k$), and voice ($r = .21–.27$, $p < .05$, $k = 3–9$). Marinova et al. (2015) also report a medium-sized relationship between job control and change-oriented proactive behaviours ($r = .25$, $p < .05$, $k = 31$). The empirical results therefore speak in favour of the hypothesis that job autonomy is related to proactive behaviours (see also Bindl & Parker, 2011, for a more qualitative review).

Another situational factor that is considered as an important antecedent of proactive behaviour is leadership. Leadership refers to the way managers and supervisors interact with subordinates in organisational contexts (Bratton & Gold, 2007; Rollinson & Broadfield, 2002). Within the OB literature on proactivity discussions on leadership are mainly concerned with supervisors' and managers' support for, as well as their general openness regarding, proactive behaviours. A culture of support and openness for proactivity strongly signals to employees that proactivity is both accepted and potentially even something that is highly desired (Tornau & Frese, 2013). It therefore follows that employees have to fear less resistance and therefore also perceive less costs ("can do" motivational state) when they engage in behaviours that try to change work practices (Ashford, Blatt, & VandeWalle, 2003). Furthermore, if a supervisor perceives proactivity as something highly desired individuals might even interpret this as a reason to engage in such behaviour.

The empirical studies concerning the influence of leadership paint a rather inconclusive picture (for a summary see also Bindl & Parker, 2011). Three studies found evidence that leadership styles that either strongly value subordinates' contributions (participative leadership) or that expect employees to question current perceptions and assumptions (transformational leadership) are indeed related to different proactive behaviours. Rank, Carsten, Unger, and Spector (2007) report that a participative leadership style positively predicts proactive service performance above a range of other individual and situational variables ($\beta = .30$, $p < .01$). In another study, Rank, Nelson, Allen, and Xu (2009) found that a transformational leadership style is a positive predictor of proactive innovation behaviours ($\beta = .33$, $p < .01$). Belschak and Den Hartog (2010) found evidence that transformational leadership is positively related to proactive behaviour focussing on the organisation (e. g., suggesting new ideas for company problems; $\beta = .29$, $p < .01$) as well as focussing on the interpersonal level (e. g., deliberately taking over colleagues' tasks in need; $\beta = .32$, $p < .01$). However, no significant relationship could be found between transformational leadership and personal proactive behaviour (e. g., career-related actions; $\beta = .17$, $p > .05$). In an early study, Morrison and Phelps (1999) reported that top management's openness to encourage and support suggestions and initiatives for change was positively related to taking charge behaviour ($\beta = .15$, $p < .01$). In addition, Ohly et al. (2006) found evidence that supervisor support is a predictor of personal initiative behaviour ($\beta = .15$, $p < .05$). However, two studies failed to find evidence for a relationship between supportive supervision and proactive work behaviour (Fay & Frese, 2001; S. K. Parker et al., 2006).

Interpersonal climate within organisations is the third context factor that has been discussed in the OB literature on proactivity. Interpersonal climate refers to the general collegial support and trust that an individual experiences when engaging in proactive behaviours. Interpersonal climate is strongly related to "affective support, confirmation of an individual's behaviour and group standing, and direct help" (Tornau & Frese, 2013, p. 55). Theoretically, a constructive interpersonal climate should foster individuals' engagement in proactive behaviour via both "can do" and "reason to" motivational states. Similarly to supervisor support, collegial support is also a strong signal for employees that proactive behaviour is accepted and something that is desired (Tornau & Frese, 2013). Collegial support and a high level of trust therefore increases psychological safety that leads to lower perceived risks that are connected to proactive behaviour (S. K. Parker et al., 2010; see also S. K. Parker et al., 2006). Furthermore, S. K. Parker et al. (2006) argue that a supportive collegial environment should also lead to more confidence in one's own actions. It is believed that other employees' trust and support enhance an agent's efficacy appraisal.

Only a few studies investigated the claimed relationships. Concentrating on proactive job search behaviours, Kanfer et al. (2001) found a medium-sized correlation of .24 ($p < .05$, $k = 15$) between social support and such activities in their meta-analysis. In their own study of 282 production employees in the U. K., S. K. Parker et al. (2006) found only a relatively small correlation between coworker trust and proactive behaviour ($r = .15$, $p < .05$). Fay and Frese (2001) cited an unpublished thesis (Vennekel, 2000) that investigated the relationship between perceived psychological safety and personal initiative behaviour in the domain of health work. This study reported a medium-sized correlation between the two measures ($r = .25$, $p < .01$). Griffin et al. (2007) reported that coworker support is positively related to proactive behaviour directed towards change at the individual ($r = .11$, $p < .01$), the team ($r = .17$, $p < .001$), and the organisational level ($r = .08$, $p < .05$) in a health care organisation. However, in an organisation that is concerned with environmental management a significant relationship could only be found between coworker support and team-level proactivity ($r = .12$, $p < .001$). The correlations between coworker support and proactive behaviour directed toward the individual as well as organisation did not reach significance. Besides other independent variables, Morrison and Phelps (1999) employed a scale that measures the extent how well change within an organisation is both supported and encouraged. However, this did not reach significance in the conducted regression analysis to explain engagement in taking charge behaviour ($p > .05$).

The last category of situational antecedents that are assumed to explain individuals' engagement in proactive behaviour is labelled job stressors. Stressors are defined as "external factors that impinge on a person and potentially result in stress" (Rollinson & Broadfield, 2002, p. 278). Job stressors are assumed to foster proactive behaviour because they are thought to represent disparities between a desired situation and the status quo (Bindl & Parker, 2011; Fay & Frese, 2001; Frese & Fay, 2001; S. K. Parker et al., 2010). Such a mismatch should give individuals a reason to engage in proactive behaviours that are directed towards the reduction of the perceived discrepancy (S. K. Parker et al., 2010; see also Carver & Scheier, 2005). A typical job stressor that was empirically considered in proactivity research is time pressure. For instance, a longitudinal study of Fay and Sonnentag (2002) found evidence that time pressure positively predicts proactive behaviour at work ($\beta = .21$, $p < .01$). Ohly and Fritz (2010) also included time pressure as an independent variable in their experience sampling study. Based on their multilevel regression analysis they found that chronic time pressure positively predicts daily proactive behaviour ($b = 0.34$, $p < .05$). Furthermore, they also report a positive relationship between daily time pressure and daily proactive behaviour ($b = 0.23$, $p < .01$).

However, it has to be emphasised that Bindl and Parker (2011) argue that job stressors might inhibit proactivity in the long run. For instance, constant time pressure can easily restrain individuals to think about new ways of working because they are just happy to get the work done in the first place. In such cases individuals might just not find the time to consider potential ways to affect the work environment. The goal generation process in particular might therefore be affected. In addition, Bindl and Parker (2011) used resources theory (e. g., Hobfoll, 2001) to suggest that repeated exposure to job stressors also easily drains individuals' resources like efficacy beliefs.

To sum up, research on proactivity generated much evidence that situational characteristics like job autonomy, supervisor support, collegial support and trust, as well as time pressure are important antecedents of self-initiated behaviour at work.

#### 2.2.3.5 Consequences of Proactivity

Within the OB literature proactive behaviour has also been argued to predict a number of outcome variables. These outcome variables can be grouped into variables that directly affect the individual (job performance, career progression, career satisfaction, and work identity) as well as consequences of proactivity that are not directly related to the individual (e. g., organisational performance). All relevant outcome variables are depicted as consequences of proactive behaviour in Figure 2.6

Individual job performance is probably the most prominent consequence of proactivity discussed and investigated by OB scholars. Job performance is used here in a rather broad sense and can be defined as an incumbent's proficiency in carrying out the tasks that were specified in the job description (Griffin et al., 2007) as well as the outcomes of these tasks that contribute to the performance of the organisation (see J. Campbell, 1990, or Sonnentag & Frese, 2002, for discussion on the performance construct). Three recent meta-analyses investigated the proposed effect of proactivity on different measures of job performance. B. Fuller and Marler (2009) found that a proactive personality is positively related to overall job performance ($r = .38, p < .05, k = 14$), performance in certain job tasks ($r = .23, p < .05, k = 8$), and even objective performance measures (e. g., sales productivity; $r = .23, p < .05, k = 6$). Quite similarly, Thomas, Whitman, and Viswesvaran (2010) reported that both measures of proactive personality based on Bateman and Crant (1993) and Frese et al. (1997) positively predicted overall job performance ($r = .21–25, p < .05, k = 15–25$). In addition, their meta-analysis showed that both voice ($r = .24, p < .05, k = 9$) and taking charge behaviour ($r = .33, p < .05, k = 4$) were also positively related to overall performance. However, the relationship between voice and objective performance measures (e. g., employee sales) did not reach significance ($p > .05, k = 4$). Tornau and Frese (2013) found evidence that taking charge ($r = .43, p < .05, k = 3–5$) and voice ($r = .52, p < .05, k = 6–9$) were positively related to supervisor-rated performance. Furthermore, medium- to large-sized correlations could also be found between personal initiative behaviour and supervisor-rated ($r = .54, p < .05, k = 6–9$) as well as objective ($r = .30, p < .05, k = 10–15$) performance.

As a possible mechanism that explains the relationship between proactivity and performance the following three potential links were proposed: First, proactive individuals should more often actively create situations that are strongly conducive to high performance working practices (Crant, 1995; see also B. Fuller & Marler, 2009; Thomas et al., 2010). Second, the active and constant engagement with different organisational problems should lead to a better understanding of one's own job as well as the whole organisation (Frese & Fay, 2001; Thomas et al., 2010). Third, proactive individuals should engage more often in deliberate efforts that are explicitly aimed at developing skills and abilities (Thomas et al., 2010; see also Chapter 3 for a discussion on the effects of such efforts). For instance, individuals might actively seek for information and feedback (Ashford & Tsui, 1991; Morrison, 1993a, 1993b; Renn & Fedor, 2001) or negotiate desired formal development opportunities (e. g., trainings; Hornung, Rousseau, & Glaser, 2008).

Career progression is another often assumed and investigated outcome of proactivity. Career progression is an umbrella term that simultaneously refers to positive outcomes of job searches as well as both subjective (e. g., career satisfaction) and objective (e. g., salary) measurements of career success. Frese et al. (1997; see also Seibert et al., 1999) explained the hypothesised relationship between these measures and proactivity as following: Proactive individuals are assumed to have a long-term future perspective that allows them to make more elaborated and detailed career plans than their less proactive counterparts. In addition, proactive individuals should also be particularly good in the transformation of goals into action plans and action plans into a set of feasible behaviours. Career progression, for instance, can be achieved by deliberately selecting promising positions or by the proactive negotiation of development opportunities. It therefore follows that, on average, proactive individuals should progress faster and further in their careers than less proactive individuals. Two meta-analyses support these claims. B. Fuller and Marler (2009) summarised several studies that investigated the relationship between proactive personality and career success measures. They found small- to medium-sized effects. Proactive personality was positively related to salary ($r = .14, p < .05, k = 10$), number of promotions ($r = .11, p < .05, k = 6$), perceived career success ($r = .26, p < .05, k = 4$), career satisfaction ($r = .31, p < .05, k = 13$), and job satisfaction ($r = .30, p < .05, k = 21$) (see also Ng, Eby, Sorensen, & Feldman, 2005, for an earlier meta-analysis that reported similar relationships). In a similar vein, Tornau and Frese (2013) found significant positive relationships between job satisfaction and personal initiative behaviour ($r = .10–.11, p < .05, k = 3–9$), taking charge ($r = .10, p < .05, k = 3–5$), and voice ($r = .14–.22, p < .05, k = 6–9$).

Proactive behaviour is not only considered to be related to outcomes on the individual but also the organisational level. In particular, the potential relationship of proactivity and organisational performance has been discussed. Organisational performance hereby refers to three potentially related outcomes that an organisation generates (Richard, Devinney, Yip, & Johnson, 2009): (a) financial performance (e. g., profits), (b) product market performance (e. g., sales), and (c) shareholder return (e. g., economic value added). Both Frese and Fay (2001) and Bateman and Crant (1999) argued that organisations benefit from proactive behaviour of their employees. For instance, proactive employees are assumed to tackle problems more independently or to come up with more innovative products, services, and processes. A proactive workforce should therefore provide a competitive advantage for organisations (see also Barney, 1991). Empirical support for these claims, however, is very limited. For instance, Koop, de Reu, and Frese (2000) reported that among the highly successful microbusiness owners in Uganda, proportionally more individuals were rated as being highly proactive (29%) than being very low on the proactivity scale (13%). Similar results were found in a sample of business owners in Eastern Germany (Zempel, 1999). In their studies with Dutch small-scale business owners, Frese, van Gelderen, and Ombach (2000) and van Gelderen, Frese, and Thurik (2000) found that a rather reactive business strategy (i. e., the opposite of proactive behaviour of the owner) was negatively related to entrepreneurial success ($\beta = -.35, p < .05$; $\beta = -.27, p < .05$).

In conclusion, much empirical evidence speaks in favour of the proposition that proactive behaviour is positively related to measures of job performance as well as career success. Whether the hypothesised link between proactive behaviour and organisational performance holds empirically is still open. Only a few studies could present convincing empirical evidence for such a relationship.

### 2.2.4 Recapitulation and Conclusion

All three research strands discuss and investigate the phenomenon that individuals are active agents who deliberately exercise control over themselves and/or the environments in which they live. This phenomenon is discussed either under the explicit notion of agency (social-cognitive theory, life-course research) or the concept of proactivity (organisational behaviour literature).

On the conceptual level agency is defined as a capacity within the literature on social-cognitive theory and life-course research. In these research strands, agency is understood as an individual quality that explains why some individuals engage more often in self-initiated behaviour than others. Within discourses of proactivity agency is mainly conceptualised as a specific set of goal-directed behaviours that aim to bring about change in the work environment or in regard to oneself. However, at the same time proactivity research acknowledges that some individuals are more agentic than others. It is assumed that individuals qualitatively differ in their tendency to engage in self-initiated behaviours. Historically this disposition has mostly been discussed under the concept of proactive personality.

Apart from these conceptual issues each of the three research strands is concerned with the identification of psychological mechanisms behind the exercise of agency, individual and situational antecedents that predict individuals' engagement in agentic behaviour, and potential consequences of individuals' agency. Moreover, all three research strands are heavily concerned with the empirical investigation of the phenomenon of agency. The key findings of these efforts can be summarised as follows:

1. Exercising agency can be understood as a process in which individuals imagine a desired and personally fitting future state that is different from the status quo, set the goal to create this desired future state, translate the goal into more concrete sub-goals, derive feasible action plans and engage in agentic behaviours that help to materialise the desired future. This process requires individuals to have the capabilities to actually follow this process from the beginning till the end (i. e., the engagement in certain actions), to be personally convinced that they are capable of engaging in the actions necessary to bring about the desired future state, and that these actions stand a chance of actually closing the gap between the status quo and the envisioned future. Individuals also need a reason to start the process in the first place.
2. Based on the proposed psychological mechanisms behind agency a range of different individual predictors of agentic behaviour were discussed in each of the three research strands. Particularly strong empirical evidence exists for the following predictors: (a) self-knowledge and self-regulation capabilities to imagine desired future states, set (sub)goals, translate these goals into a set of feasible actions, and appropriately deal with setbacks and problems; (b) control beliefs which signal to oneself that one is able to engage in the required actions to bring about the desired future state; and (c) personality traits that give a dispositional reason to engage in agentic actions.
3. Although agency is discussed mainly from an individual perspective all three research strands strongly acknowledge that social context variables also determine whether and how individuals engage in agentic behaviour.

Rather abstractly, both social-cognitive theory and life-course research conceptualise the social context as an opportunity structure. This context might either permit or constrain the exercise of agency. Within proactivity discourses this idea has been made more concrete by identifying particular situational characteristics that either foster or hinder engagement in proactive behaviour. Empirical evidence for such relationships exists for the following characteristics: job control, leadership style, coworker support, and job stressors.

4. In general, the exercise of agency is conceptualised as something positive that is supposed to relate to a range of desirable outcomes. Within the three research strands, agency could be empirically linked to individuals' educational accomplishments, career success, objective job performance, subjective job satisfaction, as well as health outcomes. Slightly different mechanisms have been proposed to explain why agentic individuals should be able to realise such positive outcomes during their life course. However, the general idea is that agentic individuals tend to take control over their life by more often setting long-term goals that match their own preferences and strengths, by being more able to actually translate those goals into appropriate actions, by being more inclined to actually engage in such actions, by being more persistent in the face of obstacles, and—in the end—by being more likely to succeed in meeting their long-term goals than their less agentic counterparts. Agentic actions might either target the individual itself (e. g., developing own competences to fit into a given social context) or the individual's social and physical context (e. g., changing work structures to fit one's own personal characteristics).

5. The theoretical discussions on agency and agentic behaviour within the three research strands promoted a large amount of empirical work. Almost all of those studies used quantitative measures of agency or agentic behaviour (subjective self-rating scales or more objective external assessments) to test hypotheses that are derived from the more theoretical literature. These studies were mostly cross-sectional in nature. However, scholars interested in life-course research especially collected impressive evidence about the positive effects of agency on certain life-course outcomes

using longitudinal datasets. Apart from correlation analysis, the most often used techniques to examine the data were regression and structural equation modelling. A range of meta-analyses summarised the most often studied relationships proposed in the literature on social-cognitive theory and proactivity.

Quite obviously, all three research strands are deeply interested in the phenomenon that individuals exercise control over themselves and/or the environments in which they live. Unfortunately, the three research strands are not well integrated with each other. The scientific community concerned with proactivity seems not to recognise the literature on life-course research and vice versa. Cross-references between both literature strands do not exist. Bandura's ideas of the important role of self-efficacy beliefs are used by both the proactivity and the life-course research. However, his theoretical ideas on the psychological mechanisms behind agency have not explicitly been taken up (although the ideas on the psychological mechanisms behind proactivity and life-course agency are quite similar to a certain point). At the same time, nevertheless, Bandura's discussion on agency also does not incorporate any ideas put forward by scholars writing about proactivity or life-course matters.

A missing integration has also to be witnessed between the literature reviewed in Sections 2.1 and 2.2. Although a few studies (including Eteläpelto et al., 2013, and van Veldhuizen, 2011) indeed recognise the central role of efficacy beliefs put forward in the social-cognitive literature as well as the conceptual ideas discussed within the life-course community, especially the discussions of psychological mechanism behind agency, the important efforts to operationalise agency, and the empirical findings of these research strands have not been taken into account. Furthermore, the discussion of proactivity within the OB literature has been almost completely ignored (for exceptions see Bryson et al., 2006; Goller & Billett, 2014; Harteis & Goller, 2014). At the same time, the discussion on agency within the workplace community has not been picked up by any of the three research strands.

To sum up, this chapter has reviewed the agency-related discussions within the social-cognitive, the life-course, and the proactivity literature. These discourses are deeply concerned with the conceptualisation, the modelling of psychological mechanisms, the identification of individual and social antecedents, as well as the empirical investigation of the phenomenon that individuals exert control over their lives by exercising choice and by engaging in intentional actions. Both the theoretical and the empirical work done in these research strands complement the agency discussion within the workplace learning literature threefold (see Section 2.1.4 for a summary and critique of this research): First, each research strand operationally defined agency either as capacity or as agentic behaviour and proposed different quantitative measures. Operational definitions and therefore also quantitative measures of agency are still missing in the workplace learning discussion. Second, all three research strands proposed nomological networks that link agency with both antecedents and outcome variables. These nomological networks have been used to derive testable hypotheses concerning agency. Such testable hypotheses do not yet exist within the workplace learning discussion on agency. Third, a large number of empirical studies already tested whether these hypotheses hold. Empirical models that attempt to investigate the relationship of agency and learning in work contexts can incorporate these research findings.

## 2.3 Deriving a Working Definition of Agency

The aim now is to use the discourses presented in the preceding sections to derive a working definition of agency and a (preliminary) conceptual framework which links agency with the development of expertise. Both the working definition and the conceptual framework are required to develop a more specific research model as well as an operational definition that will guide the empirical investigation that is planned as a later part of this thesis.

Within the reviewed literature two main conceptual perspectives of agency emerged (see Sections 2.1.4 and 2.2.4). The first perspective conceptualises agency as an individual feature that allows individuals to make choices and to engage in actions based on these choices to take control over their life or their environment. This perspective implicitly or explicitly assumes that individuals differ in the extent to which they take control over their life or their environment. The second perspective is more concerned with the intentional choices and actions as such.

In order to distinguish both conceptualisations the first one will be labelled as agency and the second one will be referred to as agentic action from here on. The consequences that follow from the engagement in agentic actions are labelled as outcomes. This conceptualisation allows for the integration of both conceptual perspectives of agency in a single conceptual framework. A graphical depiction of this conceptual framework can be found in Figure 2.7.

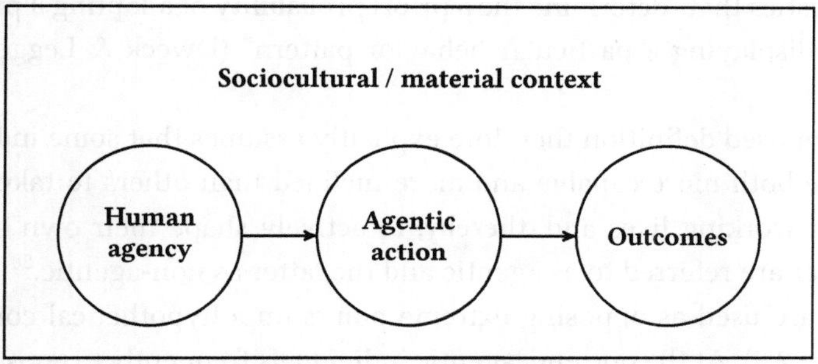


**Figure 2.7.** Conceptual framework.

Although agency plays a role in all kinds of life domains of individuals the following discussion will be constrained to work contexts. The main concept of this thesis will therefore be referred to as work agency. Work agency can be understood as a domain-specific instance of agency.

In this thesis, work agency is understood as the main driving force behind an individual's engagement in agentic actions in work contexts. Work agency will be defined as the capacity and tendency to make intentional choices, to initiate actions based on these choices, and to exercise control over the self and the environment in work-related contexts.[19] The term capacity includes both the

19 The wording of this definition has been inspired by the definition proposed by Eteläpelto, Hökkä, Vähäsantanen, and Collin (2010). In more recent publications, however, Eteläpelto et al. (2013) adapted a slightly different definition (see Section 2.1.2). This new definition conceptualises agency as something individuals do. In comparison, the definition suggested here conceptualises agency as an individual feature. It should also be emphasised that an almost identical definition of work agency was proposed by Harteis and Goller (2014).

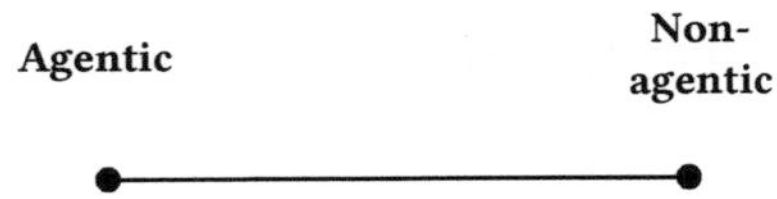


**Figure 2.8.** Hypothetical agency continuum.

actual abilities and the underlying beliefs that are required to engage in such agentic actions. Within this definition the term tendency expresses that work agency is conceptually understood as a disposition. Dispositions are individual characteristics that "determine the a priori probability of adopting a particular goal and displaying a particular behavior pattern" (Dweck & Leggett, 1988, p. 269).

The proposed definition therefore explicitly assumes that some individuals tend to be both more capable and more inclined than others to take control over their working lives and, thereby, to actively shape their own destinies. The former are referred to as agentic and the latter as non-agentic.[20] The two concepts are used as opposing extreme points on a hypothetical continuum (see Figure 2.8). At the one end, agentic individuals frequently exercise agency by making intentional choices and engaging in agentic actions. They actively take control over their lives and tune their environments in regard to their own visions. At the other end, non-agentic individuals do not exercise work agency at all. Non-agentic individuals tend to react and to comply with external forces and conditions. Quite obviously, this categorisation is purely analytical in nature. In reality neither purely agentic nor purely non-agentic individuals exist. However, this idealised continuum still allows categorisation of some individuals as more and some as less agentic.

It follows that this definition treats work agency as a latent variable that explains these differences. Within the literature on social-cognitive psychology, life-course research, and organisational behaviour three facets of such a latent

20 Such a categorisation is not a completely new one. For instance, Little, Cunningham, Shahar, and Widaman (2002) write with reference to De Charms (1970), Ryan and Deci (2000b), as well as Skinner (1995) that an "agentic individual is the origin of his or her actions, has high aspirations, learns from failures, and, overall has a greater sense of well-being. In contrast, a non-agentic individual can be a pawn to unknown extra-personal influences, has low aspirations, is hindered with problem-solving blinders, often feels helpless, and, overall, has a greater sense of ill-being" (p. 390).

variable have been described: (a) agency competence, (b) agency beliefs, and (c) agency personality. Agency competence describes the individual's ability to visualise desired future states, to set goals, translate these goals into actions, to engage in these actions, and to deal with potential problems that might occur. In other words agency competence refers to the ability to exercise agency in work contexts. Agency beliefs are concerned with the individual's perception about whether she has these abilities or not. Some scholars would also call this a sense of agency. And last but not least, agency personality describes the individual's predisposition or tendency to make choices and to engage in actions based on these choices to take control over their life. Agency personality can be understood as a psychological trait. In this thesis, the combination of these three agency facets is assumed to primarily predict whether an individual acts more or less agentically—that is, engages in more or less agentic actions. Table 2.4 summarises the characteristic of each of these three facets.

**Table 2.4.** Agency facets.

| Agency competence | Agency beliefs | Agency personality |
|---|---|---|
| • Capabilities to make decisions and to translate these decisions into actions<br>• Capabilities for self-regulation<br>• Knowledge about own preferences and capabilities | • Beliefs into one's own capabilities to exercise control over one's life and over environment<br>• Generalised expectancies about the extent to which certain means can be caused and how these means help to realise certain outcomes | • Inclination to take control over one's own life and over environment.<br>• Psychological trait<br>• Relatively stable over time |

Based on the literature discussed in this chapter it is not clear how exactly these three facets interrelate with each other. All three facets have been discussed as similarly important constituents of agency. It is therefore assumed that agency competence, agency beliefs, and agency personality are predictors that equally determine whether and how individuals engage in agentic actions. A description on how exactly these three facets are used to operationalise agency at work can be found in the methodology parts of the empirical studies described later on (see Sections 6.2.1 and 7.1.4.4).

The observable manifestations of work agency are called agentic actions. For the purpose of this thesis, agentic actions are defined as self-initiated and goal-directed behaviours that aim to take control over the work environment or the individual's work-related life course. Agentic refers to the idea that the person them self has to be the origin of these choices and actions. The individual as such has to actively make a choice and then to initiate a single action or a range of actions based on these choices. All actions that are either reflexes or mere reactions to external forces (e. g., the choices of other individuals or situational pressure) cannot be characterised as agentic. Moreover, agency requires that it be future oriented. This means that only such choices and actions can be conceptualised as agentic that aim to affect or control the future by either actively attempting to change it or by deliberately working towards maintaining a current state.

Within the literature two distinct sets of targets of agentic actions have been differentiated (see also Harteis & Goller, 2014). First, agentic actions can be directed towards the individual them self. By exercising this individual-oriented agency individuals try to take control over their personal life trajectories. For instance, an employee might want to become more proficient in a certain part of her job and therefore deliberately engages in every appropriate development opportunity she can find. Second, agentic actions can also be directed toward the individual's current environment. In work contexts, this externally-oriented agency comprises all deliberate efforts that try to take control over current work practices or organisational structures. It is assumed that agentic individuals engage more often in both individually oriented and externally oriented agentic actions. Table 2.5 gives an exemplary insight of how agentic individuals tend to act in comparison to their less agentic counterparts.

The conceptualisation of work agency and agentic actions proposed here acknowledges that individuals do not live or act in a social and/or material vacuum. Whether and how individuals engage in agentic actions does not only depend on their individual characteristics (i. e., agency competence, agency beliefs, agency personality) but also on sociocultural and material context factors.

**Table 2.5.** Conceptualisations of the behavioural tendencies of agentic vs. non-agentic individuals. Reprinted and adapted from "Harteis, C. & Goller, M. (2014). New skills for new jobs: Work agency as a necessary condition for successful lifelong learning. In T. Halttunen, M. Koivisto, & S. Billett (Eds.), *Promoting, assessing, recognizing and certifying lifelong learning: International perspectives and practices* (pp. 37–56). Dordrecht: Springer, p. 44" with permission from Springer.

| Orientation | Agentic individuals | Non-agentic individuals |
|---|---|---|
| *Individually-oriented* | Tendency to make a difference in or for the self, e. g.:<br>• Deliberately pursue learning and development activities<br>• Shaping one's own career | Tendency to:<br>• Comply with existing career patterns<br>• Accept others' definitions of self and role |
| *Externally-oriented* | Tendency to make a difference in the current work practice, e. g.:<br>• Develop or transform work practices<br>• Create new work practices<br>• Address tensions in work practices | Tendency to:<br>• Passively accept existing work practices even if problems are obvious<br>• Overlook tensions in work practices |

Such context factors are assumed to alter the a priori probabilities of adopting agentic behaviours (Dweck & Leggett, 1988). Some factors might inhibit the exercise of agency even if an individual has a strong predisposition to be agentic. For instance, a very tight leadership style might easily constrain an individual's tendency to address tensions at work. However, other context factors might encourage less-agentic individuals to take control over their working lives and their environment. For example, a supervisor who strongly supports the idea of change can easily encourage an employee to suggest new work practices. In the long run, it is also conceivable that sociocultural and material context factors directly affect an individual's capacity and tendency to exercise work agency. Individuals might develop their abilities to translate goals into action plans because of learning experiences provided in particular contexts

(e. g., family, schools). At the same time, individuals might consider themselves as less capable of influencing their lives because the socio-historic context just does not allow this. Such a deprivation of control beliefs has also been discussed under the concept of learnt helplessness (Seligman, 1972, 1992). And last but not least, context factors also affect the consequences of agentic actions. Some circumstances make it easier than others to achieve intended goals. The outcome of a goal-directed behaviour might not always be the intended one. Within Figure 2.7 the relevance of the sociocultural and material context is illustrated by the box that encloses the earlier discussed agency framework. The theorised chain of agency, agentic actions, and outcomes are embedded in the sociocultural and material context.

As could be seen in Sections 2.1 and 2.2, work agency has been related to a range of different outcomes. Within the workplace learning literature the exercise of agency is understood as a requirement for learning and development. At the same time it is acknowledged that the exercise of agency at work is associated with the development of work practices. Similar ideas have been proposed within the social-cognitive, the life-course research, as well as the organisational behaviour literature. Theoretically and empirically the notion of agency has been linked to positive health outcomes, higher qualifications levels, career attainments, as well as better functioning work processes and structures. It can therefore be summarised that—in general—the exercise of agency seems to result in a variety of desirable outcomes. However, the concrete agentic actions that help to realise these outcomes strongly vary between the different life domains. For instance, deliberately taking control of one's own health might require one to pay attention to health issues, to exercise regularly or to avoid unhealthy diets. In contrast, taking control of one's own educational career might demand individuals to actively seek learning opportunities and to deliberately invest time to improve themselves.

The focus of this thesis will now be constrained to the assumed relationship between work agency and expertise development. It is necessary to understand what agentic actions are related to learning and professional development. Furthermore, it is necessary to identify sociocultural and material context factors that either hinder or foster the engagement in such learning- and development-related agentic actions. On a theoretical level this helps to further specify the preliminary model proposed in Figure 2.7. In a later step this further specified model will be empirically tested. Chapter 3 therefore attempts to explain how individuals can agentically affect their own expertise development and what external factors influence this process.

## 2.4 Chapter Summary

As can be seen in Section 2.1 the idea of agency has been quite prominent in discussions about learning and development in work contexts. The concept has mainly been used to describe and explain individuals' choices and their engagement in learning-related activities at work. However, in spite of their centrality within these discourses, ideas of agency have mostly been discussed in a rather abstract way. Many authors do not define the concept and empirically testable research models are still largely missing. It has been only very recently that a first explicit definition was proposed by Eteläpelto et al. (2013). Empirical studies that investigate the explanatory power of the concept using hypothesis-testing methods do not yet exist.

In order to compensate for this theoretical shortcoming, social-cognitive psychology, life-course research, as well as organisational behaviour literature related to ideas of agency was reviewed and discussed in Section 2.2. Each of these research strands is heavily concerned with the role of agency in individuals' development and/or the role of agency in relation to work matters. In comparison to the WPL literature these discourses explicitly defined their agency understanding, related the concept to both antecedent and outcome variables, and proposed empirical measures of agency.

Informed by the literature reviewed in Sections 2.1 and 2.2, an individual definition of work agency as well as a preliminary conceptual model was derived. Work agency is understood as an individual characteristic that allows individuals to engage in agentic actions. Agentic actions are then defined as all kinds of self-initiated and goal-directed behaviours that aim to take control over the work environment or the individual's work-related life course. The engagement in agentic actions is assumed to result in certain kinds of outcomes. This whole causal chain is embedded in the particular sociocultural and material context that characterises the individual's situation.

# 3 The Role of Agency in Professional Development

The central aim of this chapter is to provide a theoretical framework that explains how individuals can agentically exert control over their own professional learning and development processes. At a very general level, professional learning and development hereby describes the expansion of those capacities that allow individuals to effectively and efficiently deal with the requirements of their current and future workplace (McCauley & Hezlett, 2005). For the purpose of this thesis, this learning and development process is understood as an individual's advancement from somebody who can barely deal with the requirements of her workplace to, in the best case, someone who manages to deal proficiently with almost all work-related tasks and problems. The former will be described as a novice and the latter as an expert (see also Billett, 2001a; H. L. Dreyfus & Dreyfus, 1988, 2005; Sonnentag, 2000; Tynjälä, Nuutinen, Eteläpelto, Kirjonen, & Remes, 1997). In other words, the chapter is concerned with how and what individuals—at any stage of their professional development[21]—can agentically contribute to become experts in their respective work domains.

In a first step, Section 3.1 discusses the concept of expert performance in work contexts, the characteristics that distinguish experts from novices, as well as the development processes of these characteristics. This is done by referring mainly, but not exclusively, to research that originated in cognitive psychology. In a second step, Section 3.2 is concerned with the identification and

21 Differences between the development of individuals at different stages will not be empirically investigated in this thesis. It is rather assumed that the agentic actions identified herein are relevant for individuals' advancement towards expertise regardless of their particular development stage.

classification of those activities that have been theoretically and empirically linked to the development of expert performance in work contexts. As will be seen, typical activities are the engagement in work practices, the interaction with other individuals in the workplace, the consultation of different media sources, as well as the participation in institutionalised learning opportunities. However, these activities are not always initiated by the learners themselves. It cannot automatically be assumed that they are agentic actions as defined in the last chapter. Section 3.3 therefore explicitly focuses on the question of how individuals can agentically take charge of their learning and professional development. Empirical literature is used to back up this line of reasoning. The chapter closes with a summary that complements the conceptual framework developed in Chapter 2.

## 3.1 On the Development of Professional Expertise

This section introduces the concepts of professional experts, professional expertise, and expert performance in work domains. The section, furthermore, explains how experts are able to achieve high performance in their respective work domains by outlining the differences between experts and novices. As will be seen, both the quality and the quantity of knowledge about the domain prove to be the main difference between the groups. It is followed by a discussion on how the development of such knowledge can be theoretically modelled.

### 3.1.1 Expert Performance at Work

High-performing individuals are usually referred to as experts. Broadly speaking, experts are defined as individuals who reliably show superior performance within a certain domain (Ericsson, 2006b; Ericsson & Smith, 1991; Ericsson & Towne, 2010; Gruber, 1994; Gruber & Mandl, 1996; Gruber & Ziegler, 1996; Posner, 1988). Somebody who does not (reproducibly) exhibit superior performance in such a domain is typically referred to as a non-expert. The group of non-experts hereby includes novices (i. e., individuals who have just started to engage with activities of the domain in question) and intermediates (i. e., individuals who already manage to engage in activities of their domain but do not reliably exhibit superior performance by doing so).[22] In this context, the terms novice and intermediate imply that an individual might still become an expert but is not one yet (see Section 3.1.3 for a more detailed development model of expertise). The capacity that distinguishes experts from non-experts is subsumed under the concept of expertise (Ericsson, 2006a). Thus, expertise is the individual requirement for reliable superior performance within a certain domain.

What exactly counts as superior performance is highly domain specific. A domain hereby refers to a particular area of practice that is composed of a more or less narrow set of (recurring) tasks or problems. Within the literature of expertise two different kinds of domains are distinguished: well-defined and ill-defined ones. So called well-defined domains consist mainly of problems that have only one single-best solution and tasks that have very constrained degrees of freedom concerning the underlying aims as well as the means that help to meet those goals (Eteläpelto, 1994). In such kinds of domains, performance can usually be objectively determined. In chess, for instance, the goal is always to checkmate the opponent by strictly following the predefined and well-established rules of the game. A chess expert is, therefore, a person who repeatedly wins against other high-performing chess players.

In comparison, other domains are characterised as more ill-defined in nature. Ill-defined domains comprise a range of different tasks in which the working goals as well as the appropriate choice of working methods (i. e., the means) are not always completely predefined (Eteläpelto, 1994; Gruber & Mandl, 1996; Strasser & Gruber, 2004). Practice within such domains cannot be reduced to a narrow set of well-defined tasks, rules, and goals. In ill-defined domains it is not always clear what problems have to be solved and what methods are

22 Technically, individuals who have no experience with activities of a particular domain (i. e., laypeople) are also non-experts. However, since the focus of this thesis is on employees (i. e., individuals who have at least a minimum of experience within their work domains) the discussion within this chapter is constrained to differences between experts and novices or intermediates.

appropriate to do so. Usually a certain degree of freedom exists concerning the choice of methods. Furthermore, there are often no objective performance standards that define how well a problem has been solved or a task has been approached.

Most workplaces can best be described as conglomerates of several different well- and ill-defined (sub-)domains. For instance, consider the job of a geriatric care nurse within a nursing home. The typical tasks within this domain span from administering personal care over performing health-care related duties to preparing and maintaining client records (O*NET, 2016). Obviously, some of these tasks are rather repetitive, have well-known solutions and have very few degrees of freedom in terms of their objectives or means. However, other tasks are rather complex and provide much scope for decision making. In particular, such tasks where nurses interact with residents fall into the latter category. Quite often these kinds of tasks require nurses to individually adapt their working strategies to the needs of each particular resident. This is necessary because each resident brings along a unique life course and an idiosyncratic medical history. It is not always clear what exactly has to be done in order to sustain or improve the well-being of a resident. This also sometimes leads to situations where objective performance standards are missing. Although failure to accomplish a task or to solve a problem might be obvious, the quality of a solution cannot always easily be evaluated (Goller & Billett, 2014). It is, for instance, not clear whether a certain solution to a health-related issue of a resident leads to the best possible well-being of this person. Another solution might have worked even better (or worse).

Even if work-related performance norms exist for some tasks they are often not defined as global standards. The reason for this is that workplaces are instances of a particular profession or occupation that comprise situationally specific practices and activities (Billett, 2001a). In other words, different workplaces that belong to a certain occupation or domain are not necessarily identical in terms of their specific requirements. For instance, an important part of a geriatric care nurse's job in a small rural nursing home might be to regularly cut the residents' hair. In a larger urban nursing home, however, this is not considered to be an important ability for nurses since a professional hair dresser is employed to do this job. Thus, it is the idiosyncratic circumstances of a particular workplace that determine what has to be done as well as what exactly counts as good performance and what does not (Billett, 2001a). Performance hereby refers, on a very general level, to the effectiveness and efficiency of how individuals complete the tasks and problems that are part of their particular workplace (Mieg, 2006).

For the purpose of this thesis, experts in work domains are defined as individuals who are able to effectively and efficiently deal with the whole range of different routine and non-routine tasks and problems of their respective workplace (see also Bromme, 2014; Gruber & Degner, 2016; Stark, Graf, Renkl, Gruber, & Mandl, 1995; Yielder, 2004). What exactly counts as effective and efficient depends on the particular situated norms and standards of their idiosyncratic workplace (Billett, 2001a). In this sense, professional experts are individuals who cope superiorly and reproducibly well with the specific demands of their particular work environment.

### 3.1.2 Cognitive Adaption as Foundation of Expert Performance

Research in cognitive psychology has probably been most influential in explaining superior performance of individuals. Over more than 50 years, extensive and rigorous empirical efforts were undertaken to compare outstanding individuals with less outstanding persons in a range of different domains (see for historical overviews e. g., Ericsson & Smith, 1991; Feltovich, Prietula, & Ericsson, 2006). A large body of articles and books have been published that aim to summarise and extract the generalisable findings of these research endeavours (for overviews see e. g., Chi, 2006; Ericsson, 2006a; Ericsson & Lehmann, 1996; Ericsson & Smith, 1991; Feltovich et al., 2006; Glaser & Chi, 1988; Gruber, 1994; Gruber & Mandl, 1996; Gruber & Ziegler, 1996; especially for professional domains: Berliner, 2001; Bromme, 2014; Ericsson & Towne, 2010; Ericsson, Whyte, & Ward, 2007; Norman et al., 2006; Ropo, 2004; Salas & Rosen, 2012; Sonnentag, 2000; Sonnentag, Niessen, & Volmer, 2006).

Probably the most important and prevalent finding of this research account is that expert performance can best be explained through cognitive adaptations (Ericsson & Lehmann, 1996; Feltovich et al., 2006).[23] It is the development of a large and well-structured knowledge base that ultimately allows experts to efficiently and effectively deal with tasks and problems of their specific domain of expertise (Feltovich et al., 2006; Gruber, 1999a; Gruber & Mandl, 1996; Hacker, 1992; Norman et al., 2006; Sonnentag, 2000). Experts do not only know more about their domain than novices and intermediates, but they also manage to structure and organise their knowledge according to the demands of their domain-specific environment (Ericsson & Lehmann, 1996; Feltovich et al., 2006). The effects of such a large and well-structured knowledge base can be summarised as follows:

1. Experts know more about their domain than non-experts (Chi, 2006; Feltovich et al., 2006). They know more about the typical tasks and problems that constitute a domain, about the relevant cues and variables that distinguish specific situations, about appropriate and inappropriate solutions, the role and function of other actors, the goal and norms of their domain, as well as about how the domain works in general. More knowledge about the domain helps experts to decide what task or problem characteristics are important to extract and to investigate and—at the same time—to decide what features are negligible. In addition, domain-specific knowledge permits experts to select suitable problem-solving strategies that are known to work and to avoid likely mistakes (Feltovich et al., 2006; Gruber & Mandl, 1996; see also Gartmeier & Schüttelkopf, 2012; Oser, Näpflin, Hofer, & Aerni, 2012).

2. Knowledge structures of experts are highly integrated (Sonnentag, 2000). Integrated knowledge structures can best be described as rich networks of links between encoded concepts that represent important features of their domain (Salas & Rosen, 2012). In such networks the activation of one con-

23 Please note that superior performance in some domains might also highly depend on domain-specific physiological and anatomical adaptations (e. g., certain sports or work domains that are characterised predominantly by manual labour; see for instance Ericsson & Lehmann, 1996). However, the focus of this thesis is on geriatric care nurses whose daily job is not primarily characterised by tasks and problems that require specific anatomical or physiological capacities like flexibility or strength. Any further discussions are therefore constrained to cognitive adaptations.

cept leads automatically to the activation of other connected concepts. Experts are therefore able to retrieve large amounts of relevant knowledge about familiar tasks and problems as long as certain features of a particular situation are recognised (see also Gruber & Mandl, 1996). In comparison, novices cannot reactivate their knowledge as effectively as experts. Their knowledge entities are more isolated from each other and contain less meaningful connections (Salas & Rosen, 2012; see also Feltovich, Johnson, Moller, & Swanson, 1984).

3. The knowledge of experts is predominantly structured around abstract and functional categories that represent typical problem structures in their respective domain (Chi, Feltovich, & Glaser, 1981; Feltovich et al., 2006; Salas & Rosen, 2012). Such functional representations allow experts to promptly recognise and appropriately classify encountered problems in their domain (Chi et al., 1981; Feltovich et al., 1984). The correctly identified problem type then helps experts to select appropriate strategies to deal with the present problem. Novices, on the contrary, have not yet structured their knowledge around such functional categories and can therefore not initially restrict the search to a limited set of potential solution strategies. Problem solving therefore is more challenging for them.

4. Expert knowledge is organised in such a form that allows instantaneous application. Experts possess a large range of precompiled and ready-to-use procedures that exactly define what kind of action should be executed if a specific condition in a domain-related task or problem situation is met (J. R. Anderson, 1982, 1993; Glaser & Chi, 1988). Those so-called condition-action rules permit experts to quickly react to given circumstances and to decide about appropriate reactions without consciously balancing alternatives. Put differently, the recognition of a familiar problem pattern (the activated condition) leads to the automatic recall of stereotypic reaction processes (i. e., a solution or a part of a solution). Another important advantage of experts' partial automation of certain problem-solving processes is that it frees up cognitive resources (Bereiter & Scardamalia, 1993; Eraut, 2004; Feltovich et al., 2006). Those cognitive resources can then be invested in other important cognitive functions like self-monitoring or advanced plan-

ning (in other words self-regulation; Norman et al., 2006). Due to automation of certain operations experts are therefore able to use their cognitive resources more efficiently than novices and intermediates.

All in all, cognitive psychology has presented much evidence that a large and well-structured knowledge base is the most important requirement to exhibit superior performance in any kind of domain. Knowledge hereby refers not only to memorised facts and their relation to each other (i. e., semantic knowledge; Kolodner, 1983; Tulving, 1972). It also comprises learnt routines (i. e., procedural knowledge; J. R. Anderson, 1987) as well as encoded information about personally experienced episodes (i. e., episodic knowledge; Sternberg et al., 2000; Tulving, 1972). All three types of knowledge are highly performance relevant (Sternberg et al., 2000). Procedural knowledge can directly be applied to tasks and problems and is therefore highly functional in nature. However, it can usually not be easily articulated and is therefore also sometimes referred to as tacit or implicit (Sternberg et al., 2000; see also Polanyi, 1969). Episodic knowledge is knowledge about already solved tasks and problems. Such knowledge helps to classify new problems through recognition, to plan the solution process based on successful or less successful attempts to solve similar tasks and problems encountered before, and to prevent potential mistakes that have occurred in the past (Gruber, 1999a). Episodic knowledge is—similarly to procedural knowledge—sometimes implicit in nature.[24] Domain-related semantic knowledge helps experts especially in situations where no appropriate routines or experiences are available. For instance, it has been shown that medical experts use their detailed knowledge about pathophysiological processes to diagnose diseases if similar symptoms have not been experienced before (e. g., Boshuizen & Schmidt, 1992; Schmidt & Boshuizen, 1993). However, reasoning based on semantic knowledge alone is usually very time consuming and error prone (J. R. Anderson, 1982).

24 Implicit knowledge is particularly important in situations that require fast reactions to challenging problems where alternatives cannot always be consciously balanced (Harteis & Billett, 2013; Harteis, Koch, & Morgenthaler, 2008; Harteis et al., 2012). It is often this kind of intuitive performance that distinguishes experts from non-experts (see also Section 3.1.3).

The next chapter will discuss how experts were able to construct these knowledge types and how cognitive adaptations can be explained by learning and development processes.

### 3.1.3 Developing Expertise

Another well-established finding of research on expertise is that the capacity to perform well in a domain can be learnt and developed (Ericsson, 2006b; Ericsson, Krampe, & Tesch-Römer, 1993; Ericsson & Lehmann, 1996; Gruber, 1999a; Gruber & Mandl, 1996). The large and well-structured knowledge base of experts is almost exclusively a product of a long-lasting and intensive engagement with those activities that constitute a certain domain. Other factors like favourable predispositions (i. e., talents or gifts) play only a minor role. A particular high intelligence or well-developed fine motor skills might give individuals a head start at the beginning of their career but do not explain superior performance as convincingly as a long engagement with domain-related tasks and problems (Chase & Simon, 1973; Ericsson, 2006b; Ericsson & Lehmann, 1996; Ericsson & Smith, 1991; Norman et al., 2006; however, see for a more detailed discussion on this topic: Hunt, 2006).

The term engagement hereby simultaneously refers to (a) any attempts to understand how the domain or parts of it work on a more cognitive level, as well as (b) all efforts to actually solve real-life tasks and problems that are a genuine part of the domain in question. Typical examples for activities of the first category are the participation in formalised (training) courses as well as the reading of written information sources like professional journals, textbooks or manuals. Through the engagement in those activities, individuals are able to construct elaborated networks of domain-related semantic knowledge. They mainly learn different concepts as well as how those concepts are related to each other.

In contrast, the actual engagement in tasks and problems of a domain is assumed to trigger two highly relevant but quite different cognitive development processes (second category):

1. Ongoing experience with real-life practice leads to changes in the knowledge structures of individuals who have already constructed a rich net-

work of semantic knowledge. The main idea hereby is that often used reasoning chains based upon available semantic knowledge are gradually collapsed or compiled into a limited number of higher level concepts. This process is called encapsulation (Boshuizen & Schmidt, 1992, 2008; Schmidt & Boshuizen, 1993; Schmidt & Rikers, 2007) or compilation (J. R. Anderson, 1982, 1987, 1993). The newly constructed higher-level concepts are procedural knowledge types that only contain the starting and the end-point of a previously long chain of linked concepts. They have the same explanatory power as the long chain of detailed concepts employed before by being less error-prone and much faster to use. Compilation (or encapsulation) allows the learner to make fast links between an encountered problem and a likely solution without the retrieval and interpretation of large amounts of semantic knowledge (Boshuizen & Schmidt, 1992, 2008).

2. The engagement with real-life tasks and problems leads to the construction of episodic script-type knowledge (Gruber, 1999a). Scripts are specific narrative knowledge structures that comprise information about the typical setting, the normative sequence of events, the required actions, the typical cast of characters, as well as the standard goal of commonly experienced situations (Kolodner, 1993; Schank & Abelson, 1977). In other words, scripts represent normative prototypes of recurrent situations as well as all information that is required to actually deal with these situations. However, information about the idiosyncrasy of experienced episodes is not lost due to this generalisation process. Kolodner (1983, 1993) proposed that scripts organise information about individual episodes by indexing them according to the deviations from the norms of the generalised episode. Indices are pointers to those domain-specific features that distinguish prototypical episodes from actually experienced events. Scripts are powerful episodic knowledge types that allow experienced individuals to use case-based reasoning (see also for the medical domain: Boshuizen & Schmidt, 2008; Custers, Boshuizen, & Schmidt, 1996; Feltovich et al., 1984; Schmidt & Boshuizen, 1993; Schmidt & Rikers, 2007): Each time an experienced individual faces a familiar situation the script that best describes the situation in question gets reactivated. After being activated, a script instantly provides

the practitioner with all available information of how the task or problem should be approached in general. Furthermore, the available information of the situation is matched with the indices of a retrieved script. This enables the experienced individual to also recall particular episodes that are similar to the situation at hand. These memories then help to remember what actions were helpful, less helpful or even detrimental to cope with comparable situations encountered in the past.

Based on the description just given, the development of expertise can best be described as a gradual process of acquiring more and well-structured semantic, procedural, and episodic knowledge through ongoing engagement with domain-related tasks and problems. The highly popular H. L. Dreyfus and Dreyfus (1988, 2005) model of expertise development divides this long-lasting process into five different development stages (see also Benner, 2004, for the adaptation of this model for the nursing domain): (a) novice, (b) advanced beginner, (c) competent individual, (d) proficient individual, and (e) expert. The model describes both the abilities of the learner at each stage as well as the requirement to ascend to the next stage.

At stage one, novices enter the new field of practice without any relevant experience. Any kind of behaviour of novices is governed by explicit rules encoded as semantic knowledge learnt through the engagement with codified learning material or the instruction of designated teachers. Only very poor performance can be achieved at this stage. Through ongoing experience with domain-related tasks and through encountering a sufficient number of similar situations, novices develop into advanced beginners (stage two). At this stage, learners no longer rely only on context-free rules as novices do. They also take advantage of maxims. Maxims are rules that refer to certain situational elements, like "shift up when the motor sounds like it's racing" (H. L. Dreyfus & Dreyfus, 2005, p. 783), that help to regulate their actions more effectively. Although advanced beginners start to recognise more and more features of real-life situations they often miss a sense of what is important and what can be ignored. This then leads to feelings of anxiety and exhaustion (Benner, 2004). At stage three, competent individuals have learnt to plan ahead and to adopt certain perspectives on emerging situations. Such perspectives help the learners at this stage to confine themselves to a particular set of cues and features and thereby make it easier to understand the situation and to finally act. In many cases this approach leads to appropriate actions and good results. However, the confinement to such a constrained set of situational aspects can also easily lead to misjudgements and misclassifications. At stage four, the proficient individual no longer deliberately decides which cues and features of situations are relevant and which are not. Through ongoing experience the learner has learnt to discriminate a wide variety of different domain-specific situations and accompanying responses. In other words, much of their earlier semantic knowledge has been proceduralised. However, the proficient practitioner still reverts back to rules or maxims in certain situations. At the final stage, the expert does not only immediately see what has to be done but also automatically sees how to achieve the goal that is demanded by the situation. Because of their long-lasting experience experts have encountered a large number of distinct situations and thereby constructed a large base of relevant episodic knowledge. This experience allows them to distinguish very subtle differences between situations and to activate knowledge about a variety of possible responses that have worked out either well or badly in the past. Experts therefore do not make conscious and deliberate decisions but rather respond intuitively by retrieving knowledge connected to special situations or cases they have encountered in the past. In other words "they do what normally works" (emphasis removed, H. L. Dreyfus & Dreyfus, 1988, p. 31).[25] Rules and maxims are usually not necessary any more but are still available if required.

Drawing together the discussions, the following two important propositions can be advanced. First, the construction of semantic knowledge is particularly important if one does not have any relevant experience with the class of tasks and problems at hand. This is usually the case at the beginning of a professional career (Daley, 1999). However, more experienced practitioners might also encounter completely new tasks and problems due to changes in the scope

25 A more detailed discussion on experts' intuitive decision making and problem solving can be found in Harteis and Billett (2013). However, it should also be noted that some authors are more sceptical about the notion of intuition as such (for the domain of nursing: Ericsson et al., 2007).

of their current job or all kinds of technological advancements. Thus, the acquisition of semantic knowledge might also be of relevance for individuals who work at the edge of their domain and therefore often encounter unfamiliar tasks and problems. Second, expertise as such only develops through long-lasting experience in a specific domain. Without the ongoing engagement in domain-specific activities as well as the encounter of a large number of different real-life situations the achievement of a high performance level is essentially impossible. Empirical findings back up these arguments (see e. g., Dokko, Wilk, & Rothbard, 2009; Ericsson, 2006b; Ericsson & Crutcher, 1990; Quińones, Ford, & Teachout, 1995).

### 3.1.4 Deliberate Practice

The previous section argued that long-lasting experience in a certain domain is strongly required to develop expertise. This proposition is supported both by theoretical models that emphasise the role of experience for the development of a well-structured knowledge base about a certain domain (J. R. Anderson, 1982; Boshuizen & Schmidt, 2008; H. L. Dreyfus & Dreyfus, 2005; Kolodner, 1983) as well as a range of empirical studies that showed that high-level performers have been significantly more often engaged in domain-related activities than their less expert counterparts (e. g., Dokko et al., 2009; Ericsson, 2006b; Ericsson & Crutcher, 1990; Quińones et al., 1995). At the same time, however, many individuals never reach expert performance regardless of their experience (Ericsson, 2006b). They tend to stay on a relatively stable average performance level and do not improve any more although they regularly encounter domain-related episodes. It has therefore been suggested that long-lasting experience might only be a necessary but not a sufficient condition for expertise development.

Based on this insight, Ericsson and colleagues (1993; Ericsson, 2006b) argue that not all kinds of domain-related experience equally contribute to substantial performance improvements once a certain performance level is reached. In their opinion, especially the repeated engagement in rather routine and mundane activities only leads to a certain stable performance plateau and do not help to improve further on. These claims are strongly supported by the findings of several studies that the length of experience (i. e., pure period of time) within a domain is often a relatively poor predictor of performance (Ericsson et al., 1993; Sonnentag, 1995, 1998a, 2000; Vessey, 1986).

Ericsson and colleagues (1993; Ericsson, 2006b) therefore proposed that it rather takes active efforts to overcome this average performance plateau. In their opinion the development of superior performance requires individuals to agentically invest time and effort into such activities that are qualitatively more demanding than the ones they would experience automatically. Learners have to consciously and deliberately concentrate on those practices which they have not yet mastered. Such active attempts to become better within a certain domain are usually summarised as deliberate practice (Ericsson, 2006b; Ericsson et al., 1993).

In its original narrow sense, deliberate practice is defined as the engagement in tasks that are still outside the individual's current performance and which can be mastered by "concentrating on critical aspects and by gradually refining performance through repetitions after feedback" (Ericsson, 2006b, p. 694). In well-defined domains the notion of deliberate practice usually describes activities that are specifically designed or selected to improve performance. Both the selection of such activities and the required monitoring to give performance feedback is usually done by a designated person like a coach or a trainer. The participation in such activities is described as exhausting, rather unpleasant, and time consuming.

Studies in the domains of music, chess, and sports found evidence that the engagement in such deliberate practices explains the observed performance differences in their samples. For instance, Ericsson et al. (1993) could show that violinists classified as high performers spent a significant share of their training time on the improvement of skills they had not yet fully mastered. In comparison, their less well-performing counterparts did not invest as much time in this kind of deliberate practice. A compilation of further studies that showed the relevance of deliberate practice in a range of well-defined domains can be found in Ericsson (2006b).

It is, however, questionable whether Ericsson's narrow understanding of deliberate practice has similar explanatory power in work contexts. There are at least two reasons that employees might not actually engage in any activities that can be categorised as deliberate practice (see also Goller & Billett, 2014):

1. Practitioners usually face limited time frames at work that constantly require them to engage in performance-relevant activities (van de Wiel, Van den Bossche, Janssen, & Jossberger, 2011). Work activities commonly structure around pre-set deadlines and sometimes also time-critical requirements like spontaneously arising problems or unforeseen tasks. The failure to meet deadlines or to solve emerging problems is often related to high costs in work contexts (Ericsson et al., 1993). It follows, then, that work places usually do not provide their incumbents with sufficient time resources that are required for such tedious and incremental attempts that qualify as deliberate practice. Practitioners tend therefore to be mainly concerned with the delivery of high-quality work results instead of learning or development outcomes (Boshuizen & van de Wiel, 2014; van de Wiel & Van den Bossche, 2013; see also Doornbos, Bolhuis, & Denessen, 2004).

2. Assessing one's own performance might not be easily done in work contexts. Without clear performance standards in many workplaces (see Section 3.1.1) employees might not be aware of the specific performance deficits they may actually have. It follows that practitioners are not always able to identify those skills that actually need improvement (Goller & Billett, 2014). In addition, they cannot count on designated trainers or coaches that are common in some domains like sport or music. Most workplaces do not provide access to trained instructors who invest significant time resources in the analysis of individuals' current performance levels. However, the accurate identification of shortcomings is required to find appropriate activities that help to eventually overcome them.

It is therefore not surprising that the few studies that actually investigated whether employees engage in deliberate practice at work and whether this engagement can be used to explain work-related expertise development applied a rather broad understanding of deliberate practice from the beginning. For instance, Sonnentag and Kleine (2000) defined deliberate practice at work as all efforts that are (a) performed on a regular basis during daily work practice,

(b) optional and go beyond usual task requirements, and (c) explicitly directed toward performance improvement. Typical examples of deliberate practice in their study in the domain of insurance agents are feedback seeking and mental simulations. Based on regression analyses the authors report a significant relationship between the current time spent on deliberate practice and job performance ($\beta = .29$, $p < .05$) after controlling for years of experience, the number of insurance cases handled in the past, and the time spent on activities supporting daily tasks ($R^2 = .24$). The cumulative time spent on deliberate practice in the past, however, did not significantly predict performance ($p > .05$). In a study on teachers, Dunn and Shriner (1999) explicitly used the definition given by Ericsson et al. (1993). However, retrospectively, they classified activities like preparing teaching materials and evaluation of written material as deliberate practice although these activities do not really fit their own definition. Unfortunately, the study did not investigate how they actually relate to performance or expertise development. In another study, van de Wiel, Szegedi, and Weggeman (2004) investigated the effect of deliberate practice on the expertise development of organisational consultants. In this study, the authors defined a range of work-related efforts (e. g., preparations, asking for help from a colleague) as well as developmental activities (e. g., reading professional literature, attending a further education course) as deliberate practice as long as the study participants performed those activities with a mastery goal in mind. Meaningful differences between top and average performers could only be observed for one single activity: On average the group of top performers more often read scientific literature than their non-expert counterparts ($d > 1$). However, the difference did not reach significance ($p = .06$). No other evidence was found that the engagement in deliberate learning activities is suitable to predict performance differences in the domain of consultancy. Furthermore, the participants indicated that most of their work-related and updating activities were not aimed at the development of knowledge and skills. They performed those activities mainly with a performance (i. e., to perform better than their peers within the current situation) or a professional goal (i. e., to obtain good work results) in mind (see for different achievement goals: Button, Mathieu, & Zajac, 1996, or Dweck & Leggett, 1988). In a more recent study, van de Wiel and Van den Bossche (2013) investigated the learning behaviour of physicians.

In this study all activities were categorised as deliberate practice as long as they were explicitly motivated by development and learning goals. Again, this study could find almost no evidence that physicians actually engage in activities that aim at the development of medicine-related competences. Instead, the majority of participants indicated that the focus of their work was to provide high-quality care for their patients (see also van de Wiel et al., 2011). Almost all activities (i. e., asking for advice or feedback) were directed towards the solution of specific problems emerging during the day.

In sum, the findings of these studies support the initially advanced claim that Ericsson's original notion of deliberate practice does not sufficiently help to explain the development of expert performance in work contexts. There is only very limited empirical evidence that employees actually engage in any kind of activities that can be described as deliberate practice. This is remarkable since most often the studies presented above even used a very wide and flexible understanding of the concept. In general, employees seem to engage only very seldom in activities with an explicit aim for learning and development. Their main concern in work contexts is to actually solve those problems and tasks that emerge during daily practice.

This does not mean that Ericsson's general argument is invalid. Similar to other domains, a sufficient number of studies could show that the length of experience alone is only a relatively poor predictor of expertise at work (Sonnentag, 1995, 1998a, 2000). It seems that workplaces might not automatically provide their employees with access to activities that have the potential for learning and development (Goller & Billett, 2014; Harteis & Goller, 2014). On the contrary, it is actually quite reasonable to assume that the majority of tasks and activities in many workplaces are rather repetitive in nature. Because of their routine characteristics such activities do not contribute much to the development of expertise after a certain performance level is reached (Ericsson, 2006b; Ericsson et al., 1993; see also Paloniemi, 2006; Tikkanen, 2002; see also Section 3.2.1 for a more detailed description of learning from experiences). It might therefore very well be necessary that practitioners also have to agentically contribute to their expertise development. These agentic efforts may just not satisfy Ericsson's original idea of deliberate practice. Instead of being explicitly focussed on learning and development, such activities might rather be strongly directed toward the engagement with new tasks and problems that occur at work. A more detailed discussion of the need of agentic actions in the context of professional development can be found in Section 3.3.

### 3.1.5 Recapitulation and Conclusion

Professional experts are individuals who are able to deal—at the same time highly effectively and efficiently—with the whole range of tasks and problems of their specific work environment. They do not only manage to cope superiorly and reproducibly well with routine demands. They are also capable of mastering highly ambivalent non-routine situations.

These abilities can predominantly be explained by the large and well-structured knowledge base of the expert performer. Domain-related knowledge and skills allow professional experts to overcome their working memory restrictions, to rapidly recognise and classify problem patterns, and to almost intuitively select appropriate solution strategies. Besides readily compiled routines it is the existence of encoded episodes of comparable situations experienced in the past that help experts to exhibit their superior performance within their domain. However, rich and well-structured networks of semantic knowledge might also be useful; particularly in situations that have not been experienced before.

The development of such a large and well-structured knowledge base can be almost exclusively traced back to a long-lasting and intensive engagement with domain-related activities. In other words, expert performance is, first and foremost, a product of ongoing efforts to understand the domain as well as continuous attempts to solve real-life tasks and problems that constitute the domain in question (i. e., experience). Without sufficient practice with domain-related activities no individual will develop those capacities that are required to exhibit superior performance within a particular domain.

However, experience alone is only a necessary condition for expertise development and not a sufficient one. Many individuals just do not reach expert performance levels despite their long-lasting experience within a domain. The main reason for this phenomenon is believed to lie in the nature of many domains. In most cases domains do not automatically provide individuals with sufficiently challenging tasks and problems. Many regularly occurring activities are rather repetitive and mundane in nature and therefore do not allow individuals to develop their capacities any further. It is therefore assumed that expertise development requires an active approach on the side of the learner.

## 3.2 Means of Professional Development

The previous section highlighted the important role of individuals' intensive and long-lasting engagement with domain-related activities for their expertise development. The term engagement was hereby used to simultaneously describe any kind of efforts to understand the domain as such as well as the actual participation in domain-related tasks and problems. However, apart from this specification, what kind of activities support employees to develop expertise in their respective work domain is still pretty much open. Put differently, what the concrete sources of skills and knowledge among actors in work-related domains are remains unclear. This section aims to close this gap by referring mainly to literature that originated in the field of workplace learning and professional development.

Traditionally, many scholars contrasted only two types of learning activities. So-called formal learning activities subsume all learning efforts that are organised by special institutions like schools or training providers to reach predefined learning outcomes. Usually a designated teacher is present during these learning activities and some kind of certificate is awarded to confirm learners' participation and achievement (Eraut, 2000; Malcolm, Hodkinson, & Colley, 2003). In contrast, so-called informal (or sometimes nonformal) learning activities do not meet these criteria. Marsick and Volpe (1999) describe them as "predominantly unstructured, experiential, and noninstitutional" (p. 4). However, the dichotomy of formal and informal learning has been criticised both on theoretical and empirical grounds (Billett, 2004b; Doornbos et al., 2004; Eraut, 2007; Tynjälä, 2008).

Over the years a range of different more detailed classification systems for work-related learning activities were proposed (e. g., Berings, Poell, & Gelissen, 2008; Doornbos et al., 2004; Eraut, 2007; Estabrooks et al., 2005; Kwakman,

2003; Pool, Poell, Berings, & ten Cate, 2016). In the context of this thesis it was decided to use the classification system of Pool et al. (2016). First of all, the authors' classification system was specifically created to fit the development of nurses. This is helpful since the empirical studies of this thesis will also be conducted in the domain of nursing (see Chapter 4). Second, Pool et al. developed their classification system based on several already existing typologies. They were therefore able to integrate in their own model both previous empirical findings as well as theoretical criticism brought forward by other authors. Third, the individual categories in their classification system can be characterised as largely distinct and mutually exclusive. This is not the case for some of the other categories proposed before (e. g., Berings et al., 2008). The classification system with descriptions of each category can be found in Table 3.1. For each category a more detailed description can be found in the following subsections.

### 3.2.1 Learning from Experience

On a very general level, learning from experience, sometimes also referred to as experiential learning, can be defined as the development or the adjustment of knowledge structures "through the active participation in personally relevant episodes in a natural context, e. g., a workplace" (J. Bauer, 2008, p. 22). An episode hereby describes an encountered event in a particular situation at a certain point in time (Gruber, 1999b). In work contexts such episodes are the product of individuals' participation in authentic work practices (Billett, 2001c, 2011b). Experiences can be made through the (successful or unsuccessful) engagement in work-related tasks and problems, the making of practical decisions at work, as well as the handling and operation of work-related tools and artefacts (Billett, 2001a, 2001c, 2011b; Collin, 2004; Illeris, 2007; see for the topic on learning through errors in particular: J. Bauer & Harteis, 2012; Harteis & Bauer, 2014).

In the majority of cases employees do not engage in those work practices with a learning goal in mind (Doornbos et al., 2004; see Section 3.1.4). It is rather the case that they are concerned with meeting the specific demands the particular workplace requests from them. That is why some authors charac-

**Table 3.1.** Classification system of learning activities in work contexts. Reprinted and adapted from "Pool, I. A., Poell, R. F., Berings, M. G., & ten Cate, O. (2016). Motives and activities for continuing professional development: An exploration of their relationships by integrating literature and interview data. *Nurse Education Today, 38*, 22–28, p. 23" with permission from Elsevier.

| Category | Description |
|---|---|
| *Learning from experience* | All activities connected to the engagement in actual nursing practice—i. e., task and problem solving. |
| *Learning from social interaction* | Learning through the engagement with other professional actors at work (e. g., exchange of knowledge, consultations about work matters, observations of others' work practices, and feedback). |
| *Learning from consulting media* | All activities related to the interaction with media sources like manuals, books, patient charts or the internet. |
| *Learning from institutionalised learning activities* | Formal learning activities that usually take place outside of the normal workplace like workshops, trainings or conferences. |

terise such learning as an incidental by-product (Doornbos et al., 2004; Eraut, 2000; Marsick & Watkins, 1990; Scribner & Sachs, 1991). However, the concept of experiential learning does not explicitly exclude intentional learning. Individuals at work can also encounter episodes in such situations they have created with an explicit learning goal in mind (Doornbos et al., 2004; Eraut, 2000). For instance, an employee might want to learn how to deal with a new kind of software available at her workplace. She therefore tries the new software on tasks that she has approached with another kind of software in the past. In this situation, the employee engages in work practices with both the intention to solve the task at hand and to learn something new.

On a more theoretical level, learning from experience can be described using a model developed by D. A. Kolb (1984). The model describes how individuals convert concrete episodes of experience into episodic knowledge that then can be used to guide prospective actions and thereby make new experiences in the future (Boud, Keogh, & Walker, 1999a; Segers & van der Haar, 2011). According to D. A. Kolb (1984), learning from experience follows a four-stage cyclical process involving experience, reflective observation, abstract conceptualisation, and active experimentation (i. e., action) (see also A. Y. Kolb & Kolb, 2012). This learning cycle can be found in Figure 3.1.

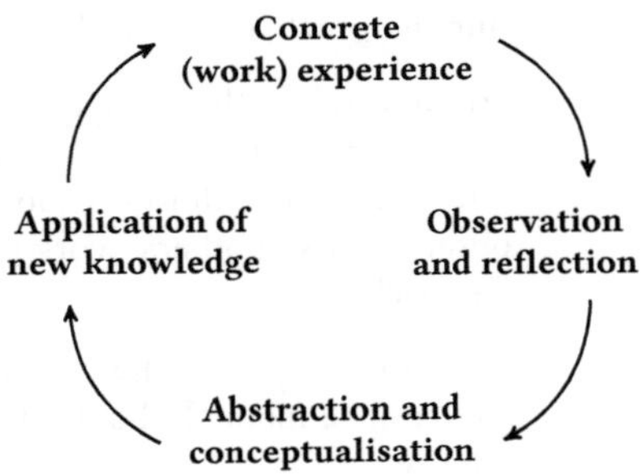


**Figure 3.1.** Kolb's learning cycle. Reprinted and adapted from "Kolb, D. A. (1984). *Experiential learning: Experience as the source of learning and development.* Englewood Cliffs: Prentice-Hall, p. 42" with permission from Pearson, Education, Inc., New York, New York.

The first stage of the model involves the individual in making a certain experience. Such experiences are a product of the individual's action and the resulting consequences of this action within the particular situation (Segers & van der Haar, 2011). In stage two, this experience is then used as the foundation for observations and reflections. In other words, the individual attempts to understand the encountered episode by analysing both the situation as well as the desired or undesired effects of her own action (J. Bauer, 2008). This reflection process is used to derive more general principles behind the relationship between her own actions and the consequences that followed out of these actions. The outcome of the third phase is then a more abstract theory of action—that is, a subjective theory of how the world works and what actions are appropriate under what kinds of circumstances (cf., Groeben, 1988)—that allows deduction of new implications for future actions in comparable situations (Segers & van der Haar, 2011). This newly derived theory of action can then be tested and validated in new situations. D. A. Kolb (1984) used the term active experimentation for this last stage of his model. The individual acts in new situations according to her new knowledge and thereby creates new experience. The cyclical model then starts from the beginning again.

There are two important implications that follow from D. A. Kolb's (1984) model. First, learning from experience requires the individual to reflect on her experiences. Without reflection, no knowledge can be constructed or modified. Reflection hereby describes the "mental activity aimed at investigating one's own action in a certain situation and involving a review of the experience, an analysis of causes and effects, and the drawing of conclusions concerning future actions" (van Woerkom, 2003, p. 40). Without the analysis of the circumstances of the situation, the causes of certain events and the appropriateness of one's own actions or experiences cannot be turned into learning. The importance of reflection for learning in work contexts has also been discussed by a range of authors (e. g., Boud et al., 1999a, 1999b; Ellström, 2006; Høyrup, 2004; Raelin, 1997; Schön, 2000).[26]

The second implication is that repeated progressions through the four stages enable the individual to refine and tune her knowledge (see also Section 3.1.3). The repeated engagement in domain-specific situations allows the individual to repeatedly apply their current theories of action and—at the same time—to analyse the viability of those theories in particular circumstances (see also Y.-J. Lee & Roth, 2005). However, repeated engagement in similar situations might lose their learning potential after some time. In order to continuously develop expertise individuals have to encounter new and increasingly challenging situations (Billett, 2001c; see also Section 3.1.4). Empirical evidence backs up this idea. For instance, Paloniemi (2006) reported that engineers perceive simple routine tasks as less relevant for their competence development (see for similar findings: Tikkanen, 2002). Learning is strongly connected to the engagement in situations that offer something "new" (Collin,

26 It should be noted that reflection is not only relevant for learning from experience. It is equally important for learning from social interaction, learning from consulting media, and learning from institutionalised learning activities (see also Pool et al., 2016, as well as Boud et al., 1999a).

2002) and simultaneously require more than the retrieval of more or less automated solution strategies already available (Paloniemi, 2006).

To sum up, learning from experience can best be described as "learning by doing one's regular job" (Berings et al., 2008, p. 445) in combination with the required reflection of one's own actions, the resulting effects, as well as the relevant social and physical circumstances. However, not all work-related experiences exhibit similar potential for the development of expertise. The sole engagement in already familiar tasks and problems does not result in much cognitive change after some time. Expertise development rather requires the individual to engage in increasingly challenging and qualitatively new work-related episodes.

### 3.2.2 Learning from Social Interaction

Social interaction describes the "process of communication and mutual influence involving contact between two or more [actors]" (Nash & Calonico, 1996, p. 68). In work contexts such contact can occur between fellow coworkers, supervisors, subordinates or other relevant stakeholders (in the case of geriatric care nurses, e. g., residents, family members of residents, doctors). Contact hereby subsumes all forms of verbal and non-verbal exchange of information, like explanations, discussions, or observations.

Within the literature social interaction has been discussed as highly relevant for learning in work and non-work contexts (e. g., Billett, 2001c, 2004b, 2014; Doornbos et al., 2004; Eraut, 2007; Eraut, Alderton, Cole, & Senker, 2002; Gerber, Lankshear, Larsson, & Svensson, 1995; Lave & Wenger, 1991; Rogoff, 1991, 1995). It is the participation in joined activities combined with the exchange of information about the shared experience that allows individuals to co-construct knowledge. On a conceptual level, there are at least four different types of such social learning activities that can be distinguished: (a) collaboration, (b) learning from narratives, (c) receiving feedback, and (d) conceptual explanations.

1. *Collaboration:* In the context of this thesis the term collaboration describes all efforts to tackle tasks and solve problems together with other individu-

als. Learning through collaboration can be explained threefold. First, learners can construct knowledge by observation and imitation. The joined engagement in work practice allows the learner to observe a role model in action and to subsequently imitate the observed strategy to solve the task or problem herself (see Bandura, 1977, 1986, and Billett, 2014, for theoretical accounts that describe such learning). Second, through the help of a more proficient other the learner is enabled to engage in practices that are still beyond her current skill level (i. e., scaffolding within the zone of proximal development; Cole, 1995; Rogoff, 1991, 1995; Vygotsky, 1978). This allows the learner to tackle yet unfamiliar (sub)tasks and (sub)problems. In other words, the assistance of other individuals permits individuals to gain highly relevant experiences and therefore to construct and refine performance-relevant knowledge. Third, shared problem solving encourages the exchange of knowledge. For instance, other professional actors can be contacted to obtain specialised knowledge, to get affirmation whether the planned action strategy seems to be reasonable or not, as well as to engage in discussions about potential solution strategies and possible pitfalls (Doornbos et al., 2004; Eraut, 2007; Estabrooks et al., 2005; Skår, 2010; see also the next two categories).

2. *Learning from narratives:* Narratives are representations of past events experienced by an individual or a group of individuals in oral, written or cinematic form (Linde, 2001). In work contexts the most important narratives are oral stories about exceptional work-related episodes told by colleagues. For instance, Oser et al. (2012; see also Oser & Spychiger, 2005) discuss the potential of such advocatory experiences in the context of mistake making. In their opinion it is not required that individuals make every kind of possible mistake. Individuals can also construct or modify their knowledge structures though the cognitive engagement with the mistakes of other individuals—for example, by listening to stories about them. The mistakes of other individuals can also help to construct knowledge about what works in certain working situations and what does not (negative knowledge). Orr (1996) also stresses the learning potential of renarrated experiences in work contexts on the basis of his ethnographic research. He found that tech-

nicians often discuss recent episodes which they encountered while repairing machines at work. The narrative representation of problem situations as well as their solutions helped the listening technicians to construct situation-specific knowledge which they did not have to experience by themselves (see also Lämsä & Sintonen, 2006; Linde, 2001; Zucchermaglio & Alby, 2016). It therefore follows that learners can benefit not only from their own experience but also from the experience of others working in the same domain.

3. *Receiving feedback:* Feedback describes all information concerning the results of an actor's actions on a certain target environment (Boero & Novarese, 2012). Opportunities to receive feedback are seen as highly important for all kinds of learning processes since feedback allows the learner to detect discrepancies between her current and desired performance (e. g., Boero & Novarese, 2012; Butler & Winne, 1995; Hattie, 2009; Kyndt, Dochy, & Nijs, 2009). Feedback can therefore be understood as a catalyst for reflection (Schley & van Woerkom, 2014) and thus an important requirement for learning from experience (see Section 3.2.1). Besides the immediate responses of the workplace itself it is mostly oral feedback of colleagues and supervisors that is perceived as important for skill and knowledge construction (Ellinger, 2005; Skår, 2010; Skule, 2004). Based on their experience, more proficient others are able to comment about the performance of the learner as well as about already mastered abilities or potential deficits.

4. *Conceptual explanations:* Explanations comprise all efforts of one individual to describe to another the cause, context, and consequences of a certain phenomenon. Such explanations help learners to understand work-related phenomena mostly on a conceptual level. This might be especially necessary in situations that involve processes of certain phenomena that are opaque or completely hidden from the observing learner (Billett, 1995, 1996). For instance, computer technology or very complex work procedures might not always be comprehensible by sole observation or trial and error (see also Berryman, 1993). It requires designated instructors or more experienced colleagues to explain on a more conceptual level what is going on and how those processes can be manipulated.

To sum up, social interaction is highly relevant for learning in work contexts. In most cases it is the contact with colleagues and supervisors that allows the learner to construct knowledge and develop skills through a range of different social learning activities (see also Klette & Smeby, 2012; Köpke, Koch, Behncke, & Balzer, 2013). However, other actors—like doctors, physiotherapists or even family members of residents in the case of geriatric nursing—are similarly important sources of knowledge (Eraut et al., 2002; Estabrooks et al., 2005; Köpke et al., 2013; Skår, 2010; Spenceley, O'Leary, Chizawsky, Ross, & Estabrooks, 2008). Discussions with them are likely to open up new perspectives on work-related matters for the learner. Furthermore, in certain other healthcare situations, specialists might be knowledgeable enough to conceptually explain particular work-related phenomena or to demonstrate new strategies to deal with specific tasks and problems that would be inaccessible without their help.

### 3.2.3 Learning from Consulting Media

On a general level, a medium is defined as a carrier (i. e., a tool) that stores or delivers information in written, pictorial, cinematographic or acoustic form. Within the literature, books and journals, different kinds of internet or intranet resources (e. g., databases, websites), and technical manuals are the most commonly mentioned media types related to professional development processes (Berings et al., 2008; Eraut, 2007; Eraut & Hirsh, 2007; Estabrooks et al., 2005; Gerber, 1998). However, especially in the domain of nursing, work-related protocols and patient charts are also acknowledged as being relevant for the development of skills and knowledge (Estabrooks et al., 2005; Skår, 2010).

All these media types can be understood as cultural artefacts (Doornbos et al., 2004) that serve employees as codified knowledge sources (Rausch, 2011). They are either used as (a) tools to solve specific problems at hand, or (b) resources to keep up with current developments in the field (see also Eraut, 2007):

1. Practitioners might encounter situations with which they are completely or partly unfamiliar. In such situations most practitioners either ask other

people from their social network (see Section 3.2.2) or they consult appropriate media resources. Media sources like professional books, manuals or journals help to find problem-specific information that can be used to understand the experienced phenomenon in more detail as well as to enumerate potential solution strategies that actually help to tackle the situation in question (Estabrooks et al., 2005; Klette & Smeby, 2012; Skår, 2010).

2. Professional journals and other periodically published publications contain information about the newest development in the corresponding domain. Practitioners can use these knowledge sources to keep pace with new technologies and new procedures, as well as new general trends concerning their practice (Gerber, 1998; Paloniemi, 2006). This is particularly important in domains that rapidly produce new insights on the base of scientific inquiry (e. g., the medical field; Sackett, Rosenberg, Gray, Haynes, & Richardson, 1996; Sackett & Rosenberg, 1995).

The important role of scientific knowledge resources for practitioners working in the domain of nursing has been acknowledged by many authors (e. g., Estabrooks et al., 2005; Klette & Smeby, 2012; Köpke et al., 2013).[27] However, it is questionable whether scientific journals are commonly used by nurses in general or by geriatric care nurses in particular. There is some evidence that nurses do not consult such knowledge resources as often as other employees in more academic professions (i. e., teacher, doctors) do (Klette & Smeby, 2012; see also Heise, 2007). One reason for this might be that nurses are often not trained to read research literature (Estabrooks et al., 2005; see especially for the German context: Köpke et al., 2013). Apart from this, missing opportunities to actually obtain research articles might also be a problem. Some nurses are just not able to access web-based databases like MEDLINE simply because there are either no computers with internet connection available (Klette & Smeby, 2012) or they do not have the skill set to do so (Estabrooks et al., 2005).

27 The main reason behind this important role is the continuing demand for evidence-based practice in all kinds of medical domains (e. g., Bund-Länder-Arbeitsgruppe Weiterentwicklung der Pflege, 2012; Meyer, Balzer, & Köpke, 2013; Robra, 2016; Sackett et al., 1996). Evidence-based practice hereby describes all practices that are "based on the findings of systematic evaluation of the evidence of the effectiveness of interventions" (Hewitt-Taylor, 2002, p. 47).

To sum up, media containing codified knowledge about phenomena, procedures, and current developments are important resources for the development of expertise. However, it is still open to discussion whether scientific literature plays the role it is assumed to play.

### 3.2.4 Learning from Institutionalised Learning Activities

In the context of this thesis, institutionalised learning activities describe all systematically arranged development opportunities that are not directly embedded in the daily production or service process of a particular workplace. They are designated endeavours that explicitly aim at participants' knowledge and skill development through the engagement in specific learning efforts usually prepared and supported by a trainer or some other qualified person. Typical examples for institutionalised learning activities are in-house seminars, external workshops, conferences, or even whole degree programmes (e. g., Berings et al., 2008; Eraut, 2007; Estabrooks et al., 2005; Pool et al., 2016; Sonnentag, Niessen, & Ohly, 2004).

For many individuals, institutionalised learning opportunities offer a first structured access to topics and phenomena of a particular domain. Designated qualification programmes (apprenticeships, vocational schools, universities) are often explicitly installed to equip novices with the knowledge and skills that are perceived as necessary to work in certain positions and occupations. Apart from this, institutionalised learning activities are also recognised as highly valuable for the ongoing professional development of practitioners. Such learning activities are perceived to possess the potential to compensate for some of the limitations of the learning activities described above—that is, learning from experience at work, learning from social interaction in work contexts, or solitary consultation of media resources (Slotte, Tynjälä, & Hytönen, 2004; Tynjälä, 2008):

1. Institutionalised learning activities are usually led by experts who are motivated to share their expertise and their insights about phenomena, tasks, and problems of a particular domain with others. Within work contexts this is not necessarily the case. Knowledge can be understood as an important source of power (French & Raven, 1959) that secures superiority or status,

as well as continued employment. Some authors therefore argue that experts within work contexts are reluctant to actually share their knowledge because of fears of losing the benefits connected to their interpersonal competitive advantage (e. g., Billett, 1995, 1996, 2004b; Huber, 2001; Szulanski, 1996).

2. Trainers, tutors or other presenters usually use institutionalised learning activities to provide participants with pedagogically rich explanations about current developments and work-related phenomena. This is important for two reasons. First, within the daily work process peers and supervisors are often incapable of delivering knowledge in an effective and efficient way. Skills and knowledge of practitioners are often tacit and not readily available (e. g., Polanyi, 1969; see also Section 3.1). Furthermore, in many work contexts employees are neither qualified nor do they find the time to prepare pedagogically rich descriptions and explanations. Taken together, these circumstances make it difficult for many practitioners to verbalise or explicate their expertise to others (see also Huber, 2001). Second, designated teachers are often capable of translating complex ideas (like theories, scientific evidence) into forms that can be easily understood by employees (see also Estabrooks et al., 2005). This is especially important in such domains where many employees do not have the abilities to access those ideas without the help of more capable others (e. g., nursing, see also Section 3.2.3).

3. Institutionalised learning activities reserve time to explore topics from multiple perspectives, to give feedback about the learners' current level of understanding, as well as to determine potential misconceptions and skill deficits. Put differently, institutionalised learning activities open up opportunities for engagement with topics and phenomena that workplaces are unable to offer in similar way (Leinhardt, McCarthy Young, & Merriman, 1995; Slotte et al., 2004; see also Section 3.1).

To sum up, institutionalised learning activities can be understood as prerequisites as well as important supplements to learning from experience, social interaction, and media as discussed above (see also Tynjälä et al., 1997).

### 3.2.5 Recapitulation and Conclusion

Within the literature on workplace learning a range of different knowledge sources and learning activities have been identified and discussed as means for employees' professional development. Based on earlier classification attempts as well as some empirical studies, Pool et al. (2016) recently proposed a typology that aims to classify those means into four distinguished categories. The first category, learning from experience, encompasses all activities directly related to the engagement in actual working practices—for example, task and problem solving, decision making or the handling of professional artefacts. Learning from social interaction, the second category, comprises all learning activities that occur as a product of communication and collaboration with different actors within the workplace. Typical examples are learning through imitation, advocatory learning via narratives or conceptual explanations offered by colleagues. The third category includes all learning that is a product of the learners' engagement with media sources, like professional journals, text books or internet databases. Last but not least, the fourth category subsumes all systematically planned learning interventions that are not directly embedded in the daily production process (e. g., workshops or seminars).

Each of these categories describes a set of rather distinct learning activities that make use of different knowledge sources employed by practitioners.[28] Empirical attempts to rank the relevance of these categories for the professional development of nurses have shown that learning from experience is rated as most important. Cooperation and collaboration with colleagues and other professional actors are ranked second, while institutionalised learning activities and the engagement with relevant media sources are positioned on third and fourth place (Klette & Smeby, 2012; Köpke et al., 2013; see also Estabrooks et al., 2005). However, theoretically it has also been emphasised how each of these learning activities might actually supplement each other (see above). For instance, experiential learning might be less effective when work-related phenomena cannot be easily observed. In such cases explanations from more profi-

28 It should be emphasised that the proposed typology has to be understood as a mostly analytical classification system. In practice many learning activities cannot always easily be classified into a single category.

cient peers or even designated teachers can easily improve the understanding of the learner. In addition, new work-related developments might not receive much attention in daily work processes. However, both professional journals and institutionalised learning activities like workshops or conferences provide learners with adequate means to actually keep pace with current trends and innovations.

All in all, the categorisation of learning activities and knowledge sources just discussed helps to further understand exactly how practitioners develop work-related knowledge and skills. These insights will be used to discuss how individuals can agentically take charge of their expertise development in the next section.

## 3.3 Agentic Actions Related to Professional Development

The last section identified a range of learning activities and knowledge sources that are important for the development of expertise. However, it has to be acknowledged that not all employees automatically have access to each of these learning activities, nor do all practitioners necessarily take advantage of them.

First of all, learning from experience and learning from social interaction especially are strongly intertwined with work itself. Thus, it is mainly the workplace structure—the division of labour, existing hierarchies, as well as certain material conditions—that determines what episodes and social interactions employees encounter during the day (see also Chapter 2). Some workplaces naturally provide their employees with a rich set of affordances but others are more restrictive in nature (see also A. Fuller & Unwin, 2004). However, just because challenging situations, work-related discussions or performance-related feedback, to list just a few examples, are not automatically part of a certain workplace does not mean they are always completely inaccessible. In many workplaces such learning opportunities are indeed available as long as they are actively sought out by their incumbents (see Chapter 2).

Second, even if employees are naturally afforded with a rich set of opportunities to engage in learning-relevant experiences, to interact with other professional actors in manifold ways, to use codified knowledge resources to solve problems or to keep up with certain developments, and to participate in institutionalised learning activities, they might still elect not to do so (see Section 2.1.1.1). In most cases, workplaces afford their employees with a certain degree of freedom regarding their daily work life (Goller & Billett, 2014). In this sense, most employees are not forced to listen to other individuals' work experience or feedback. They are also often not strictly required to read professional journals or to (enthusiastically) participate in institutionalised learning activities. It is their own decision whether they use the affordances provided for them or not (see Chapter 2). Thus, in most cases, opportunities to engage with learning-relevant affordances have to be understood as invitations and not as duties.

Based on these two arguments it follows that work-related knowledge, skills, and abilities do not develop inevitably. Without active efforts many employees may only engage in learning opportunities that are an unavoidable part of their daily work life. In other words, without learners' very own initiative the development of knowledge, skills, and abilities rapidly becomes a product of chance mostly related to the structural conditions present in their particular workplace. Practitioners working in workplaces that both afford a range of learning opportunities and simultaneously expect their staff members to actually utilise them are better off than their counterparts in less expansive work environments (see also A. Fuller & Unwin, 2004). In order to be less constrained by potentially restrictive conditions employees have to become active and to deliberately take charge of their professional development.

The aim of this section is to find out exactly how employees can do this. The main focus is hereby laid on the identification of self-initiated actions that actually help to activate or create learning affordances at work. In the sense of Chapter 2 those efforts can be interpreted as agentic actions. However, based on earlier discussions it is already known that an individual's propensity to engage in any kind of agentic action also depends on social and material context factors. This section therefore also sets out to discuss relevant workplace characteristics that either foster or hinder engagement in such efforts. A particular focus will be laid on those workplace characteristics that have already been identified as highly relevant in Section 2.2.3.4: autonomy at work, leadership and interpersonal climate, and perceived job stressors.

### 3.3.1 Crafting (Learning) Experiences at Work

As already discussed, structural factors that make up a particular workplace largely determine what experiences an incumbent can have during a work day. However, authors like Wrzesniewski and Dutton (2001), Tims and Bakker (2010), as well as Goller and Billett (2014) proposed that individuals can make both subtle and significant changes to these structural factors and thereby create new experience that would otherwise not have been afforded to them. This phenomenon is discussed either under the concept of job crafting (i. e., all efforts of an incumbent to change her current task boundaries; Wrzesniewski & Dutton, 2001) or experience crafting (i. e., all intentional actions that aim at the creation of new work-related experiences; Goller & Billett, 2014). This job and experience crafting manifests itself when incumbents discretely add new responsibilities to their job by taking over obligations of their supervisor or other individuals higher up the organisational hierarchy, engage in unfamiliar tasks by trading with colleagues, take part in or even initiate particular work-related projects (e. g., quality circles), participate in problem situations that are not primarily part of their task description, or experiment with new procedures without actually changing the scope of their current job (e. g., try out new solution strategies) (e. g., Berg, Wrzesniewski, & Dutton, 2010; Berings, Poell, & Simons, 2005; Berings et al., 2008; Bryson et al., 2006; Eraut, 2007; Goller & Billett, 2014; Kwakman, 2003; McCauley, 2006; McCauley & Hezlett, 2005; Wrzesniewski & Dutton, 2001). Incumbents who engage in such crafting efforts manage to encounter new and challenging situations more often than their counterparts who do not exercise such behaviour.[29]

29 Goller and Billett (2014) use the following example to illustrate the potential effects of job and experience crafting: A car mechanic is working in a local garage where repair work is divided between all mechanics present in a shift. Most workers in this garage prefer and therefore also tend to mostly repair those cars with which they are familiar. In contrast, the car mechanic in question deliberately attempts to repair cars she is less familiar with from time to time. This approach helps her to construct relevant knowledge about a wide variety of different cars allowing her to be much more flexible when it comes to the

Empirical evidence concerning the relationship of such crafting experiences in work contexts and professional development is still rather scarce. However, a few qualitative studies give preliminary insights that employees indeed craft learning opportunities at work and thereby take charge of their own professional development process. For instance, Bryson et al. (2006) used semi-structured interviews to investigate the learning of viticulture workers. Within their interviews they found evidence that employees in management positions identify self-initiated work projects as an important source for learning and development. Furthermore, the authors report about a vineyard worker strongly interested in the process of wine making. Because of his interest this vineyard worker deliberately sought out opportunities to work in the winery in order to learn more about wine making. In another study, Berg, Wrzesniewski, and Dutton (2010; see also Berg, Grant, & Johnson, 2010) found evidence that employees working in different profit and non-profit organisations openly associate the deliberate crafting of job tasks by altering the nature of tasks or taking on additional tasks with learning and development. In addition, they found evidence that individuals also take initiative to create additional relationships that are used to gain new knowledge.

A few quantitative studies also generated evidence that crafting behaviour positively relates to learning and development. Berings, Poell, Simons, and van Veldhoven (2007), for instance, found that nurses who frequently add something new to their job report a higher perceived development than their counterparts who do not engage in such deliberate efforts ($\beta = .29$) even when variables like work experience, information seeking or employment hours are controlled for ($R^2 = .12$). Adding something new hereby means that nurses temporarily work in other departments, take over somebody else's work or de-

division of work at the beginning of a shift. In addition, on a particular occasion, she volunteered to temporarily take over shifts in the garage's storage facilities to replace a sick colleague. This opportunity allowed her to develop an understanding of how spare parts needed to replace broken car pieces are actually ordered. She also constructed knowledge of why certain parts of certain makes are often difficult to source. This insight allows her to order parts from different manufacturers if necessary or to explain to customers why the maintenance of their car might take a little bit longer. Taken together, the just described mechanic manages to secure herself a rich set of new work experiences by deliberately shaping her task boundaries. Without her crafting efforts she would not have been able to construct the new knowledge and skills that are an important foundation of her expertise.

liberately look for new challenging situations (see also Berings et al., 2008). In a similar vein, a longitudinal study by Petrou, Demerouti, and Schaufeli (2016) could show that police officers who tend to deliberately seek out new challenges at work—like looking for new tasks or taking on more responsibilities—tend to cope better with changing demands related to their workplace than police officers who do not take such an agentic stance to their job ($\gamma = .17$, $p < .05$).

Theoretically it has been suggested that the (perceived) opportunity to make changes to one's own job is one of the most important situational antecedents of job-related crafting behaviour (Ghitulescu, 2007; Tims & Bakker, 2010; Wrzesniewski & Dutton, 2001). Incumbents are less inclined to engage in job and experience crafting if they do not have the opportunities to do so in the first place (Tims & Bakker, 2010). It therefore follows that workplaces that offer much discretion and sufficient time resources are more likely to support any kind of crafting behaviours (see also Ghitulescu, 2007). In addition, a workplace climate of trust and support should also be an important predictor of job and experience crafting. Colleagues and supervisors who approve or even actively support employees' crafting efforts reduce the perceived costs that are connected to such behaviours (Ghitulescu, 2007; see also Section 2.2.3).

Empirical results support these hypothesised relationships. For instance, Berg, Grant, and Johnson (2010) reported that individuals working in work environments with relatively low discretion do not see themselves in a position to make any changes to their job. In a more quantitative study, Lyons (2008) found evidence that sales representatives who perceive they have opportunities to make changes to their work also engage more often in actual job crafting behaviour ($r = .26, p < .01$). Similarly, Ghitulescu (2007) reported that job discretion has a significant and positive effect on efforts to craft work tasks in an automotive context ($\beta = .42$, $p < .01$). In two other studies, Hornung, Rousseau, Glaser, Angerer, and Weigl (2010) and C. C. Rosen, Slater, Chang, and Johnson (2013) could also show that employees who work in supporting and trusting climates more often tend to negotiate with their supervisors about additional responsibilities as well as new assignments that have not yet been part of their job ($\beta = .42$ and $\beta = .27$, respectively; both $p < .01$).

To sum up, much evidence exists that employees can take charge of their professional development by deliberate crafting learning experiences at work. Typical examples of such crafting behaviours are the voluntary engagement in new projects as well as tasks and responsibilities that have not yet been part of the incumbent's job description. Job and experience crafting allows employees to engage in learning-relevant experiences to which they would otherwise not have access. However, it should be noted that employees are not completely free to act at work. Low job discretion, high time pressure at work or low support from colleagues and supervisors might easily prevent employees from exhibiting any kind of crafting behaviour.

### 3.3.2 Information and Feedback Seeking

Information and feedback are critical resources for both the development of individuals and their daily work performance. Especially in unfamiliar or ambiguous situations, individuals often need information about what is technically required to perform well in a certain task or practice (so-called technical information) as well as information about existing standards and performance expectations (so-called referent information) (Miller & Jablin, 1991; Morrison, 1993b) in order to approach the task or solve the problem in the first place. In this sense, technical and referent information are nothing other than (codified) semantic knowledge not yet constructed by the incumbent. In addition, employees require information on how they perform and whether they have met the performance expectations of their organisation in the past (Ashford & Cummings, 1983; Miller & Jablin, 1991; Morrison, 1993b). Such appraisal or feedback information is an important catalyst for reflection and introspection about one's own current performance level as well as potential performance deficits (see Section 3.2.2).

Unfortunately, workplaces will not always automatically provide their employees with all required information. In order to excel at work or to progress developmentally it is often necessary that incumbents take initiative to seize and retrieve technical, referent, and appraisal information (Goller & Billett, 2014). Within the literature two different modes of seeking information and feedback are distinguished:

1. *Monitoring* subsumes all strategies where an employee deliberately seeks for informational cues and signals that are subliminally provided by the environment or the situation. These cues can arise directly from work tasks as such (e. g., failure to accomplish a task) as well as from behaviours of other actors (e. g., colleagues or supervisors might signal approval about certain performance outcomes by nodding or exhibiting other appreciative body language; Ashford & Cummings, 1983; Morrison, 1993a).

2. *Inquiry* describes all active attempts that involve directly asking other individuals to obtain required information or directly searching for relevant data in impersonal sources like books, manuals, or the internet (Ashford & Cummings, 1983; Morrison, 1993a). Inquiry is a much more overt and visible strategy in comparison to monitoring. This is especially true when other individuals are contacted to obtain certain information.

This distinction helps to understand exactly how employees seek information in work contexts. All together six analytically different information and feedback seeking strategies can be distinguished (see Table 3.2). Each of these strategies is related to learning from experience (see Section 3.2.1), learning through social interaction (see Section 3.2.2), or learning from consulting media (see Section 3.2.3).

Theoretically it has been argued that each of these six strategies should be strongly related to task mastery and professional development (e. g., Anseel, Beatty, Shen, Lievens, & Sackett, 2015; Ashford & Tsui, 1991; Goller & Billett, 2014; Morrison, 1993b). Individuals who frequently seek technical and referent information should know more about how work-related tasks and procedures are performed as well as how appropriate performance outcomes in their organisation look like. In addition, individuals who often seek feedback or other kinds of appraisal information should develop faster and better, especially in work situations where feedback is not automatically provided to them. Feedback helps them to adjust their current working strategies and to detect discrepancies between current and desired performance (see Section 3.2.2). Nevertheless, even in environments that constantly provide appraisal information, self-sought feedback should have higher potential for learning and development (Goller & Billett, 2014). The acceptance of (negative) feedback as well

**Table 3.2.** Information and feedback seeking strategies.

| Modes | Technical information | Referent information | Appraisal information |
|---|---|---|---|
| *Monitoring* | E. g., observation of how other professional actors approach a task or problem. | E. g., use of other individuals' work outcomes as reference. | E. g., searching for cues that confirm one's own approach. |
| | Mostly learning through social interaction. | Mostly learning through social interaction. | Mostly learning from experience and learning through social interaction. |
| *Inquiry* | E. g., actively asking how a task or problem should be approached or reading about it in a manual. | E. g., actively asking about the standards and expectations connected to a certain task or reading about it in a manual. | E. g., deliberately asking somebody for feedback. |
| | Both learning through social interaction and learning from consulting media. | Both learning through social interaction and learning from consulting media. | Mostly learning through social interaction. |

as the tendency to actually change one's own behaviour is usually higher in cases where the feedback is actively sought out and not only passively received (Ashford & Cummings, 1983).

A range of empirical results back up these propositions. For instance, T. N. Bauer, Bodner, Erdogan, Truxillo, and Tucker (2007) used meta-analytical procedures to investigate whether information-seeking strategies are a predictor of job-related performance measures for individuals new to their job (first 13 months). They found evidence that information seeking is weakly but significantly correlated to job performance ($r = .08, p < .05, k = 10$). Additional analyses showed that this relationship is fully mediated by increased role clarity—that is, an understanding of one's own function within an organisation. Another meta-analysis by Anseel et al. (2015) showed that feedback seeking via inquiry significantly correlates with job performance ($\rho = .13, p < .05, k = 4$). However, in the same study they found that feedback seeking based on monitoring was not significantly related to job performance ($\rho = -.03, p > .05, k = 2$). Apart from that, the results of two other recent studies that were not integrated in those meta-analyses can be described: Saks, Gruman, and Cooper-Thomas (2011) found evidence that feedback seeking is a positive predictor of task mastery ($\beta = .20, p < .05$) in their sample of Canadian interns. In a similar vein, Spagnoli, Caetano, Tanucci, and Lourenço de Sousa (2012) reported a positive relationship between implicit information-seeking strategies, defined as inquiry of written information as well as monitoring in general, and task mastery for newly employed police officers ($\beta = .16, p < .05$). Taken together these results speak in favour of the assumed relationship of individuals' engagement in information and feedback seeking behaviour and their performance development.

Apart from these positive effects, information and feedback seeking is also associated with potential costs for the individual (Ashford & Cummings, 1983; Morrison, 2002; see also Section 2.2.3.2). Inquiry strategies especially pose the risk of exposing one's own lack of skills or knowledge (Ashford & Cummings, 1983; Beenen, Pichler, & Levy, 2016). Openly looking for information about how to do a task or asking about one's own performance level might be interpreted as a skill deficit by colleagues or supervisors. It follows that individuals are less motivated to engage in information and feedback seeking if they do not feel safe to do so at work. Empirical evidence supports this proposition. A climate of trust and support are positive predictors of information and feedback seeking (e. g., Anseel et al., 2015; Beenen et al., 2016; Estabrooks et al., 2005; Spagnoli et al., 2012).

As well as these face-loss costs, information and feedback seeking also involves effort costs (Ashford & Cummings, 1983). Effort costs describe all costs related to mental or physical effort required to obtain technical, referent or appraisal information in work contexts. For instance, employees have to interrupt their work to study a book, physically move to speak with a colleague or actively make an appointment to meet with the supervisor. The more such effort is connected to an information and feedback-seeking strategy, the less often it will be exhibited (Ashford & Cummings, 1983). That is why chronic time pressure or low task autonomy may actually impede employees' intentions to seek information (Beenen et al., 2016; Savolainen, 2006). Without sufficient time resources and discretion at work, effort costs for information and feedback seeking might be quite high. However, empirical findings concerning these propositions are scarce. There are a few qualitative studies that found time pressure and other work-related stressors to be relevant factors that inhibited employees' information-seeking efforts (e. g., Lohman, 2005; Skår, 2010; Spenceley et al., 2008). In another study, Beenen et al. (2016) found evidence that task autonomy is positively and significantly correlated to feedback-seeking behaviour ($p < .01$). However, the reported relationship of $r = .14$ was rather small.

To sum up, information and feedback seeking are important strategies to access work-related knowledge sources. Individuals who frequently and deliberately engage in such behaviours should have a better chance of developing expertise in comparison to individuals who do not exhibit such efforts. Empirical evidence suggests that climates of trust and support especially promote employees' endeavours to seek technical, referent, and appraisal information. In addition, autonomy at work and the absence of constant time pressure might also be relevant factors that encourage individuals to actively take advantage of a range of different information sources.

### 3.3.3 Deliberate Engagement in Institutionalised Learning Activities

Employees usually do not have unlimited and automatic access to institutionalised learning activities. If such learning activities are not provided by the employer they have to be privately organised, and this arrangement is usually associated with effort as well as a range of costs. For instance, effort is caused because appropriate learning activities like seminars or conferences have to be found and time resources outside of normal working hours need to be reserved accordingly. In addition, if the learning activity does not take place close to the employee's home town, both travel and accommodation have to be organised. Costs may include travel expenses, accommodation costs, and participation fees. It therefore follows that only those employees who are willing to shoulder these additional efforts and financial expenses can actually benefit from potential developmental gains afforded by such privately organised learning activities.[30]

However, just because employers do not automatically provide their employees with access to institutionalised learning activities does not mean that such opportunities have to be always privately organised. Research has shown that employees are actually able to negotiate with their employers about access to development opportunities like training or workshops. For instance, Evans et al. (2004) as well as Evans and Kersh (2006) reported about employees who took the initiative to actively arrange opportunities to secure time and financial resources to undertake courses and degree programmes. They did not passively wait till they were offered these opportunities but rather actively took control over these issues. Within the organisational psychology literature such negotiation behaviour is summarised under the concept of idiosyncratic deals—that is, the self-initiated customisation of working terms that differ from standard employment conditions (Rousseau, Ho, & Greenberg, 2006). A study on accountants by Hornung et al. (2008) suggests that idiosyncratic deals that aim at the creation of development opportunities are positively and significantly related to work-related performance outcomes ($\beta = .08, p < .05$). Goller and Harteis (2014) came to similar results based on their qualitative interview study with professors. Their interviews revealed that negotiation strategies as well as active efforts to secure training opportunities are perceived as highly relevant requirement for PhDs' professional development and their academic success.

The access to institutionalised learning activities is not always the largest barrier for employees' professional development. In some contexts employers or other institutions are even required to provide employees with sufficient

30 Web-based courses are an alternative to seminar-based trainings. Although such courses do not require physical presence they might still cause costs for computer hardware, internet access, the time invested in the course, as well as potential participation fees.

access to up-dating activities like workshops or seminars. This is usually the case because of legal or quality assurance reasons (e. g., Dobischat, Fischell, & Rosendahl, 2015; Korečić, 2012). Nevertheless, just because such learning opportunities are provided does not mean that employees actually use them in an efficient and effective way. Psychological and educational research has long emphasised that learning that is solely motivated by obligation and external pressure is less effective than learning that is self-determined (e. g., Deci, Ryan, & Williams, 1996; Ryan & Deci, 2000a, 2000b). In other words, individuals who are motivated to take part in an institutionalised learning activity because they deliberately chose so should learn more and better than their counterparts who only attend because of external reasons. Moreover, empirical research has shown that it requires motivation not only to learn but also to actually transfer the learnt knowledge back into the workplace (e. g., Gegenfurtner, 2011; Gegenfurtner, Veermans, Festner, & Gruber, 2009).

A work environment that either tolerates or even encourages employees' efforts to build up learning intentions, to deliberately create access to institutionalised learning opportunities, and to eventually transfer the learnt knowledge into the workplace should be highly conducive to professional development. A few studies therefore investigated the role of social support at work on learners' intention or motivation to engage in institutionalised learning activities. For instance, Colquitt, LePine, and Noe (2000) found medium-sized correlations between supervisor as well as peer support and employees' motivation to learn ($r = .36$ and $r = .37$, respectively, $p < .05$) as well as medium-sized to large correlation between both supervisor and peer support and motivation to transfer ($r = .43$ and $r = .84$, respectively, $p < .05$). In two more recent studies, Maurer et al. (2003) and Maurer, Lippstreu, and Judge (2008) also found evidence that social support at work is positively correlated with employees' intention to engage with development-related activities ($r = .24$ and $r = .26$, respectively, $p < .001$). In addition, Kyndt, Dochy, Onghena, and Baert (2012) found positive effects of perceived employer support on employees' learning intention (main effect within an ANCOVA, $p < .001$). Within their review Gegenfurtner et al. (2009) also emphasised that social support is an important predictor of employees' motivation to transfer learnt knowledge into the workplace. For instance, Leitl and Zempel-Dohmen (2006) could show that high levels of supervisor support were positively and significantly related with maintained transfer motivation over time ($r = .18$, $p < .05$). In another study, Kirwan and Birchall (2006) showed that peer support is also positively and significantly related to motivation to transfer ($\beta = .44$, $p < .01$).

Social support as such should not be the only context factor that fosters or hinders employees' deliberate engagement in institutionalised learning activities. In particular, workplaces that openly provide their employees with autonomy and decision latitude should encourage employees to create opportunities to use new knowledge and skills learnt in institutionalised learning activities at work. If a workplace does not provide such opportunities then employees might be less inclined to attend learning activities in the first place. A study by Kyndt et al. (2011) found initial evidence that speaks in favour of this proposition. In their study on low-qualified workers they found a relationship between perceived job autonomy and individuals' learning intention ($\beta = .10$, $p < .05$). In addition, stressors like time pressure might actually prevent individuals' engagement in institutionalised learning activities. If time is a scarce resource, employees might want to concentrate their presence at work to actually approach tasks and solve problems. Participating in institutionalised learning activities or even the negotiation of such development opportunities might then have only very low priority. Unfortunately, no empirical evidence could yet be found to support this hypothesis.

To sum up, the access to institutionalised learning activities is often not automatically provided to employees. They either have to privately take charge of all planning efforts and costs of such learning opportunities or they have to actively negotiate with their supervisors or other authorised staff members to gain access to training and workshops organised by their employer. In other words, employees often have to become active in order to participate in such learning opportunities. However, even in cases when the access to institutionalised learning activities is automatically provided by an employer, these activities most likely unfold their learning potential only when employees participate on a self-determined basis. Such a self-determined intention to participate in institutionalised learning activities as well as the motivation to transfer the learning knowledge and skills into the workplace is most likely to emerge in work environments where employees feel socially supported, where they are provided with sufficient degrees of freedom, and where they feel they have the time to do so.

### 3.3.4 Recapitulation and Conclusion

This section has identified three distinct approaches to how individuals can exert control over their own professional learning and development process: (a) crafting experiences at work, (b) information and feedback seeking, and (c) deliberate engagement in institutionalised learning activities. Crafting experiences at work describes all intentional efforts to change existing task boundaries that eventually lead to new work-related experiences (see Section 3.3.1). Information and feedback seeking subsumes all self-initiated efforts to seize and retrieve work-related information (including feedback) from other individuals or impersonal sources (see Section 3.3.2). Deliberate engagement in institutionalised learning activities embraces all deliberate efforts to willingly participate in learning opportunities like seminars, workshops or conferences (see Section 3.3.3).

Each of these three approaches is related either to active efforts to deliberately and willingly use existing learning affordances (e. g., asking for feedback from a colleague) or to such efforts that aim to intentionally create access to learning opportunities that are not provided automatically (e. g., negotiating access to certain workshops). It therefore follows that the described approaches can be interpreted as agentic actions—that is, manifestations of work agency—in the sense of Chapter 2. Through the engagement in job or experience crafting, information and feedback seeking, as well deliberate participation in institutionalised learning activities, individuals agentically take control over both their own life course and their environment.

It is, however, important to note that these agentic actions are not always initiated with a learning or development goal in mind (Goller & Billett, 2014). Empirical research has shown that employees engage in a range of learning-relevant activities for several different reasons that do not necessarily include explicit learning and development goals (e. g., Bahn, 2007; Haywood, Pain, Ryan, & Adams, 2013; Pool et al., 2016; D. Watkins, 2011). For instance, some employees aim at their own career advancement and some want to improve organisational processes and structures. Still other employees want to develop a large professional network. In fact, the true motive behind one of the identified goal-directed agentic actions might not be of importance after all. All three approaches have been shown to be empirically related to learning and professional development regardless of the reason why individuals actually initiated them. In the context of this thesis it is only important whether an employee willingly and deliberately seizes learning opportunities that would not have been available without such active efforts.

The discussion in this section also strongly acknowledged that certain contextual factors affect whether and how individuals engage in (agentic) actions. Job autonomy has been identified as an important factor that allows individuals to engage in all three agentic approaches described in this chapter. Without much discretion at work it is highly unlikely that individuals are actually able to craft experiences, seek information and feedback, or engage in institutionalised learning activities. Similarly, social support has been identified as another important antecedent of all three approaches discussed in this section. Support from both colleagues and supervisors reduces (social) costs that are connected to experience crafting as well as information and feedback seeking (see Sections 2.2.3 and 3.3.2). Furthermore, social systems that actively support or at least tolerate employees' efforts to participate in institutionalised learning activities are highly conducive to individuals to do so. Time pressure at work has been identified as a barrier both for crafting behaviours as well as for information and feedback seeking. Under constant time pressure it is just hard to find the time to change task boundaries or to actively seek information. So far no empirical evidence could be found that time pressure is also related to individuals' deliberate efforts to engage in institutionalised learning activities. However, time pressure should be negatively related to such efforts on a theoretical basis.

Table 3.3 summarises the discussion presented in this section. For each of the identified agentic approaches a definition, an example, and the relevant fostering or hindering contextual factors are presented.

**Table 3.3.** Definition, example, and relevant organisational context factors for each identified agentic action related to professional learning and development.

| | Crafting experiences at work | Information and feedback seeking | Deliberate engagement in institutionalised learning activities |
|---|---|---|---|
| *Definition* | All intentional efforts aiming at the change of existing task boundaries that eventually lead to new work-related experiences. | All intentional efforts aiming to seize or retrieve work-related information from other individuals or impersonal sources. | All intentional efforts to willingly participate in institutionalised learning opportunities. |
| *Example* | Deliberately taking over new tasks at work. | Deliberately asking colleagues or supervisors for feedback about one's own performance. | Deliberately negotiating access to training opportunities. |
| *Relevant context factors* | • Autonomy (+)<br>• Social support (+)<br>• Time pressure* (-) | • Autonomy (+)<br>• Social support (+)<br>• Time pressure (-) | • Autonomy (+)<br>• Social support (+)<br>• Time pressure* (-) |

*Note.* (+) Context factor should be positively related to agentic action. (-) Context factor should be negatively related to agentic action. * No or very little empirical support.

## 3.4 Chapter Summary

This chapter was concerned with the question of how individuals can agentically exert control over their own professional learning and development processes in order to become highly proficient in their respective work domains. For this purpose, Section 3.1 discussed how superior performance at work can be conceptualised, what exactly allows individuals to achieve high performance levels at work, and whether and how such capacities can be developed. The main finding here was that superior performance of individuals can largely be explained by their cognitive adaptations. It is their comprehensive and well-structured knowledge base that allows them to deal effectively and efficiently with the whole range of tasks and problems of their specific work environment. The development of such a knowledge base can largely be traced back to a long-lasting and intensive engagement with all kinds of efforts that aim to understand either the domain or any attempts to solve real-life tasks and problems that constitute the domain in question.

Based on these findings, Section 3.2 aimed to describe how these efforts to understand the domain as well as the attempts to solve tasks and problems can be specified in a conceptually more detailed way. All together a typology of four distinct learning activities that make use of different information and knowledge sources could be identified and theoretically conceptualised: (a) learning from experience (i. e., learning as a product of engaging in actual work practices), (b) learning from social interaction (i. e., learning that occurs as a product of communication and collaboration with different workplace stakeholders), (c) learning from consulting media sources (i. e., learning that occurs as a product of the engagement with books, journals or internet resources), and (d) learning from participating in institutionalised learning activities (i. e., learning as a product of the taking part in planned learning interventions that are not a part of the daily work process). Each of these four activities is related to learning and development in professional contexts.

At the same time it was described that not all employees have access to these four activities, nor do all employees necessarily take advantage of them even if they are accessible. It was therefore argued that the large and well-structured knowledge base of experts does not develop inevitably. It rather takes initiative and active efforts to secure access to those opportunities that are not provided automatically, and/or to utilise those that are available in the best possible way. Section 3.3 identified three distinct approaches for how individuals can do this. First, incumbents can try to intentionally craft new experiences at work by actively changing existing task boundaries (job and experience crafting). Second, employees can actively seek out work-related information as well as feedback about their current performance levels (information and feedback seeking). This can be done by monitoring situational cues as well as by consulting different impersonal media sources or other knowledgeable individuals. Third, employees may also willingly and deliberately engage in institutionalised learning activities like workshops or seminars. The access to such learning opportunities can either be privately organised or negotiated with supervisors or other responsible staff members working in the same organisation. In addition, the willing and deliberate participation in institutionalised learning activities also includes participants actively trying to understand presented content as well as any attempts to eventually apply it in their particular work context (i. e., learning transfer). All three of these approaches have been theoretically and empirically connected to learning and development as well as to increased performance levels.

It should be clear that each of the three described approaches requires employees to make choices, to take initiative, and to engage in intentional efforts. For instance, in order to receive feedback an incumbent has to decide whom to ask and how to approach this person. Subsequently, the incumbent has to translate these decisions into an action plan and finally also to implement this plan—in other words, to act. It therefore follows that each of the three approaches can be interpreted as particular manifestations of work agency in the sense of Chapter 2. They necessarily incorporate self-initiated and goal-directed behaviours that aim to take control over the work environment and/or the individual's own work-related life course. Based on the argumentation of Chapter 2 it can therefore also be assumed that agentic individuals will more often engage in those approaches than non-agentic individuals.

It is important to emphasise that none of these three agentic approaches is necessarily initiated with explicit learning or performance improvement goals in mind. Some individuals might initialise them for career reasons or because they want to improve current organisational procedures. Others, on the other hand, might just engage in them because they welcome some kind of change now and again. However, the original motive behind a self-initiated action might not be of high relevance for the question of how individuals can agentically exert control over their professional learning and development process. It is only important that individuals construct new knowledge by deliberately crafting experiences, intentionally seeking information and feedback, or wilfully taking part in institutionalised learning activities. Just to give an example, acquiring feedback because one wants to solve a work-related problem might lead to the same learning outcome as similar efforts that explicitly aim at personal improvement.

Another focus of this chapter was the identification of work-related context factors that determine how and whether individuals engage in one of the three agentic approaches. This is important because context factors alter the a priori probability of adopting a certain behaviour (see Section 2.3). Context factors can directly foster or hinder whether individuals engage in certain agentic actions. However, they can also operate as moderators between individuals' general inclination to take control over their work environment and/or their own life course and the actual engagement in corresponding activities. In accordance with the discussion of Chapter 2 the following three important context factors could be identified: (a) job autonomy, (b) social support as part of the prevalent interpersonal climate as well as the predominant leadership approach at work, and (c) time pressure as an important work-related stressor. Job autonomy and social support have been argued to be positive predictors of each of the three agentic approaches discussed here. Time pressures, on the other hand, have mainly been discussed as a negative predictor. Empirical evidence speaks much in favour of these propositions.

To sum up, employees can take charge of their professional learning and development by deliberately crafting new experiences at work, by intentionally seeking information about work-related matters and feedback about their current work performance, as well as by wilfully taking part in institutionalised learning activities. Agentic individuals are assumed to engage more often in such endeavours than non-agentic individuals. Furthermore, work environments that provide their staff with sufficient job autonomy and time resources as well as social support are more likely to promote such agentic endeavours. A central outcome of these propositions is that the conceptual model developed in Chapter 2 can now be extended and concretised. Based on the argument presented above the former abstract construct "agentic actions" can now be replaced with the three agentic approaches just described: job and experience crafting, information and feedback seeking, and deliberate participation in institutionalised learning activities. In addition, the outcome of those agentic actions will be replaced with expertise. And last but not least, the rather abstract notion of sociocultural and material context can now be substituted with the three identified social context factors that either directly predict employees' engagement in the three agentic actions or moderate the relationship between work agency and the three approaches. A more detailed discussion as well as a graphical depiction of this newly derived research model can be found in the next chapter.

# 4 Research Questions, Research Model, and Research Approach

## 4.1 Research Questions

The main research goal of this thesis is to provide a first attempt to empirically investigate the role of human agency in work-related learning and professional development processes by using hypothesis-testing methods. Such an attempt is highly justified since, while human agency has been intensively discussed within the WPL literature as an essential construct to explain learning and development in professional contexts (see Section 2.1), there has been no such investigative study to date. The overarching research question of this thesis is therefore as follows:

- How does human agency explain work-related learning and professional development?

Based on the theoretical discussion provided in Chapter 2, two separate conceptual perspectives of human agency have been identified: human agency as an individual feature and as something that individuals do. Within this thesis both perspectives are combined. The first perspective is integrated in the central construct of work agency, which is defined as the capacity and tendency to make intentional choices, to initiate actions based on these choices, and to exercise control over the self and the environment in work-related contexts. The second perspective is subsumed under the concept of agentic actions. These are manifestations of work agency and can be defined as self-initiated and goal-directed behaviours aiming at either (a) making a difference in or for the self, or (b) making a difference in the current work practice. It is assumed that agentic individuals—that is, individuals who tend to be more capable and more inclined to take control over their working lives—more often engage in agentic actions than their less-capable and less-inclined counterparts.

Within the WPL literature, both conceptualisations of human agency (i. e., agency as an individual feature and something that individuals do) have been associated with work-related learning and professional development. For the purpose of this thesis it has been hypothesised that agentic individuals will more often engage in certain agentic actions that contribute to their learning and development. In other words, agentic individuals are more likely to become highly proficient and therefore to develop expertise in their respective work domain than less-agentic individuals. Based on theoretical discussions presented in Chapter 3, three distinct agentic actions could be identified that are considered to be strongly related to professional learning and development: (a) deliberate job and experience crafting (i. e., intentionally creating new work experience by actively changing existing task boundaries), (b) intentional information and feedback seeking (i. e., actively seeking out work-related information and feedback), and (c) wilful participation in institutionalised learning activities (i. e., all intentional efforts to participate in workshops or courses). Individuals who engage in these agentic actions should learn more and therefore are more prone to developing expertise than individuals who do not engage in these agentic actions.

Agentic actions have been mainly discussed as being the product of individuals' capacities and tendencies to take control over their working lives. However, at the same time it was repeatedly emphasised that individuals do not live or act in a social or material vacuum. In other words, whether and how individuals engage in agentic actions does not depend on their capacities and tendencies alone. These individual factors only determine the a priori probability of whether and to what extent an individual actually exercises agency. Social and material context factors are assumed to alter this a priori probability. Some factors might inhibit individuals' tendency to adopt certain behaviours and other factors encourage individuals to do so even if they have a relatively low tendency at the beginning. Based on the discussion in Chapters 2 and 3, the following factors could be identified as relevant in work contexts: (a) autonomy at work, (b) social support, and (c) job-related stressors like time pressure.

Based on these theoretical insights the overarching research question can now be broken down into three separate research questions (RQ):

RQ1. How does agency as an individual-level feature explain employees' engagement in agentic actions?

RQ2. How does engagement in agentic actions relate to the development of work-related expertise?

RQ3. How do organisational context factors affect engagement in agentic actions?

## 4.2 Hypotheses and Research Model

The theoretical discussion provided in Chapters 2 and 3 can now be used to derive preliminary answers to the questions raised in the last section. These hypotheses will later be used to test whether the theoretical assumptions concerning the relationships between work agency, agentic actions, expertise development, and organisational context factors derived in the previous chapters hold empirically. In the following, each research question will briefly be readdressed with the aim of deriving a set of testable hypotheses.

**RQ1. How does agency as an individual-level feature explain employees' engagement in agentic actions?**

As discussed earlier, it is assumed that highly agentic individuals more often engage in agentic actions like (a) job and experience crafting, (b) information and feedback seeking, as well as (c) wilful participation in institutionalised learning activities. However, it has also been argued that agentic individuals are more likely to initiate constructive change at work (see Sections 2.1 and 2.2). The first four hypotheses are therefore:

*Hypothesis 1.1:* Work agency will be positively associated with employees' job and experience crafting behaviours.

*Hypothesis 1.2:* Work agency will be positively associated with employees' information- and feedback-seeking behaviours.

*Hypothesis 1.3:* Work agency will be positively associated with employees' wilful participation in institutionalised learning activities.

*Hypothesis 1.4:* Work agency will be positively associated with employees' efforts to initiate constructive change at work.

It should be noted that Hypothesis 1.4 is not directly required to answer the overarching research question. However, it was decided to include this hypothesis because it gives information about whether the later employed operationalisation of work agency is indeed a valid one. A measure of work agency should be a positive predictor of both agentic actions that are primarily directed towards the individual and agentic actions that are primarily directed towards the individual's environment.

**RQ2. How does engagement in agentic actions relate to the development of work-related expertise?**

It has been assumed that individuals who deliberately engage in job and experience crafting, information and feedback seeking, and wilful participation in institutionalised learning activities are more likely to develop expertise. It follows that the next three hypotheses are:

*Hypothesis 2.1:* Job and experience crafting behaviours will be positively associated with employees' expertise development.

*Hypothesis 2.2:* Information- and feedback-seeking behaviours will be positively associated with employees' expertise development.

*Hypothesis 2.3:* Wilful efforts to participate in institutionalised learning activities will be positively associated with employees' expertise development.

Employees' efforts to initiate constructive change at work are not assumed to contribute directly to learning and development. It is rather hypothesised that work agency and expertise jointly predict such behaviours. Agentic individuals who have already managed to develop expertise are therefore more likely to initiate constructive change at work.

*Hypothesis 2.4:* Expertise will be positively associated with employees' efforts to initiate constructive change at work.

**RQ3. How do organisational context factors affect engagement in agentic actions?**

Job autonomy, social support, and time pressure have been identified as relevant organisational context factors that affect how individuals engage in agentic actions in the context of their work. Empirically there has been evidence that the first two context factors should be positive direct predictors of all three identified agentic actions that are hypothesised to relate to work-related learning and professional development as well as to individuals' efforts to initiate constructive change at work. The next eight hypotheses are therefore as follows:

*Hypothesis 3.1:* Autonomy at work is positively associated with employees' job- and experience-crafting behaviours.

*Hypothesis 3.2:* Autonomy at work is positively associated with employees' information- and feedback-seeking behaviours.

*Hypothesis 3.3:* Autonomy at work is positively associated with employees' wilful participation in institutionalised learning activities.

*Hypothesis 3.4:* Autonomy at work is positively associated with employees' efforts to initiate constructive change at work.

*Hypothesis 3.5:* Social support at work is positively associated with employees' job- and experience-crafting behaviours.

*Hypothesis 3.6:* Social support at work is positively associated with employees' information- and feedback-seeking behaviours.

*Hypothesis 3.7:* Social support at work is positively associated with employees' wilful participation in institutionalised learning activities.

*Hypothesis 3.8:* Social support at work is positively associated with employees' efforts to initiate constructive change at work.

The relationship between time pressure as a specific job stressor and individuals' engagement in agentic actions is not as clear. Some studies showed that time pressure is positively associated with some agentic actions (see Section 2.2.3.4). However, there are also some theoretical arguments as well as some empirical evidence that time pressure might actually be negatively associated with individuals' engagement in agentic actions (see Sections 3.3). It follows that only non-directional hypotheses can be derived:

*Hypothesis 3.9:* Time pressure at work is associated with employees' job- and experience-crafting behaviours.

*Hypothesis 3.10:* Time pressure at work is associated with employees' information- and feedback-seeking behaviours.

*Hypothesis 3.11:* Time pressure at work is associated with employees' wilful participation in institutionalised learning activities.

*Hypothesis 3.12:* Time pressure at work is associated with employees' efforts to initiate constructive change at work.

Apart from being direct predictors, the three context factors might also moderate the relationship between work agency and agentic actions. Sufficient job autonomy and social support are assumed to strengthen the relationship between work agency and agentic actions. The effect of time pressure, however, remains unclear. Accordingly the hypotheses are:

*Hypothesis 3.13:* Autonomy at work moderates the relationship between work agency and employees' job- and experience-crafting behaviours. Autonomy at work is expected to strengthen the relationship between work agency and employees' job- and experience-crafting behaviours.

*Hypothesis 3.14:* Autonomy at work moderates the relationship between work agency and employees' information- and feedback-seeking behaviours. Autonomy at work is expected to strengthen the relationship between work agency and employees' information- and feedback-seeking behaviours.

*Hypothesis 3.15:* Autonomy at work moderates the relationship between work agency and employees' wilful participation in institutionalised learning activities. Autonomy at work is expected to strengthen the relationship between work agency and employees' deliberate participation in institutionalised learning activities.

*Hypothesis 3.16:* Autonomy at work moderates the relationship between work agency and employees' efforts to initiate constructive change at work. Autonomy at work is expected to strengthen the relationship between work agency and employees' efforts to initiate constructive change at work.

*Hypothesis 3.17:* Social support at work moderates the relationship between work agency and employees' job- and experience-crafting behaviours. Social support at work is expected to strengthen the relationship between work agency and employees' job- and experience-crafting behaviours.

*Hypothesis 3.18:* Social support at work moderates the relationship between work agency and employees' information- and feedback-seeking behaviours. Social support at work is expected to strengthen the relationship between work agency and employees' information- and feedback-seeking behaviours.

*Hypothesis 3.19:* Social support at work moderates the relationship between work agency and employees' wilful participation in institutionalised learning activities. Social support at work is expected to strengthen the relationship between work agency and employees' deliberate participation in institutionalised learning activities.

*Hypothesis 3.20:* Social support at work moderates the relationship between work agency and employees' efforts to initiate constructive change at work. Social support at work is expected to strengthen the relationship between work agency and employees' efforts to initiate constructive change at work.

*Hypothesis 3.21:* Time pressure at work moderates the relationship between work agency and employees' job- and experience-crafting behaviours. Time pressure at work is expected to either strengthen or weaken the relationship between work agency and employees' job- and experience-crafting behaviours.

*Hypothesis 3.22:* Time pressure at work moderates the relationship between work agency and employees' information- and feedback-seeking behaviours. Time pressure at work is expected to either strengthen or weaken the relationship between work agency and employees' information- and feedback-seeking behaviours.

*Hypothesis 3.23:* Time pressure at work moderates the relationship between work agency and employees' wilful participation in institutionalised learning activities. Time pressure at work is expected to either strengthen or weaken the relationship between work agency and employees' deliberate participation in institutionalised learning activities.

*Hypothesis 3.24:* Time pressure at work moderates the relationship between work agency and employees' efforts to initiate constructive change at work. Time pressure at work is expected to either strengthen or weaken the relationship between work agency and employees' efforts to initiate constructive change at work.

Taken together, these 32 hypotheses can be translated into the final research model presented in Figure 4.1. This research model is an extended version of the conceptual framework presented at the end of Chapter 2.

## 4.3 Research Approach and Implementation

The research model presented in Figure 4.1 will be tested in the domain of inpatient geriatric care nursing. This domain was chosen because of three interdependent reasons. First, a combination of sinking birth rates and constantly increasing life spans results, for most Western countries including Germany, in a steadily growing share of the population above the retirement age (Eurostat, 2011; Werner, 2011). Simultaneously, traditional family relationships that build on long-standing mutual intergenerational transfer are less and less common in many countries. Economic developments—like a higher demand for geographic flexibility or a higher female participation in the labour market—often make it impossible for younger generations to physically care for their parent generation (e. g., Blinkert & Klie, 2004). Taken together, institutionalised care

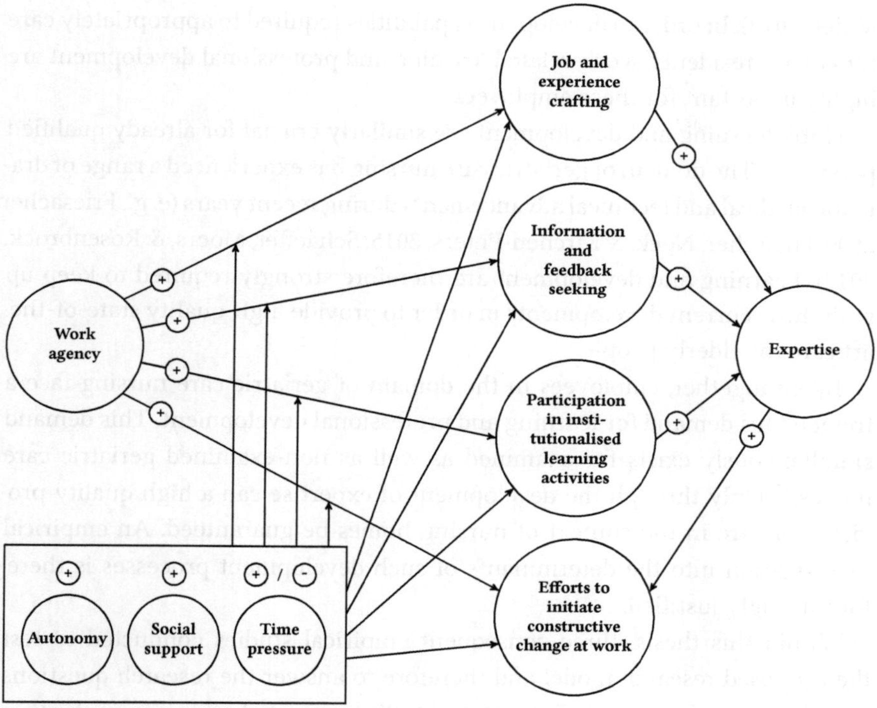


**Figure 4.1.** Final research model. For reasons of clarity the hypothesised effects of the three organisational context factors have not been printed on the path. These effects are instead printed above each organisational factor. They apply to all arrows indicating a direct or a moderator effect originating between the organisational context factors and the agentic actions in the model.

for the elderly becomes more and more important in Western countries (see also Hussein & Manthorpe, 2005).

Second, many countries face skill shortages of elderly care personnel. In particular, there are often insufficient numbers of nurses who are competent and qualified to take care of the elderly in nursing homes (Hussein & Manthorpe, 2005; Sheets, 2012). A common strategy for nursing homes is therefore to employ staff who are not trained or certified as geriatric care nurses (Afentakis &

Maier, 2010). In order to develop the capabilities required to appropriately care for elderly residents, work-related learning and professional development are highly important for these employees.

Third, learning and development are similarly crucial for already qualified personnel. The domain of geriatric care nursing has experienced a range of dramatic medical and technical advancements during recent years (e. g., Friesacher, 2009; Hielscher, Nock, & Kirchen-Peters, 2015; Schaeffer, Moers, & Rosenbrock, 2012). Learning and development are therefore strongly required to keep up with those current developments in order to provide high-quality state-of-the-art care for elderly people.

Taken together, employees in the domain of geriatric care nursing face a tremendous demand for learning and professional development. This demand simultaneously exists for examined as well as non-examined geriatric care nurses.[31] Only through the development of expertise can a high quality provision of care in the context of nursing homes be guaranteed. An empirical investigation into the determinants of such development processes is therefore strongly justified.

Within this thesis, three consequent empirical studies conducted to test the proposed research model and therefore to answer the research questions stated above are reported. These three studies strongly build upon each other. Each study will be shortly described below. A more detailed description, however, can be found in the next three chapters.

1. *Study 1: Initial insights into work agency in the domain of geriatric care nursing (Chapter 5).* This study aimed to provide an initial insight into geriatric care nurses' agency at work. This was necessary since not much is known about how geriatric care nurses exercise their agency at work. It is especially unclear whether geriatric care nurses indeed exercise their agency through engagement in job and experience crafting, information and feedback seeking, wilful participation in institutionalised learning activities, as well as efforts to initiate change. It is also unclear whether the identified context factors—job autonomy, social support, and time pressure—are as

31 Examined nurses have acquired a state-organised medical qualification based on a 3-year apprenticeship. This is not the case for non-examined nurses.

relevant as theoretically argued. It was therefore decided to conduct a qualitative interview study about geriatric care nurses' agency. The main aim of this study was to investigate whether the proposed research model could be tested in the domain of geriatric care nursing. Moreover, the insights of this study are thought to advance the proposed research model if necessary and yield additional information about how to operationalise the constructs included in the model.

2. *Study 2: Proposed study design, instrument development, and pilot study (Chapter 6).* This study aimed to develop and test both the quantitative research design and the survey instrument that was then used to answer the research questions posed in this chapter. This was necessary because most of the measures planned to be used in the data collection have not yet been psychometrically investigated. In addition, the study design intended to use social network analysis to obtain different indicators for the participants' level of expertise. Such a social network analysis, however, had not previously been conducted in the nursing homes taking part in this research project. It was therefore decided to test whether this particular type of method could be applied in the present research context and whether it would result in data usable for further investigation. The data examination comprised mainly psychometric and correlation analyses. Based on the insights of this pilot study the study design as well as the questionnaire was to be revised if necessary.

3. *Study 3: Work agency and its effects on expertise development (Chapter 7).* This study tested the revised model based on Study 1 using the study design and survey instrument developed in Study 2. All together it was planned to gather data from more than 800 geriatric care nurses working in German nursing homes. The data of this study were then analysed using psychometric methods (i. e., exploratory and confirmatory factor analysis) as well as variance-based structural equation modelling. Structural equation modelling allows testing of all the proposed hypotheses at once. The results of the analyses conducted in this study were used to answer the research questions stated above.

The next three chapters are used to describe these studies in more detail. Each chapter will contain a short theoretical framework, a description of the methodological approach applied, a description of the main study results, as well as a discussion of the findings in relation to the theoretical framework developed in Chapters 2 and 3 as well as the succeeding studies.

# 5 Study 1: Initial Insights into Work Agency in the Domain of Geriatric Care Nursing

So far not much is known about how geriatric care nurses exercise their agency in work contexts, how these agentic actions explain their work-related learning and development, or what contextual factors foster or hinder their engagement in those agentic actions. Large parts of the theoretical discussion presented in Chapters 2 and 3 have not been explicitly focussed on geriatric care nurses.[32] Moreover, almost no empirical results about the agency of geriatric care nurses exist. It is therefore necessary to empirically investigate whether the still domain-unspecific model developed in the previous chapters can be used as a foundation for a quantitative questionnaire study later on. In addition, it is still not fully clear what counts as expert performance in the domain of geriatric care nursing. It is therefore also necessary to gain further insights into how to conceptualise and later measure expertise of geriatric care nurses.

The aim of this first study is to fill this research gap by getting initial empirical insights about geriatric care nurses' agency at work as well as their professional expertise development. Such insights will (a) help to make clear whether the theoretically derived research model can be used to answer the main research questions of this thesis, and (b) give further information on how to operationalise the concepts included in this model. In other words, this study helps to further contextualise the derived research model and to

32 Parts of Chapter 3 referred to literature about the professional learning of nurses in general. However, it has to be acknowledged that nurses working in hospitals might exercise their agency differently and they might also learn differently from nurses working in nursing homes.

develop a survey instrument that is suited for testing the hypotheses in the domain of inpatient geriatric care nursing. It should, however, be noted that the empirical results of this study might indeed indicate that the proposed model cannot be used in its current form. The insights of this study are then used to advance the research model in such a way that it can be tested in the domain of geriatric care nursing.

This chapter is structured as follows: Section 5.1 describes the methodological approach of Study 1. A detailed report of the most relevant findings of this study is given in Section 5.2 and then discussed in Section 5.3. The chapter concludes with a summary that highlights the most important implications for the further research process in Section 5.4.

## 5.1 Methodology

To gain preliminary insights into the topic of agency at work in the domain of inpatient geriatric care nursing an explorative interview study was conducted. The next section describes the sample characteristics of this study. Section 5.1.2 will then describe how the interviews were conducted. The analyses of the interview material are outlined in Section 5.1.3.

### 5.1.1 Sample

Highly experienced staff nurses in inpatient geriatric care were chosen as interview partners. All participants were selected based on managerial experience (at least head of nursing for a residential area) and extensive work experience in the domain of elderly care in nursing homes (at least 20 years of experience). Staff nurses were perceived as experts on expertise development and self-initiated behaviours of nurses as well as affecting organisational context factors in the domain of geriatric care. Because of their supervisory position staff nurses are responsible for the operation of their care unit. Part of their daily work is to observe and evaluate work performance of nurses working under their supervision. Furthermore, due to their long work experience staff nurses are assumed to have worked closely with a range of different employees. All participants are thought to be able to answer interview questions not only in regard to their own development and behaviours but also to the observed development and behaviours of other nurses with whom they have worked in the past.

All together nine study participants were interviewed in August and September 2013. The first interview was used for piloting purposes and was later removed from the interview corpus. Based on this first interview the initial interview guideline was slightly revised and restructured.

At the end, eight interviews with eight nurses from six different nursing homes could be used for this study. Of those interviewees seven were female and only one was male. However, a high share of female employees is quite characteristic for the domain of geriatric care nursing (Federal Employment Agency, 2014). All participants had extensive work experience (*M* = 23.9, *SD* = 5.4) and most of them also had long-lasting managerial experience (*M* = 10.3, *SD* = 5.6). Two interviewees (both female) had only 2 years of managerial experience. However, both of these have worked in geriatric care nursing for more than 25 years. On average the study participants were 49.5 years (*SD* = 2.0) old and had worked in nursing homes in both rural and urban areas. Two study participants worked in a small nursing home with only 20 nurses. The other five interviewees worked in medium or large nursing homes with more than 45 nurses. The largest nursing home employed 100 nurses. One interviewee (P2) was no longer employed in elderly care at the time of the interview. She is now working in a care unit for disabled individuals. The interview was not removed from the corpus since she answered most of the questions with regard to her long-lasting experience as a geriatric care nurse. The employing nursing homes of all study participants were geographically located in the German state of North Rhine-Westphalia.

Six out of the eight interview partners were recruited based on recommendations of a local provider of further education in the context of nursing. This gatekeeper (see e. g., Bortz & Schuster, 2010; Merkens, 2004) provided a list of 10 experienced geriatric care nurses from which one nurse declined to participate because of time issues and one nurse was excluded by the author because she worked in outpatient instead of inpatient care. Another interview partner could be approached based on the recommendation of other study participants. All participants agreed to participate in the interview study after the first phone contact with the author of this thesis.

### 5.1.2 Interview Procedure

All interviews were conducted face-to-face by the author himself. Four interviews were conducted in a seminar room of a local hotel were the interview partners were accommodated during a work-related training course. All other interviews were conducted at the subjects' workplace. All interview partners were sufficiently accustomed to the interview location and felt visibly comfortable during the interviews. It can therefore be assumed that the participants perceived the interview location as a safe room in which to answer the questions.

A semi-structured interview guideline was used to ask several open-ended questions to obtain empirical insights about work agency in the domain of geriatric care nursing (see Appendix A). The guideline was developed according to well-established principles: good comprehensibility, interviewee adequacy, use of open questions, goal-orientedness, and activating participants' experience (e. g., Gläser & Laudel, 2008).

The guideline started with a question concerning the work of elderly care nurses in general in order to accommodate the study participants with the interview situation. The second and third questions concerned how superior work performance can be conceptualised in the domain of elderly care and how employees develop necessary expertise to perform on a superior level. The fourth question focussed on how nurses can deliberately affect their own development. The fifth question asked the subject to distinguish between agentic and non-agentic employees and to describe their different work behaviours. Organisational factors that either hinder or foster agentic behaviours at work were addressed in question six. Question seven asked the participants whether they believe that superior work performance depends mainly on organisational or individual factors. Question eight ended the interview asking whether the interviewees might want to add anything that had not been a focus in the interviews so far.

The interview guideline was used in a rather flexible and open way. In particular, the sequence of questions was often adjusted due to the topics brought up by the study participants. Furthermore, quite often unexpected topics emerged in the interviews. In cases where those topics seemed to contribute to the research questions they were followed up. The interviews lasted 61 minutes (*SD* = 19) on average. With prior approval all interviews were recorded for later transcription.

The interviews were transcribed verbatim by two student assistants. The recorded interviews were converted into text using standard orthography without the use of phonetic notations (e. g., Gläser & Laudel, 2008; Mayring, 2002). Accent and dialect were transferred into standard German. Verbal and non-verbal features (like laughing or meaningful pauses) were commented upon using brackets and capital letters (e. g., "(LAUGHING)"). Both student assistants were experienced in transcribing similar interview material based on former empirical projects. After the transcription each transcript was proof-read by the author of this thesis. Identification of acoustically incomprehensible or unclear interview passages was attempted by the author in cooperation with the student assistants. However, fully incomprehensible passages were marked in the transcripts with three question marks. Names of individuals, places or nursing homes were replaced with generic labels (e. g., "Name-A", "Place-F") in the transcript for purposes of anonymity of study participants.

The text units within each interview were continuously numbered; a text unit consists of an uninterrupted interview part by either the study participant or the interviewer. Text units beginning with "MG" are parts spoken by the interviewer (Michael Goller) and text units beginning with "P" (for participant) followed by an integer were parts spoken by the interviewee (e. g., "P1" for the first participant, "P2" for the second participant).

### 5.1.3 Analysis

The comprehensive text material of 146 pages was analysed using Mayring's (2002, 2004, 2015) qualitative content analysis and followed the procedures outlined by Schreier (2012) using MAXQDA 10 (VERBI, 2012). In particular, a combination of structuring and summarising content analysis was used. The main aim of the procedure described below was to identify and summarise relevant content within the data to obtain sufficient empirical insights to contextualise the research model of this thesis and to develop a survey instrument that helps to test the hypotheses posed in the Chapter 4 (Schreier, 2012).

1. At first, a preliminary deductive category system was derived from the theoretical considerations presented in Chapters 2, 3, and 4. This category system was designed to categorise propositions within the interview material that allowed sufficient empirical insights about geriatric care nurses' agency at work to be obtained. The category system contained three main categories (expertise, manifestations of work agency, and contextual factors). All except one of those main categories were then divided into sub-categories (e. g., information and feedback seeking, and deliberate participation in institutionalised learning activities). A definition was assigned to each category.

2. All transcripts were used to test the preliminary category system and to inductively extract additional categories. The interviews were coded by the author using the preliminary category system.

3. Based on the insights from the first coding cycle (i. e., steps 1 and 2) the preliminary category system was revised. The aim of this step was to improve the quality and applicability of the category system. Some of the categories were refined or redefined. Text material that was found to be interesting but that could not be assigned to any existing categories was used to derive new categories (inductive category building). Additionally, for each category that was not further divided into any sub-categories a key example was assigned (i. e., a prototypical text passage that would be coded with this category) and—if necessary—a coding rule (a rule specifying how to deal with certain text passages). The final category system (four main categories, 14 sub-categories, and seven categories on the lowest level) including the category definition, key examples, and coding rules can be found in Appendix B. In addition, the first column of Table 5.1 lists all categories.

4. After the final category system was established all interviews were (re)coded by the author of this thesis. As a minimal coding unit, a propo-

sition to one topic was defined (i. e., a clause). If possible a full sentence should be coded. The maximal coding unit (context unit in terms of Mayring, 2002, 2015) was defined to be a set of thematically linked propositions. If necessary to assist understanding, the question of the interviewer should be included in the coding.

5. In order to check the reliability of the coding procedure a second coder—one of the student assistants who had already transcribed the interviews—recoded all coding units that were categorised in step 4. After initial training on how to apply the category system using interviews 3 and 8, the second coder independently recoded all remaining interviews. It was only indicated to her that certain text parts were coded but not what category was assigned ("blind coding"; Schreier, 2012). After that, each coding that did not match was discussed between the author and the second coder. If both coders agreed upon a unique coding the text unit was recategorised. If no agreement could be reached the different codings were maintained to calculate the inter-coder reliability but were then excluded from any further analysis. Based on both coding systems Krippendorff's $\alpha$ ($\alpha^k$; Krippendorff, 2004) and the percentage of agreement (*PoA*, Schreier, 2012) were calculated as measures of reliability (see Krippendorff, 2004, on the discussion on what measure of reliability to use). $\alpha^k$ yielded a value of .88 and the *PoA* was 88.81%. Based on those values the reliability of the analysis can be assessed as sufficiently good (Krippendorff, 2004; Lombard, Snyder-Duch, & Bracken, 2002; Neuendorf, 2002).[33]

6. In the last step, all coded text units were individually paraphrased and eventually summarised.[34] The paraphrasing allowed the different nature of propositions to be brought into line by preserving the information content. The abstraction was used to reduce similar text units to their core proposi-

33 *PoAs* and $\alpha^k$s of higher than 90% or .90, respectively, indicate a good reliability. Values above 80% or .80, respectively, however, still indicate an acceptable fit (Krippendorff, 2004; Lombard et al., 2002; Neuendorf, 2002).

34 In contrast to Mayring (2015), summarising was not used to derive categories. Instead, the summary of the obtained paraphrases was used to reduce the text material and to uncover the core propositions included in the interview material.

**Table 5.1.** Category system and distribution for reported categories and study participants.

| Categories | Study participants | | | | | | | | |
|---|---|---|---|---|---|---|---|---|---|
| | P1 | P2 | P3 | P4 | P5 | P6 | P7 | P8 | *Total* |
| 1 Expertise | | | | | | | | | |
| Performance | 6 | 4 | 6 | 5 | 9 | 7 | 8 | 8 | *53* |
| Knowledge | 3 | 2 | 2 | – | 1 | – | 1 | – | *9* |
| 2 General statements concerning work agency* | 5 | 3 | 3 | 2 | 3 | 2 | – | 1 | *19* |
| 3 Manifestations of work agency | | | | | | | | | |
| Participation in institutionalised learning activities | 6 | 3 | 10 | 2 | 7 | 7 | 1 | 11 | *47* |
| Information and feedback seeking | | | | | | | | | |
| from other individuals* | 10 | – | 2 | 3 | – | 1 | 7 | 1 | *24* |
| from impersonal resources* | 2 | – | – | 2 | 1 | 4 | 1 | 2 | *12* |
| Job and experience crafting | | | | | | | | | |
| Job enlargement* | 2 | 6 | – | 1 | – | 2 | 4 | – | *15* |
| Job enrichment* | 1 | 4 | 2 | 3 | 1 | 1 | – | 2 | *14* |

*Continued on next page*

Table 5.1 – *Continued from previous page*

| Categories | Study participants | | | | | | | | |
|---|---|---|---|---|---|---|---|---|---|
| | P1 | P2 | P3 | P4 | P5 | P6 | P7 | P8 | *Total* |
| Initiating change | 6 | 2 | 4 | – | – | 4 | 6 | 7 | *29* |
| Overtime and addititional work assignments* | 3 | 2 | 5 | – | 1 | – | – | 3 | *14* |
| Misc | – | 1 | – | – | – | 4 | 1 | – | *6* |
| 4 Organisational contextual factors | | | | | | | | | |
| Job autonomy | 2 | 2 | – | – | – | 1 | – | – | *5* |
| Support | | | | | | | | | |
| Coworkers* | 1 | – | – | 1 | 2 | – | 3 | 2 | *9* |
| Supervisors* | 2 | 1 | 2 | – | 1 | 2 | 3 | 3 | *14* |
| Unclear* | 2 | – | – | 1 | – | 2 | 1 | – | *6* |
| Time resources | 1 | 2 | 2 | 1 | – | 1 | 3 | 2 | *12* |
| Appreciation from the employer* | – | 1 | 1 | – | 1 | 2 | – | 1 | *6* |
| Legal issues* | – | – | – | – | – | – | 2 | – | *2* |
| Misc | 2 | – | 1 | 1 | 1 | – | – | 2 | *7* |
| *Total* | *54* | *33* | *40* | *22* | *28* | *40* | *41* | *45* | *303* |

*Note.* All categories marked with an asterisk (*) have been derived trough inductive coding in step 3. A hyphen (–) indicates that this category did not occur in a particular interview.

tions within each subcategory. The resulting core propositions were used for further analyses.

Table 5.1 contains a summary of the coded text units for each category and each interview participant. As can be seen, not all interviewees spoke about all themes of interest. However, for all categories at least three different interview partners mentioned certain aspects that could be assigned to the concerning category.

## 5.2 Findings

In this section the main findings of the qualitative content analysis will be reported. Each finding will be illustrated by a few short text examples from the interviews. Since the original interviews were conducted in German each provided text example was translated into English by the author of this thesis. After each quote an identifier indicates the speaking interview partner as well as the number of the text unit within the corresponding transcript as a reference (e. g., “P3, 97” = “Participant 3, text unit 97”).

This section is structured as follows: Section 5.2.1 presents all findings about what geriatric care nurses have to be able to do at work and what exactly counts as superior performance in the domain of geriatric care nursing. Section 5.2.2 identifies agentic actions that are exhibited by geriatric care nurses. A focus is laid on presenting interview material that connects those agentic actions with expertise development. Finally, Section 5.2.3 presents interview material about relevant context factors at work that foster or hinder nurses' engagement in the agentic actions identified earlier.

### 5.2.1 Expertise in Geriatric Care Nursing

All interviewees described the job of geriatric care nurse as a challenging activity that comprises a highly diverse range of different tasks (Category: Expertise – Performance). Geriatric care nurses have to perform well in (a) medical tasks like measurement of health related data, treatment of wounds, and infusions or provision of drugs; (b) basic care like personal hygiene, food preparation, and support for basic activities (going to the toilet, eating, getting dressed, etc.); (c) social care like conversations, counselling, taking residents for a stroll, and the provision of entertainment programs; (d) diagnosis of basic needs, illnesses, emotional states, and current abilities; (e) communication with doctors, relatives, other medical professionals, and other institutions; as well as (f) administrative tasks like maintaining resident records and general care planning. One of the interviewees described the job in the following way:

> Well, an examined nurse has to do the basic care, counselling, work with relatives, administrative tasks like care planning, the whole care documentation, admission interviews, as well as palliative care if somebody is dying—also with the relatives—contacts with the doctors, with the therapists, well to represent the nursing home to the public [...] The medical stuff, well I would say, infusions, measuring blood pressure, the whole stuff, blood sugar. The non-examined nurses have to engage more into the care activities. I would say like the daily things like going to toilet, going for stroll, social care, feeding residents, but, sure, supporting the examined nurses. Assistance in a way. (P6, 8)

It is important to note that the responsibilities are described as somehow different for examined and non-examined nurses. Non-examined nurses are usually not allowed to engage in certain medical tasks or to communicate with doctors. They are more responsible for basic and social care activities. Examined nurses, however, usually take on the activities that are perceived to require more knowledge. Nevertheless, examined nurses also engage in basic and social care tasks if required.

Interestingly, some interviewees emphasised that a number of non-examined nurses are similarly capable, or even more capable, than their examined counterparts. These non-examined nurses then take on the tasks usually handled by examined nurses.

> Well, just because they are examined does not mean that they are the top employees. Surely, they have the knowledge—or should have—and the responsibilities. But sometimes, because of cost saving, I leave a ward to one of my capable non-examined nurses. [...] Those non-examined nurses are so capable, they can easily manage a ward for themselves, they really do. (P3, 97)

Concerning the question of what exactly characterises superior performance in the domain of geriatric care, a range of interesting answers was given. Probably the most recurring theme is the ability to adequately solve tasks and problems. Experts do not only work by the book but are able to adjust their behaviour to the current requirements of spontaneously changing problem situations. They manage to rapidly adapt their working strategies to the daily changing medical and age-related conditions of their residents. Some of the interviewees argued that expert nurses succeed in setting priorities based on the specific situation at hand. On the contrary, non-expert nurses tend to blindly follow pre-set work schedules as well as codified rules.

> What does good mean? Well, you have to be able to work under pressure and you have to adapt to people. You have to be able to always adapt to those individuals. Even if they have the same symptoms. The care as well as the illness is always a different one. Well, you really have to be able to adjust. (P3, 10)

> ... to be able to react spontaneously without having a bad conscience. You have to be able to postpone some tasks, to do them later or to abolish them completely. (P7, 2)

> Well, that we do not necessarily measure blood pressure this morning. This is something we can postpone till tomorrow, yes? We measure blood pressure once a month. Whether it is today or tomorrow is irrelevant. That is something we don't do now. However, the relative of the deceased resident is more important now, that's just it. [...] The expert is capable to set priorities in this moment. In contrast, the non-expert just sees her work without thinking about it, that she really has to set priorities; maybe postponing something or delegate something else. She only sees her part without looking right or left. (P6, 16)

Another important theme was the experts' abilities to deal with stress and time pressure. Time pressure has been reported to be a frequent phenomenon in many geriatric care homes. Experts, however, seem to be less affected by time constraints than their non-expert counterparts. They still manage to adequately respond to the needs of the residents. In addition, they manage to work in such a manner that the residents do not realise that the nurse works under time pressure. This is usually done through better time management as well as faster working style in general. Furthermore, they keep track of all the things happening in the workplace without forgetting anything. All in all, these abilities help superior nurses to get along much better with the residents than less superior ones.

> I think they do it in a different way. They manage their time in a better way. She just recognises how much time is required for a resident. (P5, 12)

> ... they manage this much better. They are not just fast but they do their job well, fast and in such a way that the resident does not become aware that things get hectic. (P3, 18)

The following quote indicates that expert nurses take the role of (unofficial) supervisors as well as acting as approachable colleague when it comes to questions. Again, both roles are not necessarily bound to the qualification of the nurse.

> She [a good non-examined nurse] has, essentially, the overview about all the tasks. She can even instruct other nurses, yes, she completely keeps track. She sets the tone, not in a bad way, yes? She just takes other nurses along. There are many non-examined nurses that just approach her: "What do we have to do now?" (P6, 20)

A few interview partners also talked about knowledge required to show such superior performance (Category: Expertise – Knowledge). They mainly referred to medical knowledge about illnesses and symptoms, and knowledge about appropriate treatments as well as drugs. Moreover, geriatric care-specific knowledge was also mentioned. For instance, nurses have to know about the placing of patients, the transfer from one place to another, as well as kinaesthetics (i. e., how to control one's body motions when lifting residents). Lastly, some nurses also talked about so-called expert standards. These standards are codified processes of how to deal with certain problems that occur in geriatric care homes.

### 5.2.2 Geriatric Care Nurses' Manifestations of Agency

Almost all interviewees emphasised that some nurses act more agentically than others (Category: General statements concerning work agency). Agentic individuals have been described as being more interested in work matters in general and much more self-reliant. They try to constantly keep up with new developments in their own domain and tend to participate more often in further education courses. Furthermore, these nurses really want to get involved by taking initiative at work.

> Well, I do have those employees that are really really active, really agile and they get involved, they have ideas, they want to realise them, just want to sort things out. If there is something new coming up, they are the ones that are the eager ones. That's where I say: "Those are the ones that stand out, they feel like to get involved." Sure, that's connected to more workload because those things are indeed additional work. Still, they want to do that. I think it is not that common, but—yes—they do exist. (P2, 58)

> There are the ones—you really notice that—they really like their job. […] They are like "I will do that!", they are always there and industrious, but even beyond that: "I am going to develop something!" or "I do have an idea!". (P5, 140)

On the contrary, less agentic nurses tend only to work to rule and do not show much interest in work matters. Although they might actually notice tensions in work practice they usually neither suggest any ideas to tackle these issues nor do they take any initiative to actually change anything. The following quotes illustrate this distinction more clearly:

> Well, those are the ones that always go to in-house trainings and to whom we can say "We would like you to go there for three days." And they say "Yes, I can do that." […] And then you have the ones that do not participate in any staff event, they are absent from any meeting and they seldom go to any in-house training, and even say: "Me? No, not me!" (P3, 65)

> Ok. There are always two types. There are some people, they do the job as a calling and they really like it. And then you have the ones that do the job because of the money. And you really notice that if you deal with them on a day-to-day basis. You can really notice that. That is for instance, like that, are you interested in trainings, do you want to keep up-to-date, do you want to develop? And the others, they just work to rule and go home. I think that's the difference. They do their job, they really do, but they are missing that certain interest, I would say. (P1, 20)

It is worth noting that the interview partners described the less-agentic individuals not necessarily as the inferior nurses as such. These nurses do indeed work sufficiently well. However, they do not move beyond the necessity. Agentic individuals are described as the ones who try to develop or transform work practices and organisational structures. Typical examples are that nurses make suggestions about how to change work procedures, how to improve the well-being of residents in general or about acquiring books or new medical equipment (Category: Manifestations of work agency – Initiating change). They develop ideas, make suggestions about how to tackle certain issues, and—if necessary—defend their ideas against rejections or certain reservations brought forward by other organisational stakeholders.

> We have some of these colleagues, they just inform themselves, think for themselves and then just come and say: "Could we buy this? Couldn't we change that?" (P1, 58)

> The ones that react interested when it comes to new developments and then want to take charge. I mean when it comes to change, they don't just want to adapt, they want, if new things are introduced at work, they want to actively implement, they want to have the opportunity to shape: "How can I implement that and how do I put that into action?" (P2, 146)

> And she already has ideas, really concrete ideas. Not just saying: "Everything goes wrong." Instead, having tangible ideas… (P7, 174)

The interview partners were also asked whether they think that nurses can actively contribute to their learning and professional development. Without exception all interviewees answered that nurses can develop by participating in a huge range of different formal learning activities like in-house training, external training that either lead to specialisations (e. g., dementia, psychological illnesses, palliative medicine), career advancements (e. g., staff nurse, chief nursing officer), or enhancement of one's own skill set (e. g., kinaesthetics, conversational skills), as well as tertiary education (e. g., nurse education, nursing science) (Category: Manifestations of work agency – Participation in institutionalised learning activities). Agentic nurses tend to take part in most of the provided learning activities and even negotiate additional training opportunities. If required they willingly accept that some of these opportunities are connected to additional effort and costs. Less agentic individuals, on the contrary, are more reserved when it comes to training opportunities.

> Those are the people that like to participate in training and who are really enthusiastic about them. Even if it means additional work hours. (P1, 30)

> You also have it like that: "Ahh, do I really have to go?" That's just seen as additional effort. And, you try to motivate them and you try, but sometimes it is just not that easy. […] They really have that kind of attitude: "I just spend seven hours here, and now I am supposed to sit there? No, I am not interested." Or they just do not see the sense in it: "Why?" That does exist. (P5, 80–86)

> And she would say: "Yes, I have experience." And I would ask "Further training? Further education?"—"No, no really, I am just not interested." Then she is not up-to-date. In such a case, no professional development will happen. (P8, 44)

Within the interviews almost all interview partners spoke about the importance of verbal exchange between colleagues and other stakeholders at work (Category: Manifestations of work agency – Information and feedback seeking – from other individuals). They emphasised that nurses can indeed develop further through active efforts to obtain information and seek knowledge from other individuals within their work contexts. Agentic individuals have been described as being more inquisitive. They tend to ask questions about unknown procedures or new developments. They do so not only with colleagues but also with doctors or nurses from other wards or even other nursing homes. They next quotes illustrate these findings.

> Or these colleagues, they ask the doctors quite intensively: "Why exactly this prescription? What else can we do? Aren't there any alternatives?" And the others, they just wait till the doctor explains it to them. They do not enquire. I think those are different types of employees. (P1, 160)

> Those are the attentive ones, they keep a close eye, they try to get the bigger picture, they also take a look what is happening on other wards and they communicate with the adequate people… (P3, 101)

> MG: Are there differences between the nurses?
> P4: I would say yes, there are a few, who are really interested, the ones who enquire if there are illness symptoms. And you have the other ones, they just do their work, and they are not necessarily the low performance employees, but they are just not interested. That surely depends on the person. (P4, 59–60)

> Well, there are the colleagues that think, they know it all. And you have those people, they already know a lot, but they enquire and they come to you during discussions like: "How do you do that? How do you go about here? Where did you learn that?" That's a little bit different. (P7, 154)

Surprisingly, not one of the participants explicitly spoke about feedback seeking of geriatric care nurses.

Deliberate access to impersonal knowledge resources was also frequently named as an important means for professional development in the domain of geriatric care (Category: Manifestations of work agency – Information and feedback seeking – from impersonal resources). The interview partners indicated that agentic nurses more often read journals and professional books. They also tend to use the internet more often as an information resource. One nurse (P7) emphasised that there are no big differences between nurses who are examined and those who are not. She experienced non-examined nurses who read at least as much as their examined counterparts.

> You can Google things, or just buy some textbooks, I can also subscribe to professional journals. Sure, that leads to costs, but those are the things, where I think, that when I am interested in a certain area, then I can buy a book, read through it or just look for an article on the web. (P5, 60)

> I can subscribe to professional journals, there are surely enough in the domain of geriatric care or DBFK [German association for care professions] or something like that, where you can find really good articles. We have a full library in our nursing home. I can use it. We monthly get the new "The Nurse" or "The Carer", they come from the DBFK, we get them, geriatric care books but also things like social care, that is also a part of all of our jobs. (P6, 66)

> If they are interested, if they—for instance—hear about new developments, they then read about those developments, in the internet or in journals about care issues. And it doesn't matter whether they are examined or non-examined nurses. We have non-examined nurses who are interested and they read quite a lot. And because of that they are better with the residents, because they know the illnesses and they ask and observe and read. (P7, 26)

The job as geriatric care nurse provides much potential to take over additional tasks and activities that go beyond the normal duties. The majority of the interview partners stressed that nurses can indeed agentically craft opportunities for new experiences at work (Category: Manifestations of work agency – Job and experience crafting – Job enlargement). On the one hand, nurses can apply for institutionalised positions like wound manager or practical instructor that usually require a certain training beforehand. On the other hand, interview partners also named a range of informal responsibilities that can be taken over: communication with relatives, coordination of the duty roster or incontinence manager. These supplementary duties usually do not require special training.

> Or somebody who says I want to become responsible for the wounds (wound manager). We have one colleague, who implemented that here and does it now in the whole nursing home. He does it in an advisory kind of function. (P1, 48)

> Like the advisory nurse that is an additional task here for the examined nurses. Then, we also have those practical instructors. That is also an additional task for examined nurses. Sure, we could go through the whole list. Wound management. Those are all additional tasks, which has to be done throughout the normal day. [...] definitely it's a special task, a special responsibility. (P2, 114)

> ...I am thinking about one particular non-examined colleague at the moment—she takes on many responsibilities for her team and she asks me: "Am I allowed to give this information to the relatives?" Then we spoke about what she is allowed to do. And the relatives like communicating with her, because she gives informed answers. And if she would not be allowed to take on responsibilities she would be unhappy, if she would have to work just by the rule. (P7, 74)

> If you like—for instance—the topic hygiene, then you can go into this direction and go to your supervisor and say: "If there is something going on, then I would like to participate and want to do it in advance and maybe take up some responsibilities." (P7, 130)

Apart from that the interviewees spoke about participation in work-related projects that are also a means to gain new insights into the job. It should also be emphasised that not all of the reported episodes tell about nurses who independently initiated their engagement in such additional duties. However, the interviewees emphasised that more agentic nurses tend to use available chances to participate in new projects or to take over new tasks more often. Less agentic nurses, on the other hand, tend not to use such chances even if they are present at work.

The additional duties enumerated so far have not been connected to any career-related advancements. All of the added tasks and activities were located on the same hierarchical level as the nurse in question has been before. However, the interviewees also spoke about deliberate efforts towards career advancement as a geriatric care nurse. These efforts are sought to lead to new work experience through the engagement in new tasks on a higher hierarchical level (Category: Manifestations of work agency – Job and experience crafting – Job enrichment).

> You have opportunities for career advancement. You can start as a non-examined nurse and then graduate as an examined one and then maybe go even further, take on a supervisor role. [...] Management of geriatric care homes, work as the manager of a nursing home. The ones that I know, they have just sought out these developments. (P4, 44–48)

> He always said: "I want to become head nurse of a ward. I just want to take on the responsibilities". (P6, 70)

It is not always necessary to move up the career ladder first to engage in the activities that are usually a part of the role of head nurses or ward managers. One interviewee also described how nurses can take on these tasks temporarily.

> If you have the vacation period or some kind of multiple sick leaves at the same time. Then you have the one that takes matters into her own hand. [...] If, I don't know, if you have shortage of staff, that is somebody, I don't know, who just takes charge of all the organisation. (P2, 56–60)

Agentic individuals have also been described as being more involved in their work (Category: Manifestations of work agency – Overtime and additional work assignments). This involvement manifests itself through a tendency to work more hours than necessary, to be more often available if other nurses are on sick leave, to participate in certain special events like summer festivals or even to meet with apprentice nurses in their own leisure time. These agentic individuals also tend to act as multipliers in terms of teaching other nurses the knowledge that they have learnt through an institutionalised learning activity.

> We have quite a lot of practical instructors, who are really agentic when it comes to the teaching of our apprentices. They, they intensively accompany them, they even—some of them—meet with the apprentices after their work day and really take the time. And they really do a good job and are on it with much dedication. (P1, 42)

> They are more dedicated, they even stay half an hour or a full hour longer, and do not record their overtime, they do it voluntarily. They, maybe, also participate in special events in the evening... (P3, 16)

### 5.2.3 Relevant Organisational Context Factors

Within the interviews a few highly relevant organisational context factors were named and further discussed. All interviewees strongly emphasised the important role of social support at work (Category: Organisational context factors – Support). Social support included both supervisors and coworkers' general openness towards new ideas as well as change. Unless nurses face a culture of openness that allows them to bring in ideas irrespective of their hierarchical position, they will not act agentically. The following quotes illustrate this proposition mostly with regard to collegial support:

> I think, you need to have the opportunities on the team level to address issues that you think that cause problems. (P1, 82)

> I think, if you have a really agentic employee, somebody who is really dedicated at the beginning and this employee starts working in a bad environment, where they constantly thwart new ideas. And this employee tries to bring in new ideas, but they are constantly discarded, I think, this employee will change and not bring in ideas after a while. (P1, 182)

> Even if I have this ability, or this need [to be agentic], but I just don't find the breeding ground, or the space, where I can prove myself, then even if I have much need for this—that will just not do. But if there is the room for that and I do not want it, then this will also not work. You need to have both. (P2, 180)

> Well, the most ideas address how to organise things at work, how you can organise work in a better way, to think about, even if it is not easy to actually apply, because you have some colleagues that prefer the old way. It's like passive resistance, they don't say "No!". But still, these are the employees that hinder us to try something new. (P5, 74)

A special role is attributed to the support granted by direct supervisors and other individuals with executive power. Supervisors have to take their subordinates seriously, they need to be open to new ideas, and work towards the implementation of proposals made by their employees. Trust was discussed as an important issue in association with such a supporting environment.

> Well, I think that very much depends on the supervisors and that they give the signal "I do support if somebody wants to participate in a training and such stuff that come from the employees". You have to take them seriously. (P2, 170)

> They have to realise that, yeah to notice that if you say something, that it is taken seriously and implemented when applicable. (P3, 113)

> And that is important. And if you have a boss like that, yes? Then you can implement ideas. If she is open for such things. There are also those supervisors, that reject everything they didn't come up with by themselves, like: "Oh, sh**, that could have been a good idea that I could have had. But no, we won't do that." Like that. They just do not do that then. But if you have the whole package, if the employees can count on their supervisor, if they can trust her, then yes, I think then you can implement such things. (P8, 78)

Apart from support the interview partners also named general autonomy or job discretion as an important context factor (Category: Organisational context factors – Job autonomy).

> You need to have the opportunity, I just said that, that you are allowed to realise something, to bring in own ideas. Not only to have strict rules and guidelines—there are enough that you have to follow—but outside of these limits you need to have opportunities to go either right or left. (P1, 132)

> Trial and error, yes, that they are allowed to try, even when they fail. (P6, 104)

A recurring theme in almost all interviews was the general lack of time during the work day (Category: Organisational context factors – Time resources). The basic message of these discussions was that there is hardly enough staff to do all the required tasks at work appropriately. This time pressure leads to missed opportunities to exchange information or to engage in efforts that go beyond the necessities. The next quotes will illustrate the issues raised:

> MG: What do you mean with not enough time?
> P2: Being understaffed. Well, the workload that has to be managed nowadays is just tremendous. Quite often we are understaffed, I have to say that, that's very often an issue, respectively, the employee-to-resident ratio is just very tight, that I don't think you can really live up to the expectations. Well, idealism is left behind, probably. (P2, 5–6)

> Sure, that would be desirable [to deliberately seek information from colleagues and other stakeholders], if you would have that more often, however—you know that—time resources are really tight. (P7, 148)

> We have these shift handovers, the focus there is work. Breaks during working time are seldom possible and even if, you do them alone, right? […] So basically, we cannot really exchange ideas, apart from those shift handovers, but even there we do not have the time. (P8, 26)

Employee appreciation was also discussed as an important context factor that determines whether nurses engage in agentic efforts or not (Category: Organisational context factors – Appreciation from the employer). Some interviewees stressed that without a deep appreciation of the nurses' work shown by the employer, agentic efforts that go beyond the necessity are highly unlikely:

> Well, I just can imagine if your work is not appreciated in your nursing home, if I suggest something, that I will give up eventually. (P6, 102)

> That the employee, well, I would say, they should not feel oppressed, they should feel being appreciated, respected, yes? (P8, 78)

A few other context factors were also named as potentially relevant. For instance, one interview partner mentioned that legal issues might also hinder nurses from engaging in efforts to initiate constructive change. In her opinion, laws or legally binding rules might sometimes prevent employees from making innovative suggestions because they think they could get in trouble. Furthermore, the general budget of a nursing home might be a factor if it comes to deliberate engagement in institutionalised learning activities. If there is no money available, then efforts to negotiate access to such learning opportunities might be condemned to fail from the outset.

## 5.3 Discussion

The next four sections will discuss the findings of this interview study with regard to the theoretical framework presented in Chapters 2 to 4.

### 5.3.1 Conceptualisation of Expert Performance in the Domain of Geriatric Care Nursing

All interview partners unanimously described geriatric care nursing as a job that consists of a range of complex and distinct activities. Geriatric care nurses have to engage in different care-related and administrative tasks during a normal working day. Because all study participants emphasised the variety of the job it can be concluded that expert nurses are expected to perform well in all the activities discussed in the interviews. The ability to deal with the whole range of tasks and problems of a certain workplace has already been discussed in Section 3.1.1 as an important part of work-related expertise.

Some of the mentioned activities might occur because they are intentionally scheduled around the working day. However, others emerge very spontaneously. The ability to perform flexibly in regard to unexpectedly changing circumstances was explicitly mentioned as a sign of expertise by the interview partners. Expert nurses are capable of deviating from prescheduled work routines in order to deal effectively and efficiently with the problem situation at hand. Effectively and efficiently hereby mainly means to respond adequately to the specific needs of the residents in a ward. This description fits well in the general discussion of expert performance at work presented in Chapter 3 (see also Benner, 2004; H. L. Dreyfus & Dreyfus, 2005).

Within the interviews the study participants often referred either to examined or non-examined nurses. Non-examined nurses are usually employed to assist their examined counterparts. However, several study participants stressed that non-examined nurses often do the same work as the examined ones, and that their performance is often as least as good, if not even better, than the performance of the examined nurses. There were even reports about non-examined nurses who managed whole wards autonomously and/or took the role of informal supervisors. This can be interpreted as cases where expertise was recognised by other nurses within a nursing home regardless of the employee's actual qualification and hierarchical position.

Idiosyncratic circumstances within a nursing home were not mentioned to determine what exactly counts as good performance and what does not. This is an interesting finding. It either means the study participants do not perceive large differences between different nursing homes in regard to the definition of good performance, or that they are just unaware of those differences (see Section 3.1.1 as well as Billett, 2001a, for a theoretical discussion on the relevance of idiosyncratic circumstances of a workplace for the definition of performance criteria within a certain domain).[35]

### 5.3.2 Exercising Agency at Work in the Domain of Geriatric Care Nursing

All interviewees described differences between nurses with regard to their tendency and ability to take control over their life and their environment. Agentic nurses have been described as more self-reliant, taking more initiative, and more interested in the development of their work-related knowledge, skills, and abilities. Non-agentic individuals, on the other hand, were described as being more reactive and compliant in nature: Although they tend to notice

35 It should be noted that all interviewees reported experience with more than one single nursing home at least.

tensions in work practices, they do not actively address them. They rather complain about problems without making concrete suggestions for how to tackle them. This description fits well with the conceptualisation of work agency derived in Chapter 2 (see also the conceptualisations of Bandura, 2012; Eteläpelto et al., 2013; Harteis & Goller, 2014).

The interviews were structured mainly around observable behaviours which agentic nurses tend to exhibit more often than non-agentic nurses. Such behaviours can be interpreted as manifestations of agency—that is, agentic actions—in the sense of Chapter 2. All together six conceptually different agentic actions were discussed in the interviews:

1. *Initiating constructive change at work:* Agentic nurses more often try to make a difference at work by questioning inefficient work procedures, by attempting to restructure non-functional organisational system, and by advertising new equipment or information material. They do not only address observed issues but also make concrete suggestions for how to implement their own ideas. In addition, they also defend their ideas against reservations of colleagues or supervisors. This behaviour syndrome can be interpreted as proactive work behaviour as discussed in Section 2.2.3 (especially: taking charge behaviour; e. g., Morrison & Phelps, 1999).

2. *Participation in institutionalised learning activities:* Agentic nurses are in general more open to participating in institutionalised learning activities like in-house or external training as well as certain degree programmes. However, they are open not only to participating in such learning opportunities but also to actively organising their participation. Within the interviews, institutionalised learning activities were only discussed in terms of classical tertiary and quaternary education. Conferences, for instance, were not mentioned as being relevant in the domain of geriatric care nursing. Nevertheless, the described behavioural syndrome fits well with the description given in Section 3.3.3 (deliberate engagement in institutionalised learning activities) as well as partly with the idea of idiosyncratic deals brought forward by Rousseau et al. (2006; see also Hornung et al., 2008).

3. *Information and feedback seeking:* Agentic individuals are described as seeking more information from (a) colleagues or supervisors, and (b) impersonal resources like books, journals or internet databases. Within the interviews most participants reported about episodes of deliberate enquiry of either technical or referent information (see Section 3.3.2 as well Ashford & Cummings, 1983; Morrison, 1993b). A few interviewees also reported about episodes where nurses used monitoring strategies to gain technical information (mostly learning through observation). However, based on the interview material it was not possible to decide whether those strategies were used in an agentic sense or if they were just something that naturally occurs at work. Furthermore, within the interviews no reports about nurses' efforts to deliberately monitor or enquire about appraisal information could be found. A possible explanation might be that the interview partner subsumed these feedback-seeking strategies within their reports about nurses' deliberate discussions of problems and cases.

4. *Job and experience crafting:* Agentic nurses have been described as being more inclined to take on additional tasks, to apply more often for institutionalised positions like wound or quality managers, and to participate more often in certain short-term projects at work. This behaviour can be labelled as deliberate job enlargement. In a classical sense, job enlargement describes all means that increase the scope of employees' daily jobs (Bratton & Gold, 2007; Hulin & Blood, 1968). In addition, agentic nurses also engage in deliberate job enrichment. They are keen to take over responsibilities from supervisors or other individuals on a higher hierarchical level (see also Bratton & Gold, 2007; Herzberg, 1968). This can be done on a short-term basis (e. g., replacing someone who is on sick leave) or by trying to advance within the geriatric care career ladder. Both deliberate job enlargement as well as enrichment can be understood as two distinct facets of job and experience crafting behaviour described in Sections 2.2.3.1 and 3.3.1 (see also Goller & Billett, 2014; Wrzesniewski & Dutton, 2001).

5. *Going beyond the necessity of their job:* Agentic nurses tend to take their job more seriously and are willing to spend more time on job-related activities. For instance, they have been described as working overtime more often,

willingly replacing other colleagues on sick leave or investing leisure time to meet with apprentices. Such a behaviour syndrome has not yet been discussed as a manifestation of agency within the literature. At the same time, it might be possible that the described individuals are not agentic as such. The willingness to take on overtime or to replace sick colleagues could also be explained by compliance.

6. *Taking on the role of multipliers:* The last manifestation of agency described in the interviews is the tendency to act as multipliers at work. Multipliers are individuals who actively attempt to distribute information and knowledge recently gained from institutionalised learning activities. If this behaviour is self-initiated and goal directed it could indeed be understood as agentic in nature. However, such behaviour has not yet been discussed in the literature on agency in work contexts.

Four of these six agentic actions have already been included in the theoretically derived research model described in Chapter 4. However, the findings of this study allow the model to be further advanced.

First, the study findings indicate that the concept of information and feedback seeking should be divided in two separate concepts: (a) reading professional literature (i. e., enquiry of codified information like books, journals or internet databases), and (b) deliberate interaction with different professional actors like colleagues, supervisors, therapists or doctors. Both concepts can be interpreted as facets of the larger construct of information and feedback seeking. Furthermore, learning from social interaction and learning from consulting media has already been discussed as two different means for professional development in Section 3.2 (see also Pool et al., 2016). It should be noted that deliberate interaction might include not only information but also feedback seeking. Although feedback seeking was not explicitly mentioned in the interviews it was decided not to exclude this important aspect of deliberate interaction. Feedback seeking has been argued to be an important catalyst for reflection processes and, therefore, professional learning and development (see Section 3.3.2; see also Goller & Harteis, 2014).

Second, job and experience crafting should also be split into two different concepts: (a) deliberate job enlargement, and (b) deliberate job enrichment.

Deliberate job enlargement subsumes all self-initiated behaviours that aim to expand tasks horizontally within a nurse's current job. In contrast, deliberate job enrichment subsumes all agentic behaviours that aim to add tasks that are usually done by someone on a higher hierarchical level or to advance within the hierarchical geriatric care nursing system. This distinction makes the idea of job and experience crafting more concrete. Individuals who engage in either of these two agentic actions are able to craft new experiences that would have otherwise not been afforded to them (see Section 3.3.1).

Third, the deliberate participation in institutionalised learning activities will be constrained to training and study opportunities. Other institutionalised learning activities do not seem to play an important role in the domain of geriatric care nursing in Germany.

Two additional agentic actions could be identified: (a) going beyond the necessity of their job, as well as (b) taking on the role of a multiplier. Both agentic actions have not yet been discussed within the literature. Since the research model described in Chapter 4 now already includes six different agentic actions (participation in training opportunities, reading professional literature, interaction with other professional stakeholders, job enlargement, job enrichment, and initiating constructive change at work) it was decided not to expand the already quite complex model any further. However, both agentic actions should be included in future studies.[36]

### 5.3.3 Agentic Actions Relevant to Expertise Development in the Domain of Geriatric Care Nursing

Based on the interviews, work agency and expertise in geriatric care nurses can be perceived as being conceptually different. Some of the study participants emphasised that it is not exclusively the group of expert nurses who exercise agency at work. Agency is also exercised by nurses who have not (yet) reached expertise. However, at the same time participants acknowledged

36 Apart from the increased complexity of the model the inclusion of new constructs would have substantially extended the survey instrument. As will be seen in the next chapter, the survey instrument is already quite long and takes about 30 minutes to complete.

that geriatric care nurses who exercise agency are more prone to reaching expertise than nurses who do not exercise agency.

First and foremost, nurses' deliberate participation in training opportunities has been mentioned as an important predictor of professional learning and development. Second, the interview participants also described nurses who more often seek information both from colleagues or other work-related stakeholders (like doctors or therapists) and from impersonal resources as having a higher chance of developing expertise than nurses who do not engage in such agentic actions. This is not surprising since all these activities have already been associated with learning and development within the literature (see Sections 3.2 and 3.3). They all allow employees to keep up with current developments in the field of geriatric care nursing as well as to co-construct relevant knowledge that is required to care for residents in an effective and efficient way.

Deliberate job enlargement and job enrichment were not directly related to learning and development in the interviews. However, the interview participants acknowledged that nurses can get new insights about their occupation through new tasks and new responsibilities. Both job enlargement and job enrichment are means to craft new experiences that would not otherwise have been afforded (see Section 3.3.1).

It therefore follows that deliberate participation in training opportunities, deliberate reading of professional literature, deliberate interaction with different professional actors, deliberate job enlargement, as well as deliberate job enrichment can all be interpreted as agentic actions that are relevant predictors of work-related expertise development in the domain of geriatric care nursing. However, there was no evidence within the interviews that the initiation of constructive change at work also predicts the development of expertise.

### 5.3.4 Organisational Context Factors That Affect Geriatric Care Nurses' Engagement in Agentic Actions

All interviewees acknowledged that organisational context factors affect whether and how nurses engage in certain kinds of actions. Based on their argumentation, however, it was not possible to derive explicit information about whether they described the organisational context factors as direct predictors of the mentioned agentic actions or as moderators between work agency and the actions in question. Since both types of relationships have been hypothesised in Chapter 4 and both types of relationships can be read into the interview statements, the next paragraphs will use the term antecedents to avoid the usage of the terms predictor and moderator.

Social support was discussed as the most important organisational context factor within the interviews. Without the support of both colleagues and supervisors, engagement in agentic actions is perceived as highly unlikely. However, the interview findings indicate that the support of colleagues and the support of supervisors might slightly differ from each other conceptually. Collegial support has mainly be discussed as coworkers' general openness to bringing in ideas as well as to change in general. Such openness plays a particularly important role when agentic nurses want to initiate constructive change at work. Supervisor support was discussed in a broader manner as supervisors' tendency to take their subordinates seriously, to trust them, and to be open to new ideas, as well as an inclination to implement suitable ideas proposed to them. Supervisor support might be important not only if nurses want to initiate constructive change at work. It rather prepares the ground for all kinds of actions which are self-initiated and somehow also influence the day-to-day business of a nursing home. Based on these insights it was decided to split the larger concept of social support into two difference facets: (a) coworker support, and (b) supervisor support. Both coworker and supervisor support are hypothesised to be important antecedents of all agentic actions included in the research model (see also Sections 2.2.3.4 and 3.3 for further discussion of the role of social support for individuals' engagement in agentic actions).

Quite similarly, autonomy at work has also been discussed as a relevant organisational context factor. Without freedom, independence, and discretion to schedule and execute one's work, agentic actions are unlikely to occur. Sufficient autonomy could be some kind of signal towards the employees that self-initiated behaviour is not generally forbidden or deprecated (see also Section 2.2.3.4). Further evidence for this hypothesis is given because laws and legally binding guidelines have also been mentioned as affecting whether and how individuals engage in agentic actions. Tight laws and guidelines might easily restrict nurses' perceived potential to take initiative and thereby deviate from standard procedures. It can therefore be argued that job autonomy is, as already hypothesised in the theoretically derived research framework, a relevant antecedent of all agentic actions included in the model.

Another organisational context factor that has been both theoretically discussed in Chapters 2 and 3 as well as mentioned in the interviews is time pressure. Time pressure has been described as a general lack of time during the day. The interviews indicated that insufficient time hinders individuals' engagement in every kind of activity that goes beyond the absolutely necessary like medical treatments, basic care, and administration. Without sufficient time resources there is a big chance that nurses do not exchange information with each other, do not ask for further learning activities that take place during working hours, do not read about emerging problems during the day, do not add even more tasks to their job or engage in any kind of time-consuming projects to initiate constructive change at work. Based on the interviews, time pressure can therefore be conceptualised as a negative antecedent of the agentic actions included in the model. This is an important insight since some empirical studies as well as some theoretical arguments also speak in favour of conceptualising time pressure as a positive predictor of agentic actions (see Section 2.2.3.4 as well as Fay & Sonnentag, 2002; Fritz & Sonnentag, 2009).

In addition to the already theoretically derived organisational context factors, both the available budget of a nursing home and a culture of appreciation have been mentioned as possible organisational context factors. First, low budgets might prevent nurses from engaging in any agentic actions that are connected to substantial costs. Without a sufficient budget available, nurses might not attempt to negotiate expensive training opportunities or to initiate change that could cause additional costs (see the context of PhDs for similar findings: Goller & Harteis, 2014). Second, a culture of appreciation might motivate individuals to go beyond the necessity of their job. However, if appreciation is missing at work, agentic individuals might invest their agency in other life domains. Although both these organisational context factors are perceived as highly plausible it was decided not to include them in the research model. Again, the reason for this decision lies in the already high complexity of the model. An even more complex model could easily lead to estimation problems in the structural equation framework employed in Studies 2 and 3. This is especially the case since organisational context factors are not only modelled as direct predictors but also as moderators between work agency and expertise in the research model of this thesis. In addition, a more complex model would also translate into a longer survey instrument and, therefore, potentially lower response rates. Both context factors should however be considered for inclusion in future studies.

### 5.3.5 Methodological Approach and Limitations

An exploratory interview approach was chosen to get insights into how geriatric care nurses exercise agency at work, how the exercise of work agency is related to their professional learning and development, and what organisational context factors affect whether and how they engage in agentic actions. In total, nine interviews with highly experienced staff nurses were conducted. The first interview was used for piloting reasons and was later removed from the interview corpus. The remaining eight interviews were analysed using qualitative content analysis following the procedures outlined by Mayring (2002, 2004, 2015) and Schreier (2012).

At least three major limitations of this study have to be pointed out. First, all study participants answered the interview questions with regard to their personal interpretation of colleagues' and subordinates' behaviours, motives, and tendencies. These interpretations might not necessarily represent the reality of past events in an adequate way. It was not always quite clear whether the interviewees described cases based on past experience or rather prototypical conceptions of nurses (e. g., agentic vs. less agentic individuals). Some descriptions could have been based on very ideal types of employees that do not exist in such a way in reality. Second, all findings are based on a relatively small sample size. A large sample size might have led to other findings in regard to the identified agentic actions as well as organisational context factors. It is therefore not clear how generalisable are the findings of this study. Third, the interview partners were not sampled randomly. Such a non-random sampling of participants could easily lead to sample-selection problems (cf., Collier & Mahoney, 1996). For instance, it is conceivable that only such participants who are strongly interested in the topic of agency at work took part in this study (all interviewees knew the main topic of the interviews in advance). Individuals who are not as interested in this topic might not have described how agentic individuals are prone to develop expertise because they might not be aware of this fact. However, they would then have explained expertise development with other factors that are more in their focus of interest.[37]

All findings presented in this study have to be interpreted against the background of these potential limitations. At the same time, however, it has also to be generally emphasised that interviews with supervisors can indeed give insights into topics related to why employees engage in behaviours, what organisational context factors affect their behaviour, and what kinds of employees tend to develop better than others. Supervisors can be understood as experts of these topics. Because of their organisational position they have to regularly assess performance issues as well as developmental needs of their subordinates. In addition, because of their long work experience they are able to answer interview questions in regard to a wide range of other nurses with whom they have worked in the past. Moreover, due to their experience they usually have worked in more than one ward and even more than one nursing home. They therefore have good insights into how different organisational context factors determine behaviour of their colleagues or subordinates.

## 5.4 Chapter Summary

This chapter has described the first empirical study of this thesis. The focus of this study was to give preliminary insights into how geriatric care nurses exercise agency at work, how work agency is related to the development of expertise, and what organisational factors affect geriatric care nurses' engagement in the identified agentic actions. In addition, the study asked how expert performance is conceptualised in the domain of geriatric care nursing. The answers to these questions are thought to validate and advance the theoretically

37 It is worth considering that only one of the staff nurses interviewed in this study was interested in taking part in either the pilot test or the main study (see Section 6.1). This might give first evidence that interest in the topic of agency might not have been a major issue and therefore did not bias the interviews too much.

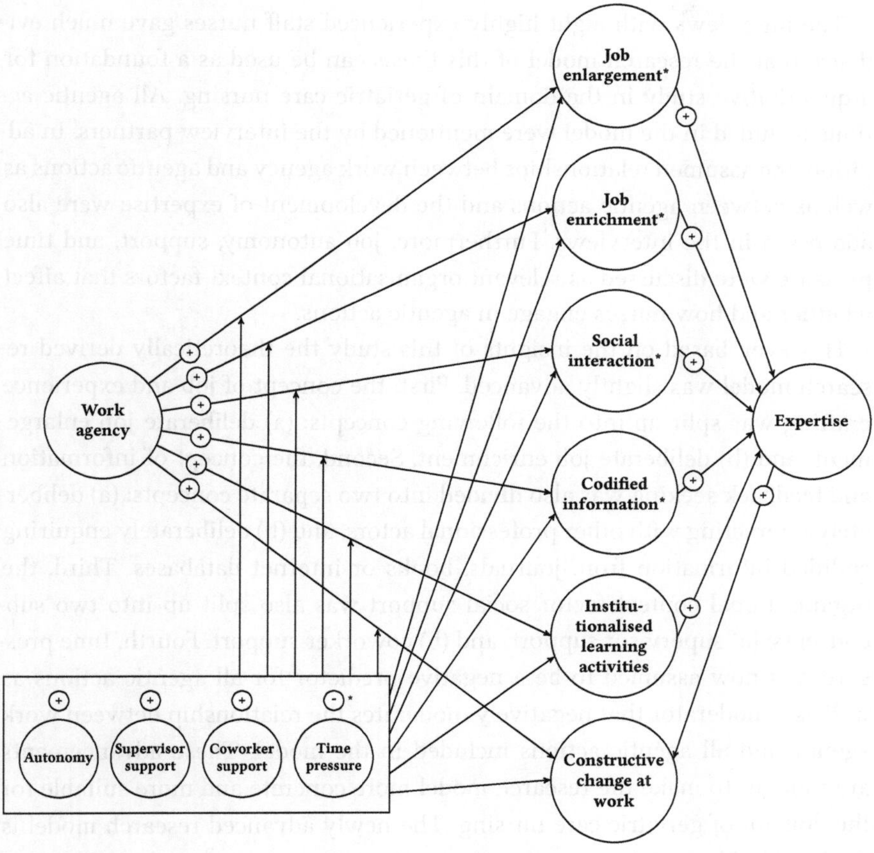


**Figure 5.1.** Advanced research model. Changes to the model described in Chapter 4 are indicated by an asterisk (*). For reasons of clarity the assumed effects of the four organisational context factors have not been printed on the path. They apply to all arrows indicating a direct or a moderator effect originating between the organisational context factors and the agentic actions in the model. Please note that the labels for the agentic actions have been slightly shortened. This was done for reasons of visual clarity.

derived research model presented in Chapter 4 and to give additional insights on how to operationalise the concepts included in this model.

The interviews with eight highly experienced staff nurses gave much evidence that the research model of this thesis can be used as a foundation for a quantitative study in the domain of geriatric care nursing. All agentic actions included in the model were mentioned by the interview partners. In addition, the assumed relationships between work agency and agentic actions as well as between agentic actions and the development of expertise were also addressed in the interviews. Furthermore, job autonomy, support, and time pressure were discussed as relevant organisational context factors that affect whether and how nurses engage in agentic actions.

However, based on the insights of this study the theoretically derived research model was slightly advanced. First, the concept of job and experience crafting was split up into the following concepts: (a) deliberate job enlargement, and (b) deliberate job enrichment. Second, the concept of information and feedback seeking was also divided into two separate concepts: (a) deliberately interacting with other professional actors, and (b) deliberately enquiring codified information from journals, books or internet databases. Third, the organisational context factor social support was also split up into two subconcepts: (a) supervisor support, and (b) coworker support. Fourth, time pressure was now assumed to be a negative predictor for all agentic actions as well as a moderator that negatively moderates the relationship between work agency and all agentic actions included in the model. These advancements are thought to make the research model more concrete and more suitable for the domain of geriatric care nursing. The newly advanced research model is depicted in Figure 5.1.

In addition, the interview study allowed interesting insights into how the agentic actions, the organisational context factors, as well as professional expertise can be operationalised in a way that fits the domain of geriatric care nursing. Table 5.2 lists each of the relevant constructs with a new revised definition as well as some remarks on how to operationalise the construct in order to answer the research questions posed in Chapter 4.

**Table 5.2.** Construct definitions and remarks for operationalisation.

| Concept | Definition | Remark for operationalisation |
|---|---|---|
| *Deliberate job enlargement* | All efforts that increase the scope of a nurse's daily job by adding new tasks. | Includes the engagement in institutionalised positions like wound managers, the engagement in non-institutionalised positions like being in charge of hygiene products, the engagement in tasks that have not been done before, as well as the participation in short-time projects. |
| *Deliberate job enrichment* | All efforts to take over additional responsibilities from supervisors or other individuals on a higher hierarchical level. | Includes all efforts that aim to increase opportunities to exercise additional discretion at work by taking hold of supervisor positions (short-term and long-term). |
| *Deliberate social interaction* | All efforts to obtain work-related information from other individuals. | Includes all efforts to obtain feedback, to discuss unclear tasks and emerging problems as well as to ask for advice from colleagues, supervisors, and/or other professional stakeholders. |
| *Deliberate enquiry of codified information* | All efforts to obtain work-related information from impersonal information resources. | Includes all efforts to read in professional journals, books or internet databases in order to obtain relevant information or to keep up with current developments. |

*Continued on next page*

Table 5.2 – *Continued from previous page*

| Concept | Definition | Remark for operationalisation |
| --- | --- | --- |
| *Deliberate participation in institutionalised learning activities* | All efforts to participate in institutionalised learning activities related to professional learning and development. | Includes all efforts to participate in institutionalised learning activities if they are offered, to actively (privately) organise these learning opportunities, as well as to actively negotiate access to them with their supervisors. |
| *Deliberate efforts to initiate constructive change at work* | All efforts to initiate change at work that constructively affects organisational procedures or structures. | All efforts to introduce new working procedures, to acquire new tools or information material as well as to improve non-functional and inefficient work procedure or structures. |
| *Job autonomy* | The "degree to which the job provides substantial freedom, independence, and discretion to the employee in scheduling the work and in determining the procedures to be used in carrying it out" (Hackman & Oldham, 1975, p. 162) | The perception of how the workplace allows the nurse to take initiative and to exercise agency in general. |
| *Supervisor support* | Supervisors' general openness for personal initiative as well as their tendency to encourage and assist employees to act agentically. | No additional remarks. |

*Continued on next page*

Table 5.2 – *Continued from previous page*

| Concept | Definition | Remark for operationalisation |
|---|---|---|
| *Coworker support* | Coworkers' general openness for personal initiative as well as their tendency to encourage and assist other employees to act agentically. | No additional remarks. |
| *Time pressure* | The subjective experience of having not enough time to complete the assigned work tasks. | Time pressure manifests itself if nurses have the feeling of being not able to do the work in the time provided by their employer. In addition, nurses might not be able to take their breaks from work or to finish their work within the normal working time. |
| *Expertise* | All individual prerequisites that allow nurses to effectively and efficiently deal with the whole range of different routine and non-routine tasks of their respective workplace. | Nurses with more expertise might be asked more often for advice by other nurses irrespective of their hierarchical position in the organisation. |

It is important to note that the proposed advancements lead to changes in the following hypotheses described in Chapter 4: 1.1, 1.2, 2.1, 2.2, 3.1, 3.2, 3.5, 3.6, 3.7, 3.8, 3.9, 3.10, 3.11, 3.12, 3.13, 3.14, 3.17, 3.18, 3.19, 3.20, 3.21, 3.22, 3.23 and 3.24. Because of the new concepts introduced they will be replaced by the following hypotheses:

**RQ1. How does agency as an individual-level feature explain employees' engagement in agentic actions?**

*Hypothesis 1.1a:* Work agency will be positively associated with employees' deliberate job enlargement.

*Hypothesis 1.1b:* Work agency will be positively associated with employees' deliberate job enrichment.

*Hypothesis 1.2a:* Work agency will be positively associated with employees' deliberate interactions with other professional actors.

*Hypothesis 1.2b:* Work agency will be positively associated with employees' deliberate enquiry of codified information.

**RQ2. How does engagement in agentic actions relate to the development of work-related expertise?**

*Hypothesis 2.1a:* Deliberate job enlargement will be positively associated with employees' expertise development.

*Hypothesis 2.1b:* Deliberate job enrichment will be positively associated with employees' expertise development.

*Hypothesis 2.2a:* Deliberate interactions with other professional actors will be positively associated with employees' expertise development.

*Hypothesis 2.2b:* Deliberate enquiry of codified information will be positively associated with employees' expertise development.

**RQ3. How do organisational context factors affect engagement in agentic actions?**

*Hypothesis 3.1a:* Autonomy at work is positively associated with employees' deliberate job enlargement.

*Hypothesis 3.1b:* Autonomy at work is positively associated with employees' deliberate job enrichment.

*Hypothesis 3.2a:* Autonomy at work is positively associated with employees' deliberate interactions with other professional actors.

*Hypothesis 3.2b:* Autonomy at work is positively associated with employees' deliberate enquiry of codified information.

*Hypothesis 3.5a:* Supervisor support at work is positively associated with employees' deliberate job enlargement.

*Hypothesis 3.5b:* Supervisor support at work is positively associated with employees' deliberate job enrichment.

*Hypothesis 3.5c:* Coworker support at work is positively associated with employees' deliberate job enlargement.

*Hypothesis 3.5d:* Coworker support at work is positively associated with employees' deliberate job enrichment.

*Hypothesis 3.6a:* Supervisor support at work is positively associated with employees' deliberate interactions with other professional actors.

*Hypothesis 3.6b:* Supervisor support at work is positively associated with employees' deliberate enquiry of codified information.

*Hypothesis 3.6c:* Coworker support at work is positively associated with employees' deliberate interactions with other professional actors.

*Hypothesis 3.6d:* Coworker support at work is positively associated with employees' deliberate enquiry of codified information.

*Hypothesis 3.7a:* Supervisor support at work is positively associated with employees' deliberate participation in institutionalised learning activities.

*Hypothesis 3.7b:* Coworker support at work is positively associated with employees' deliberate participation in institutionalised learning activities.

*Hypothesis 3.8a:* Supervisor support at work is positively associated with employees' efforts to initiate constructive change at work.

*Hypothesis 3.8b:* Coworker support at work is positively associated with employees' efforts to initiate constructive change at work.

*Hypothesis 3.9a:* Time pressure at work is negatively associated with employees' deliberate job enlargement.

*Hypothesis 3.9b:* Time pressure at work is negatively associated with employees' deliberate job enrichment.

*Hypothesis 3.10a:* Time pressure at work is negatively associated with employees' deliberate interactions with other professional actors.

*Hypothesis 3.10b:* Time pressure at work is negatively associated with employees' deliberate enquiry of codified information.

*Hypothesis 3.11:* Time pressure at work is negatively associated with employees' deliberate participation in institutionalised learning activities.

*Hypothesis 3.12:* Time pressure at work is negatively associated with employees' efforts to initiate constructive change at work.

*Hypothesis 3.13a:* Autonomy at work moderates the relationship between work agency and employees' deliberate job enlargement. Autonomy at work is expected to strengthen the relationship between work agency and employees' deliberate job enlargement.

*Hypothesis 3.13b:* Autonomy at work moderates the relationship between work agency and employees' deliberate job enrichment. Autonomy at work is expected to strengthen the relationship between work agency and employees' deliberate job enrichment.

*Hypothesis 3.14a:* Autonomy at work moderates the relationship between work agency and employees' deliberate interactions with other professional actors. Autonomy at work is expected to strengthen the relationship between work agency and employees' deliberate interactions with other professional actors.

*Hypothesis 3.14b:* Autonomy at work moderates the relationship between work agency and employees' deliberate interactions with other professional actors. Autonomy at work is expected to strengthen the relationship between work agency and employees' deliberate enquiry of codified information.

*Hypothesis 3.17a:* Supervisor support at work moderates the relationship between work agency and employees' deliberate job enlargement. Supervisor support at work is expected to strengthen the relationship between work agency and employees' deliberate job enlargement.

*Hypothesis 3.17b:* Supervisor support at work moderates the relationship between work agency and employees' deliberate job enrichment. Supervisor support at work is expected to strengthen the relationship between work agency and employees' deliberate job enrichment.

*Hypothesis 3.17c:* Coworker support at work moderates the relationship between work agency and employees' deliberate job enlargement. Coworker support at work is expected to strengthen the relationship between work agency and employees' deliberate job enlargement.

*Hypothesis 3.17d:* Coworker support at work moderates the relationship between work agency and employees' deliberate job enrichment. Coworker support at work is expected to strengthen the relationship between work agency and employees' deliberate job enrichment.

*Hypothesis 3.18a:* Supervisor support at work moderates the relationship between work agency and employees' deliberate interactions with other professional actors. Supervisor support at work is expected to strengthen the relationship between work agency and employees' deliberate interactions with other professional actors.

*Hypothesis 3.18b:* Supervisor support at work moderates the relationship between work agency and employees' deliberate enquiry of codified information. Supervisor support at work is expected to strengthen the relationship between work agency and employees' deliberate enquiry of codified information.

*Hypothesis 3.18c:* Coworker support at work moderates the relationship between work agency and employees' deliberate interactions with other professional actors. Coworker support at work is expected to strengthen the relationship between work agency and employees' deliberate interactions with other professional actors.

*Hypothesis 3.18d:* Coworker support at work moderates the relationship between work agency and employees' deliberate enquiry of codified information. Coworker support at work is expected to strengthen the relationship between work agency and employees' deliberate enquiry of codified information.

*Hypothesis 3.19a:* Supervisor support at work moderates the relationship between work agency and employees' deliberate participation in institutionalised learning activities. Supervisor support at work is expected to strengthen the relationship between work agency and employees' deliberate participation in institutionalised learning activities.

*Hypothesis 3.19b:* Coworker support at work moderates the relationship between work agency and employees' deliberate participation in institutionalised learning activities. Coworker support at work is expected to strengthen the relationship between work agency and employees' deliberate participation in institutionalised learning activities.

*Hypothesis 3.20a:* Supervisor support at work moderates the relationship between work agency and employees' efforts to initiate constructive change at work. Supervisor support at work is expected to strengthen the relationship between work agency and employees' efforts to initiate constructive change at work.

*Hypothesis 3.20b:* Coworker support at work moderates the relationship between work agency and employees' efforts to initiate constructive change at work. Coworker support at work is expected to strengthen the relationship between work agency and employees' efforts to initiate constructive change at work.

*Hypothesis 3.21a:* Time pressure at work moderates the relationship between work agency and employees' deliberate job enlargement. Time pressure at work is expected to weaken the relationship between work agency and employees' deliberate job enlargement.

*Hypothesis 3.21b:* Time pressure at work moderates the relationship between work agency and employees' deliberate job enrichment. Time pressure at work is expected to weaken the relationship between work agency and employees' deliberate job enrichment.

*Hypothesis 3.22a:* Time pressure at work moderates the relationship between work agency and employees' deliberate interactions with other professional actors. Time pressure at work is expected to weaken the relationship between work agency and employees' deliberate interactions with other professional actors.

*Hypothesis 3.22b:* Time pressure at work moderates the relationship between work agency and employees' deliberate enquiry of codified information. Time pressure at work is expected to weaken the relationship between work agency and employees' deliberate enquiry of codified information.

*Hypothesis 3.23:* Time pressure at work moderates the relationship between work agency and employees' deliberate participation in institutionalised learning activities. Time pressure at work is expected to weaken the relationship between work agency and employees' deliberate participation in institutionalised learning activities.

*Hypothesis 3.24:* Time pressure at work moderates the relationship between work agency and employees' efforts to initiate constructive change at work. Time pressure at work is expected to weaken the relationship between work agency and employees' efforts to initiate constructive change at work.

# 6 Study 2: Proposed Study Design, Instrument Development, and Pilot Study

This chapter intends to propose a research design and to compose a quantitative survey instrument suitable for answering the research questions posed in Chapter 4. Both are necessary since—until now—no comparable study exists that has investigated a similar set of research questions in the domain of geriatric care nursing. It follows that both the research design as well as the survey instrument have to be newly developed. This will be done by taking the theoretical framework described in Chapters 2 to 4 as well as the findings of the qualitative study presented in Chapter 5 into account. As far as possible, an attempt will be made to find existing measures to operationalise the concepts included in the advanced research model. Where this is not possible, either existing scales will be adapted or completely new scales will be developed.

It has been strongly recommended to examine newly developed research designs and survey instruments before using them in larger studies (Bortz & Döring, 2006; De Vaus, 2002). Such a piloting phase is the focus of the second study of this thesis. More concretely, Study 2 aims to obtain information about the feasibility and acceptance of the proposed research design as well as the quality of the measures used to operationalise the theoretical concepts included in the main research model. Three criteria were used to assess to what extent the research design and the survey instrument fulfil these requirements. First, a high response rate is a good indicator that the general research design is both feasible and accepted by the relevant target group. Low response rates might indicate substantial problems with the planned survey procedure. Second, all measures included in the questionnaire should satisfy established psychometric quality standards (e. g., Bühner, 2011; Hair, Black, Babin, & Anderson, 2014). Failure to satisfy those standards indicates problems with the scales and the corresponding items used in the survey instrument. Third, it is expected that the relationships between the measures of the constructs included in the model will follow the hypothesised relationships derived in Chapters 4 and 5. Results that are consistent with these hypotheses give preliminary evidence about the validity of the underlying research model. In addition, such results can also be interpreted as indicators for construct validity.

The chapter is structured as follows: Section 6.1 presents and discusses the general research procedure developed to test the hypothesised research model. The development of the survey instrument as well as a description of all scales used in this instrument can be found in Section 6.2. Following these considerations, Section 6.3 describes the methodological approach of the pilot study. The results of this study are then presented and discussed in Sections 6.4 and 6.5 respectively. The chapter closes with a summary that points out the most important findings as well as potential implications for the main study to be presented in Chapter 7.

## 6.1 Proposed Study Design and Sampling Strategy of the Main Study

The research model described in Chapters 4 and 5 assumes that agentic nurses are more prone to developing expertise through the engagement in learning-relevant agentic action in comparison to their less agentic counterparts. To test this causal development assumption a longitudinal research approach with several measurement points over time would be required (Bortz & Döring, 2006). However, such a research approach would have exceeded the scope of this thesis. In addition, the contacted nursing homes exhibited a general unwillingness to participate in such a multi-wave study, which is why only a cross-sectional design was adapted. Although, strictly speaking, no causal inferences can be drawn from such a study design, it is still eligible to show whether proposed relationships between different variables statistically exist (Bortz & Döring, 2006). Those relationships can then be interpreted as initial indicators for potentially existing causal relationships based on the underlying theoretical rationale (Bortz & Döring, 2006; Check & Schutt, 2012).

Data collection was conducted through the administration of self-administered questionnaires containing closed questions that could be answered on a predetermined rating scale. This kind of data collection was chosen for three reasons. First, geriatric care nurses are accustomed to completing self-administered questionnaires containing closed questions. In many cases such questionnaires have been used before in employee attitude surveys or in other kinds of research projects. Second, the quality of the answers to closed questions is usually not affected by participants' articulacy. As long as the descriptions on the questionnaire as well as the questions as such are phrased in simple language it can be expected that nurses with limited language capabilities are also able to participate in the study. Third, self-administered questionnaires allow for gathering of relatively large amounts of data in a relatively short time. This is an important advantage, since data collection was planned to take place during normal work days of the participating nurses, thus only a relatively small fraction of their working time had to be reserved for this study. All together, a high acceptance of this method of data collection from both the nursing homes and the single study participants could be expected. This acceptance should then lead to a high response rate.

Personal discussions with head nurses revealed a low affinity and acceptance of computer technology for many geriatric care nurses. Furthermore, in many nursing homes access to computers is very limited. It was therefore decided to collect data using a paper-and-pencil-based instrument instead of an online survey. To ensure confidentiality and privacy each questionnaire was accompanied by an envelope. The questionnaire was to be placed into the envelope and then to be put into a centrally located and sealed ballot box.

The aim was to collect a sample of at least 800 participants in the domain of inpatient geriatric care nursing for the main study. Such a sample was necessary to robustly test the advanced research model derived in Chapters 4 and 5. A detailed description of the data analyses will be given in Chapter 7. However, a sample size of 800 was considered to be adequate for the following two reasons:

1. It was planned to employ elaborated statistical analysis techniques like confirmatory factor analysis (CFA) and structural equation modelling (SEM) based on a partial least squares (PLS) approach to check the quality of the survey instrument and to test the proposed research model respectively. Unfortunately, due to missing information on expected effect sizes a power analysis could not be performed in order to calculate the exact sample size required for this study. However, within the literature a range of rules of thumb can be found that help to determine the number of cases necessary for the purpose of this thesis. First, Westland (2010) recommends calculating the required sample size using an equation based on the ratio of indicators to latent variables as well as on simulation results of prior studies (see Section 7.1.4.3 for more details). Based on his recommendation a minimum sample size of 222 for the CFA could be obtained (see Section 7.1.4.3). Second, it has been proposed that the sample size for PLS-SEM should exceed 10 times the maximum number of paths directed at a single construct included in the model (Hair, Hult, Ringle, & Sarstedt, 2014). The highest number of structural paths in the research model is 30 (formative operationalisation of work agency employing the repeated-indicator approach; see Section 7.1.4.4). A sample size of at least 300 is therefore required for this approach. In order to assure the convergence and the robustness of both the CFA and the PLS estimation it was decided not stay with the minimal required sample size but rather to obtain at least 400 cases.

2. Many authors (e. g., J. C. Anderson & Gerbing, 1988; Bagozzi & Yi, 1988) recommend cross-validation of findings based on a first sample (calibration sample) with the findings of an independent additional sample (validation sample). Such a cross-validation approach allows for testing the robustness of findings reported in a single study without an explicit replication attempt. In addition, such an approach also allows advancement of a research model based on the findings in the calibration sample and then testing whether the empirically advanced model still holds in an independent validation sample (e. g., Cabrera-Nguyen, 2010). However, because each analysis has to be performed twice, an additional sample of 400 participants was required for

the purpose of this thesis. It therefore follows that data of 800 geriatric care nurses had to be collected.

In order to collect the proposed sample, different strategies were used to find nursing homes that were willing to participate in the study. At first, all interview partners from Study 1 (see Chapter 5) were asked whether their employer wanted to participate. However, only one nursing home could be acquired this way. The research study was then presented in a local further education course on nursing management with 10 participating head nurses. Five nursing homes could be persuaded to participate this way. In the next step, information about the study was distributed using two mailing lists containing CEOs or head nurses in parts of North Rhine-Westphalia as well as to personal contacts established by the author. As an incentive to participate, each nursing home was offered a report comparing their individual results with the average results as a benchmark. Altogether, 33 nursing homes agreed to participate in the research project.

## 6.2 Development of the Survey Instrument

Based on the findings of the interview study presented in Chapter 5 as well as the theoretical model proposed in Chapter 4, a standardised survey instrument was developed. The development of the instrument followed guidelines proposed in the literature (e. g., Bühner, 2011; Worthington & Whittaker, 2006).

The questionnaire started with a short briefing about the purpose of the study, a description about the information asked, instructions on how to fill in the questionnaire, indication of the time required to complete the questionnaire, as well as a statement about the confidentiality of the study. All questionnaires contained information on how to contact the author. After this introductory section, the questionnaire was divided into five distinct question parts: (a) socio-demographic information, (b) agency facets, (c) agentic actions, (d) organisational context factors, and (e) expertise measures.

Part one included items on personal information about the participants like gender, age, work experience in years, work experience at the current employer in years, volume of employment, highest educational attainment, further education certificates, the number of further education courses undertaken in the last year, as well as whether the participant was in a supervisory position. Some of these variables were used to describe the obtained sample (gender, age, volume of employment, highest educational attainment, supervisory position). Others, however, were intended to be used as control variables in the following statistical analyses (work experience, work experience at current employer, the number of further education courses).[38] The exact operationalisation of those attributes can be found in Appendix C.

Parts two to four measured different constructs about individual characteristics, work behaviours, and organisational context factors. Each single construct was operationalised based on the definitions presented in Table 5.2 in Chapter 5. At first, a literature review was conducted to find established and already validated scales that could be used for the purpose of this study. If no German version of an already existing scale could be obtained then all items were translated by the author of this thesis. This translation was then discussed with colleagues working in the same scientific discipline as the author. However, where no appropriate scales could be found, either completely new items were developed or items from existing but not fully fitting scales were modified. For each scale a pool of potential items was generated (Worthington & Whittaker, 2006). This item pool was then discussed with colleagues of the author. Based on this discussion the most appropriate items were chosen to operationalise the scale in question. All scales in these three parts used a 5-point Likert scale answer format with the end points 1 = *Do not agree at all* and 5 = *Fully agree*. Based on the recommendation of some authors each scale was operationalised with at least five different items (e. g., Hair, Black, et al., 2014; Hinkin, 1998). This was assumed to improve the measurement accuracy of the scales used in the newly developed instrument as well as to guarantee

38 Section 3.1 discussed a range of different prerequisites of expertise development besides the hypothesised set of agentic actions. The most important identified antecedent hereby was experience within the domain of interest. That is why both general work experience as well as work experience at the current employer were included in the questionnaire as potential control variables for the following statistical analyses. Moreover, designated training programmes might also help to develop expertise (e. g., Ericsson et al., 2007). It follows that the number of training courses undertaken should also be controlled for in any statistical analysis.

the stability of the employed statistical methods used in the main study (e. g., Kline, 2011).

Particular care was taken to ensure that all items were formulated in a language capable of being understood by a wide range of individuals working in inpatient geriatric care nursing. This was especially necessary since many geriatric care nurses have only low educational backgrounds and/or speak German as a non-native language. All items were checked for appropriateness with a former geriatric care nurse now working in a nurse training academy.

The next sections (6.2.1 to 6.2.3) describe the scales used in parts two to four of the questionnaire in more detail (source, modifications made, example items). Part five contained an expertise measure based on social network analyses (SNA). A description of the items used for this SNA as well as the main idea behind this operationalisation can be found in Section 6.2.4.

### 6.2.1 Work Agency Facets

Part two of the questionnaire contained scales on the three facets of work agency described at the end of Chapter 2: agency competence, agency beliefs, and agency personality. The three facets are understood to capture different aspects of work agency and are used to obtain a composite measure of work agency.

In this specific case, work agency is operationalised as a second-order construct that is constituted by three different reflectively measured first-order constructs (agency competence, agency beliefs, agency personality) containing 10 items each. Such a formative type of operationalisation assumes that the latent construct (i. e., work agency) is caused by its underlying facets (e. g., Becker, Klein, & Wetzels, 2012; Diamantopoulos & Winklhofer, 2001; Jarvis, MacKenzie, & Podsakoff, 2003). Mathematically speaking, this approach measures work agency as a weighted linear sum of the estimated factor scores of the three agency facets. Within the later employed PLS framework such a higher order measurement approach has an important advantage: Both the reflectively measured agency facets and the formatively measured second-order construct work agency can be operationalised as latent constructs. This allows for testing of the psychometric properties of the reflective scales used and empirical estimation of the weights of the three facets. These weights then give information about the relative importance of each agency facet in the prediction of the agentic actions included in the structural equation model.

The formative measurement model of work agency is depicted in Figure 6.1. A more detailed description of how the formative construct of work agency was modelled in the PLS-SEM analysis can be found in Section 7.1.4.4 of the next chapter.

The three facets were operationalised as follows:

- *Agency competence:* Since no appropriate existing scale for this facet could be found, 10 new items were developed for this study. The scale measures the ability to visualise desired future states, to set goals, to translate these goals into actions, to engage in these actions, and to deal with potential problems that might occur (see Section 2.3 in Chapter 2). A sample item of this scale is "I find it easy to work towards my professional goals".

- *Agency beliefs:* The personal belief to be agentic in the work context was operationalised by using an adapted scale on general self-efficacy by Schwarzer and Jerusalem (1995). The original scale measures "the belief of being able to control challenging environmental demands by means of taking adaptive action" (Schwarzer, Bäßler, Kwiatek, Schröder, & Zhang, 1997, p. 70) and is conceptually strongly overlapping with the definition of agency beliefs given in Section 2.3 of Chapter 2. A sample item of this 10-item scale is "I can solve most problems if I invest the necessary effort". The scale was slightly adapted by adding "at work" to each item (e. g., "I can solve most problems at work if I invest the necessary effort").

- *Agency personality:* The individual tendency to exercise agency was operationalised by using a German adaption (Jacobi, Brand-Jacobi, Westenhöfer, & Weddige-Diedrichs, 1986) of the desirability of control scale by Burger and Cooper (1979). The scale was developed to "measure individual differences in the general level of motivation to control the events in one's life" (Burger & Cooper, 1979, p. 381). The original German version contained 19 items. However, the scale was reduced to 10 items to shorten the length of the questionnaire. Items were selected in order to fit into workplace settings, so items like "I enjoy political participation because I want to have as much of a say in running government as possible" were excluded. The scale was furthermore slightly adapted by adding "at work" or "work" to each item. A sample item of this scale is "I prefer work activities where I have a lot of control over what I do and when I do it".

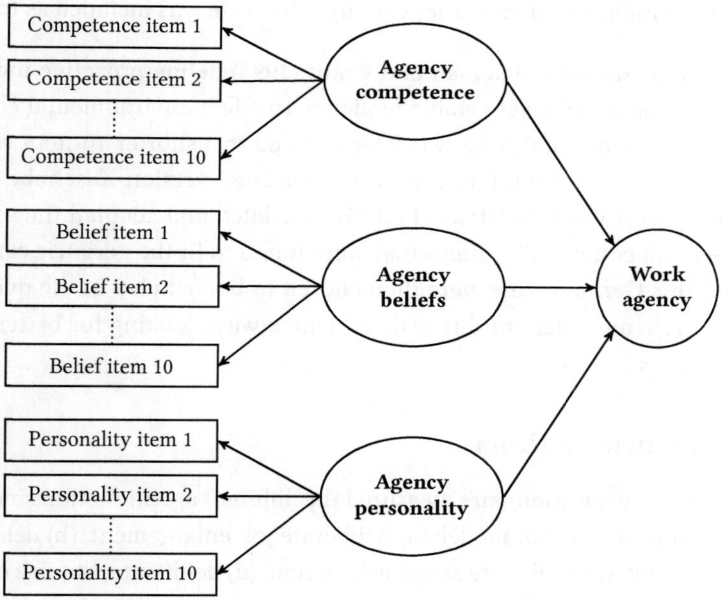


**Figure 6.1.** Formative second-order measurement model of work agency.

It was decided not to operationalise agency personality with the proactive personality scale developed by Bateman and Crant (1993). Although the authors argue that their scale assesses a personality trait, many items seem to rather measure a broad range of general agentic activities in the sense of Chapter 2. Instead, it was decided to use the desirability for control scale of Burger and Cooper (1979). The scale measures individuals' time-stable inclination to take control over their lives and their environments. The items of this scale are developed in such a way that fit the idea of an agency personality trait in the sense of the definition presented in Section 2.3 much better than the proactive personality scale.

A shortened version of Bateman and Crant's (1993) proactive personality scale was nevertheless included in the questionnaire. It was assumed that the formative agency measure should moderately to highly correlate with the latent construct of proactive personality. Such a correlation could then be interpreted as an indicator of construct validity. The scale was included as follows:

- *Proactive personality:* Bateman and Crant (1993) define proactive individuals as having a "relatively stable tendency to effect environmental change" (p. 103). Their original scale was later reduced to a shorter 10-item version by Seibert et al. (1999). Based on this shortened version Kaschube (2003) and Lang-von Wins and Triebel (2005) translated and adapted the scale to the German context. Five items that were found to fit the geriatric care context of this German scale were then chosen to be included in the questionnaire.[39] A sample item of this scale is "I am always looking for better ways to do things".

### 6.2.2 Agentic Actions

Part three of the questionnaire measured the different agentic actions included in the advanced research model: (a) deliberate job enlargement, (b) deliberate job enrichment, (c) deliberate social interaction, (d) deliberate enquiry of codified information, (e) deliberate participation in institutionalised learning activities, and (f) deliberate efforts to initiate constructive change at work. These agentic actions were operationalised as follows:

- *Deliberate job enlargement:* Any effort to increase job challenges by adding new tasks to one's current position at work is called job enlargement (Hulin & Blood, 1968). This construct was operationalised by using four items of the subscale "increasing challenging job demands" of Tims, Bakker, and Derks' (2012) job-crafting instrument (e. g., "I regularly take on extra tasks even though I do not receive extra salary for them"). All items were translated

39 Only five instead of the 10 original items were chosen in order to limit the length of the already quite extensive survey instrument.

into German by the author of this thesis. The fifth item of this scale was perceived to be ill-fitting for the domain of geriatric care nursing. A new item ("If I have the opportunity, I try to take on tasks still unknown to me") was therefore developed to replace the fifth item of the original subscale.

- *Deliberate job enrichment:* In comparison to job enlargement this construct comprises all efforts of nurses that aim to increase opportunities to exercise discretion at work (Ivancevich & Matteson, 1993). This can be arranged by purposefully taking hold of supervisory positions or other tasks that broaden the scope for decision-making. A new scale with five items was developed since no existing scale was available for this construct. A sample item of this scale is "I try to take on such tasks at work that provide me with much decision latitude".
- *Deliberate social interaction:* This scale measures all efforts to obtain work-related information about performance expectations and standards at work, feedback about current performance levels, and information on how to perform required job tasks via deliberate interaction with colleagues, supervisors, and other professional actors. The construct was operationalised with five items. Three items could be used from Tims et al.'s (2012) "increasing social job resource" subscale of their job crafting instrument. However, two items of this originally 5-item scale did not fit the geriatric care domain and were replaced by two newly developed items (e. g., "I discuss problems and difficult cases with my coworkers") that were based on insights from the interview study reported in Chapter 5.
- *Deliberate enquiry of codified information:* This scale measures all deliberate efforts to obtain work-related information from impersonal information resources like books, journals, and internet databases. Since no existing scale was available, five new items were developed based on the findings of Study 1. A sample item of this scale is "In order to keep up to date in regard to developments in the domain of geriatric care I often deliberately read professional literature".
- *Deliberate participation in institutionalised learning activities:* This scale measures to what extent nurses deliberately enquire and/or participate in fur-

ther education courses related to their profession. No existing scale could be found for this purpose. Five new items based on the findings of Study 1 were therefore developed to measure this construct (e. g., "I am proactively discussing my further education needs with my employer or supervisor").

- *Deliberate efforts to initiate constructive change at work:* This construct was measured using the "taking charge" scale of Morrison and Phelps (1999). Taking charge is defined as "discretionary behavior intended to effect organizationally functional change" (Morrison & Phelps, 1999, p. 403) and therefore strongly overlaps with the definition of deliberate efforts to initiate constructive change at work presented in Section 5.4. Morrison and Phelps (1999) developed and tested a 10-item scale for measuring this construct. In order to limit the length of the questionnaire only five items of this scale were chosen to be included in the questionnaire. The five items with the highest factor loadings reported by Morrison and Phelps (1999) were selected (e. g., "I often try to bring about improved procedures for the work unit or department"). All items were then translated by the author.

### 6.2.3 Organisational Context Factors

Organisational context factors at work contribute to part four of the questionnaire. Based on the advanced research model described in Chapter 5, scales that measure (a) job autonomy, (b) supervisor support, (c) coworker support, and (d) time pressure were included in the survey instrument. These constructs are operationalised as follows:

- *Job autonomy:* Job autonomy describes the subjectively perceived decision latitude that allows for the exercising of agency at work. The construct was operationalised using Stegmann et al.'s (2010) translated subscale "decision-making autonomy" of the "work design questionnaire" developed by Morgeson and Humphrey (2006). The original scale contained only three items (e. g., "The job gives me a chance to use my personal initiative or judgement in carrying out the work"). Another three items were developed to make the scale more robust (e. g., "To bring in own ideas and visions into my work is not a problem").

- *Supervisor support:* The extent to which the employees feel supported by their supervisors to exercise agency at work is called supervisor support. Support is defined as a general openness for personal initiative, a tendency to assist other individuals when they want to take initiative, and a culture of encouragement to bring in personal ideas and suggestions. This construct was operationalised by six self-developed items (e. g., "If I want to bring in new ideas at work I get support from my supervisors").
- *Coworker support:* This scale is similar to the one before, although it measures the social support that is offered by peers (coworkers, colleagues) at work. It is measured by the same items used to operationalise supervisor support. However, in these items the term "supervisor" is replaced with "coworker". A sample item for this scale is "My coworkers are open for constructive change I suggest".
- *Time pressure:* Time pressure describes the subjective experience of having not enough time to complete assigned work tasks. Time pressure might result in a feeling of stress, missed breaks or even overtime hours. The construct was measured using a 5-item subscale of Semmer, Zapf, and Dunckel's (1999) inventory for stress-related task analyses (ISTA). A sample item of this subscale is "Because of too much work I either miss or postpone breaks".

### 6.2.4 Expertise Measures

Part five of the questionnaire was developed to measure the current expertise level of the geriatric care nurses participating in this study. Different approaches for this task have been proposed in the literature on professional development and workplace learning:

1. *Available ranking lists:* Ranking lists sort individuals based on their performance within a certain domain. Such rankings mostly exist for well-defined domains (e. g., chess and sports) and are either based on rating systems that directly take the past performance of individuals into account (e. g., Elo rating system), on external assessments of other knowledgeable stakeholders (e. g., fans or certain judges) or on market values of the experts themselves

(e. g., in football). Although some researchers managed to transfer this approach to work domains (e. g., van de Wiel et al., 2004) such lists do not exist for geriatric care nurses.

2. *Self-reporting measures:* Another approach that has been used in studies on learning in work contexts are self-reporting measures (e. g., Stoker & Van der Heijden, 2001; van der Heijden, Boon, van der Klink, & Meijs, 2009). Self-reporting measures rely on individuals' ability to correctly self-assess their expertise level. This ability might be severely limited. For instance, empirical evidence exists that experts often tend to underestimate their abilities while novices tend to overestimate theirs (e. g., Kruger & Dunning, 1999). In addition, equally performing individuals tend to judge their own performance lower in environments with many other high-performing individuals in contrast to environments with many other low-performing individuals (big-fish-little-pond effect; Marsh, 1987; Marsh & Parker, 1984). However, the advantage of such measures is that they are highly accepted by study participants.

3. *Supervisor ratings:* Other researchers used supervisor ratings as measures of expertise (e. g., Sonnentag, 2000). The typical procedure to obtain such measures is to ask supervisors within an organisational unit to rate the performance of their subordinates. However, personal discussions with several head nurses revealed that the acceptance of such an approach can be expected to be very low (i. e., accepted to be low by head nurses and/or CEOs). First of all, any kind of written performance assessment is usually only allowed to be done in the context of yearly employee appraisal interviews that affect salary negotiations as well as career advancements. Second, a ward in a typical German nursing home usually employs between 10 and 35 employees (see Chapter 7 for information on the number of employees of the nursing homes participating in Study 3). The rating effort for the supervisors would therefore be perceived as too time consuming.

4. *Peer nominations:* Sonnentag (1998b) advocates nominations from peers instead of supervisors as yet another alternative measure for expertise in work contexts. The idea is relatively similar to the one using supervisor rat-

ings. However, in this case the performance of an individual is assessed by their coworkers. This can be done directly via the same survey instrument used to get data to measure the other relevant constructs. It only takes a list of all employees within a single organisational unit (e. g., a ward). Each participant is then asked to either rank or directly assess their coworkers in terms of their expertise. Such an approach has two important advantages: First, no additional source of data (e. g., ranking list, questionnaire filled in by supervisors) is required. Second, the data resulting from such peer nominations can be analysed using social network analysis (SNA). Such analysis strategies allow not only use of frequencies of nomination but also calculation of centrality measures (e. g., Bonacich & Lloyd, 2001; Freeman, 1978). Measures of centrality make it possible to account for information of who exactly nominated somebody else in their social network. This way, individuals can be ranked higher when they are nominated by other high-ranked experts (see also Sparrowe, Liden, Wayne, & Kraimer, 2001),[40] so a much finer expertise score can be obtained for each single participant. However, the disadvantage of this method is that each participant has to indicate her own name on the survey instrument. In other words, the survey is not anonymous any more.

Based on the advantages, disadvantages, and the availability of expertise measures it was decided to use the peer-nomination approach. The peer-nomination approach was assessed to result in the most appropriate expertise measure. The feasibility of this approach was judged to be high by several head nurses (based on personal discussions) as long as the study participants are convinced that all data handling and data analysis is done by researchers not directly connected to their employers. The peer-nomination approach was implemented as follows (see Appendix D for a more detailed example of this operationalisation):

40 The main idea behind such a ranking is the plausible assumption that experts tend mostly to ask for advice from colleagues who have either a similar or a higher expertise level than themselves (e. g., Borgatti & Cross, 2003; van der Rijt, van de Wiel, Van den Bossche, Segers, & Gijselaers, 2012). It follows that individuals who are often asked by other well-performing colleagues should receive higher expertise scores than individuals who are only asked by low-performing colleagues.

- *Peer appraisal based on the ability to help with problems and difficulties at work:* This question presents each participant with a list of the coworkers on their ward. The participants are then asked to choose five of their coworkers whom they would contact in order to receive professional advice in cases of problems or difficulties at work. In the next step they were asked to rank the five chosen coworkers from 1 to 5, whereby 1 represents the coworker perceived as most competent to give advice and 5 represents the one perceived as least competent from the chosen colleagues. The participants were also asked to indicate their own name.
- *Peer appraisal based on the ability to introduce colleagues into the work of geriatric care:* To increase reliability another question focussing on peer nomination was included. Similarly to the first question each participant was presented with a list of their coworkers. The participants were then asked to nominate those five colleagues whom they perceive could teach students and non-experienced colleagues the most about geriatric care. It was emphasised that the question focusses on professional aspects and not on teaching abilities.

## 6.3 Purpose and Methodological Approach of the Pilot Study

Pilot testing of the developed questionnaire and proposed study design before conducting a main study has been strongly recommended (Bortz & Döring, 2006; De Vaus, 2002). A pilot test allows identification of problems with the planned research approach. In addition, the insights from a pilot test can be used to revise both the study design and the scales used in the survey instrument if necessary.

The main aims of this pilot study were (a) to test the acceptance and feasibility of the research design, (b) to assess the psychometric quality of the selected or developed scales, and (c) to obtain initial insights about the proposed relationships between the variables included in the research model.

For this purpose, a nursing home with a total of 94 geriatric care nurses was chosen. The particular nursing home is located in an urban environment and is composed of four different wards. After the first contact with the head nurse, the purpose as well as the process of the study was explained to the executive personnel in a team meeting one month before data collection. In this team meeting, supervisors for each ward as well as both the CEO and the head nurse were present. Based on the reaction of all participants of this meeting it could be inferred that the purpose of the study had been understood and the questionnaire as well as the study design had been judged as suitable for the particular context.

Each ward received a separate set of questionnaires with the individual ward name printed on the first page and the individual list of employees for the peer-nomination questions on the last few pages. Data collection was conducted over a time span of 3 weeks in March and April 2014. Each employee received a questionnaire accompanied by an envelope from their direct supervisor. A ballot box was put in a position easily accessible for all participants. Each participant was asked to fill in the questionnaire, place it into the envelope, seal the envelope, and then put the envelope into the ballot box. In total, 21 questionnaires were returned.

After the survey period ended, data were entered by the author. All negative items were recoded after data entry. Participation analyses as well as missing value analyses were chosen to test for the acceptance and feasibility of the research design. The psychometric quality was analysed using scale means and standard deviations, minimum and maximum values, corrected item-total correlations, mean item correlation and Cronbach's $\alpha$. Although desirable, no exploratory or confirmatory factor analyses could be conducted, since the obtained sample size of $n = 21$ was too low (for sample size requirements see Section 7.1.4 in the next chapter as well as Kline, 2011; Westland, 2010). The assumed relationships between the model variables were tested using bivariate product-moment correlations.

All analyses were conducted with R v3.2.5 (R Core Team, 2016) using mainly the psych v1.4.5 package (Revelle, 2015). Again, because of the small sample size no other—more elaborated—type of statistical methods could be used to analyse the data.

## 6.4 Findings of the Pilot Study

In this section the findings of the pilot test of the planned study to answer they research questions posed in Chapter 4 are reported. Section 6.4.1 presents all findings concerning the acceptance and the general feasibility of the research design. Section 6.4.2 then reports all information required to assess the psychometric quality of the scales used in this study. The assumed relationships between the different constructs included in the research model are presented in Section 6.4.3.

### 6.4.1 Participation, Sample Information, and Missing Values

In total, 21 filled-in questionnaires were returned. Because 94 geriatric care nurses received a questionnaire in the first place this corresponds to a total response rate of 22.34%. Table 6.1 reports the response rate for each ward. As can be seen, the response rates differ extensively among the four wards: Ward 1 has the highest response rate while Ward 4 has the lowest.

**Table 6.1.** Response rates.

| Ward | Population | Sample | Response rate |
|---|---|---|---|
| 1 | 34 | 12 | 35.29% |
| 2 | 16 | 4 | 25.00% |
| 3 | 25 | 4 | 16.00% |
| 4 | 19 | 1 | 5.26% |
| *Total* | *94* | *21* | *22.34%* |

Of the 21 study participants 18 were female. On average, the respondents were 35.1 years old ($SD$ = 13.4) and had 11.7 years of work experience in the domain of geriatric care ($SD$ = 8.5). About 45% worked part-time and 55% worked as full-time nurses. Forty-five percent of the participants worked as examined nurses and 14.29% worked in a supervisory position.

Missing data analyses were conducted separately for variables in parts one to four and variables in part five, since the question structure of the peer nomination differs extensively from the other questions. Furthermore, the imputation of missing values is generally possible for all items in parts one to four but not part five.

In parts one to four, 3.12% of data was missing. Missing values occurred in 66.67% of cases and 50.47% of variables. The majority of cases ($n = 18$) showed less than 5% of missing values. However, two cases exceeded 15% of missing values. Missing data distributed relatively equally over all variables. Only three variables (number of further education courses in the last year; items 4 and 5 from the supervisor support scale) showed more than 10% of missing values.

In part five, 16.67% of data was missing. Missing values occurred in 52.38% of cases and all variables were affected. Much data was missing in the question where participants are supposed to indicate their own identity (38.10% missing values). The second highest percentage of missing data (24.76%) could be observed for the ranking of coworkers who are perceived as most competent to give advice in the face of problems or difficulties.

Unfortunately, the number of missing values of part five implied that no SNA could be conducted (see e. g., Costenbader & Valente, 2003; Kossinets, 2006; Stork & Richards, 1992; for general discussions on issues of missing data in SNA). In total, eight out of 21 participants did not indicate their own identity. Because of the missing identity information, no centrality measure or other expertise indicator could be assigned to almost 40% of the participants. Put differently, within the dataset of this pilot study no expertise measure was available for a large group of participants. It was therefore decided to exclude the social network data from any further analysis in this study.

### 6.4.2 Item and Scale Analyses

To assess the psychometric quality of the scales, item and scale analyses including the investigation of standardised Cronbach's α (α), mean inter-item correlations (*MIC*), corrected item-to-total correlation, scale range (minimum to maximum value), means (*M*), and standard deviations (*SD*) were employed. Following the suggestions made in the literature (e. g., Bühner, 2011; Raubenheimer, 2004; Schnell, Hill, & Esser, 2011) items were excluded if they caused α—as a measure of internal consistency—to be below .70 (Hair, Black, et al., 2014). Another rule of thumb often cited in the literature (e. g., Bühner, 2011) suggests that the corrected item-to-total correlation for each item within a scale should exceed .30. However, this rule was not followed if α showed a sufficient internal consistency ($\alpha > .70$). This way no additional variance was removed in the resulting mean scale. Some authors argue that the *MIC* should be between .20 and .40 (e. g., Bühner, 2011; Piedmont, 2014). However, since the *MIC* is a measure for item homogeneity, large values indicate evidence that each item is measuring the same construct. *MIC* values above .40 are therefore not seen to cause any problems (see also Bollen & Lennox, 1991). Table 6.2 reports relevant statistics for each final scale used for further analyses.

Both the agency competence and the agency belief facet result in αs exceeding .80 and .90, respectively. In addition, the *MIC* for both scales is above the threshold of .20. The corrected item-total correlations between each item and its corresponding scale are between .47 and .92 as well as .22 and .75, respectively. Two items of the agency belief scale did not reach the corrected item-to-total correlation threshold of .30 (items 1 and 3). However, since the scale otherwise exhibits sufficient psychometric quality it was decided to keep both items. The small standard deviations ($SD = .77$, $SD = .44$, respectively) are indicators for relatively small variation within the employed scales for both agency facets.

The scale measuring the third agency facet, agency personality, initially did not result in a α above .60. Although all negative items were recoded, additional analyses showed that four items of the scale (items 4, 5, 7, and 9) were negatively related to the remaining ones. Only one of the observed 16 negative correlations reached significance (correlation between item 3 and item 4; $r = -.57, p > .01$). Eventually, all four items were excluded from the scale for all further analyses. The new 6-item scale resulted in a sufficiently high α of .77. Moreover, the 6-item scale also met both the criteria for *MIC* as well as the corrected inter-item correlation for each item included in the scale. The small standard deviation ($SD < 0.80$) points out a relatively small variation within the scale.

**Table 6.2.** Descriptive and reliability statistics for each scale included in the model.

| Scale | Items | α | *MIC* | Range: Potential | Range: Actual | *M* | *SD* |
|---|---|---|---|---|---|---|---|
| *Agency facets* | | | | | | | |
| Agency competence | 10 | .94 | .62 | 1–5 | 1.9–5.0 | 3.4 | 0.77 |
| Agency beliefs | 10 | .82 | .31 | 1–5 | 2.8–4.5 | 3.7 | 0.44 |
| Agency personality | 6 | .77 | .35 | 1–5 | 2.5–4.5 | 3.3 | 0.62 |
| *Agentic actions* | | | | | | | |
| Job enlargement | 5 | .91 | .67 | 1–5 | 1.0–4.8 | 3.0 | 1.10 |
| Job enrichment | 5 | .76 | .39 | 1–5 | 1.0–4.8 | 3.1 | 0.96 |
| Social interaction | 4 | .71 | .38 | 1–5 | 1.0–5.0 | 3.2 | 0.94 |
| Codified information | 5 | .91 | .66 | 1–5 | 1.0–5.0 | 3.0 | 1.00 |
| Inst. learning activ. | 5 | .85 | .53 | 1–5 | 1.0–4.4 | 2.7 | 1.20 |
| Constructive change | 5 | .97 | .85 | 1–5 | 1.0–5.0 | 3.2 | 1.20 |
| *Contextual factors* | | | | | | | |
| Job autonomy | 6 | .92 | .65 | 1–5 | 1.2–5.0 | 3.5 | 0.90 |
| Supervisor support | 6 | .98 | .90 | 1–5 | 1.0–5.0 | 3.0 | 1.10 |
| Coworker support | 6 | .96 | .80 | 1–5 | 2.0–5.0 | 3.5 | 0.87 |
| Time pressure | 5 | .89 | .61 | 1–5 | 1.0–5.0 | 3.5 | 1.20 |
| *Other scales* | | | | | | | |
| Proactive personality | 5 | .74 | .37 | 1–5 | 1.8–4.5 | 3.2 | 0.66 |

*Note.* All values are reported after items were dropped based on item and scale analyses. α = Standardised Cronbach's α; *MIC* = Mean item correlation; *M* = Mean; *SD* = Standard deviation.

All scales but one measuring agentic actions showed sufficient (α > .70), good (α > .80) or even very good (α > .90) internal consistencies. Deliberate social interaction results in an initial α of only .66. Further investigation showed that the item "I seek to interact with external experts (e. g., doctors, pharmacists, physiotherapists) that I encounter at work" correlated relatively little with the mean scale score of the remaining items ($r = .11$). After the item was dropped from the scale, α increased to .71. Both the *MIC*s as well as the corrected item-to-total correlations exceeded their respective cut-off values for the items of each of the six scales. The only exception was item 5 of the job enrichment scale. For this item the corrected item-to-total correlation was only .28. The means of all scales varied between 2.7 and 3.2. Observed standard deviations exceeded .94.

The internal consistency of the scales job autonomy, supervisor support, coworker support, and time pressure could be assessed as good and very good. All $\alpha$ were above .89. In addition, both the *MIC*s as well as the corrected item-to-total correlations exceeded their cut-off values without exception. The observed means ($M_{Autonomy} = M_{Cow.\ support} = M_{Time\ pressure} = 3.5$, $M_{Superv.\ support} = 3.0$) indicate participants' minor tendency to agree on these scales. Standard deviations varied between $SD_{Coworker\ support} = 0.87$ and $SD_{Time\ pressure} = 1.20$.

The 5-item scale on proactive personality yielded a $\alpha$ of .74, a *MIC* of .37, a mean of 3.2 and a standard deviation of 0.66. Further analyses revealed that the first item of this scale ("Nothing is more exciting than seeing my ideas turn into reality") correlated comparable lower with the mean score of the item ($r = .18$) than the other items (all $r > .51$).

All in all, the scales used in the questionnaire showed relatively good psychometric qualities. Because of the small sample size no further analyses (e. g., exploratory or confirmatory factor analyses) could be conducted. The scales were therefore constructed based on the insights just presented. For further analyses mean scores for each scale and participant were calculated.

### 6.4.3 Testing Assumed Relationships

To gain preliminary insights concerning the relationships assumed in the research model, bivariate product-moment correlations between the scales were calculated (see Table 6.3). All significance levels were based on two-tailed tests. Although the research model explicitly states hypothesised directions between most variables, strictly speaking, the pilot test was conducted for exploratory reasons. In such cases two-sided significance tests are commonly used (Bortz & Schuster, 2010). To interpret the correlations Cohen's (1992) effect size guidelines were followed. Correlations between .10 and .30 were interpreted as small, correlations between .30 and .50 as medium sized, and correlations above .50 as large.

**Table 6.3.** Correlations between main constructs.

| Measure | 1 | 2 | 3 | 4 | 5 | 6 | 7 | 8 | 9 | 10 | 11 | 12 | 13 |
|---|---|---|---|---|---|---|---|---|---|---|---|---|---|
| 1 Agency competence | | | | | | | | | | | | | |
| 2 Agency beliefs | .42 | | | | | | | | | | | | |
| 3 Agency personality | .56** | .42 | | | | | | | | | | | |
| 4 Job enlargement | .12 | .35 | .15 | | | | | | | | | | |
| 5 Job enrichment | .59** | .27 | .32 | .12 | | | | | | | | | |
| 6 Social Interaction | .46* | .26 | .77*** | .31 | .32 | | | | | | | | |
| 7 Codified information | .61** | .44* | .70*** | .22 | .30 | .68*** | | | | | | | |
| 8 Instit. learning activities | .22 | .54* | .27 | .88*** | .22 | .29 | .39 | | | | | | |
| 9 Constructive change | .31 | .51* | .44* | .01 | .54* | .33 | .48* | .25 | | | | | |
| 10 Job autonomy | .32 | .46* | .61** | −.11 | .24 | .18 | .34 | .21 | .52* | | | | |
| 11 Supervisor support | .61** | .23 | .52* | .18 | .64** | .41 | .48* | .34 | .46* | .39 | | | |
| 12 Coworker support | .59** | .12 | .69*** | −.27 | .33 | .28 | .41 | −.09 | .16 | .51* | .51* | | |
| 13 Time pressure | −.09 | .01 | −.32 | .28 | −.04 | −.25 | .01 | .34 | .22 | −.29 | .02 | −.32 | |
| 14 Proactive personality | .44* | .35 | .54* | −.10 | .26 | .50* | .34 | −.06 | .35 | .34 | .19 | .26 | −.26 |

*Note.* Product-moment correlations are calculated using pairwise complete observation. Two-tailed significance tests: * $p < .05$, ** $p < .01$, *** $p < .001$.

The correlations between the three agency facets were all positive and medium to large in size. However, only the correlation between agency competence and the agency personality facet reached significance ($p < .01$).

Within the agentic actions only two correlations were below .20 (job enrichment with job enlargement and job enlargement with efforts to initiate change at work). No negative correlations occurred. Four scales were positively and significantly correlated with large effect sizes: social interaction with enquiry of codified information ($r = .68$, $p < .001$), enquiry of codified information with efforts to initiate change at work ($r = .48$; $p < .05$), participation in institutionalised learning activities with job enlargement ($r = .88$, $p < .001$), and job enrichment with efforts to initiate change at work ($r = .54$, $p < .05$).

Within the organisational context factors only two correlations reached significance: Coworker support was positively related to both job autonomy and supervisor support (both $r = .51$, $p < .05$; large effect size). Supervisor support and job autonomy were positively related ($r = .39$; medium effect size). Time pressure was negatively related to both job autonomy and coworker support ($r = -.29$ and $r = -.32$, respectively; medium effect size).

All agency facets were positively related to each of the measured agentic actions. The correlations between the competence facet and social interaction ($r = .46$, $p < .05$; medium effect size), enquiry of codified information ($r = .61$, $p < .01$; large effect size), and job enrichment ($r = .59$, $p < .01$; large effect size) all reached significance. Significant relationships were also observed for the correlations between the agency belief facet and enquiry of codified information ($r = .44$, $p < .05$; medium effect size), participation in institutionalised learning activities ($r = .54$, $p < .05$; large effect size), and efforts to initiate change at work ($r = .51$, $p < .05$; large effect size). The agency personality facet was significantly related to social interaction ($r = .77$, $p < .001$; large effect size), enquiry of codified information ($r = .70$, $p < .001$, large effect size), and efforts to initiate change at work ($r = .44$, $p < .05$; medium effect size). All other correlations did not reach significance.

The correlations between the situational factors and the agentic actions revealed a mixed pattern. From the 24 correlations only four reached significance: Job autonomy with efforts to initiate change at work ($r = .52$, $p < .05$; large effect size) as well as supervisor support with job enrichment ($r = .64$,

$p < .01$; large effect size), enquiry of codified information ($r = .48$, $p < .05$; medium effect size), and efforts to initiate change at work ($r = .46$, $p < .05$; medium effect size). Three correlations had very small or essentially zero effect sizes: Coworker support with participation in institutionalised learning activities ($r = -.09$), and time pressure with job enrichment ($r = .04$) as well as with enquiry of codified information ($r = .01$). All other correlations resulted in small to medium effect sizes. Two of these correlations were negative: Time pressure with social interaction ($r = -.25$) and coworker support with job enlargement ($r = -.27$).

The correlations between the three agency facets and the proactive personality measure were all positive. Significant correlations were found for the relationship of proactive personality with agency competence ($r = .44$, $p < .05$; medium effect size) and agency personality ($r = .54$, $p < .05$; large effect size). However, the correlation between proactive personality and agency belief did not reach significance although a medium effect size could be found ($r = .35$).

## 6.5 Discussion

The overall response rate of this pilot test was slightly above 22% and can be assessed as mediocre. In a large meta-analysis on compatible studies the average response rate was found to be 35.7% with a standard deviation of 18.8 (Baruch & Holtom, 2008). It seems that some geriatric care nurses could not be sufficiently motivated to take part in this study. One possible explanation for this phenomenon might be that only nurses who are highly agentic and/or interested in the larger topic of this thesis completed questionnaires while less agentic and/or less interested nurses did not. This would lead to a sample selection bias because randomised sampling can no longer be guaranteed (e. g., Tomaskovic-Devey, Leiter, & Thompson, 1994). In addition, a sample selection bias could occur because the response rate substantially differed among the four wards. In the worst case this response behaviour was caused by particular characteristics of the ward (e. g., commitment of the supervisor, etc.). However, based on the data available it is not possible to empirically explore whether a sample bias really exists and what reasons might have caused it. Still, all empirical results of this study should be interpreted with caution.

In order to increase response rates and, therefore, to minimise the likelihood as well as the potential effects of a sample selection bias in the main study, an incentive system could be used. Incentives are stimuli that are thought to motivate individuals to participate in a study who would otherwise have not been participated. Although the efficacy of incentives is highly contested (Baruch & Holtom, 2008) they might indeed improve the response rate of questionnaire studies (Singer & Ye, 2013; Stadtmüller & Porst, 2005). For the purpose of this study a group incentive scheme was chosen: Within each nursing home the ward with the highest response rate was promised a gift basket. This was thought to reframe the survey into a small competition between the wards within a nursing home and therefore to motivate additional nurses to take part in the main study.

The missing data analyses resulted in a mixed picture. Within the first four parts of the questionnaire only a very negligible number of items were not appropriately answered. A discussion with the head nurse of the nursing home indicated that nurses felt comfortable filling in the items and accepted the general survey procedure. However, a significant amount of data for the peer-nomination approach used in part five of the questionnaire was missing. About 40% of the respondents did not indicate their own identity while completing the peer-nomination questions. This caused substantial problems for analysing the data. Without sufficient information about the identity of a respondent none of the proposed expertise measures (number of nominations, degree of centrality) could be calculated and assigned. The high rate of missing values in this part of the questionnaire was interpreted as a low acceptance towards the employed measurement approach. This could partly be confirmed based on personal discussions with the head nurse of the participating nursing home. In contrast to the a priori expectations the participating nurses seemed to interpret the social network questions as an invasion of privacy.

A possible reason for this low acceptance could be that the nurses did not fully trust the procedures that were supposed to guarantee their privacy and confidentially. Another explanation, however, would be that nurses did not feel comfortable nominating and rating their coworkers if they had to disclose their own identity. Both reasons could have easily led to a general reluctance to complete some of the questions in part five. Moreover, distrust might have also been a reason for not submitting a questionnaire in the first place. Part five of the questionnaire could therefore have contributed to the relatively low general response rate. Based on this interpretation it was decided not to employ the peer-nomination approach anymore. Because expertise ranking lists were not available and supervisor ratings could not be utilised, a self-reporting approach had to be used. The development of a new expertise measure will be described in the next chapter, in Section 7.1.3.

The psychometric quality of the Likert-type scales used in the pilot study can be assessed as sufficiently good for the most part. Only three scales indicated some minor problems: (a) agency personality, (b) social interaction, and (c) proactive personality. First, some items of the agency personality scale were negatively related to the remaining scales. A closer inspection of the trouble-causing items of the agency personality scales did not reveal why these negative correlations occurred. It was decided neither to remove the items from the main study nor to rephrase them since they were selected from an already validated scale by Jacobi et al. (1986). In addition, it was not fully clear whether the negative correlations might have only been caused because of the small number of respondents in the pilot study. Only one of the observed negative correlations reached significance; the non-significant correlations cannot be assumed to be negative in the population. Second, item 5 of the social interaction scale ("I am looking to exchange information with external experts I come in touch with at work [e. g., doctors, pharmacists, or psychotherapists]") did not correlate with the other items of this scale as expected. However, no theoretical explanation could be found for this low correlation. It was decided to keep the item in the questionnaire since the exchange with other professional actors has been theoretically and empirically argued to be an important facet of deliberate social interaction at work (e. g., Estabrooks et al., 2005; Köpke et al., 2013; Spenceley et al., 2008; see also Chapter 5). Third, the first item of the proactive personality scale exhibited a very low correlation with the other items used for this scale. Because the proactive personality scale was composed only out of a subset of the whole scale proposed by Bateman and Crant (1993) it was decided to replace the first item with another one of the same scale that was thought to work better in the domain of geriatric care ("Nothing is more exciting than seeing my ideas turn into reality").

To sum up, the item and scale analysis conducted in this pilot test indicated that the employed scales could be used for the main study. However, at the same time, it should be emphasised that—because of the small sample size—only very basic indicators of their psychometric properties could be obtained. There is indeed a chance that the scales used might not withstand more elaborated evaluation based on statistical methods like exploratory or confirmatory factor analyses. Such analyses are conducted in the main study (see Chapter 7).

Bivariate correlations were used to test the relationships assumed in the advanced research model derived in Chapters 4 and 5. Because of the small sample size only medium to large correlations reached significance ($r > .43$). It was therefore decided to interpret the correlations mainly based on the effect size measure. Correlations below .10 were perceived as negligible. All in all, the correlations exhibited an expected pattern. All the agency facets were positively correlated to all agentic actions (small to large effect sizes). This speaks in favour of Hypotheses 1.1a, 1.1b, 1.2a, 1.2b, 1.3, and 1.4. In addition, all three facets positively correlated with the proactive personality scale (medium to large effect size). Almost all correlations between job autonomy, supervisor support and coworker support, as well as the agentic actions, were positive (small to medium effect sizes). This is first evidence for the accuracy of Hypotheses 3.1b, 3.2a, 3.2b, 3.3, 3.4, 3.5a, 3.5b, 3.5c, 3.5d, 3.6a, 3.6b, 3.6c, 3.6d, 3.7a, 3.8a, and 3.8b. However, deliberate job enlargement was negatively correlated both with job autonomy and coworker support. Both correlations speak against Hypotheses 3.1a and 3.5c. It will be interesting to see whether these results also hold in the main study. Time pressure was positively correlated with deliberate job enlargement, deliberate participation in institutionalised learning activities, and efforts to initiate constructive change at work (small to medium effect sizes). This gives evidence about the potential inaccuracy of Hypotheses 3.9a, 3.11, and 3.12. However, time pressure was negatively correlated with deliberate social interaction (medium effect size). This speaks in favour of Hypothesis 3.10a. These findings give first evidence that time pressure might affect nurses' engagement in different agentic actions differently.

Unfortunately, because of the small sample size none of the moderator hypotheses could be empirically tested.

To conclude, the direction as well as the effect size of most of these correlations supported the research model. In addition, assumed relationships that empirically hold can be interpreted as signs of construct validity. Nevertheless, it has to be emphasised that only a very small sample was available to calculate the correlations.

## 6.6 Chapter Summary

The main aim of this chapter was to develop a research design as well as a survey instrument that could be used to answer the research questions posed in Chapter 4. In addition, it was aimed to pilot test both the general research design as well as the scales used in the survey instrument.

The pilot test indicated that the planned study design was—in many parts—accepted by the participants and the employed scales exhibited sufficient psychometric qualities. However, the pilot test also resulted in a relatively low response rate as well as considerable problems with the chosen operationalisation of expertise. In addition, smaller problems with two other scales emerged. The correlation analyses provided evidence in favour of construct validity of the scales included in the survey instrument. Moreover, the analysis gave initial insights about the potential accuracy and/or inaccuracy of the hypotheses derived in Chapters 4 and 5.

Based on these insights the following implications for the main study of this thesis were derived: (a) introduction of a contest-based incentive system to increase the response rate, (b) replacement of the peer-nomination approach of measuring expertise with self-reporting measures, and (c) replacement of one item in the proactive personality scale. These implications were thought to increase the response rate by simultaneously reducing the number of missing values in the main study. In addition, the implications also aimed to obtain scales with improved psychometric characteristics.

# 7 Study 3: Work Agency and Its Effect on Expertise Development

This chapter describes the third and final study of this thesis. The main aim of this study is to test the hypotheses underlying the advanced research model derived in Chapters 4 and 5. This will be done by employing hypothesis-testing methods on data gathered in the domain of geriatric care nursing. The research approach of this study follows the design developed and pilot tested in the last chapter. However, based on the insights of the pilot test certain changes to the general study design—including the survey instrument—have been carried out (e. g., new expertise measure, incentive system). All changes will be described below.

Data analyses followed a cross-validation approach using structural equation modelling. In a first step, exploratory and confirmatory factor analyses (EFA and CFA) were used to test the psychometric quality of the survey instrument employed in this study. Based on the insights of these analyses a statistical model was constructed that allowed for testing of the hypothesised research model using partial least square structural equation modelling (PLS-SEM). These analyses were conducted using half of the data collected in this study (calibration sample). In a second step, both the CFA as well as the PLS-SEM were replicated in the second half of the dataset (validation sample). This procedure allowed for testing whether the hypothesised research model holds and whether the findings are robust across two different samples.

The chapter is structured as follows: Section 7.1 describes the methodological approach of this study including sampling, data collection, and analyses.

Section 7.2 then reports the most relevant findings of this study. These findings are discussed in Section 7.3. The chapter closes with a summary in Section 7.4.

## 7.1 Methodology

As foreshadowed, this study follows the general research approach developed in the last chapter. All data were gathered via self-administered paper-and-pencil questionnaires in the domain of geriatric care nursing. Although a longitudinal study design would have been more appropriate to answer the research questions only a cross-sectional study could be conducted. This was because of nursing homes' general unwillingness to participate in a two- or even three-wave study. In order to acquire sufficient nursing homes as well as subjects to participate in this research project a cross-sectional study design was judged to be acceptable. Although such a research design does not allow causal inferences concerning development processes to be drawn, it gives preliminary evidence of whether hypothesised relationships between different variables statistically exist (Bortz & Döring, 2006; Check & Schutt, 2012).

All statistical analyses were conducted with base R v3.2.5 (R Core Team, 2016) if not explicitly stated otherwise. All R packages used for data analyses will be separately mentioned.

This section describes the general methodological approach employed in this study. In a first step, Section 7.1.1 is concerned with the survey procedure as well as the sample characteristics. In a second step, the data entry, preparation, and screening procedure (Section 7.1.2) as well as the survey instrument (Section 7.1.3) are described. A more detailed description of the strategies used to analyse the obtained data can be found in Section 7.1.4.

### 7.1.1 Sample

After the pilot study all remaining 32 nursing homes were informed about the changes in the questionnaire as well as the introduction of the incentive scheme described at the end of Study 2. No objections concerning these changes were raised.

**Table 7.1.** Sample information.

| Nursing home | Population ($N$) | Sample ($n$) | Response rate |
|---|---|---|---|
| 1 | 125 | 76 | 60.80% |
| 2 | 76 | 39 | 51.32% |
| 3 | 79 | 27 | 34.18% |
| 4 | 76 | 40 | 52.63% |
| 5 | 67 | 27 | 40.30% |
| 6 | 28 | 17 | 60.71% |
| 7 | 120 | 34 | 28.33% |
| 8 | 48 | 20 | 41.67% |
| 9 | 56 | 45 | 80.36% |
| 10 | 23 | 18 | 78.26% |
| 11 | 68 | 51 | 75.00% |
| 12 | 22 | 14 | 63.64% |
| 13 | 43 | 7 | 16.28% |
| 14 | 68 | 10 | 14.71% |
| 15 | 70 | 36 | 51.43% |
| 16 | 62 | 38 | 61.29% |
| 17 | 64 | 17 | 26.56% |
| 18 | 42 | 20 | 47.62% |
| 19 | 60 | 35 | 58.33% |
| 20 | 48 | 33 | 68.75% |
| 21 | 100 | 44 | 44.00% |
| 22 | 21 | 13 | 61.90% |
| 23 | 77 | 56 | 72.73% |
| 24 | 48 | 6 | 12.50% |
| 25 | 40 | 25 | 62.50% |
| 26 | 39 | 31 | 79.49% |
| 27 | 56 | 8 | 14.29% |
| 28 | 40 | 13 | 32.50% |
| 29 | 55 | 18 | 32.73% |
| 30 | 52 | 10 | 19.23% |
| 31 | 52 | 30 | 57.69% |
| 32 | 57 | 51 | 89.47% |
| *Total* | *1 882* | *909* | *48.30%* |

Subsequently, all 32 nursing homes agreed to take part in the main study. Questionnaires were distributed to 1 882 employees and 909 employees returned completed questionnaires. This represents an overall response rate of 48.3%. The response rates for each nursing home can be found in Table 7.1. The data collection in each nursing home lasted 5.1 weeks on average (*Min* = 2, *Max* = 12) and took place during April to September 2014.

From these 909 geriatric care nurses, 88.9% were female. On average respondents were 41.3 years old (*SD* = 12.0) and had 12.7 years of work experience (*SD* = 9.7). Around 40% of the nurses worked part-time and 60% worked in full-time positions. Of the subjects in the sample, 54.2% worked as examined nurses. Only about 16% of the 1 882 nurses worked in a supervisory position.

The representativeness of the data was assessed using available data from the German Federal Employment Agency (2014) on the distribution of gender and qualification level (examined vs. non-examined nurses). In Germany, 86% of geriatric care nurses are female and 56% work as examined employees. The $\chi^2$ test showed a significant difference between the distribution of males and females in the population and the sample, $\chi^2(1, 598\,884) = 5.99$, $p = 0.014$, Cramer's $V = .003$. The test on differences regarding the qualification level, however, did not reach significance, $\chi^2(1, 456\,082) = 1.64$, *ns*, Cramer's $V = .002$. Strictly speaking, due to the significant result of the first test the sample in this study cannot be considered to be representative. However, the differences between the sample and the population are marginal. First, the test on the distribution of the qualification level does not show any differences between the sample and the population. Second, for both tests, Cramer's $V$ indicates very small effect sizes. Third, $\chi^2$ are very sensitive to large sample sizes. In other words, $\chi^2$ reaches significance even when the compared samples differ only slightly as long as the size of at least one sample is large (Hair, Black, et al., 2014). Since the participants in population numbered almost 600 000 individuals a significant result is not surprising here. It therefore follows that the sample does not substantially differ from the population in terms of gender and qualification level.

## 7.1.2 Data Entry, Preparation, and Screening

Data entry was managed by three student assistants and the author of this thesis. The first 220 questionnaires were entered by the author and later checked by one student assistant. The remaining cases were then entered by the same student assistant and checked by two others. All detected input errors (e. g., typographical errors) were manually corrected by the author. All negative items were recoded after data entry.

During data entry 14 atypical cases had to be removed. Cases were defined to be atypical if they met at least one of the following criteria: (a) respondents were not working as geriatric care nurses, (b) respondents did not take the survey seriously (e. g., by writing copious comments in the questionnaire), or (c) respondents predominantly indicated only certain scores on the rating scales (e. g., only 3s on a 1 to 5 rating scale). Another 16 cases had to be removed since more than 30% of values were missing. The final sample therefore consisted of 879 usable cases.

Missing data analysis on the final sample resulted in 2.2% missing values within the whole dataset. Missing values occurred in 49.9% of cases and each single variable was affected. Within the literature missing data is not seen as a problem for further analysis as long as the number of missing values does not exceed 5% for each variable as well as the dataset as a whole (e. g., Schendera, 2007; Tabachnick & Fidell, 2007). Only three variables within the socio-demographic part of the questionnaire reached this limit. Table 7.2 lists the variables and the according percentage of missing values. Because of the high count of missing values in these variables they were excluded from any further analyses.

**Table 7.2.** Variables with high percentage of missing values.

| Variable | Missing values |
|---|---|
| *Number of further education courses participated in the last year* | 19.1% |
| *Number of obtained further education certificates* | 7.4% |
| *Work experience at the current employer* | 5.9% |

The remaining missing values were treated with expectation maximisation (EM) imputation using the R package Amelia II v1.6.4 (Honaker, King, & Blackwell, 2011). Imputation is necessary since both confirmatory factor analyses with Satorra-Bentler correction as well as PLS-SEM, which was later employed (see Section 7.1.4), require complete data without any missing values. EM imputation was chosen because it is argued to be the superior technique even in cases where the pattern of missing data cannot be assumed to be completely at random (e. g., Hair, Black, et al., 2014). It was then investigated whether the imputed dataset differed significantly from the dataset with missing values regarding the socio-demographic variables reported above. No significant differences between the datasets could be found. Table 7.3 summarises the results of the significance tests. It can therefore be assumed that the imputation process did not significantly change the sample characteristics. All further analyses used the imputed dataset.

**Table 7.3.** Comparison of raw and imputed dataset.

| Variable | Test statistic | $p$ |
|---|---|---|
| *Gender* | $\chi^2(1, 1\,763) = 0.00$ | *ns* |
| *Age* | $W(909, 879) = 387\,263.00$ | *ns* |
| *Work experience* | $W(909, 879) = 379\,096.50$ | *ns* |
| *Working hours* | $\chi^2(2, 1\,761) = 0.25$ | *ns* |
| *Qualification level* | $\chi^2(1, 1\,761) = 0.03$ | *ns* |
| *Supervisor position* | $\chi^2(1, 1\,748) = 0.08$ | *ns* |

*Note.* $W$ = Wilcoxon rank-sum test statistic; *ns* = Not significant.

Both CFA and PLS-SEM assume that cases are independent from each other (see, e. g., Bowen & Guo, 2012, for a discussion). However, this assumption often does not hold for clustered data—that is, data where subsets of participants are grouped into some kind of higher level units (e. g., nurses in nursing homes). Non-independence occurs if participants of the same subset tend to have more similar characteristics than participants of different subsets and can easily lead to deflated standard errors that result in wrong *p* values using ordinary least square estimators (like PLS-SEM).

The severance of clustering within the dataset can be assessed using the intra-class correlation coefficient (*ICC*). The *ICC* measures how much variance within the dataset has to be attributed to the higher level unit. However, no clear guidelines exist for determining at what *ICC* a statistical adjustment (e. g., multilevel modelling) for the clustering effect is necessary. For example, V. E. Lee (2000) argues that adjusting for clustering effects might only be necessary if *ICC*s are above .10. Others (e. g., Kreft, 1996, in Bowen & Guo, 2012) argue that only *ICC*s greater than .25 require methods that take clustering into account. *ICC*s for all variables within the research model with nursing home affiliation as grouping variable were calculated using the R package multilevel v2.5 (Bliese, 2013). No *ICC* exceeded .10 ($M = .03$, $SD = 0.02$, $Min = .00$, $Max = .09$). It follows that the extent of clustering within the dataset was not expected to pose much of a problem for further analyses.

However, even small *ICC*s are capable of causing alpha inflation. Barcikowski (1981) estimated that an *ICC* of .05 results in a real alpha level of about .19 if the average number of observations with a cluster is about 25.[41] In order to compensate for such an effect it was decided to reduce the alpha level for this study to .01. Based on the results published by Barcikowski (1981) the alpha inflation would therefore lead to a real alpha level of about .04 and is therefore still below the standard value of .05.

Due to additional assumptions of CFA all variables included in the main research model were tested on multivariate normality. A Shapiro-Wilk multivariate test on normality was calculated using the R package mvnormtest v0.1-9 (Jarek, 2012). The test showed that the data cannot be assumed to be multivariate normally distributed, $W = 0.57$, $p < .01$. Implications of this finding for further data analysis will be discussed below.

### 7.1.3 Instrument

As already discussed, the survey instrument remained quite similar to the one used in Study 2. It still consisted of five distinct question parts: (a) socio-

41 The average number of observations within each group for this study was 28.4.

demographic information, (b) agency facets, (c) agentic actions, (d) organisational context factors, and (e) expertise measures including a preliminary briefing about the study, a short description of the questions, instructions on how to fill in the questionnaire, as well as a statement about the confidentiality and anonymity of the study. In addition, each questionnaire was accompanied by an envelope[42] as well as a note describing the newly introduced incentive system. More specifically, the note stated that within each nursing home the ward with the highest relative participation rate would receive a gift basket after the survey phase was completed. In small nursing homes where nurses' affiliation to their wards was not collected, the note promised a gift basket for all employees if the participation rate exceeded 70%.

Parts one to four of the survey instrument were essentially identical to the ones employed in the pilot test. Only the first item of the proactivity scale was replaced with another item that was thought to fit the domain of geriatric care nursing better (see Section 6.5). Table 7.4 presents a definition, a reference, and a sample item for each scale used in these parts.

Because of the findings of the pilot test reported in Chapter 6, it became necessary to discard the peer-nomination approach initially selected to measure expertise in part five of the survey instrument. As an alternative it was decided to use an approach that is solely based on self-reports. Self-reports require neither indication of one's own identity nor rating of other nurses. This new approach was hoped to be more accepted by the participants and therefore to result in both a higher participation rate and a smaller number of missing values in part five (see also Section 6.5).

42 Similarly to the pilot study, the questionnaire was to be placed and sealed into this envelope. The sealed envelope could then be put into a centrally located ballot box that was easily accessible for each participant.

**Table 7.4.** List of scales used in part two to four in the survey instrument.

| Scale | Definition | Sample item |
|---|---|---|
| *Agency competence* (self-developed; 10 items) | Individuals' ability to visualise desired future states, to set goals, translate these goals into actions, to engage in these actions, and to deal with potential problems that might occur. | "I find it easy to work towards my professional goals." |
| *Agency beliefs* (adapted from Schwarzer & Jerusalem, 1995; 10 items) | Individuals' perception of being able engage in goal-directed and self-initiated behaviour. | "I can solve most problems at work if I invest the necessary effort." |
| *Agency personality* (adapted from Jacobi et al., 1986; 10 items) | Individuals' predisposition or tendency to make choices and to engage in actions based on these choices to take control over their life and/or environment. | "At work I prefer to take on tasks where I am much in control over what I am doing and how I am doing it." |
| *Proactive personality* (adapted from Kaschube, 2003; Lang-von Wins & Triebel, 2005; 5 items) | "[R]elative stable tendency to effect environmental change." (Bateman & Crant, 1993, p. 103) | "I am always looking for better ways to do things." |
| *Deliberate job enlargement* (adapted from Tims et al., 2012; 5 items) | All efforts that increase the scope of a nurses daily job by adding new tasks. | "I regularly take on extra tasks even though I do not receive extra salary for them." |

*Continued on next page*

Table 7.4 – *Continued from previous page*

| Scale | Definition | Sample item |
| --- | --- | --- |
| *Deliberate job enrichment* (self-developed; 5 items) | All efforts to take over additional responsibilities from supervisors or other individuals on a higher hierarchical level. | "I try to take on such tasks at work that provide me with much decision latitude." |
| *Deliberate social interaction* (adapted from Tims et al., 2012; 5 items) | All efforts to obtain work-related information from other individuals. | "I discuss problems and difficult cases with my coworkers." |
| *Deliberate enquiry of codified information* (self-developed; 5 items) | All efforts to obtain work-related information from impersonal information resources. | "In order to keep up to date in regard to developments in the domain of geriatric care I often deliberately read professional literature." |
| *Deliberate participation in institutionalised learning activities* (self-developed; 5 items) | All efforts to participate in institutionalised learning activities related to professional learning and development. | "I am proactively discussing my further education needs with my employer or supervisor." |
| *Deliberate efforts to initiate constructive change at work* (adapted from Morrison & Phelps, 1999; 5 items) | All efforts to initiate change at work that constructively affects organisational procedures or structures. | "I often try to bring about improved procedures for the work unit or department." |

*Continued on next page*

Table 7.4 – *Continued from previous page*

| Scale | Definition | Sample item |
|---|---|---|
| *Job autonomy* (adapted from Stegmann et al., 2010; 6 items) | The "degree to which the job provides substantial freedom, independence, and discretion to the employee in scheduling the work and in determining the procedures to be used in carrying it out" (Hackman & Oldham, 1975, p. 162) | "The job gives me a chance to use my personal initiative or judgement in carrying out the work." |
| *Supervisor support* (self-developed; 6 items) | Supervisors' general openness for personal initiative as well as their tendency to encourage and assist employees to act agentically. | "If I want to bring in new ideas at work I get supported from my supervisors." |
| *Coworker support* (self-developed; 6 items) | Coworkers' general openness for personal initiative as well as their tendency to encourage and assist employees to act agentically. | "My coworkers encourage me to bring in new ideas into work." |
| *Time pressure* (adapted from Semmer et al., 1999; 6 items) | The subjective experience of having not enough time to complete the assigned work tasks. | "Because of too much work I either miss or postpone breaks." |

Unfortunately, no existing self-reporting scale measuring expertise in the domain of geriatric care nursing could be found. However, a literature research revealed the Nurse Competence Scale (NCS). The NCS aims to measure subjects' abilities to deal with the whole range of tasks and problems in the domain of general nursing. These tasks and problems are divided into seven distinct areas of expertise: (a) help and care, (b) giving advice, (c) diagnostic functions, (d) handling emergency situations, (e) assuring high-quality medical treatment, (f) cooperation, and (g) coaching and teaching. The scale was originally developed by Meretoja, Isoaho, and Leino-Kilpi (2004) based on expertise research conducted by Benner (1984) and later adapted to the German nursing context by Martin, Sugarman, and Hickinbottom (2010) as well as again by Girbig and Bauer (2011). Only the adaptation by Girbig and Bauer (2011) has been adequately documented in the literature.

The original version of Meretoja et al.'s (2004) scale was reported to comply sufficiently with psychometric quality standards whereby Müller (2013) questioned the psychometric properties of the scale translated by Martin et al. (2010). Information about the psychometric quality of the German NCS translated by Girbig and Bauer (2011) does not exist. Because of the insufficient documentation as well as the questionable psychometric properties of the NCS translation by Martin et al. (2010), it was decided to use the German NCS version developed by Girbig and Bauer (2011).

Because the NCS was originally developed for general nurses working in hospitals it was decided to adapt the scale to the geriatric care nursing context. In cooperation with one head nurse as well as one experienced geriatric care nurse now working as a nurse trainer, each item was investigated for whether it could be used for this study. All items that did not represent the domain of geriatric care nursing were removed from the scale (15 of the original 57 items, e. g., "Co-ordinating multidisciplinary team's nursing activities"). In addition, the term "patient" was replaced with the word "resident" in all items. Apart from that, only one item had to be changed: Instead of speaking only about "consequences of illnesses" in item 3 of the giving advice dimension the phrase "consequences of illnesses and ageing" was inserted.

Within the survey instrument of this study each nurse was asked to assess how well she could deal with the situation described in each single item. In line with Meretoja et al. (2004) as well as Girbig and Bauer (2011), a 7-point Likert scale was used as the answer format (1 = *Not at all* and 7 = *Very well*). The number of items for each expertise area as well as one sample item can be found in Table 7.5. The full set of items can be found in Appendix E.

Because the psychometric quality of the adapted NCS could not be investigated in a pilot test (and was not psychometrically tested in previous studies) another scale was developed to measure expertise in the domain of geriatric care nursing. This scale used five items to measure how often other team mem-

**Table 7.5.** Expertise areas measured in the NCS including the number of items and a sample item.

| Scale | No. of items | Sample item |
|---|---|---|
| *Help and care* | 9 | "Planning resident care according to individual needs." |
| *Giving advice* | 5 | "Supporting residents to cope with consequences of illnesses and ageing." |
| *Diagnostic functions* | 6 | "Analysing patient's well-being from many perspectives (e. g., care, nutrition, mobility, housing)." |
| *Handling emergency situations* | 3 | "Recognising situations posing a threat to life early." |
| *Assuring high-quality medical treatment* | 6 | "Check procedures for their medical and care-related safety." |
| *Cooperation* | 9 | "Recognising colleagues' need for support and help." |
| *Coaching and teaching* | 9 | "Coaching others in duties within my responsibility area." |

bers ask the respondent for advice and help concerning work-related problems and challenging situations. Based on the findings of Study 1 this can be interpreted as an indicator of expertise. Individuals who are more often asked for advice and help at work should have more expertise than individuals who are not asked as often. A sample item of this scale is "When coworkers need advice or want to discuss a problem, they come more often to me than to others" (the full set of items can be found in Appendix E). Respondents could answer these items on a 5-point Likert scale (1 = *Do not agree at all* and 5 = *Fully agree*).

This scale is referred to as "Expertise (Advice-seeking)" in the following discussions.

## 7.1.4 Data Analyses

### 7.1.4.1 General Considerations

To test the proposed research model and, therefore, the derived hypotheses, a structural equation modelling (SEM) approach was employed. SEM allows simultaneous estimation and investigation of a set of complex dependency relationships (e. g., mediation and moderation) between different variables of interest. Such a set of relationships between variables is usually referred to as a structural model. Another important characteristic of SEM is its capacity to incorporate unobserved latent constructs that are operationalised based on particular manifest indicator variables. Thus, SEM explicitly allows for specification of a measurement model that defines the correspondence between latent constructs and observed indicator variables (Hair, Black, et al., 2014; Tabachnick & Fidell, 2007). Since the proposed research model assumes multiple relationships between latent constructs that are measured using manifest indicator variables, SEM is an appropriate method for this study.

Two different techniques for estimating structural equation models exist:

1. *Covariance-based SEM (CB-SEM):* This approach is often described as a combination of factor analysis and multiple regression that uses the covariance structure between all observed variables as a starting point. CB-SEM aims to derive a hypothetical covariance matrix between all observed variables that is theoretically implied by the structure of the research model. All relevant model parameters (e. g., path coefficients between two latent variables) are estimated in such a way that the difference between this hypothetical (or model-implied) covariance matrix and the observed (or data-implied) covariance is minimised. The most common procedure for this is the maximum likelihood (ML) method. Unfortunately, this estimation method is only efficient and unbiased if the underlying data come from a multivariate normal distribution. Distribution-free estimation methods (e. g., ADF) also exist but require very large data sets (e. g., more than 5 000 cases) (Hu,

Bentler, & Kano, 1992; Kline, 2011). A more feasible approach for dealing with non-normality is to use correction methods and robust standard errors (Kline, 2011; Satorra & Bentler, 1994). After the estimation procedure CB-SEM allows the model adequacy to be examined by comparing the differences between the model-implied and the observed covariance matrix. Several fit indices can be provided to assess the model validity (e. g., CFI, see Section 7.1.4.3) based on this comparison. Another advantage of CB-SEM is that measurement errors of the latent constructs can be taken into account. This way more accurate parameter estimates for the structural model can be calculated (Hair, Black, et al., 2014; Hair, Ringle, & Sarstedt, 2011; Kline, 2011).

2. *Variance-based SEM or partial least squares SEM (PLS-SEM):* PLS-SEM is an alternative approach to estimating hypothesised relationships in a structural equation model (see Esposito Vinzi, Chin, Henseler, & Wang, 2010, or Hair, Hult, et al., 2014, for an overview of this analysis technique). This approach is based on ordinary least squares regression and exploits all available data to estimate path relationships. Its main goal is to find path coefficients that maximise the explained variance ($R^2$) of all endogenous constructs (i. e., all variables in the model that are explained through other variables). A main advantage of PLS-SEM is that the data are not required to stem from a (multivariate) normal distribution. Significance tests are based on bootstrapping. Furthermore, PLS-SEM is argued to have higher levels of statistical power to detect significant relationships between variables if they exist in the population (Hair, Hult, et al., 2014). Yet another advantage is that PLS-SEM allows incorporation of both lower order and higher order formative constructs which cannot be achieved simply with CB-SEM. However, two important disadvantages have also to be noted. First, PLS-SEM is not able to correct for measurement errors. This drawback results in the problem that parameters for the measurement model are typically overestimated, while the parameter estimates for the structural models are usually underestimated. This issue is known as PLS-bias. Second, no accepted fit index exists that allows for assessment of the global model adequacy similar to CB-SEM. A goodness-of-fit index (*GoF*) was proposed (Tenenhaus, Am-

ato, & Vinzi, 2004; Tenenhaus, Vinzi, Chatelin, & Lauro, 2005) but is also currently highly debated (Henseler & Sarstedt, 2013). The current literature advocates avoiding its use (Hair, Hult, et al., 2014; Henseler & Sarstedt, 2013). Nevertheless, the adequacy of the estimated model can still be evaluated using the explained variances ($R^2$) of the endogenous variables, the significance of hypothesised path coefficients, and effect size measures ($f^2$) (Chin, 2010; Hair, Hult, et al., 2014; Hair et al., 2011).

Although CB-SEM and PLS-SEM are conceptually and mathematically quite different, simulation studies show that both methods often result in very similar path estimates (e. g., Reinartz, Haenlein, & Henseler, 2009). The choice in favour or against one of these methods is argued to be based on both theoretical and model-building reasons: CB-SEM should be used when the main goal is to test an established theory and a global goodness-of-fit criterion is required. The use of PLS-SEM is suggested if the research is more aimed at theory development and/or if formative constructs are part of the model (Hair, Hult, et al., 2014; Hair et al., 2011; Reinartz et al., 2009).

This study is a first attempt to quantitatively investigate the relationship between work agency and expertise. Although the research model was based on theoretical considerations, such a task has still to be characterised as exploratory in nature. Furthermore, work agency has been operationalised as a second-order formative construct in this study (see Chapter 6 as well as Figure 7.2 in Section 7.1.4.4). Both reasons therefore speak strongly in favour of the PLS-SEM approach. However, the PLS-SEM approach is still prone to so-called PLS-bias. An overestimation of the measurement model might give wrong evidence about the quality of the measurement instrument. It was therefore decided to additionally conduct a CFA to adequately assess how well the indicator variables used measure the latent constructs. CFA uses CB-SEM and is therefore not prone to any PLS bias. Furthermore, the CB-SEM approach is able to investigate the quality of the instrument using global goodness-of-fit criteria (Bühner, 2011; Hair, Black, et al., 2014). To sum up, this study uses CFA (i. e., CB-SEM) to test the hypothesised measurement model and PLS-SEM to test the hypothesised structural model. This combination allows for exploitation of the advantages of both approaches by—similarly—avoiding their disadvantages.

To validate the robustness of SEM findings, a cross-validation approach has been proposed (e. g., Bagozzi & Yi, 1988; Bowen & Guo, 2012). Cross validation is a technique to investigate whether a model estimated based on a certain sample can be replicated in another independent sample from the same population (Bagozzi & Yi, 1988). The sample used in the first step is called the calibration sample. The second dataset used is called the validation sample. A research model is claimed to be robust if it reaches adequate fit and features similar parameter estimates both in the calibration and the validation sample (Bowen & Guo, 2012).

Furthermore, a cross-validation approach allows the calibration sample for preliminary item and scale analyses to be used. This is especially important since the sample size of the pilot study (see Study 2) was too small to investigate the quality of the instrument using elaborated techniques like EFA. In addition, new scales were introduced in the survey instrument that have not been analysed in regard of their psychometric qualities at all.

EFA is a technique that tries to "examine the underlying patterns or relationships for a large number of variables and to determine whether the information can be condensed or summarized in a smaller set of factors" (Hair, Black, et al., 2014, p. 89). EFA is especially useful for investigating whether the different items used in a newly developed questionnaire adequately represent a set of theoretically assumed constructs (Henson, 2006). Based on the results of the EFA, items that do not meet certain quality standards (see Section 7.1.4.2) can be removed in order to increase the psychometric properties of the instrument in use. However, testing the adequacy of the revised instrument using CFA in a new sample has been highly recommended (e. g., Cabrera-Nguyen, 2010). This study follows this suggestion. An EFA was used to revise the measurement model using the calibration sample. Based on the results of the EFA a CFA was then run using data from both the calibration and the validation sample, respectively.

The final sample of 879 cases was split in half using a random selection procedure. From each of the 32 participating nursing homes half of the employees were randomly[43] selected to create the calibration sample ($n_A = 432$). The remaining employees then built up the validation sample ($n_B = 447$). This procedure allowed the original data to be subset in a way that both the variance between the nursing homes as well as the variance within each nursing home was equally reflected in both subsamples. The following sections give more detail about the analysis procedure as well as criteria for interpretation of the results of these analyses.

#### 7.1.4.2 Exploratory Factor Analyses

EFA was used to identify those items that most adequately represent the theoretical constructs of the proposed research model. Furthermore, it was employed to investigate the assumed unidimensionality of each scale used in the questionnaire.

Different factor extraction methods exist within the EFA framework (e. g., principal component analysis, principal factor analysis, maximum likelihood). It was decided to use principal factor analysis (PFA) because it takes measurement errors into account and is therefore especially recommended if the goal is to extract latent factors behind a battery of measured variables (Conway & Huffcutt, 2003; Fabrigar, Wegener, MacCallum, & Strahan, 1999). Another advantage of PFA is that it does not require data to be normally distributed (Schmitt, 2011). Since the underlying factors are not assumed to be orthogonal (i. e., statistically uncorrelated) an oblique rotation method (Promax; Hendrickson & White, 1964) was applied. The number of retained factors was selected based on the MAP test (O'connor, 2000; Velicer, 1976) as well as the scree test (Cattell, 1966). Both Bartlett's test ($p < .05$) and the Kaiser-Meyer-Olkin measure of sampling adequacy criterion ($MSA > .50$, but better above .70) were employed to test whether the underlying data structure was adequate to use EFA (see Hair, Black, et al., 2014; Kaiser, 1974).

Unidimensionality is assumed if all items of one scale only load on a single theoretical latent factor (Hair, Black, et al., 2014). Items with cross loadings (loadings on more than one factor with a loading above .32; Tabachnick &

43 The splitting and random sampling was done with the R package sampling v2.6 (Tillé & Matei, 2013).

Fidell, 2007) as well as loadings below .40 were, therefore, excluded from any further analysis. Cronbach's $\alpha$ was used as an additional measure of unidimensionality of the scales. $\alpha$ should be above .70 (Hair, Black, et al., 2014).

Four different EFAs for each individual model part (agency dimensions, agentic actions, organisational context factors, and expertise measures) were calculated using the R package psych v1.5.8 (Revelle, 2015). This way the factor structure of the conceptually most similar items could be analysed in a very compact way. Since a CFA was later employed to test the whole measurement model it was decided not to run a single EFA on all items at once. In addition, the research model assumes strong correlations between the variables of the different model parts. A single EFA might therefore result in a factor structure with several cross loadings that are only due to high correlations between the latent constructs and not the items as such. These cross loadings, however, might then falsely indicate psychometric problems with the affected scales.

#### 7.1.4.3 Confirmatory Factor Analyses

CFA was employed to confirm the fit of the measurement model used in this study. To ensure the overidentification of the model estimated with CFA the loading of the first indicator of each latent variable was fixed to one. This resulted in a final model with 501 free parameters to estimate and 8 679 degrees of freedom. The model is therefore overidentified.

The ratio of indicators to latent variables in the hypothesised measurement model is $s = 135/22 = 6.14$. Westland (2010) recommends a sample size of at least $n = 50s^2 - 450s + 1100$ based on simulation results of Marsh and colleagues (Marsh, Balla, & Hau, 1996; Marsh, Balla, & McDonald, 1988; Marsh, Hau, Balla, & Grayson, 1998). In the case of this study the equation results in a minimum sample size of 222 which is far below the size of each subsample. It can therefore be concluded that the sample size requirements to estimate CFA models using the two subsets was met.

As described above, the data used in this study cannot be assumed to come from a multivariate normal distribution. It was therefore decided to employ robust ML estimation with Satorra-Bentler $\chi^2$ correction (Satorra & Bentler, 1994), robust standard errors, and scaled fit indices. This procedure is usually recommended if data are not normally distributed (Curran, West, & Finch, 1996; Finney & DiStefano, 2006; Kline, 2011; Tabachnick & Fidell, 2007). All calculations were conducted with the R package lavaan v0.5.20 (Rosseel, 2012) and semTools v0.4-11 (semTools Contributors, 2016).

**Convergent Validity.** Convergent validity describes to what extent the manifest items of a latent variable can all be assumed to measure the same thing. In other words, do the items within scale share a high proportion of common variance (Hair, Black, et al., 2014)? To empirically test this criterion both the factor loadings ($\lambda$) of the CFA model as well as the construct reliabilities were investigated. First, factor loadings should be higher than .50 or, ideally, even higher than .70 (Hair, Black, et al., 2014). Second, construct reliabilities should be .70 and higher. However, construct reliabilities between .60 and .70 may also be acceptable (Hair, Black, et al., 2014). Coefficient $\omega$ (Raykov, 2001) was used to estimate construct reliabilities.

**Discriminant Validity.** Discriminant validity describes to what extent the measured constructs are empirically distinct from each other (Hair, Black, et al., 2014). The Fornell-Larcker criterion (Fornell & Larcker, 1981) was used to assess this requirement. This criterion proposes that the average variance extracted (*AVE*) for any two latent variables should be higher than the square of their correlation. The rationale behind this requirement is that each latent variable should share more variance with its items than it shares with any other latent construct.

**Global Model Diagnostics.** As argued before, CFA provides several fit indices that can be used to assess the overall quality of the measurement model. In accordance with the literature (Beauducel & Wittmann, 2005; Hair, Black, et al., 2014; Kline, 2011) a range of different fit indices are presented in this study to investigate different model fit aspects: (a) $\chi^2$ with $p$ value, (b) $\chi^2/df$, (c) *CFI*, (d) *RMSEA* with confidence interval (*CI*), and (e) *SRMR*.

The deviance between the observed and the model implied covariance matrix is measured by $\chi^2$. The larger the $\chi^2$ the worse the model fit; $\chi^2$ can be used to test whether a significant difference exists between the proposed model and the data. However, this test is very sensitive both for models with a high number of indicators as well as large datasets (i. e., $n > 250$; Bowen & Guo, 2012; Hair, Black, et al., 2014; Tabachnick & Fidell, 2007). It is therefore recommended to use additional fit indices. The normed $\chi^2$ ($\chi^2/df$) sets the obtained $\chi^2$ in relation to the degrees of freedom of the model in question (i. e., of the mathematical information available to estimate the model). The smaller the normed $\chi^2$ the better the model fit. The comparative fit index (*CFI*) measures how well the proposed model fits the data in comparison to a null model where all observed variables are assumed to be uncorrelated (Hair, Black, et al., 2014). A large *CFI* is desirable. The root mean square error of approximation (*RMSEA*) investigates how similar the observed and the model-implied covariance matrix are, taking the model complexity and the sample size into account. The smaller the *RMSEA* the better the model fit. The standardised root mean square residual (*SRMR*) is a measure for the "average differences between the sample variances and covariances and the estimated population variances and covariances" (Tabachnick & Fidell, 2007, p. 720). Small *SRMR* values indicate a good fit. Table 7.6 depicts recommended cut-off values for each of the described fit indices (Bowen & Guo, 2012; Hair, Black, et al., 2014; Tabachnick & Fidell, 2007). The presented cut-off values were used as criteria to evaluate the model fit.

**Table 7.6.** Measurement model fit evaluation criteria: Fit indices and cut-off values.

| | | Recommended cut-off | |
|---|---|---|---|
| Fit index | Possible range | Acceptable fit | Good fit |
| $\chi^2$ | $0 - \infty$ | As small as possible | Not significant |
| $\chi^2/df$ | $0 - \infty$ | $< 3.00$ | $< 2.00$ |
| *CFI* | $0 - 1$ | $> 0.90$ | $> 0.95$ |
| *RMSEA* | $0 - 1$ | $< 0.07$ | $< 0.05$ |
| *SRMR* | $0 - 1$ | $< 0.08$ | $< 0.05$ |

*Note. df* = Degrees of freedom; *CFI* = Comparative fit index; *RMSEA* = Root mean square of error approximation; *SRMR* = Standardised root mean square residual.

**Common Method Variance.** All constructs within the research model of this thesis were measured using self-reports within a single questionnaire. It was therefore necessary to test whether common method variance posed problems. Common method variance describes the phenomenon that variance within the dataset cannot only be attributed to either the latent constructs of interest or random measurement error but also to the measurement method itself (D. T. Campbell & Fiske, 1959; Podsakoff, MacKenzie, Lee, & Podsakoff, 2003). In other words, the shared variance between two variables in the dataset might exist only because both variables were measured via a single method. Such a systematic error variance might then cause common method bias. Common method bias describes the phenomenon that estimated parameters (e. g., correlations between predictor and criterion variables) might strongly diverge from real parameters in the population (Doty & Glick, 1998; Podsakoff et al., 2003). Both the inflation and deflation of parameter estimates is possible (Doty & Glick, 1998; Williams & Brown, 1994).

Common method variance can be explained through different psychological processes that affect respondents' questionnaire completion (see for an overview: Podsakoff et al., 2003). For instance, individuals might want to answer all items consistently, might have implicit theories about the relationships of certain variables, might answer in a socially desired manner, or might tend to answer all items either with high or low ratings (acquiescence). In cases where no assumptions about the source of a possible method bias exist, Podsakoff et al. (2003) recommend the use of the single-common-method-factor approach to diagnose and control for common method bias.

The single-common-method factor approach is based on the estimation and comparison of four different measurement models (Williams, Cote, & Buckley, 1989; see also: Widaman, 1985, and for a similar application, Facteau, Dobbins, Russell, Ladd, & Kudisch, 1995). Model 1 is the null model where all indicators (i. e., items) are uncorrelated and no latent factors are specified. Within Model 2, all indicators load on one single-method factor. This means that Model 2 assumes that a single-method factor explains all variance within the data. Model 3 is the original measurement model based on the conceptual research model of this study. Model 4 is similar to Model 3 but it additionally introduces the single-method factor from Model 2. The correlation between the method factor and all other latent constructs is set to zero. Model 4 assumes that not only the hypothesised factor structure of the measurement model accounts for variance in the data but also a common method factor. All models are separately estimated and compared using CFA. If Model 2 fits the data better than Model 1, and Model 4 fits better than Model 3, the existence of common method variance can be assumed. The fit of each of the four models is assessed using the fit indices described above as well as Cohen's $w$ as effect sizes measure.[44] Cohen's $w$ of about .10 will be interpreted as small, .30 as medium, and .50 as large (Bortz & Döring, 2006). Figure 7.1 depicts the four models (please note that for illustration purpose only two hypothesised latent factors each with three indicators are included in the figure.).

The use of CFA also allows for estimation of how much of the variance within the dataset can be attributed to the assumed factor structure, the common method factor, as well as unsystematic measurement error (see Facteau et al., 1995; Widaman, 1985; Williams et al., 1989). Model 4 was used for this calculation. To calculate the variance attributed to the hypothesised factor structure the loadings of all items on their corresponding latent factor are squared, summed, and then divided by the number of items. Similarly, the variance attributed to the common method factor is calculated by squaring and summing the respective items loadings and dividing by the number of items. The unique variance that can be attributed neither to the factor structure nor the common method factors is calculated by subtracting both prior estimated variances from one. Based on a prior study (Williams et al., 1989), some authors argue that common method bias does not cause too much problem as long as the variance accounted for by the common method factor is below 25%–30% (e. g., Facteau et al., 1995).[45]

#### 7.1.4.4 PLS Modelling

**Model Specification.** As described in Section 6.2.1 in the previous chapter, work agency is defined as a composite index based on three facets: agency com-

44 $w = \sqrt{\Delta\chi^2/(n \cdot \Delta df)}$ whereby $\Delta\chi^2 = |\chi_1^2 - \chi_2^2|$, $n$ = sample size, and $\Delta df = |df_1 - df_2|$.

45 See Richardson, Simmering, and Sturman (2009) for a critical discussion of the whole common method variance detection issue.

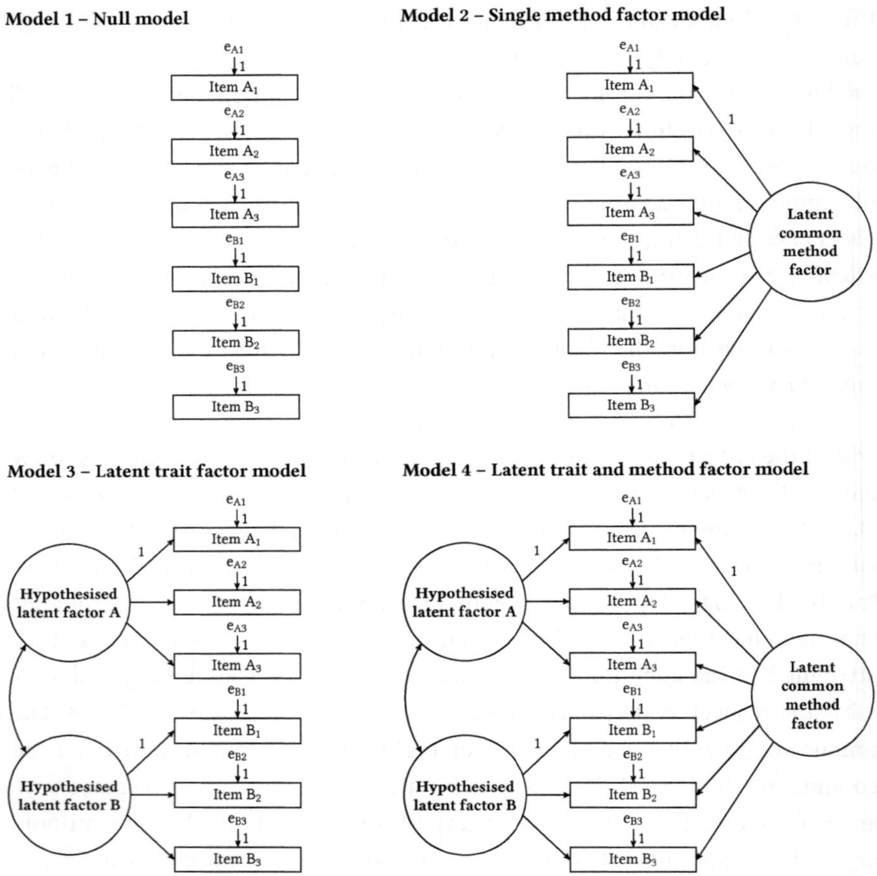


**Figure 7.1.** Models estimated to diagnose common method variance. Model 1 depicts the null model where all items are uncorrelated. Model 2 shows the single-method factor model where all items load on one single latent common method factor. In the latent trait factor model (Model 3) all items load on their theoretically derived latent trait factor. Model 4 is a combination of models two and three where all items load on their related latent trait factor and on a latent common method factor. All hypothesised latent trait factors are allowed to correlate. Measurement errors are abbreviated with e. Reprinted and adapted from "Williams, L. J., Cote, J. A., & Buckley, M. R. (1989). Lack of method variance in self-reported affect and perceptions at work: Reality or artifact? *Journal of Applied Psychology, 74*(3), 462–468, p. 464" with permission from APA.

petence, agency beliefs, and agency personality. These three facets are understood to capture different aspects of work agency and therefore constitute—or in other words, cause—the construct of interest. Within the SEM context such constructs are referred to as second-order hierarchical latent variables that follow the reflective-formative model (Becker et al., 2012; Jarvis et al., 2003). In such models, the second-order construct (work agency in the case of this thesis) is operationalised as a latent formative variable constituted by different reflectively measured latent first-order constructs (agency competence, agency beliefs, and agency personality in this study). Figure 7.2 depicts the relationship between the first-order and second-order constructs.

Three different approaches to model hierarchical latent variables exist within the PLS framework (Becker et al., 2012; Lohmöller, 1989; Wetzels, Odekerken-Schröder, & van Oppen, 2009): (a) the repeated indicator approach, (b) the two-stage approach, and (c) the hybrid approach. The repeated indicator method specifies the second-order construct as a linear function of all manifest indicator variables used for the underlying first-order constructs. This means that the manifest indicator variables of the first-order constructs are used twice to measure the latent second-order construct. The two-stage approach estimates the latent variables' scores of the first-order construct in a first-stage model that does not contain the higher order construct. Those scores are then used in the second-stage model as manifest indicators of the second-order construct. The hybrid method splits the manifest indicators for each first-order construct in half and uses the first half to estimate the first-order constructs and the second half for the higher order construct. It was decided to use the repeated indicator approach in this study because it estimates all constructs simultaneously and thereby takes the whole nomological network into account (Becker et al., 2012).

The repeated indicator approach can be implemented in two different ways. The manifest indicators of the higher order construct can be assigned using either a formative or a reflective mode (Becker et al., 2012; Hair, Hult, et al., 2014). Based on a simulation study, Becker et al. (2012) strongly recommend using the repeated indicator approach with formative measurement mode on the higher order construct for reflective-formative hierarchical models. They argue that this approach leads to less biased parameter estimates and more reliable higher order scores. It was decided to follow their suggestion. Figure 7.2 depicts the measurement approach used in this study.

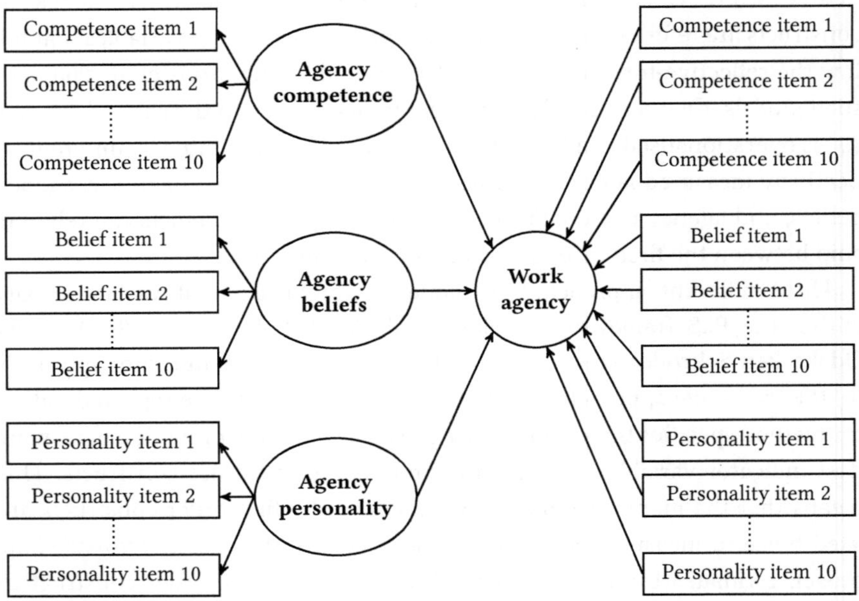


**Figure 7.2.** Formative second-order measurement model of work agency based on repeated indicator approach.

A possible disadvantage of the repeated indicator approach has to be noted. The number of indicators should be similar across the lower order constructs. The estimated weights for the lower order constructs on the higher order construct might otherwise be severely biased (Becker et al., 2012; Hair, Hult, et al., 2014). Although all three facets are measured with 10 manifest indicators, this bias can still occur if certain items have to be eliminated from their scale because of their psychometric properties. In such cases item parcelling (see Little et al., 2002) might be an appropriate strategy to adjust the number of items.

Because the hypothesised research model contains a formative higher order construct, all moderators were modelled using the two-stage approach (Hair, Hult, et al., 2014; Henseler & Chin, 2010; Henseler & Fassott, 2010): In a first step, the research model was estimated without the moderators (i. e., main effect model only). In a second step, the latent factor scores of all included variables were extracted from the estimated main effect model. A new indicator—in other words an interaction term—for each moderator was built by multiplying the latent factor score of the corresponding exogenous variable with the latent factor score of the corresponding moderator variable. This newly obtained moderator indicator was then used as an additional predictor for the endogenous variable. For instance, in order to model that job autonomy moderates the relationship between work agency and deliberate job enlargement, the factor scores of work agency and job autonomy were multiplied. This moderator variable (referred to as "work agency * job autonomy") was then included in a new model as an additional predictor of deliberate job enlargement. All other variables were measured by means of their extracted latent factor scores obtained in step one. The estimated standardised path coefficient of the moderator variable then indicated the strength of the moderation effect.

Following the recommendation of Hair, Hult, et al. (2014) as well as Becker et al. (2012), the path weighting scheme was applied to estimate the structural model. It is argued to be the most appropriate weighting scheme for models containing higher order constructs. Bootstrapping with 5 000 resamples was applied to test whether path coefficients, factor loadings, and outer weights[46] were significantly different from zero.

PLS does not require data to be normally distributed. Furthermore, sample size requirements are less strict than for CB-SEM estimation. Hair, Black, et al. (2014) propose that the required sample size can be determined by means of power analyses (e. g., Cohen, 1992) focussing on the part of the model with the highest number of manifest or latent antecedents. In this study, due to the repeated indicator approach with formative measurement mode, the highest number of antecedents was 30. Using R's pwr package v1.1-3 (Champely, 2015) a minimum sample size of 321 was determined to achieve a statistical power

46 Outer weights represent how strongly the different indicators of a formative construct define their construct. In other words, weights are the equivalent of factor loadings in the case of reflective measures. Mathematically, they can be interpreted as standardised regression coefficients ($\beta$).

of 80% for detecting $R^2$ values of at least .10 on a significance level of 1%.[47] The minimum sample size requirement was therefore met for both subsamples.

The structural equation model tested with PLS-SEM included all hypothesised relationships described in the final research model depicted in Figure 5.1 in Chapter 5. In addition, work experience in years was included in all analyses as a global control variable. In other words, work experience was modelled as a direct predictor of each other variable included in the structural equation model. Unfortunately, neither work experience at the current place of employment nor the number of further education courses could be used as additional control variables. Both variables had to be excluded from any further analysis because of a high percentage of missing values (see Section 7.1.2).

PLS estimation was done with the R package plspm v0.4.7 (Sanchez, Trinchera, & Russolillo, 2015).

**Evaluation of the PLS Measurement Model.** Similarly to the evaluation of a CFA (see above) the convergent validity (based on the factor loadings and construct reliability) and discriminant validity (based on the Fornell-Larcker criterion) were investigated for each reflective measurement model (Hair, Hult, et al., 2014) used in this study. However, due to the PLS bias the results from the CFA are the more strict and conservative ones. Since both convergent and discriminant validity could already be established, deviant evaluation results were not expected.

Hair, Hult, et al. (2014) proposed checking whether the newly introduced formative construct (work agency) exhibits convergent validity (see also Chin, 1998a). Convergent validity is said to be established if the formative construct highly ($\beta > .80$) and significantly relates to a reflective measurement that is thought to measure something similar or something identical. The shortened proactive personality scale was chosen as a suitable reflective measure to perform this analysis.

Additionally, the formative measurement model of work agency had to be checked for collinearity of its latent indicators. Collinearity can easily lead to

47 $R^2 = .10$ was chosen because the absolute average correlation between all exogenous and endogenous model variables in the pilot study was $r = .34$ (see Chapter 6). This average correlation is the equivalent of $R^2 = .12$.

inflated standard errors as well as incorrectly estimated (outer) weights. To assess the level of collinearity between the three facets of work agency the corresponding variance inflation factors (*VIF*) were calculated. *VIF*s below 5 are perceived as acceptable (Hair, Black, et al., 2014; Hair, Hult, et al., 2014).

Furthermore, it was necessary to check the significance and the relevance of the outer weights of the formative measurement model (Hair, Hult, et al., 2014). If the outer weights significantly differ from zero ($p < .05$) they are said to significantly contribute to the formation of the formative construct. The sizes of the weights can then be used to derive information about the relative contribution of each agency facet to the formation of the latent work agency construct. The facet with the highest outer weight contributes the most to the work agency construct.

**Evaluation of the Structural Model.** To assess how well the theoretical research models fit the empirical data the structural model had to be evaluated. This evaluation included (a) the assessment of the significance and the size of the path coefficients between predictor and criterion variables, (b) the assessment of the $R^2$ values of each endogenous variable, and (c) the assessment of partial effect sizes $f^2$ (Chin, 2010; Hair, Hult, et al., 2014).

Before these evaluation steps, the structural model had also to be checked for collinearity (Hair, Hult, et al., 2014). For each endogenous variable within the structural model the *VIF* for all corresponding predictors were calculated. The same criterion applies as described above (i. e., $VIF < 5$).

Within the structural model the standardised path coefficients ($\beta$) represent the empirically estimated relationship between two latent variables (Chin, 2010; Hair, Hult, et al., 2014). The standardised path coefficient can vary between $-1$ and $+1$. A $\beta$ close to $+1$ represents a strong positive linear relationship between both variables. Vice versa, a $\beta$ close to $-1$ represents a strong negative linear relationship between two variables. A $\beta$ close to zero represents a non-existing linear relationship. No acknowledged effect size categorisation exists for standardised path coefficients. In this thesis $\beta$ larger than .10 are interpreted as meaningful. To test whether the estimated standardised path coefficients differ significantly from zero a bootstrapping procedure was applied (see above; one-tailed tests).

In a next step, the coefficient of determination ($R^2$) of each endogenous variable was calculated and interpreted. This coefficient represents the amount of variance of an endogenous variable that is explained by all its corresponding exogenous variables in the model. In other words, the coefficient explains how much variation of the endogenous variable can be predicted by all linked exogenous variables. $R^2$ ranges from 0 to 1. The higher $R^2$ the more variance is explained. The percentage of unexplained variance of the endogenous variable can be calculated as follows: $100 \cdot (1 - R^2)$. Cohen (1988) defines $R^2$s of .02, .13, and .26, respectively, as small, medium, and large.[48] However, Chin (1998b) as well as Hair, Hult, et al. (2014) use far stricter effect size definitions. Chin (1998b) describes $R^2$ of .19 as small, .33 as medium, and .66 as large effects. Hair, Hult, et al. (2014) use .25, .50, and .75 as corresponding thresholds. At the same time, Hair, Hult, et al. (2014) remark that especially in scientific disciplines that are concerned with human behaviour, $R^2$ of .20 might already be considered as high. Here Götz, Liehr-Gobbers, and Krafft (2010) opinion is followed that a generalisable effect size characterisation of $R^2$ does not exist and strongly depends on the individual study. Within the proposed research model only a small number of possible predictors were included for each endogenous variable. High $R^2$ are therefore not expected. $R^2$ that exceed .20 will be perceived as being substantial.

In addition to the coefficient of determination, the calculation of partial $f^2$ effect sizes gives information about whether a single variable or a set of variables has or have substantive impact on an endogenous construct of interest. Partial $f^2$ is defined as $(R^2_{incl} - R^2_{excl})/(1 - R^2_{incl})$; whereby $R^2_{incl}$ denotes the coefficient of determination that is based on all linked predictor variables and $R^2_{excl}$ is the coefficient of determination with the set of selected predictor variables excluded from the model (Hair, Hult, et al., 2014). Based on Cohen (1988), $f^2$s of .02, .15, and .35 can be characterised as small, medium, and large effect sizes, respectively.

**Cross Validation.** As described in Section 7.1.4.1 the evaluation of the measurement and the structural model were first performed with the calibration

48 Based on the relationship $f^2 = R^2/(1 - R^2)$ (see also Bortz & Schuster, 2010).

sample. The validation sample was then used to check whether the obtained path coefficients as well as the $R^2$ values could be replicated in an independent dataset.

Multigroup analysis based on the resampling parametric approach (e. g., Hair, Hult, et al., 2014; Sanchez, 2013) was used to test whether the standardised path coefficients estimated in the calibration and the validation sample significantly differed from each other. This approach estimates the standardised path coefficients for both samples, then uses bootstrapping to calculate standard error estimates (5 000 resamples), and finally calculates a two-tailed *t* value for each compared path coefficient. This *t* value is then used to obtain a corresponding *p* value (Hair, Hult, et al., 2014; Sanchez, 2013).

## 7.2 Findings

The main findings of Study 3 are reported in this section. The focus is principally on answering the research questions posed in Chapter 4. For this purpose, Section 7.2.1 reports on the psychometric quality of the survey instrument used in this study. Initially, the results of the EFAs are described (Section 7.2.1.1). At the second step, a CFA is conducted and reported. Both analyses are based upon the calibration sample (Section 7.2.1.2). The results of the CFA are then cross validated using the validation sample (Section 7.2.1.3). After the psychometric quality of the measurement model has been established, PLS-SEM analysis are conducted and described in Section 7.2.2. After a short assessment of the PLS-based measurement model (Section 7.2.2.1) the structural research model is tested both in the calibration and the validation sample (Section 7.2.2.2). The results are then statistically compared in Section 7.2.2.3.

### 7.2.1 Measurement Model

#### 7.2.1.1 Exploratory Factor Analyses

As described above, four different PFAs for each model part (agency facets, agentic actions, organisational context factors, and expertise measures), as well as the proactive personality measure were calculated. However, before the factor structure could be analysed it had to be tested whether the data were suitable for performing PFAs in the first place. Table 7.7 shows the results of Bartlett's test and Kaiser-Meyer-Olkin measures of sampling adequacy criterion for each single calculated PFA.

**Table 7.7.** Results of Bartlett's test and the Kaiser-Meyer-Olkin measure of sampling adequacy criterion.

| Model part | *p* | *MSA* |
|---|---|---|
| *Agency facets* | < .001 | .91 |
| *Agentic actions* | < .001 | .88 |
| *Organisational context factors* | < .001 | .93 |
| *Expertise measures* | | |
| Advice seeking | < .001 | .81 |
| Nurse competence scale | < .001 | .96 |
| *Proactivity measure* | < .001 | .61 |

*Note.* *p* = *p* value of Bartlett's test; *MSA* = Overall measure of sampling adequacy.

As can be seen, Bartlett's test reached significance ($p < .001$) for all tested constructs. The *MSA* values were all above the proposed cut-off value (> .50 or even > .70). In other words, the correlation pattern among the included items in the measurement model indicated that the data could be used to calculate PFAs.

In a next step, a PFA for each model part was calculated using all items that were intended to operationalise the theoretical constructs included in the particular model part. If necessary, this first PFA was used to exclude items with high cross loading as well as items with loadings below .40.[49] Based on the set of items retained, the MAP test and the scree test were used to determine the appropriate number of factors. A second PFA was calculated to further investigate the factor structure based on the number of factors indicated by both the MAP and the scree test.

49 The first PFA was calculated using the number of theoretical underlying constructs as the number of factors to extract.

**Agency Facets.** The first PFA indicated that five items (agency beliefs 1, agency personality 4, agency personality 7, agency personality 9, and agency personality 10) had to be excluded from any further analysis because their factor loadings were below .40. After removing these items, both the scree test and the MAP test confirmed the theoretically assumed three-factor solution. The factor loadings of the second PFA can be found in Table 7.8. As can be seen, the empirical factor structure resembles the theoretical item-construct association quite well. All three factors explain 46% of the items' original variance.

**Table 7.8.** Factor loadings for PFA with Promax rotation of the agency facets scales.

| Item | FA1 | FA2 | FA3 |
|---|---|---|---|
| Agency competence 1 | **.75** | −.14 | .04 |
| Agency competence 2 | **.84** | −.06 | −.07 |
| Agency competence 3 | **.84** | −.08 | −.06 |
| Agency competence 4 | **.55** | .11 | −.15 |
| Agency competence 5 | **.72** | .10 | −.12 |
| Agency competence 6 | **.65** | .01 | .03 |
| Agency competence 7 | **.81** | −.07 | .01 |
| Agency competence 8 | **.81** | −.07 | .06 |
| Agency competence 9 | **.60** | .08 | .11 |
| Agency competence 10 | **.58** | .03 | .25 |
| Agency beliefs 2 | .23 | **.41** | −.05 |
| Agency beliefs 3 | .24 | **.40** | −.05 |
| Agency beliefs 4 | −.14 | **.79** | .00 |
| Agency beliefs 5 | −.10 | **.80** | −.04 |
| Agency beliefs 6 | −.09 | **.76** | .03 |
| Agency beliefs 7 | −.13 | **.80** | .06 |
| Agency beliefs 8 | .09 | **.67** | .00 |
| Agency beliefs 9 | .06 | **.70** | −.01 |
| Agency beliefs 10 | .14 | **.53** | .09 |
| Agency personality 1 | .09 | .08 | **.49** |
| Agency personality 2 | −.01 | −.06 | **.71** |

*Continued on next page*

Table 7.8 – *Continued from previous page*

| Item | FA1 | FA2 | FA3 |
|---|---|---|---|
| Agency personality 3 | −.01 | .00 | **.63** |
| Agency personality 5 | −.10 | .10 | **.66** |
| Agency personality 6 | .04 | .09 | **.54** |
| Agency personality 8 | −.05 | −.13 | **.49** |
| *Explained variance* | *.21* | *.16* | *.09* |

*Note.* FA1–FA3 = Extracted factors; Factor loadings ≥ .40 are in boldface.

**Agentic Actions.** All together six items (social interaction 2, social interaction 4, social interaction 5, institutionalised learning activities 1, institutionalised learning activities 3, and job enrichment 1) had to be excluded from any further analysis because either their factor loadings were below .40 or cross loadings were above .32 in the first PFA. After removing these items, both the scree test and the MAP test confirmed a six-factor solution. The obtained pattern matrix with all factor loadings can be found in Table 7.9. All items load on their theoretical construct. Only one item (institutionalised learning activities 2) has a loading of only .39. However, because the threshold of .40 was almost met it was decided to not exclude the item. In total all six factors explain 60% of the items' original variance.

**Table 7.9.** Factor loadings for PFA with Promax rotation of the agentic action scales.

| Item | FA1 | FA2 | FA3 | FA4 | FA5 | FA6 |
|---|---|---|---|---|---|---|
| Social interaction 1 | −.09 | .01 | .03 | .00 | −.01 | **.73** |
| Social interaction 3 | .08 | −.07 | −.02 | −.03 | .00 | **.82** |
| Codified information 1 | .10 | **.56** | .01 | .02 | −.03 | .05 |
| Codified information 2 | −.02 | **.84** | −.02 | .05 | −.04 | −.07 |
| Codified information 3 | −.01 | **.83** | .10 | −.08 | −.10 | −.03 |
| Codified information 4 | .05 | **.50** | −.05 | −.02 | .11 | .08 |
| Codified information 5 | −.06 | **.89** | −.03 | .03 | .07 | .00 |

*Continued on next page*

Table 7.9 – *Continued from previous page*

| Item | FA1 | FA2 | FA3 | FA4 | FA5 | FA6 |
|---|---|---|---|---|---|---|
| Inst. learning activities 2 | .05 | .12 | .08 | −.01 | **.39** | −.01 |
| Inst. learning activities 4 | −.12 | −.01 | −.02 | .01 | **1.01** | .00 |
| Inst. learning activities 5 | .12 | −.04 | −.02 | .00 | **.77** | −.01 |
| Job enlargement 1 | −.03 | −.02 | **.65** | −.06 | .17 | .04 |
| Job enlargement 2 | .05 | .00 | **.66** | .04 | .14 | −.01 |
| Job enlargement 3 | .01 | .02 | **.84** | −.04 | −.07 | −.01 |
| Job enlargement 4 | .00 | −.01 | **.74** | .01 | −.09 | −.02 |
| Job enlargement 5 | .00 | .04 | **.71** | .10 | −.09 | .03 |
| Job enrichment 2 | .05 | −.05 | .09 | **.52** | .00 | .07 |
| Job enrichment 3 | −.11 | −.01 | .10 | **.83** | −.06 | −.05 |
| Job enrichment 4 | −.07 | .01 | .00 | **.82** | .06 | −.01 |
| Job enrichment 5 | .21 | .03 | −.15 | **.69** | .03 | .02 |
| Constructive change 1 | **.86** | −.01 | .00 | −.05 | −.08 | .10 |
| Constructive change 2 | **.80** | .04 | −.05 | .07 | −.04 | .02 |
| Constructive change 3 | **.78** | −.08 | .12 | −.04 | .06 | −.04 |
| Constructive change 4 | **.93** | −.01 | −.02 | −.05 | −.02 | .00 |
| Constructive change 5 | **.76** | −.02 | .05 | .04 | −.03 | −.09 |
| *Explained variance* | *.15* | *.12* | *.11* | *.09* | *.08* | *.05* |

*Note.* FA1–FA6 = Extracted factors; Factor loadings ≥ .40 are in boldface. Please note that factor loadings above 1.00 are not uncommon for correlated (oblique) factors (see Jöreskog, 1999).

**Organisational Context Factors.** Three items had to be excluded based on the first PFA that investigated the factor structure within the items measuring organisational context factors. Items "job autonomy 4", "job autonomy 5", and "job autonomy 6" exhibited cross loadings ($\lambda > .40$) with the factor representing supervisor support. After those items were excluded the MAP and the scree test confirmed the theorised four-factor solution. The factor loadings of this solution can be found in Table 7.10. All four factors account for 75% of the included items' original variance.

**Table 7.10.** Factor loadings for PFA with Promax rotation of the organisational context factor scales.

| Item | FA1 | FA2 | FA3 | FA4 |
|---|---|---|---|---|
| Autonomy 1 | .04 | .02 | −.01 | **.73** |
| Autonomy 2 | −.03 | .01 | .01 | **.97** |
| Autonomy 3 | .01 | −.01 | −.01 | **.87** |
| Supervisor support 1 | **.81** | −.01 | .01 | .04 |
| Supervisor support 2 | **.92** | .01 | .02 | −.02 |
| Supervisor support 3 | **.95** | .01 | .04 | −.03 |
| Supervisor support 4 | **.89** | .00 | −.05 | −.01 |
| Supervisor support 5 | **.94** | −.01 | .00 | .01 |
| Supervisor support 6 | **.92** | −.01 | −.02 | .00 |
| Coworker support 1 | .16 | **.72** | .04 | .00 |
| Coworker support 2 | −.02 | **.90** | −.02 | .04 |
| Coworker support 3 | −.06 | **.93** | .00 | .03 |
| Coworker support 4 | .04 | **.91** | −.04 | −.04 |
| Coworker support 5 | −.03 | **.97** | .02 | −.01 |
| Coworker support 6 | .00 | **.93** | .01 | .00 |
| Time pressure 1 | −.02 | .00 | **.79** | −.02 |
| Time pressure 2 | .04 | .05 | **.82** | −.06 |
| Time pressure 3 | −.01 | .04 | **.78** | −.02 |
| Time pressure 4 | .01 | −.04 | **.78** | .08 |
| Time pressure 5 | −.03 | −.07 | **.76** | .04 |
| *Explained variance* | *.25* | *.24* | *.15* | *.11* |

*Note.* FA1–FA4 = Extracted factors; Factor loadings ≥ .40 are in boldface.

**Expertise Measure (Advice Seeking).** The first PFA for this expertise measure resulted in the factor structure that is depicted in Table 7.11. Both the MAP and the scree test confirm the assumed unidimensionality of this scale. The extracted factor accounts for 57% of the five items' original variance.

**Table 7.11.** Factor loadings for PFA with Promax rotation of the expertise (advice seeking) scale.

| Item | FA1 |
|---|---|
| Expertise (advice seeking) 1 | **.70** |
| Expertise (advice seeking) 2 | **.76** |
| Expertise (advice seeking) 3 | **.84** |
| Expertise (advice seeking) 4 | **.78** |
| Expertise (advice seeking) 5 | **.69** |
| *Explained variance* | *.57* |

*Note.* FA1 = Extracted factor; Factor loadings ≥ .40 are in boldface.

**Expertise Measure (CNS).** The first PFA on the competence nursing scale did not resemble the assumed seven-factor structure. Several items exhibited severe cross loadings. For example, three of the giving advice items loaded on factor one and six items loaded on factor three. Furthermore, eight other items (help and care 3, help and care 4, help and care 6, diagnostic functions 3, diagnostic functions 4, diagnostic functions 5, diagnostic functions 6, cooperation 7) simultaneously loaded on at least two factors. After removing the cross-loading items the MAP test indicated a four-factor solution. The scree test could not be unambiguously interpreted. The second PFA was therefore calculated based on a predefined four-factor structure indicated by the MAP test. The factor loadings of this solution can be found in Table 7.12. In a first step, all problematic items had to be identified. Item "help and care 7" and "coaching and teaching 3" cross loaded on more than one factor and were removed from any further interpretation and analysis. Both items "help and care 1" and "help and care 2" did not sufficiently load on any factor and therefore were also removed. In a second step, the new factor structure had to be interpreted. As can be seen, all remaining coaching and teaching items load on factor 4, the majority of the cooperation items load on factor 3, and all assuring high-quality medical treatment items load on factor 2. These three factors can therefore be interpreted as coaching and teaching facet (FA4), cooperation facet (FA3), and assuring high-quality medical treatment facet (FA1), respectively. The items "cooperation 1" and "cooperation 8" both strongly load on factor 2. Because those items did not match the description of the assuring high-quality medical treatment scale it was decided to remove them from any further analyses. The remaining 10 items all load on factor 1. The items are mainly concerned with core duties of medical care within the geriatric care context. It was therefore decided to interpret the first factor as core medical care expertise facet. The extracted factors account for 70% of the items' original variance.

**Table 7.12.** Factor loadings for PFA with Promax rotation of the CNS scales.

| Item | FA1 | FA2 | FA3 | FA4 |
|---|---|---|---|---|
| Help and care 1 | .17 | .30 | .19 | .04 |
| Help and care 2 | .29 | **.33** | .08 | .02 |
| Help and care 5 | **.54** | .07 | .26 | −.12 |
| Help and care 7 | **.65** | −.31 | **.33** | −.03 |
| Help and care 8 | **.77** | −.12 | .10 | .02 |
| Help and care 9 | **.76** | −.20 | .15 | .04 |
| Giving advice 3 | **.61** | −.02 | .14 | .06 |
| Giving advice 4 | **.65** | −.02 | .09 | .06 |
| Handling emergency situations 1 | **.84** | .20 | −.17 | −.07 |
| Handling emergency situations 2 | **.90** | .11 | −.15 | −.08 |
| Handling emergency situations 3 | **.83** | .26 | −.29 | .05 |
| Diagnostic functions 1 | **.73** | .13 | .03 | −.03 |
| Diagnostic functions 2 | **.61** | .31 | −.17 | .06 |
| Assuring high-quality medical treatment 1 | .15 | **.83** | −.17 | .05 |
| Assuring high-quality medical treatment 2 | −.10 | **.81** | .10 | .02 |
| Assuring high-quality medical treatment 3 | .03 | **.83** | .07 | −.02 |
| Assuring high-quality medical treatment 4 | −.15 | **.89** | .19 | −.10 |
| Assuring high-quality medical treatment 5 | .22 | **.63** | .06 | −.04 |
| Assuring high-quality medical treatment 6 | .23 | **.64** | −.06 | .03 |
| Cooperation 1 | .14 | **.53** | .28 | −.01 |
| Cooperation 2 | −.05 | −.07 | **.86** | −.02 |
| Cooperation 3 | −.19 | .16 | **.95** | −.18 |
| Cooperation 4 | −.06 | −.01 | **.83** | .03 |
| Cooperation 5 | .12 | .07 | **.58** | .01 |

*Continued on next page*

Table 7.12 – *Continued from previous page*

| Item | FA1 | FA2 | FA3 | FA4 |
|---|---|---|---|---|
| Cooperation 6 | .09 | .04 | **.58** | .11 |
| Cooperation 8 | .07 | **.50** | .19 | .13 |
| Cooperation 9 | −.01 | .14 | **.44** | .30 |
| Coaching and teaching 1 | −.07 | −.06 | −.04 | **1.00** |
| Coaching and teaching 2 | .05 | .06 | −.11 | **.88** |
| Coaching and teaching 3 | −.08 | **.32** | −.10 | **.74** |
| Coaching and teaching 4 | .09 | −.14 | .14 | **.77** |
| *Explained variance* | *.22* | *.19* | *.19* | *.10* |

*Note.* FA1–FA4 = Extracted factors; Factor loadings ≥ .40 are in boldface. Please note that factor loadings above 1.00 are not uncommon for correlated (oblique) factors (see Jöreskog, 1999).

**Proactive Personality.** The first PFA calculated on the proactive personality scale resulted in a factor structure where two items did not reach the factor loading threshold of .40 (proactive personality 1, proactive personality 2). Both the scree and the MAP test including the remaining three items indicated the appropriateness of a single-factor solution. The item loadings of the second PFA can be found in Table 7.13. The factor accounts for 35% of the items' original variance.

**Table 7.13.** Factor loadings for PFA with Promax rotation of the proactive personality scale.

| Item | FA1 |
|---|---|
| Proactive personality 3 | **.50** |
| Proactive personality 4 | **.76** |
| Proactive personality 5 | **.48** |
| *Explained variance* | *.35* |

*Note.* FA1 = Extracted factor; Factor loadings ≥ .40 are in boldface.

To sum up, based on the exploratory factor analyses a range of items had to be excluded from any further analysis and interpretation. However, the first evidence in favour of the unidimensionality of each scale used in this study could be found after these items were excluded.

Only two items remained in the "social interaction" scale. The minimum recommended number of items to measure latent constructs is three within the CFA framework (e. g., Hair, Black, et al., 2014; Hinkin, 1998). Constructs measured with fewer than three items often cause estimation problems (Kline, 2011). Because of this it was decided to exclude the social interaction scale from any further analysis.

In addition to the EFA results, Table 7.14 gives further information about each scale. As can be seen, α is above .70 for each scale but proactive personality (α = .59). Based on this new information the psychometric quality of the proactive personality scale had to be severely questioned. It was therefore decided to exclude this scale from any subsequent analysis.

**Table 7.14.** Descriptive and reliability statistics for each scale included in the model (calibration sample).

| | | | Range | | | |
|---|---|---|---|---|---|---|
| Scale | Items | α | Potential | Actual | *M* | *SD* |
| *Agency* | | | | | | |
| Agency competence | 10 | .91 | 1-5 | 1.0-5 | 3.6 | 0.67 |
| Agency beliefs | 9 | .88 | 1-5 | 1.7-5 | 3.8 | 0.63 |
| Agency personality | 6 | .76 | 1-5 | 1.0-5 | 3.3 | 0.75 |
| *Agentic actions* | | | | | | |
| Job enlargement | 5 | .85 | 1-5 | 1.0-5 | 3.3 | 0.95 |
| Job enrichment | 4 | .82 | 1-5 | 1.0-5 | 3.1 | 1.05 |
| Codified information | 5 | .85 | 1-5 | 1.0-5 | 3.3 | 0.97 |
| Inst. learning activities | 3 | .77 | 1-5 | 1.0-5 | 3.5 | 1.11 |
| Constructive change | 5 | .91 | 1-5 | 1.0-5 | 3.3 | 0.96 |

*Continued on next page*

Table 7.14 – *Continued from previous page*

| Scale | Items | α | Range Potential | Range Actual | *M* | *SD* |
|---|---|---|---|---|---|---|
| *Organisational characteristics* | | | | | | |
| Job autonomy | 3 | .90 | 1-5 | 1.0-5 | 3.4 | 1.06 |
| Supervisor support | 6 | .96 | 1-5 | 1.0-5 | 3.4 | 1.07 |
| Coworker support | 6 | .96 | 1-5 | 1.0-5 | 3.5 | 0.96 |
| Time pressure | 5 | .89 | 1-5 | 1.0-5 | 3.8 | 1.03 |
| *Expertise* | | | | | | |
| Expertise (advise seeking) | 5 | .87 | 1-5 | 1.0-5 | 3.5 | 0.83 |
| Core medical care facet | 10 | .94 | 1-7 | 1.3-7 | 5.7 | 0.99 |
| Cooperation facet | 6 | .89 | 1-7 | 1.5-7 | 5.7 | 0.95 |
| Quality management facet | 6 | .93 | 1-7 | 1.0-7 | 5.1 | 1.34 |
| Coaching and teaching facet | 3 | .90 | 1-7 | 1.0-7 | 5.1 | 1.47 |
| *Other scales* | | | | | | |
| Proactive personality | 3 | .59 | 1-5 | 1.0-5 | 3.6 | 0.77 |

*Note.* α = Standardised Cronbach's alpha; *M* = Mean; *SD* = Standard deviation.

The number of items of the agency facets (agency competence, agency beliefs, agency personality) is not equal any more. An equal number of indicators, however, is necessary to obtain correctly estimated path coefficients in the later employed PLS-SEM (see Section 7.1.4.4). To reestablish this requirement a randomised item-parcelling approach was implemented (see Little et al., 2002). An item parcel was calculated as the average of two randomly selected items that belong to a single scale (Kishton & Widaman, 1994).[50] To obtain exactly five indicators for each scale, five parcels, four parcels, and one parcel had to be calculated for the agency competence facet, the agency beliefs facet, and the agency personality facet, respectively. All remaining items were used as non-parcelled indicators. The newly obtained indicator structure can be found in Table 7.15.

50 For instance, agency beliefs parcel 1 = $\frac{\text{agency beliefs 4+agency beliefs 10}}{2}$.

**Table 7.15.** Indicator structure of latent agency facets.

| Scale | Parcelled | Items |
|---|---|---|
| *Agency competence* | | |
| Indicator 1 | Yes | Agency competence 5, Agency competence 6 |
| Indicator 2 | Yes | Agency competence 2, Agency competence 7 |
| Indicator 3 | Yes | Agency competence 3, Agency competence 10 |
| Indicator 4 | Yes | Agency competence 1, Agency competence 4 |
| Indicator 5 | Yes | Agency competence 8, Agency competence 9 |
| *Agency beliefs* | | |
| Indicator 1 | Yes | Agency beliefs 4, Agency beliefs 10 |
| Indicator 2 | Yes | Agency beliefs 5, Agency beliefs 7 |
| Indicator 3 | Yes | Agency beliefs 2, Agency beliefs 6 |
| Indicator 4 | Yes | Agency beliefs 8, Agency beliefs 9 |
| Indicator 5 | No | Agency beliefs 3 |
| *Agency personality* | | |
| Indicator 1 | Yes | Agency personality 3, Agency personality 6 |
| Indicator 2 | No | Agency personality 1 |
| Indicator 3 | No | Agency personality 2 |
| Indicator 4 | No | Agency personality 5 |
| Indicator 5 | No | Agency personality 8 |

#### 7.2.1.2 Confirmatory Factor Analyses

In a next step, it was tested whether the measurement model fits the data from the calibration sample using confirmatory factor analysis. The tested measurement model was derived based on the insights from the EFA. This means that, first, only those items that supported the assumed factor structure in the EFA were included in the model. Second, the factor-item relationship of the nursing competence scale was also based upon the findings of the EFA presented above and not the original factor structure. Third, all three agency facets were measured with parcelled items. Because correlations between the latent constructs were thought to be plausible they were not constrained to zero. The new model has 312 free parameters to estimate and 3 604 degrees of freedom. The model is therefore overidentified.

The CFA model converged normally and all estimated parameters appeared to be plausible. The fit indices indicated only a moderate model fit, $\chi^2(3\,604) = 6\,073.91$, $p < .001$, $\chi^2/df = 1.69$, $CFI = .893$, $RMSEA = .040$ with 90% $CI = .038–.041$, $SRMR = .051$. All factor loadings significantly differed from zero. However, the item "agency personality 8" had a loading of only .39. Twelve items had a loading between .50 and .70. The remaining 76 items all had loadings above .70 (see Appendix F for a detailed list of all factors loadings).

Because the *CFI* indicated a poor fit the empirical modification indices (*MI*) were investigated to identify possible measurement model misspecifications. *MI*s above 50 are considered to be substantial. The *MI*s indicated that the model fit would improve substantially if the error terms of 21 different items were allowed to covary.[51] This finding gives evidence that the affected items share variance that is not yet explained by the theoretical factor structure specified in the measurement model. Since only items within their respective scale are affected (i. e., no items between different scales) this finding speaks against unidimensionality of the underlying factor. Evidence against unidimensionality can especially be found for the NCS: 15 of the 21 affected items stem from this scale. Due to this finding it was decided to exclude the NCS from any further analyses. For all other affected item pairs, it was decided to exclude the item of each correlated pair with the smallest factor loading from any further analysis.

In addition, the item "agency personality 8" was removed because of its small factor loading ($\lambda = .39$). This had the advantage that it was not necessary any more to parcel indicator 1 of this scale (see Table 7.15). Both items "agency personality 3" and "agency personality 6" could now separately be included in the measurement model of the agency personality facet.

51 The following items are affected: "constructive change 1" and "constructive change 2", "time pressure 3" and "time pressure 4", "expertise (advice seeking) 1" and "expertise (advice seeking) 2", "help and care 8" as well as "help and care 9", "giving advice 3" and "giving advice 4", "handling emergency situations 1" and "handling emergency situations 2", "handling emergency situations 2" and "handling emergency situations 3", "cooperation 2" and "cooperation 3", "cooperation 5" and "cooperation 6", "assuring high-quality medical treatment 5" and "assuring high-quality medical treatment 6", as well as "coaching and teaching 1" and "coaching and teaching 2".

Based on the changes just described a new CFA was calculated. Figure 7.3 depicts a graphical representation of the estimated model. The new model has 169 free parameters to estimate and 1 574 degrees of freedom. The model is therefore overidentified. Again, the CFA converged normally and estimated parameters were in order. The fit indices improved substantially and now indicated a good model fit, $\chi^2(1\,574) = 2\,256.58$, $p < .001$, $\chi^2/df = 1.43$, $CFI = .95$, $RMSEA = .032$ with 90% $CI = .029–.034$, $SRMR = .047$. All factor loadings within this model reached significance and were above .50: 14 items have a loading between .50 and .70, while the remaining 45 items have loadings above .70 (a list of all factor loadings can be found in Appendix G). Furthermore, all construct reliabilities are above .70 (see Table 7.16).

Within the next step discriminant validity of the measured constructs was assessed. Table 7.16 shows the latent factor correlations in the lower left triangle as well as the square root of *AVE* on the diagonal. The square root of each factor's *AVE* is higher than its highest correlation with any other factor. The Fornell-Larcker criterion therefore provides evidence in favour of the latent constructs' discriminant validity.

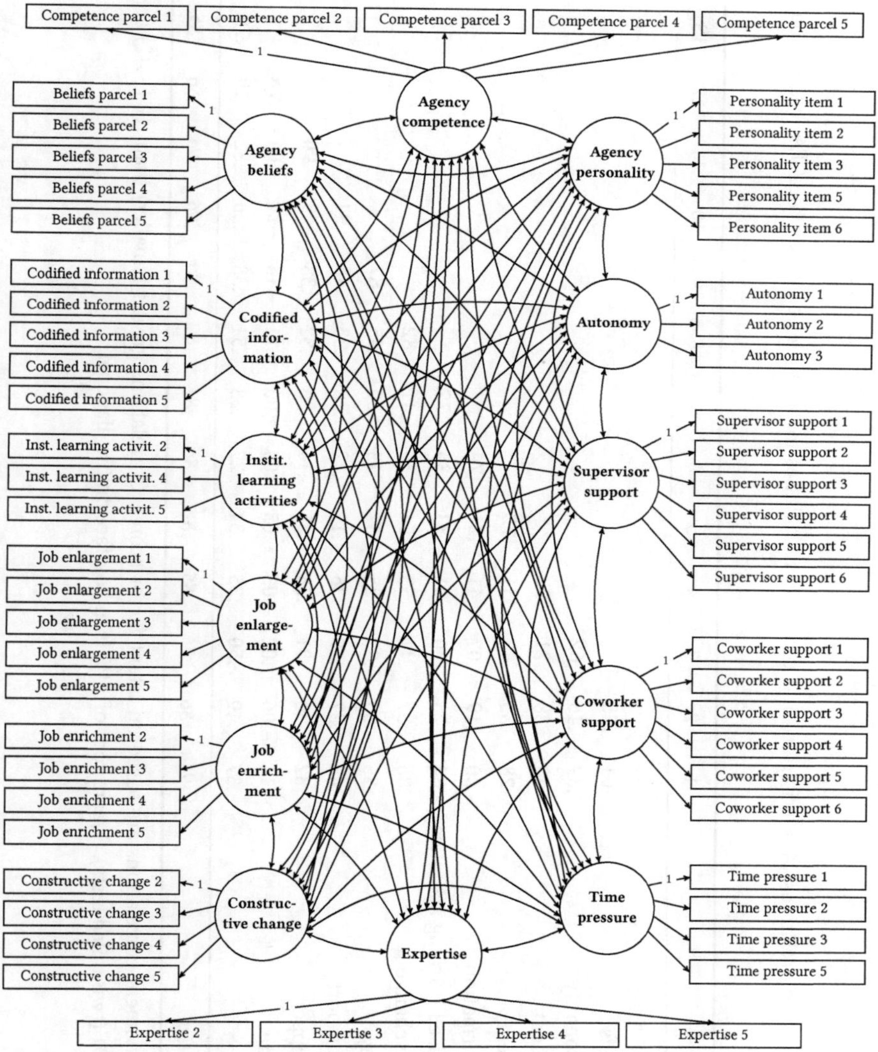


**Figure 7.3.** Hypothesised measurement model containing all scales later used in the PLS analysis. Latent variables are depicted as ellipses and observed indicators are shown as rectangles. Please note that the error terms of the observed indicators are not included in the figure. Each latent factor is allowed to correlate with all other latent factors included in the model.

**Table 7.16.** Inter-factor correlations, *AVE* criterion, and construct reliabilities for all scales based on the CFA (calibration sample).

| | Measure | 1 | 2 | 3 | 4 | 5 | 6 | 7 | 8 | 9 | 10 | 11 | 12 | 13 |
|---|---|---|---|---|---|---|---|---|---|---|---|---|---|---|
| 1 | Agency competence | **.82** | | | | | | | | | | | | |
| 2 | Agency beliefs | .64 | **.75** | | | | | | | | | | | |
| 3 | Agency personality | .39 | .46 | **.62** | | | | | | | | | | |
| 4 | Job enlargement | .40 | .38 | .21 | **.73** | | | | | | | | | |
| 5 | Job enrichment | .28 | .33 | .42 | .51 | **.73** | | | | | | | | |
| 6 | Codified information | .30 | .19 | .07 | .41 | .21 | **.74** | | | | | | | |
| 7 | Institutionalised learning activities | .34 | .25 | .30 | .51 | .33 | .35 | **.77** | | | | | | |
| 8 | Constructive change | .36 | .37 | .41 | .53 | .54 | .39 | .41 | **.82** | | | | | |
| 9 | Job autonomy | .35 | .35 | .37 | .25 | .32 | .15 | .29 | .45 | **.87** | | | | |
| 10 | Supervisor support | .41 | .27 | .19 | .36 | .19 | .22 | .28 | .33 | .48 | **.91** | | | |
| 11 | Coworker support | .32 | .30 | .21 | .38 | .25 | .14 | .22 | .32 | .38 | .55 | **.90** | | |
| 12 | Time pressure | −.11 | −.06 | .02 | −.03 | −.05 | .04 | .00 | .11 | −.13 | −.24 | −.04 | **.78** | |
| 13 | Expertise | .37 | .49 | .50 | .35 | .34 | .27 | .28 | .51 | .38 | .26 | .32 | .19 | **.77** |
| | *Construct reliabilities* | *.91* | *.86* | *.76* | *.85* | *.82* | *.86* | *.81* | *.89* | *.90* | *.96* | *.96* | *.86* | *.85* |

*Note.* All product-moment correlations are based on latent factor scores. Correlations greater (smaller) than .12 (−.12) are significant at $p < .01$ (two-tailed tests). Square root of *AVE* is in boldface on the diagonal.

In a last step it was investigated whether the measurement model was affected by common method variance. As described above (see Section 7.1.4.3), four different measurement models (1 = null model, 2 = single-method factor model, 3 = assumed measurement model, and 4 = assumed measurement model including a single-method factor) were estimated. The fit indices of the four models can be found in Table 7.17. It should be noted that Model 3 is identical to the adjusted measurement model estimated above. It can be seen that Model 2 fits the data significantly better than Model 1, $\Delta\chi^2(59) = 7\,552.5$, $p < .001$. The effect of this improvement is large, $w = .54$. Furthermore, Model 4 also fits the data significantly better than Model 3, $\Delta\chi^2(59) = 197.7$, $p < .001$. However, the fit indices improved only marginally: $\Delta CFI = .009$, $\Delta RMSEA = -.003$, $\Delta SRMR = -.009$. The small improvement was also indicated by a rather small effect size, $w = .09$. In addition to this analysis, variance partitioning was used to estimate the variance attributed to the assumed factor structure and the common method factor. The method factor accounted for 16.1% of the items' variance. The assumed factor structure accounted for 47.7% of the original variance. About 36.2% of the original variance was attributed to unsystematic measurement errors. In conclusion, the data were mildly affected by common method variance. Based on the analysis just conducted it can be concluded that the impact of common method variance does not pose serious problems for this study.

**Table 7.17.** Results of model comparison to detect common method variance.

| Model | $\chi^2$ | *df* | *CFI* | *RMSEA* | *SRMR* | $\Delta\chi^2$ | *p* | *w* |
|---|---|---|---|---|---|---|---|---|
| 1 Null | 16 510.7 | 1 711 | | | | | | |
| 2 Single method factor | 11 302.7 | 1 652 | .35 | .12 | .13 | 7 552.5† | < .001 | .54 |
| 3 Measurement model | 2 256.6 | 1 574 | .95 | .03 | .05 | | | |
| 4 Measurement model + Single method factor | 2 058.9 | 1 515 | .96 | .03 | .04 | 197.7‡ | < .001 | .09 |

*Note. df* = Degrees of freedom; *CFI* = Comparitive fit index; *RMSEA* = Root mean square of error approximation; *SRMR* = Standardised root mean square residual; $\Delta\chi^2$ = Scaled $\chi^2$-difference between models; $p$ = $p$ value of the test whether $\Delta\chi^2$ significantly differs from zero; $w$ = Effect size Cohen's *w*. † Comparison of model 1 and 2. ‡ Comparison of model 3 and 4.

**Table 7.18.** Inter-factor correlations, *AVE* criterion, and construct reliabilities for all scales based on the CFA (validation sample).

| | Measure | 1 | 2 | 3 | 4 | 5 | 6 | 7 | 8 | 9 | 10 | 11 | 12 | 13 |
|---|---|---|---|---|---|---|---|---|---|---|---|---|---|---|
| 1 | Agency competence | **.84** | | | | | | | | | | | | |
| 2 | Agency beliefs | .71 | **.77** | | | | | | | | | | | |
| 3 | Agency personality | .41 | .35 | **.64** | | | | | | | | | | |
| 4 | Job enlargement | .45 | .44 | .41 | **.67** | | | | | | | | | |
| 5 | Job enrichment | .37 | .37 | .60 | .59 | **.69** | | | | | | | | |
| 6 | Codified information | .40 | .28 | .30 | .53 | .39 | **.77** | | | | | | | |
| 7 | Inst. learning activities | .39 | .33 | .32 | .62 | .40 | .45 | **.81** | | | | | | |
| 8 | Constructive change | .44 | .37 | .61 | .45 | .57 | .37 | .40 | **.82** | | | | | |
| 9 | Job autonomy | .50 | .40 | .43 | .31 | .44 | .28 | .37 | .41 | **.89** | | | | |
| 10 | Supervisor support | .44 | .33 | .26 | .35 | .26 | .28 | .29 | .28 | .49 | **.89** | | | |
| 11 | Coworker support | .41 | .29 | .21 | .27 | .25 | .28 | .21 | .24 | .35 | .52 | **.89** | | |
| 12 | Time pressure | −.14 | −.15 | .11 | −.03 | .01 | −.06 | −.05 | .14 | −.14 | −.29 | −.16 | **.79** | |
| 13 | Expertise | .42 | .46 | .55 | .41 | .46 | .37 | .46 | .60 | .40 | .29 | .37 | .15 | **.79** |
| | *Construct reliabilities* | *.92* | *.88* | *.78* | *.80* | *.78* | *.88* | *.84* | *.89* | *.92* | *.96* | *.96* | *.87* | *.87* |

*Note.* All product-moment correlations are based on latent factor scores. Correlations greater (smaller) than .12 (−.12) are significant at $p < .01$ (two-tailed tests). Square root of *AVE* is in boldface on the diagonal.

#### 7.2.1.3 Cross Validation

The exploratory and confirmatory factor analyses just described used the data of the calibration sample to check the psychometric quality of the proposed measurement model. The findings of these analyses were then used to revise the measurement model with the aim to improve its fit to the maximum possible extent. The validation sample was now used to check whether the adjusted measurement model still held in a new and independent dataset. This way evidence could be presented that the good model fit in the calibration sample was not just a methodological artefact due to the adjustment procedure.

The CFA model estimated with data of the validation sample converged normally and all estimated parameters were plausible. The fit indices indicated an acceptable to good model fit, $\chi^2(1\,574) = 2\,590.64$, $p < .001$, $\chi^2/df = 1.65$, $CFI = .94$, $RMSEA = .038$ with 90% $CI = .036–.040$, $SRMR = .048$. All factor loadings were above .50 and reached significance. The number of items with loadings between .50 and .70 was 15. The remaining 44 items all had loadings above .70 (see Appendix H for more details on the factor loadings). As can be seen in Table 7.18, all construct reliabilities exceeded the desired threshold of .70. Furthermore, the *AVE* criterion for all constructs was successfully fulfilled (see Table 7.18). These results therefore again supported both convergent and discriminant validity of the measurement model used. To conclude, all presented analyses strongly support the measurement model. It could therefore be used to test the full structural equation model employing the partial least square approach.

### 7.2.2 PLS Analyses

#### 7.2.2.1 Measurement Model

Similar to the CFA results just presented the evaluation of the PLS-based measurement model gave strong evidence for convergent and discriminant validity of all reflectively measured constructs. All factor loadings of the items used to measure the latent constructs in the PLS model reached significance. Only two of these 59 items had loadings below .70 (agency beliefs parcel 5: $\lambda = .64$; agency personality 1: $\lambda = .69$; a detailed list of all factor loadings based on the

PLS estimation can be found in Appendix I). All construct reliabilities were well above the suggested threshold of .70 (see Table 7.19). Furthermore, the Fornell-Larcker criterion was also fulfilled for all constructs (see Table 7.19 for the square root of the *AVEs*).[52] As expected, the PLS-based measurement model showed a slightly better fit than the CFA-based measurement model. This is due to the so called PLS bias.

In the next step, the quality of the second-order formative measurement model of work agency had to be tested. Unfortunately, the convergent validity of this second-order formative construct could not be evaluated because of the unsatisfying psychometric properties of the proactive personality scale. However, work agency correlated positively and significantly with all agentic actions included in the research model. This could also be interpreted as an indicator of convergent validity.

Based on the analysis of the variance inflation factors for each agency facet ($VIF_{Competence} = 1.56$, $VIF_{Beliefs} = 1.63$, $VIF_{Personality} = 1.19$) collinearity could be ruled out as an issue. Furthermore, all three outer weights of the agency facets reached significance ($p < .001$). The agency competence facet ($\beta = .51$) contributed only slightly higher to the work agency construct than the agency personality facet ($\beta = .44$). With a weight of .30, the agency beliefs facet contributed considerably less to the work agency construct than the agency competence and the agency personality facet.

Based on this analysis it can be argued that both the reflective measures as well as the second-order formative measure of work agency satisfy the necessary requirements to estimate the assumed relationships between the latent construct in the structural model.

52 Please note that correlations with the construct of work agency were not used to check the Fornell-Larcker criterion. The correlations between the three agency facets and work agency in particular were expected to be very high since the factor score of work agency is a weighted linear sum of the estimated factor scores of the three agency facets.

**Table 7.19.** Inter-factor correlations, *AVE* criterion, and construct reliabilities for all scales based on the PLS analysis (calibration sample).

| | Measure | 1 | 2 | 3 | 4 | 5 | 6 | 7 | 8 | 9 | 10 | 11 | 12 | 13 | 14 | 15 |
|---|---|---|---|---|---|---|---|---|---|---|---|---|---|---|---|---|
| 1 | Experience | **NA** | | | | | | | | | | | | | | |
| 2 | Agency competence | .01 | **.86** | | | | | | | | | | | | | |
| 3 | Agency beliefs | .05 | .59 | **.81** | | | | | | | | | | | | |
| 4 | Agency personality | .05 | .33 | .38 | **.71** | | | | | | | | | | | |
| 5 | Work agency | .05 | .84 | .77 | .72 | **NA** | | | | | | | | | | |
| 6 | Job enlargement | −.14 | .36 | .33 | .19 | .40 | **.79** | | | | | | | | | |
| 7 | Job enrichment | −.11 | .25 | .30 | .35 | .38 | .43 | **.80** | | | | | | | | |
| 8 | Codified information | .08 | .28 | .18 | .09 | .25 | .36 | .19 | **.79** | | | | | | | |
| 9 | Inst. learning activit. | −.01 | .32 | .25 | .28 | .38 | .46 | .29 | .35 | **.83** | | | | | | |
| 10 | Constructive change | .05 | .33 | .33 | .35 | .45 | .47 | .49 | .37 | .39 | **.87** | | | | | |
| 11 | Job autonomy | .08 | .33 | .33 | .33 | .42 | .22 | .31 | .14 | .28 | .42 | **.91** | | | | |
| 12 | Supervisor support | .04 | .39 | .26 | .18 | .39 | .34 | .18 | .21 | .25 | .31 | .46 | **.92** | | | |
| 13 | Coworker support | −.06 | .30 | .29 | .19 | .34 | .36 | .24 | .17 | .21 | .31 | .37 | .54 | **.92** | | |
| 14 | Time pressure | .11 | −.09 | −.05 | .03 | −.06 | −.03 | −.05 | .04 | .02 | .09 | −.12 | −.23 | −.05 | **.84** | |
| 15 | Expertise | .21 | .33 | .42 | .41 | .48 | .30 | .30 | .27 | .31 | .45 | .34 | .23 | .29 | .20 | **.83** |
| | *Construct reliabilities* | NA | *.94* | *.91* | *.84* | NA | *.90* | *.88* | *.90* | *.87* | *.92* | *.94* | *.97* | *.97* | *.91* | *.90* |

*Note.* All product-moment correlations are based on latent factor scores. Correlations greater (smaller) than .12 (−.12) are significant at $p < .01$ (two-tailed tests). Square root of *AVE* is in boldface on the diagonal. NA = Not applicable because the scale was measured with only one item or was formatively measured.

#### 7.2.2.2 Structural Model

As described above the structural model evaluation was based upon the assessment of the significance and the size of the path coefficients, the assessment of $R^2$ values, and the assessment of partial effect sizes $f^2$. However, in a first step, collinearity issues within the structural model had to be ruled out.

Table 7.20 shows the variance inflation factors for each set of variables that jointly predict a common endogenous variable in the structural equation model. As can be seen, all *VIF*s are far below the critical threshold of 5. This is strong evidence against collinearity.

**Table 7.20.** Variance inflation factors (calibration sample).

| First set (All agentic actions) | | Second set (Expertise) | | Third set (Construct. change) | |
|---|---|---|---|---|---|
| Predictors | *VIF* | Predictors | *VIF* | Predictors | *VIF* |
| Work Agency | 1.30 | Codified inform. | 1.23 | Work Agency | 1.31 |
| Job autonomy | 1.42 | Inst. learning act. | 1.35 | Expertise | 1.37 |
| Superv. support | 1.52 | Job enlargement | 1.55 | Experience | 1.05 |
| Cow. support | 1.73 | Job enrichment | 1.25 | | |
| Time pressure | 1.09 | Experience | 1.05 | | |
| Experience | 1.04 | | | | |

*Note. VIF* = Variance inflation factor.

Figure 7.4 depicts the estimated research model. The standardised path coefficients that represent the strength of the relationship between two latent variables are printed on the corresponding arrows. The respective resampled *t* value is displayed in brackets following each path coefficient. The adjusted $R^2$ values can be found below each latent variable printed in boldface. Please note that for the sake of clarity, only significant paths ($p < .01$) are included in Figure 7.4. Furthermore, control variables are not included in this figure. All standardised path coefficients as well as the corresponding *t* values, *p* values, and significance levels can be found in Appendix J.

Job experience has been included as a control variable. Only the relationships between experience and expertise ($\beta = .25$), deliberate job enlargement

($\beta = -.16$), as well as deliberate job enrichment ($\beta = -.14$) reached significance on the 1% level.

Only one of the included moderator variables reached significance at the 1% level. Time pressure significantly moderates the relationship between work agency and deliberate participation in institutionalised learning activities ($\beta = -.12$). The negative sign of the path coefficient indicates that in work contexts with high time pressure, agentic individuals participate deliberately in institutionalised learning activities less often than in work contexts with low or no time pressure. No other moderator reached significance. In consequence, the direct relationships between work agency and all agentic efforts (except deliberate participation in institutionalised learning activities) as well as all organisational characteristic variables and the agentic efforts can directly be interpreted.

As expected, work agency was positively and significantly related to all included agentic actions ($p < .001$). In relative terms, the estimated relationship between work agency and deliberate participation in institutionalised learning activities ($\beta = .31$) is the strongest. The estimated relationships between work agency and deliberate job enlargement ($\beta = .30$) as well as between work agency and deliberate job enrichment ($\beta = .30$) are of similar strength. The estimated standardised path coefficients between work agency and deliberate enquiry of codified information as well as deliberate efforts to initiate constructive change are .20 and .22, respectively.

Only a few path coefficients between the included organisational context factors and the agentic actions in the model reached significance at the 1% level: job autonomy was positively and significantly related to deliberate job enrichment ($\beta = .19$) as well as to deliberate efforts to initiate constructive change ($\beta = .21$). Furthermore, coworker support was positively and significantly related to deliberate job enlargement ($\beta = .19$).

The following three agentic actions were positively and significantly related to the expertise measure in the model: deliberate job enrichment ($\beta = .20$), deliberate job enlargement ($\beta = .14$), and deliberate participation in institutionalised learning activities ($\beta = .15$). The relationship of deliberate enquiry of codified information with the expertise measure ($\beta = .11$) was positive but did not reach significance ($p = .014$). Furthermore, deliberate efforts to initiate

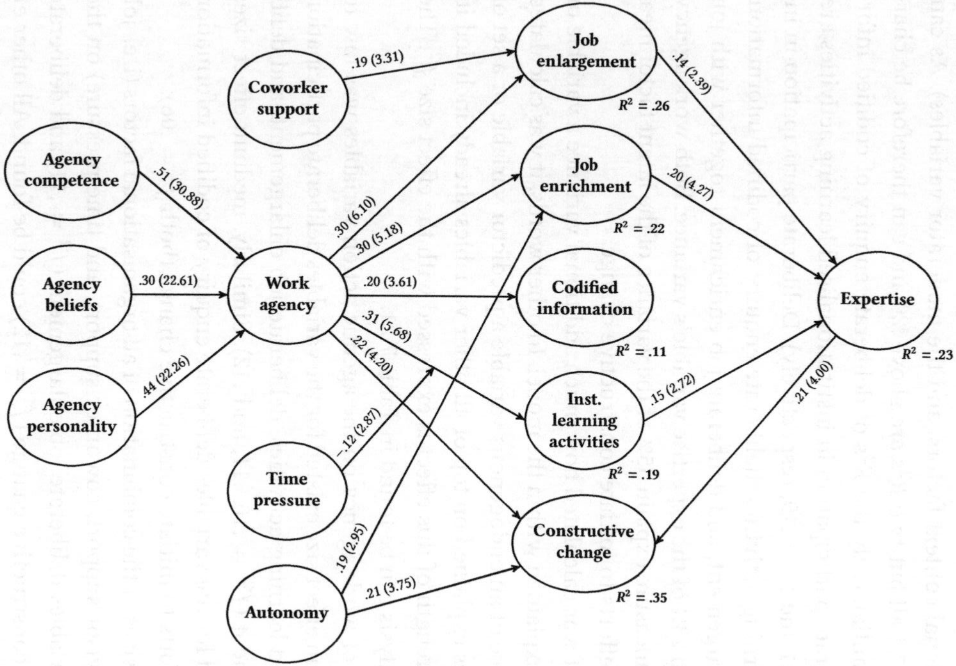


**Figure 7.4.** Estimated PLS structural equation model with standardised path coefficients and $R^2$ values (calibration sample). The standardised path coefficients are printed above each path. The corresponding resampled $t$ value can be found in brackets. $R^2$ values are printed in boldface below each endogenous variable. Please note that non-significant paths ($p \geq .01$, one-tailed tests), paths from the control variable (job experience), and observed indicators are not included in the figure.

constructive change was significantly and positively predicted by the expertise level of an employee (β = .21, $p < .001$).

The $R^2$ values of the agentic actions give information of how much of the construct's variance is explained through all modelled predictors (work agency, organisational context factors, and the moderator variables). As can be seen in Figure 7.4 all but two $R^2$s are above .20 and can therefore be characterised as substantial. Only the $R^2$s of deliberate enquiry of codified information and deliberate participation in institutionalised learning activities are below .20 ($R^2 = .11$ and $R^2 = .19$, respectively). Deliberate participation in institutionalised learning activities, deliberate enquiry of codified information, deliberate job enlargement, and deliberate job enrichment together with job experience explain 23% of the expertise variable's variance. Both work agency and the expertise measure explain 35% of the variance of the latent factor measuring deliberate efforts to initiate constructive change.

In a final step, it was calculated how much additional variance a variable or a set of variables explained within the model. In other words, it was calculated how much variance of an endogenous variable a predictor variable or a set of predictor variables explained on top of all other variables already included in the model. The strength of this effect is expressed with the effect size $f^2$. The results of this analysis can be found in Table 7.21.

The effect size of work agency on the agentic action variables was low to medium. A medium effect size existed for the variables deliberate participation in institutionalised learning activities, deliberate job enlargement, and deliberate job enrichment ($f^2 = .10$, .11, and .12). Similarly, medium effect sizes could be observed for the variables deliberate enquiry of codified information and deliberate efforts to initiate constructive change (both $f^2 = .06$).

Medium effect sizes of the combination of all organisational factors (i. e., job autonomy, supervisor support, coworker support, and time pressure) on the agentic action variables deliberate job enlargement ($f^2 = .11$) and deliberate efforts to initiate constructive change ($f^2 = .12$) could be found. All other effect sizes of the organisational context factors on agentic actions were low. The effect size of the control variable job experience was non-existent or small for all variables. However, the strongest effect size could be found for the variable expertise ($f^2 = .08$).

**Table 7.21.** Partial effect sizes (calibration sample).

| | $R^2$ | | | | | | $f^2$ | | |
|---|---|---|---|---|---|---|---|---|---|
| | | Model without | | | | | | | |
| Endogene variable | Full model | Organisational context factors | Work agency | Job experience | Expertise | Expertise and organ. context factors | Organisational context factors | Work agency | Experience |
| *Job enlargement* | .26 | .18 | .18 | .24 | .26 | .18 | .11 | .11 | .03 |
| *Job enrichment* | .22 | .16 | .13 | .20 | .22 | .16 | .08 | .12 | .03 |
| *Codified information* | .11 | .07 | .06 | .10 | .10 | .07 | .04 | .06 | .01 |
| *Inst. learning act.* | .19 | .14 | .11 | .19 | .19 | .14 | .06 | .10 | .00 |
| *Constructive change* | .35 | .27 | .31 | .35 | .32 | .20 | .12 | .06 | .00 |
| *Expertise* | .23 | .23 | .23 | .17 | NA | NA | .00 | .00 | .08 |

*Note.* $R^2$ = Coefficient of determination; $f^2$ = Effect size Cohen's $f^2$.

#### 7.2.2.3 Cross Validation

In order to check whether the findings presented here also hold in an independent dataset the PLS model was again estimated with data of the validation sample. Similarly to the calibration sample, strong evidence in favour of convergent and discriminant validity could be found. Almost all reflective indicators had significant factor loadings above .70. Only the factor loadings of the indicators "agency beliefs 4" ($\lambda = .67$), "agency personality 1" ($\lambda = .68$), and "job enlargement 4" ($\lambda = .69$) were slightly below this threshold (Appendix K). All estimated construct reliabilities exceeded .70. Furthermore, the Fornell-Larcker criterion was also fulfilled for all constructs (see Table 7.22).

The *VIF*s for the formative measurement model as well as the structural model indicated that collinearity did not pose any problems. Apart from this, all three outer weights of the agency facets reached significance ($p < .001$). In conclusion, presentation and interpretation of the estimated findings of the structural model could now proceed.

Figure 7.5 shows the estimated research model based on the validation sample. Again, for the sake of clarity, both insignificant paths (i. e., $p > .01$) and paths from the control variable (experience) are excluded from Figure 7.5. A summary of all standardised path coefficients, the corresponding $t$ values, and $p$ values can be found in Appendix L.

Instead of a detailed description, only significant deviations between the model based on the calibration sample (see above) as well as the just estimated model based on the validation sample are reported. Table 7.23 lists all significant deviations including the estimated standardised path coefficients for both models, the standard errors, the difference between the standardised path coefficients, the standard error of this difference, the $t$ value, as well as the corresponding $p$ value.

The results of the comparison of both models show that the parameter estimates were relatively stable. Only six standardised path coefficients differed significantly ($p < .05$). It is noteworthy that the relationship between all three work agency facets significantly differed between the calibration and the validation sample. In the validation sample, both the agency competence facet ($\beta_A = .51$, $\beta_B = .43$, $\Delta\beta = -.09$) and the agency beliefs facet ($\beta_A = .30$,

$\beta_B = .22$, $\Delta\beta = -.09$) had a significant smaller outer weight than in the calibration sample. However, the outer weight of the agency personality facet was significantly higher in the validation sample than in the calibration sample ($\beta_A = .44$, $\beta_B = .60$, $\Delta\beta = .16$). In other words, within the validation sample the personality facet contributed more strongly and both the belief and the capacity facets contributed somewhat less to the formative construct of work agency than in the calibration sample. A general overview of the partial effect sizes of the estimated model using the validation sample can be found in Appendix M.

Furthermore, three other path coefficients significantly differed between the two samples: (a) coworker support on deliberate job enlargement ($\beta_A = .19$, $\beta_B = .03$, $\Delta\beta = -.16$), (b) work agency * supervisor support on deliberate job enlargement ($\beta_A = .14$, $\beta_B = -.08$, $\Delta\beta = -.23$), and (c) work agency * time pressure on deliberate efforts to initiate constructive change ($\beta_A = -.11$, $\beta_B = .05$, $\Delta\beta = .15$). In the latter two cases even the direction of the relationship changed. This result indicates that a sound interpretation of the effect of these both moderators is not possible.

**Table 7.22.** Inter-factor correlations, *AVE* criterion, and construct reliabilities for all scales based on the PLS analysis (validation sample).

| | Measure | 1 | 2 | 3 | 4 | 5 | 6 | 7 | 8 | 9 | 10 | 11 | 12 | 13 | 14 | 15 |
|---|---|---|---|---|---|---|---|---|---|---|---|---|---|---|---|---|
| 1 | Experience | **NA** | | | | | | | | | | | | | | |
| 2 | Agency competence | .02 | **.88** | | | | | | | | | | | | | |
| 3 | Agency beliefs | .10 | .66 | **.83** | | | | | | | | | | | | |
| 4 | Agency personality | .18 | .36 | .30 | **.73** | | | | | | | | | | | |
| 5 | Work agency | .15 | .79 | .68 | .82 | **NA** | | | | | | | | | | |
| 6 | Job enlargement | −.08 | .39 | .37 | .33 | .48 | **.92** | | | | | | | | | |
| 7 | Job enrichment | −.02 | .33 | .32 | .47 | .51 | .49 | **.91** | | | | | | | | |
| 8 | Codified information | .03 | .37 | .26 | .28 | .40 | .46 | .33 | **.91** | | | | | | | |
| 9 | Inst. learning activit. | .05 | .38 | .32 | .29 | .43 | .54 | .36 | .44 | **.85** | | | | | | |
| 10 | Constructive change | .12 | .40 | .33 | .51 | .57 | .40 | .48 | .35 | .39 | **.75** | | | | | |
| 11 | Job autonomy | .12 | .46 | .38 | .37 | .50 | .28 | .39 | .28 | .36 | .36 | **.78** | | | | |
| 12 | Supervisor support | .02 | .42 | .32 | .24 | .41 | .31 | .24 | .27 | .27 | .26 | .48 | **.82** | | | |
| 13 | Coworker support | −.05 | .40 | .29 | .20 | .38 | .27 | .25 | .28 | .20 | .23 | .33 | .51 | **.85** | | |
| 14 | Time pressure | .02 | −.13 | −.11 | .07 | −.03 | .02 | .01 | .00 | .01 | .15 | −.14 | −.26 | −.15 | **.85** | |
| 15 | Expertise | .24 | .39 | .41 | .46 | .56 | .35 | .39 | .35 | .42 | .54 | .36 | .28 | .35 | .17 | **.87** |
| | *Construct reliabilities* | *NA* | *.94* | *.92* | *.85* | *NA* | *.95* | *.97* | *.97* | *.92* | *.87* | *.87* | *.91* | *.89* | *.91* | *.92* |

*Note.* All product-moment correlations are based on latent factor scores. Correlations greater (smaller) than .12 (−.12) are significant at $p < .01$ (two-tailed tests). Square root of *AVE* is in boldface on the diagonal. NA = Not applicable because the scale was measured with only one item or was formatively measured. Please note that correlations with work agency were not used to check whether the Fornell-Larcker criterion was fulfilled (see Footnote 52 this chapter).

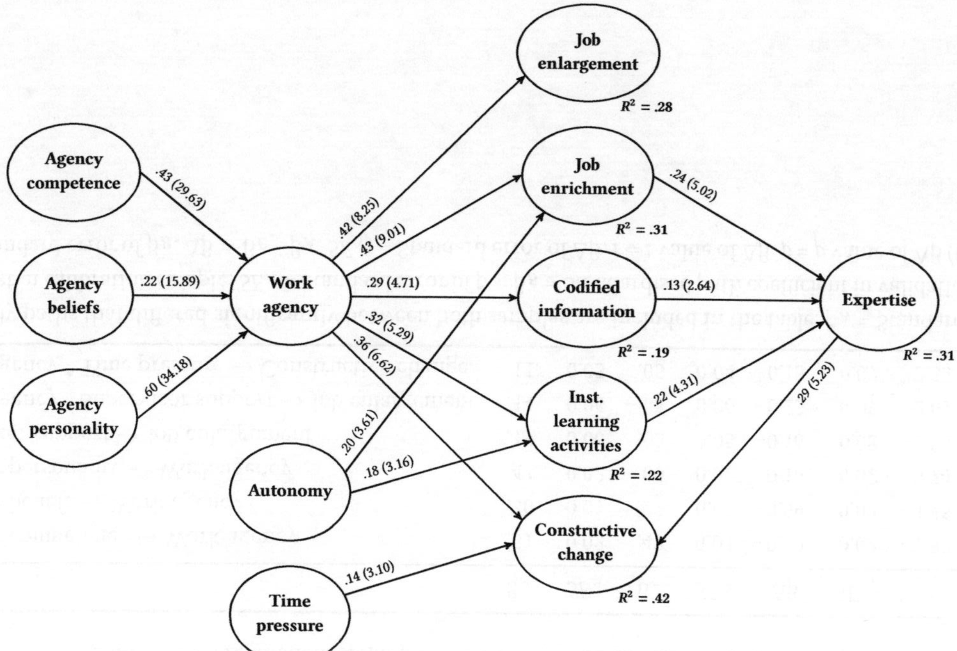


**Figure 7.5.** Estimated PLS structural equation model with standardised path coefficients and $R^2$ values (validation sample). The standardised path coefficients are printed above each path. The corresponding resampled $t$ value can be found in brackets. $R^2$ values are printed in boldface below each endogenous variable. Please note that non-significant paths ($p \geq .01$, one-tailed tests), paths from the control variable (job experience), and observed indicators are not included in the figure.

**Table 7.23.** PLS model comparison between calibration and validation sample.

| Path | $\beta_A$ | $SE_A$ | $\beta_B$ | $SE_B$ | $\Delta\beta$ | $SE_{\Delta\beta}$ | $t$ | $p$ |
|---|---|---|---|---|---|---|---|---|
| Agency competence → Work agency | .51 | 0.02 | .43 | 0.01 | −0.09 | 0.02 | −3.87 | <.001 |
| Agency beliefs → Work agency | .30 | 0.01 | .22 | 0.01 | −0.09 | 0.02 | −4.45 | <.001 |
| Agency personality → Work agency | .44 | 0.02 | .60 | 0.02 | 0.16 | 0.02 | 6.74 | <.001 |
| Coworker support → Job enlargement | .19 | 0.06 | .03 | 0.05 | −0.16 | 0.08 | −2.05 | .041 |
| Work agency * Supervisor support → Job enlargement | .14 | 0.06 | −.08 | 0.06 | −0.23 | 0.09 | −2.67 | .008 |
| Work agency * Time pressure → Constructive change | −.11 | 0.05 | .05 | 0.04 | 0.15 | 0.07 | 2.35 | .019 |

*Note.* Only paths that differed significantly between both samples are included in the table. $\beta_A$ = Standardised path coefficient in calibration sample; $SE_A$ = Standard error of $\beta_A$; $\beta_B$ = Standardised path coefficient in validation sample; $SE_B$ = Standard error of $\beta_B$; $\Delta\beta = \beta_B - \beta_A$, $SE_{\Delta\beta}$ = Standard error of $\Delta\beta$; $t$ = $t$ value of $\Delta\beta$; $p$ = $p$ value of $\Delta\beta$ (two-tailed tests).

## 7.3 Discussion

This section aims to summarise and discuss all empirical findings reported in this chapter. Section 7.3.1 concentrates on the psychometric quality of the survey instrument. Section 7.3.2 then focusses on the test of the research model. Finally, Section 7.3.3 discusses the appropriateness of the methodological approach used in this study, including potential limitations.

### 7.3.1 Psychometric Quality of the Survey Instrument

Separate exploratory factor analyses for each model part (agency facets, agentic actions, organisational context factors, expertise measures) as well as Cronbach's α were used to check whether the scales exhibit unidimensionality in the calibration sample (see Section 7.2.1.1).

The analyses revealed that not all items used in the survey instrument worked as expected. In almost all of the different scales some items loaded on more than one empirical factor simultaneously and/or did not sufficiently load on any factor. These items were excluded from any further analysis because both cross loadings and insufficient loadings violate the assumption of unidimensionality (Hair, Black, et al., 2014). Particularly affected were all dimensions of the NCS, the deliberate social interaction scale, as well as the proactive personality scale. First, it was impossible to reproduce the assumed theoretical factor structure of the NCS (help and care, giving advice, handling emergency situations, diagnostic functions, assuring high-quality medical treatment, cooperation, coaching and teaching). The EFA revealed a four-factor structure. The empirically derived factors were interpreted as follows: (a) core medical care facet, (b) cooperation facet, (c) quality management facet, and (d) coaching and teaching facet. Second, because only two items of the social interaction scale remained after the EFA it was decided to completely remove the social interaction scale from all following analyses. Third, the proactive personality items were removed from any subsequent analyses because a low Cronbach's α indicated that the scale could not be assumed to be unidimensional.

Based on the newly derived item-factor structure a CFA was estimated for the whole measurement model using the data from the calibration sample (see

Section 7.2.1.2). This CFA revealed substantial psychometric problems with some of the items included in the measurement model. In particular, the items of the NCS were affected. Consequently, it was decided to completely exclude the items of the NCS and also to remove three other affected items from any further analyses. A new CFA without these items indicated a good fit of the newly derived measurement model with the data as well as evidence for both convergent and discriminant validity of the different scales used in the survey instrument. This result could be replicated with another CFA estimated using the data from the validation sample (see Section 7.2.1.3).

To sum up, nine of the original 22 scales as well as a few single items used in the survey instrument did not exhibit sufficient psychometric properties to be used for further analyses (all NCS dimensions, proactive personality, and deliberate social interaction). Nevertheless, the remaining scales and their respective items (agency competence, agency beliefs, agency personality, deliberate job enlargement, deliberate job enrichment, deliberate enquiry of codified information, deliberate participation in institutionalised learning activities, efforts to initiate constructive change at work, job autonomy, supervisor support, coworker support, time pressure, and advice seeking expertise) proved to be appropriate measures for the constructs included in the research model of this thesis. The psychometric quality of these scales and items could be confirmed in both the calibration and the validation sample.

## 7.3.2 Test of the Research Model

The theoretically derived research model was tested using a PLS-SEM approach. This approach simultaneously allowed estimation and investigation of the specified relationships between all unobserved latent constructs included in the research model. The robustness of the findings of this model test was checked through a cross-validation approach. Only findings that hold both in the calibration and the validation sample are interpreted to be robust. Within this section the findings of the PLS-SEM approach will be summarised and discussed, with a focus on the rejection or confirmation of the hypotheses derived in Chapters 4 and 5.

In this study, work agency was operationalised as a formative construct with three distinct agency facets: (a) agency competence, (b) agency beliefs, and (c) agency personality. All three facets proved to be important and significant empirical constituents of work agency. This means that individuals can only be characterised as agentic if they simultaneously have (a) the capacity to make decisions and to translate these decisions into feasible actions, (b) the beliefs in their own capabilities to exercise control over their lives and their environments, and (c) an inclination to actually take control. This is in line with the theoretical framework elaborated in Chapter 2.

In both samples, agency beliefs' relative contribution to the work agency construct was the lowest. In contrast, agency competence and agency personality contributed most to the construct. It therefore seems that strong capacities to make decisions and to translate these decisions into action plans as well as a general tendency to take control over one's own life and environment are more important for actually engaging in self-initiated behaviours than the beliefs about one's own capabilities. This is an interesting finding since almost all theoretical models and frameworks discussed in Chapter 2 emphasised the important role of agency beliefs (e. g., Bandura, 2001; Gecas, 2003; Grant & Ashford, 2008; Hitlin & Elder, 2007b; S. K. Parker et al., 2010).

The high relative contribution of agency competence and agency personality can be interpreted twofold. First, strong agency competences might lower the perceived costs of engaging in self-initiated behaviours (see Section 2.2.3.2). Individuals who know how to make plans to reach goals and to implement them might face lower costs in terms of lost time or energy. In addition, knowledge about strategies to translate goals into appropriate action plans might also lower the risk of failing or meeting resistance from colleagues and supervisors. In the context of the model depicted in Figure 2.6 (Chapter 2) a strong agency competence might therefore increase the "can do" motivational state of an individual (see also Chapter 2; Bindl & Parker, 2011; J. B. Fuller et al., 2012; S. K. Parker et al., 2006). Second, a strong inclination to take control over one's life and over one's environment can be interpreted as a distal[53] reason

53 Agency personality can only be characterised as a distal antecedent. In comparison, situational utility judgements and motivational variables as well as felt responsibility to engage in certain actions are psychologically much closer antecedent (see Figure 2.6, Chapter 2).

to engage in agentic actions in the first place. Individuals in need of control are strongly motivated to initiate behaviours that contribute to actually taking control. The engagement in agentic actions is the first step towards meeting this need.

However, the difference between the relative contributions of the three agency facets should be interpreted with care. All three parameter estimates significantly differed between the calibration and the validation sample. While agency competence and agency personality almost equally contributed to work agency in the calibration sample ($\beta_A = .51$ and .44, respectively) the relative contributions differed more strongly in the validation sample ($\beta_B = .43$ and .60, respectively). Similarly, the relative contribution of agency beliefs differed considerably between the samples ($\beta_A = .30$, $\beta_B = .22$). This is evidence that the absolute strength of the contributions of the three facets might not be globally valid. For some (groups of) individuals agency competence might be the most important prerequisite for engaging in self-initiated behaviours. For others, however, their agency personality might be the most important one. Furthermore, for some nurses agency beliefs might be a more important antecedent for the engagement in agentic actions than for others. Future studies should investigate whether the relative contributions of the three facets are stable between different samples and/or whether other variables can explain potential differences.

One of the most important findings of this study is that work agency is significantly and positively related to all agentic actions included in the research model. In other words, agentic nurses engage more often in self-initiated and goal-directed behaviours like deliberate job enlargement, deliberate job enrichment, deliberate enquiry of codified information, deliberate participation in institutionalised learning activities, and efforts to initiate constructive change at work than their less agentic counterparts.[54] This relationship could be found in both the calibration and validation samples and therefore speaks strongly in favour of Hypotheses 1.1a, 1.1b, 1.2b, 1.3, and 1.4. Unfortunately, no empirical information in favour or against Hypothesis 1.2a could be obtained since the

54 The effects of the moderator variable found in the calibration sample are interpreted later. However, the moderator does not change the interpretation given at this moment.

social interaction measure had to be excluded from any kind of SEM analyses because of its insufficient psychometric properties (see Section 7.2.1.1).

Work agency in combination with job experience explained between 7% and 20% (calibration sample) and 16% and 32% (validation sample) of the variance of the agentic actions included in the model (see Table 7.21 and Appendix M). It follows that work agency was found to be a substantial and important antecedent of most of the agentic actions included in the research model. The lowest influence of work agency was consistently found on deliberate enquiry of codified information ($R^2$ = .07 and .16, for both samples respectively). It seems that the decision to read professional journals and books or to study medical information in internet databases is affected by other important variables not included in the model. For instance, the competence to obtain information from codified information could be such a variable. Authors like Köpke et al. (2013) emphasised that nurses in Germany are usually not trained to read or understand research-related literature. Furthermore, not all nurses might have the skill-set to actually access web databases because of low computer literacy (Estabrooks et al., 2005). Another potential determinant is the general availability of access to certain information resources. For instance, Klette and Smeby (2012) argue that not all nurses have similar access to databases that contain medical information. In other words, a nurse might be agentic but might not engage in deliberate enquiry of codified information because she does not know how or does not have the opportunity to do so.

The strongest effect of work agency in terms of explained variance could be found for deliberate efforts to initiate constructive change ($R^2$ = .20 and .32, for both samples respectively; see Table 7.21 and Appendix M). This speaks in favour of the assumption that agentic individuals do not try to take control only over their life but also want to shape the organisational structures and processes they have to deal with on a daily basis. Work agency is a substantial antecedent of all efforts that try to make a difference in the current work practice. However, being agentic is not the only requirement for engaging in such efforts. It could also be shown that expertise is a similarly important antecedent of all deliberate efforts towards constructive change in both samples (evidence in favour of Hypothesis 2.4). In other words, experts are more likely to develop or transform new work practices and to constructively address tensions at work than non-experts. Taken together, evidence was found that individuals who are simultaneously highly agentic and highly competent are most likely to engage in deliberate efforts to initiate constructive change at work.

Within the study it was also tested how the other four agentic actions related to expertise. It was hypothesised that deliberate job enlargement, deliberate job enrichment, deliberate enquiry of codified information, and deliberate participation in institutionalised learning activities are all positively related to individuals' levels of expertise.[55] Across both samples evidence was found that only deliberate job enrichment and deliberate participation in institutionalised learning activities are robust predictors of expertise. In other words, it was found that geriatric care nurses who more often take over additional responsibilities from supervisors or other staff members on a higher hierarchical level and individuals who deliberately participate in professional training and courses exhibit a higher expertise level than individuals who do not engage in such efforts. These findings are in line with the assumptions made in Chapter 3 (see also Goller & Harteis, 2014; Hornung et al., 2008) and strongly support both Hypotheses 2.1b and 2.3.

Deliberate efforts to increase the scope of one's own daily job by adding new tasks did not predict expertise in the validation sample. A significant and positive effect of deliberate job enlargement on expertise could be found only in the calibration sample. It was therefore decided to reject Hypothesis 2.1a. It is surprising that a tendency to craft new experiences at work by taking on unfamiliar tasks and by participating in work-related projects does not contribute to the development of expertise in the domain of geriatric care nursing. There are at least two possible explanations for this finding. First, some nurses might deliberately enlarge their jobs but do not reflect on the experiences that result from these efforts. Without reflection, work-related experiences might not easily lead to the construction or the modification of knowledge (see Section 3.2; D. A. Kolb, 1984; van Woerkom, 2003). However, this explanation leaves open why nurses manage to develop expertise through deliberate job enrichment but not job enlargement. Efforts to take on more responsibilities also only lead

55 An interpretation of the relationship of deliberate efforts to initiate constructive change and expertise has just been presented.

to new knowledge when new experiences are reflected upon. Second, some nursing homes might provide institutionalised job rotation programmes (Est, 2010) which periodically shift employees from one task or position to another (Bratton & Gold, 2007). Through such programmes employees automatically make new work-related experiences and a deliberate approach towards job enlargement is no longer required for expertise development.

The relationship between deliberate enquiry of codified information and expertise reached significance in the validation but not in the calibration sample. It follows that deliberate efforts to read professional journals, books, and other kinds of web resources are not found to be robust predictors of expertise in this study (resulting in the rejection of Hypothesis 2.2b). A similar finding was reported by van de Wiel et al. (2004). In their study on organisational consultants they could not find any significant differences between top and average performers concerning their habits in reading professional literature.

A potential explanation for a missing link between efforts to seek out codified information and measures of expertise is the general fact that reading as such often only leads to the construction of inert knowledge. Information presented in literature sources might be retrievable but cannot easily be applied to tasks and problems emerging in the workplace (Renkl, Mandl, & Gruber, 1996a, 1996b). In this sense, reading might have no direct effect on performance because nurses are not able to transfer newly obtained information into their work contexts. The potential inability of many nurses to read scientific literature might contribute to this problem (see for this issue e. g., Estabrooks et al., 2005; Köpke et al., 2013). In other words, because of a general lack of scientific training a range of professional literature sources might not be accessible to many nurses. Without capacities to understand research literature and to translate such complex information into working strategies no performance gains can be expected (see for instance, Renkl, 2015; Rost & Schilling, 2006).

Taken together, all four agentic actions as well as job experience as a control variable explained 23% of the variance of expertise in the calibration sample and 31% in the validation sample. Without job experience the four agentic actions still explained 17% (calibration sample) and 26% (validation sample) of the variance of expertise. This speaks in favour of the assumption that the exercise of agency at work indeed benefits the development of expertise. However, more than 70% of the observed variance of the expertise measure was explained by other factors not included in the investigated research model. This is not completely surprising since the PLS model included neither a measure of social interaction (because of the already explained psychometric reasons) nor a number of other potential predictors of expertise development: the quality of the training offered in the particular nursing homes (e. g., Ericsson et al., 2007), the quantity of training in which a nurse participated, the learning potential of specific workplaces (i. e., scope of action, challenges, task interdependence, feedback etc.; e. g., Ketterl, 2014; Rausch, 2013), and the particular nursing homes' learning and/or error culture (e. g., Fischer & O'Connor, 2014; Putz, Schilling, & Kluge, 2012), just to name a few. In addition, the survey instrument only asked whether the participants generally tend to engage in the particular agentic actions. It was neither asked how often they engage in these activities nor about the quality of the learning experience that resulted from the engagement. In addition, it was not asked whether the participating nurses reflected on the experiences that came out of the agentic actions in which they engaged. As argued before, reflection is strongly required in order to learn from experiences, social interaction, consulting media, and institutionalised learning activities (see Section 3.2; e. g., Boud et al., 1999b; D. A. Kolb, 1984; Pool et al., 2016).

The theoretical model included four organisational context factors (job autonomy, supervisor support, coworker support, and time pressure) as direct predictors of each of the six initial agentic actions. Because the social interaction items had to be excluded from any kind of SEM analyses no empirical information in favour or against hypotheses including this construct could be obtained. It is therefore neither possible to reject nor to confirm Hypotheses 3.2a, 3.6a, 3.6c, and 3.10a. Of the remaining 19 hypotheses concerning the direct relationship between organisational context factors and agentic actions 14 hypotheses (3.1a, 3.2b, 3.5a, 3.5b, 3.6b, 3.6d, 3.7a, 3.7b, 3.8a, 3.8b, 3.9a, 3.9b, 3.10b, 3.11) had to be rejected because neither in the calibration nor the validation sample did any empirical evidence support the assumed direct effects. Another three hypotheses (3.3, 3.4, 3.5c) had to be rejected because evidence for the existence of a relationship was found in only one of the two samples: job autonomy on deliberate efforts to participate in institutionalised learning activities ($\beta_B$ = .18), job autonomy on deliberate efforts to initiate constructive change ($\beta_A$ = .21), and coworker support on deliberate job enlargement ($\beta_A$ = .19). Another hypothesis (3.12) had to be rejected because the observed relationship in the validation sample was positive although a negative relationship was hypothesised (time pressure on deliberate efforts to initiate constructive change; $\beta_B$ = .14). In addition, no significant relationship between time pressure and constructive change could be found in the calibration sample.

Only the relationship between job autonomy and deliberate job enrichment reached significance in both the calibration and the validation sample. This finding support the assumption that nurses tend to take over additional responsibilities at work as long as it is possible to do so (e. g., S. K. Parker & Turner, 2002; Tornau & Frese, 2013). It follows that Hypothesis 3.1b can be confirmed.

Besides being incorporated as direct predictors all context factors have also been included as moderators between work agency and the five agentic actions in the research model. Of the 24 assumed moderation effects none could be confirmed. Again because social interaction had to be excluded from any further analyses, no evidence against or in favour of Hypotheses 3.14a, 3.18a, 3.18c, and 3.22a could be obtained. Of the remaining 20 hypothesis 19 had to be rejected because neither in the calibration nor the validation sample was there any empirical evidence to support the assumed moderation effects (3.13a, 3.13b, 3.14b, 3.15, 3.16, 3.17a, 3.17b, 3.17c, 3.17d, 3.18b, 3.18d, 3.19a, 3.19b, 3.20a, 3.20b, 3.21a, 3.21b, 3.22b, 3.24).

Time pressure negatively moderated nurses' deliberate efforts to participate in institutionalised learning activities in the calibration sample. In other words, the higher the perceived time pressure at work the less often nurses wanted to participate in training or other kinds of courses even if they were highly agentic. This might give evidence that high time pressure does not allow nurses to engage in any kind of additional activities (like training) that are not directly related to assigned tasks and problems. However, this interpretation has to be made with care. Time pressure did not significantly moderate the relationship between work agency and nurses' deliberate participation in institutionalised learning activities in the validation sample. So strictly speaking, Hypothesis

3.23 had also to be rejected because no robust evidence for the assumed moderator effect could be found.

Taking all these results into account it can be argued that organisational context factors seem to only negligibly affect whether and how nurses engage in agentic actions at work. First of all, work environments that are conducive to work agency do not automatically foster individuals' engagement in self-initiated behaviours. This study found almost no evidence that nurses engage more often in deliberate job enlargement, deliberate job enrichment, deliberate enquiry of codified information, deliberate participation in institutionalised learning activities, or deliberate efforts to initiate constructive change in work environments that offer considerable job autonomy, support from supervisors and coworkers as well as sufficient time resources (apart from the relationship of job autonomy and deliberate job enrichment). Second, organisational context factors do not inhibit the engagement in agentic actions as long as a nurse has a strong disposition to exercise agency in the first place. Agentic nurses engage more often in self-initiated behaviours than their less agentic counterparts regardless of the sociocultural and material context factors at work. This was unexpected since all theoretical frameworks reviewed in Chapter 2 discuss the strong interdependency of context factors and agency (e. g., Billett, 2006, 2008b; Elder, 1998; Elder & Shanahan, 2007; Eteläpelto et al., 2013; Vähäsantanen, 2013). It was assumed that employees exercise more agency in such work environments that offer favourable conditions (many affordances, few constraints). This assumption could not be confirmed in this thesis.

At the same time, it has to be stressed that organisational context factors were only included as direct predictors of agentic actions and as moderators between work agency and agentic actions in the research model. In addition, only a cross-sectional research design was employed (see next section for methodological criticism). This study therefore could not test whether sociocultural and material context factors have lagged effects on nurses' general capacity and tendency to exercise agency in the first place. Work environments with favourable conditions (e. g., high job autonomy, high social support, sufficient time resources) might allow employees to increase their agency beliefs as well as their agency competences which then lead to more engagement in agentic actions in the future.[56] It has already been suggested in the literature that opportunities to successfully exercise agency in the past should lead to mastery experiences that strengthen self-efficacy beliefs in the long run (e. g., Bandura, 1989, 2001; Frese & Fay, 2001; Gecas, 2003; S. K. Parker et al., 2006). Similarly, opportunities to exercise agency should allow individuals to build up meta-cognitive knowledge about (a) own preferences and life-course objectives, as well as (b) strategies to translate decisions and goals into action plans (also called self-knowledge; e. g., Markus, 1983; T. D. Wilson, 2009). On the contrary, situations that do not provide opportunities for exercising agency deprive individuals of the chance to construct meta-cognitive knowledge. In such situations individuals also tend to learn to be reactive rather than proactive because they know they do not have much choice or their choices cannot be successfully translated into actions (e. g., Seligman, 1972, 1992).

### 7.3.3 Methodological Approach and Limitations

All findings reported in this chapter have to be interpreted in consideration of potential limitations or weaknesses of the study design, the survey instrument employed, as well as the analysis procedures utilised. It is therefore necessary to point out these potential limitations and discuss them in relationship to the conclusions drawn in sections above:

1. The employed cross-sectional design does not allow for testing of causal development hypotheses. Causal development hypotheses describe assumed relationships where one variable causes (i. e., produces) variation in another variable over time (Bortz & Döring, 2006; Jaccard & Jacoby, 2010). For instance, within the research model it is assumed that work agency causes individuals to engage in agentic actions and that some of these agentic actions cause learning and therefore the development of expertise. Such kinds of causal development relationships require that the variation in the dependent variable (e. g., expertise) occurs after the variation in the independent variable(s) (e. g., deliberate job enlargement) (Check & Schutt, 2012).

56 Both agency competence and agency beliefs are conceptualised as malleable concepts. On the contrary, agency personality is conceptualised as a stable and immutable trait-like concept that cannot be easily changed (see Chapter 2).

Because all constructs in the research model have been measured at one single measurement point this requirement cannot be tested for. It follows that—strictly speaking—the implied causal development relationships between the variables in the model cannot be empirically investigated. However, this study did provide information about the empirical association of some of the assumed relationships using PLS-SEM analyses. Empirical associations are a necessary precondition for a potential causal (development) relationship between any of two variables (Bortz & Döring, 2006; Check & Schutt, 2012). This is especially true if a causal mechanism exists that thoroughly describes why the independent variables cause the dependent one and if a larger context has been identified in which the causal relationships are hypothesised to occur (see Check & Schutt, 2012). The causal mechanism between all variables in the research model has been described in Chapters 2, 3, and 4. Moreover, Study 1 found initial evidence about the appropriateness of the relationships between the variables in the research model in the context of geriatric care nursing. To conclude, this study found first evidence that a causal (development) relationship between certain variables included in the model could exist. Future studies should investigate the assumed relationships in more detail using experimental or longitudinal research designs.

2. Neither the nursing homes that agreed to take part in this study nor the participating nurses were randomly selected from the population. Data could only be obtained from nurses who (a) worked in one of the 32 nursing homes that were willing to take part in this study, and (b) voluntarily decided to complete a questionnaire. It is therefore questionable whether the findings of this study can be generalised beyond this specific sample and/or the domain of geriatric care nursing. In addition, it cannot be ruled out that some of the findings are the sole product of sample selection biases (cf., Berk, 1983; Winship & Mare, 1992). For instance, Bortz and Döring (2006) emphasise that voluntary research participants are often better educated and have a higher intelligence in comparison to individuals who do not voluntarily participate in surveys. It is therefore conceivable that voluntary participants might more often reflect on experiences than non-participants.

This, however, could mean that deliberate job enrichment does not positively relate to the development of expertise in the population, in which individuals might be—on average—less prone to reflect on work-related experiences than the sample used for the analyses in this chapter. Deliberate job enrichment without reflection upon experienced problems and tasks will most likely not lead to learning or work-related development.

3. Only self-reporting measures were used to operationalise the constructs included in the research model. Self-reports are prone to bias empirical findings for three potential reasons. Firstly, participants tend to answer self-reporting measures in socially desirable ways (Donaldson & Grant-Vallone, 2002; Holtgraves, 2004). For instance, nurses might indicate a high tendency to deliberately participate in institutionalised learning activities because they assume this is expected and highly valued in their professional domain. Similarly, time pressure might be rated too highly since absence of sufficient time resources is an ongoing topic within the domain of geriatric care nursing (see Section 5.2.3). Such response patterns could easily lead to over- or under-estimation of certain behaviours or phenomena. Although the questionnaire asked the respondents to complete all questions as honestly as possible and guaranteed anonymity to all participants beforehand, the existence of social desirability biases cannot be fully ruled out. Secondly, self-reports might not be valid (Podsakoff, 1986). It is questionable whether self-report measures of organisational characteristics like job autonomy really measure autonomy at work or only an individual's personal perception of autonomy. This is especially a problem if the validity of a measure used in a study could not be established beforehand (e. g., by correlating it with another already established measure) and/or the measure in question claims to objectively operationalise a certain construct. Fewer problems occur when past studies have already presented evidence that a measure is indeed a valid one and/or only subjective assessment of certain constructs is required (e. g., not the objective lack of time is relevant for the study but the subjective perception of being under time pressure). Within this study it is particularly unclear whether the employed advice seeking expertise scale is a valid measure for operationalising expert performance. A valida-

tion of all measures used in this study would be highly desirable. Finally, the use of self-reports within a single questionnaire can easily lead to common method variance (see also Section 7.1.4.3). Common method variance describes the phenomenon that the shared variance between two variables in a dataset only exists partly because they were measured with the same single method (D. T. Campbell & Fiske, 1959; Podsakoff et al., 2003). Such common method variance can easily lead to biased parameter estimates in correlative analyses like PLS-SEM. Based on the test conducted in Section 7.2.1.2 only very limited evidence was found that common method variance really poses a problem for this study. However, it cannot be completely ruled out that some of the estimates reported in this study are slightly biased because of common method variance.

4. PLS-SEM does not provide a widely accepted fit index to assess the global model adequacy similarly to CB-SEM (Henseler & Sarstedt, 2013). It was therefore only possible to evaluate the adequacy of the estimated model using the size of the path coefficients, their $p$ values, share of explained variance ($R^2$), as well as effect size measures ($f^2$). It follows that only limited evidence could be presented that the assumed model actually fits the data. Nevertheless, PLS-SEM was used because of its advantages in the context of this study. CB-SEM would not have easily allowed for use of a second-order formative agency construct in combination with a large number of interaction effects in SEM as theoretically and empirically derived in Chapters 2, 3, 4, and 5. In other words, any disadvantages connected to PLS-SEM are offset by its advantages in comparison to other estimation procedures.

To sum up, several limitations concerning the study design, the survey instrument employed, and the analysis approaches could be identified. All findings of this study have to be interpreted in the face of these limitations. Nevertheless, this study provided initial insights into the role of work agency on the process of expertise development of geriatric care nurses by employing hypotheses-testing methods. A particular strength of this study is its cross-validation approach. Cross validation allowed testing of whether the relationships found between different variables in the calibration sample also exist in the validation sample. Within this study, a hypothesis was only confirmed if empirical evidence supporting the assumed relationship could be found in both of the samples. Such an approach towards hypothesis testing is much more rigorous than using only one single sample.

## 7.4 Chapter Summary

This chapter described the third study conducted as part of this thesis. The main aim of this study was to test the hypotheses posed in Chapters 4 and 5. For this purpose, usable data of 879 geriatric care nurses working in 32 different German nursing homes were gathered. These data were then randomly split into two separate datasets (calibration and validation sample) in order to cross validate all findings. A combination of exploratory and confirmatory factor analyses was used to analyse the psychometric quality of the questionnaire. A PLS-based structural equation modelling approach was used to test all hypotheses included in the underlying research model after the psychometric quality of the measurement model was established. A more detailed description of the methodological approach employed in this study can be found in Section 7.1. All findings concerning the quality of the measurement model as well as the PLS-SEM analyses can be found in Section 7.2. These findings were then discussed in Section 7.3.

The findings of this study can be summarised as following. First, robust evidence was found that work agency is indeed a positive predictor of all agentic actions included in the research model. In other words, agentic individuals engage more often in deliberate job enlargement, deliberate job enrichment, deliberate enquiry of codified information, deliberate participation in institutionalised learning activities, and efforts to initiate constructive change at work. Second, three of the five agentic actions included in the model are positively related to expertise. Both deliberate job enrichment and deliberate participation in institutionalised learning activities are positive predictors of expertise. Conversely, expertise was found to be a positive predictor of deliberate efforts to initiate constructive change at work. All three relationships were predicted in the research model. Unfortunately, only limited evidence could be found for the association between deliberate job enlargement and deliberate enquiry of codified information (a significant relationship could be observed in only one of the two samples). It was therefore concluded that this study could not reliably confirm the assumed relationships. Third, almost no evidence was found that the included organisational context factors affect individuals' engagement in self-initiated behaviour. All together it was assumed that autonomy at work, supervisor and coworker support, as well as time pressure directly predict whether individuals' engage in agentic actions and/or moderate the relationship between work agency and agentic actions. Only the direct relationship between job autonomy and deliberate job enrichment proved to be robustly significant in both samples. No, or only limited, evidence was found for all the other assumed direct relationships. In addition, almost no evidence was found for the moderated relationship between work agency and the five included agentic actions. A more detailed overview of all the findings of this study can be found in Table 7.24. This table lists all hypotheses as well as the corresponding findings for each of the two samples (CS = calibration sample, VS = validation sample, OA = overall).

To sum up, this study presented evidence in favour of some of the hypotheses included in the research model presented in Chapters 4 and 5 and evidence against others. The next chapter aims to discuss these findings in regard to the overarching research questions posed in this thesis.

**Table 7.24.** Synopsis of hypotheses tests.

| Hypothesis | | CS | VS | OA |
|---|---|---|---|---|
| *Relationships between work agency and agentic actions* | | | | |
| 1.1a: | Work agency $\xrightarrow{\oplus}$ Job enlargement | ✓ | ✓ | ✓ |
| 1.1b: | Work agency $\xrightarrow{\oplus}$ Job enrichment | ✓ | ✓ | ✓ |
| 1.2a: | Work agency $\xrightarrow{\oplus}$ Social interaction | NA | NA | NA |
| 1.2b: | Work agency $\xrightarrow{\oplus}$ Codified information | ✓ | ✓ | ✓ |
| 1.3: | Work agency $\xrightarrow{\oplus}$ Inst. learning activities | ✓ | ✓ | ✓ |
| 1.4: | Work agency $\xrightarrow{\oplus}$ Constructive change | ✓ | ✓ | ✓ |

*Continued on next page*

Table 7.24 – *Continued from previous page*

| Hypothesis | | CS | VS | OA |
|---|---|---|---|---|
| *Relationships between agentic actions and expertise* | | | | |
| 2.1a: | Job enlargement $\xrightarrow{\oplus}$ Expertise | ✓ | × | × |
| 2.1b: | Job enrichment $\xrightarrow{\oplus}$ Expertise | ✓ | ✓ | ✓ |
| 2.2a: | Social interactions $\xrightarrow{\oplus}$ Expertise | NA | NA | NA |
| 2.2b: | Codified information $\xrightarrow{\oplus}$ Expertise | × | ✓ | × |
| 2.3: | Inst. learning activities $\xrightarrow{\oplus}$ Expertise | ✓ | ✓ | ✓ |
| 2.4: | Expertise $\xrightarrow{\oplus}$ Constructive change | ✓ | ✓ | ✓ |
| *Relationships between organisational context factors and agentic actions* | | | | |
| 3.1a: | Job autonomy $\xrightarrow{\oplus}$ Job enlargement | × | × | × |
| 3.1b: | Job autonomy $\xrightarrow{\oplus}$ Job enrichment | ✓ | ✓ | ✓ |
| 3.2a: | Job autonomy $\xrightarrow{\oplus}$ Social interaction | NA | NA | NA |
| 3.2b: | Job autonomy $\xrightarrow{\oplus}$ Codified information | × | × | × |
| 3.3: | Job autonomy $\xrightarrow{\oplus}$ Inst. learning activities | × | ✓ | × |
| 3.4: | Job autonomy $\xrightarrow{\oplus}$ Constructive change | ✓ | × | × |
| 3.5a: | Supervisor support $\xrightarrow{\oplus}$ Job enlargement | × | × | × |
| 3.5b: | Supervisor support $\xrightarrow{\oplus}$ Job enrichment | × | × | × |
| 3.5c: | Coworker support $\xrightarrow{\oplus}$ Job enlargement | ✓ | × | × |
| 3.5d: | Coworker support $\xrightarrow{\oplus}$ Job enrichment | × | × | × |
| 3.6a: | Supervisor support $\xrightarrow{\oplus}$ Social interaction | NA | NA | NA |
| 3.6b: | Supervisor support $\xrightarrow{\oplus}$ Codified information | × | × | × |
| 3.6c: | Coworker support $\xrightarrow{\oplus}$ Social interaction | NA | NA | NA |
| 3.6d: | Coworker support $\xrightarrow{\oplus}$ Codified information | × | × | × |
| 3.7a: | Supervisor support $\xrightarrow{\oplus}$ Inst. learning activities | × | × | × |
| 3.7b: | Coworker support $\xrightarrow{\oplus}$ Inst. learning activities | × | × | × |
| 3.8a: | Supervisor support $\xrightarrow{\oplus}$ Constructive change | × | × | × |
| 3.8b: | Coworker support $\xrightarrow{\oplus}$ Constructive change | × | × | × |
| 3.9a: | Time pressure $\xrightarrow{\ominus}$ Job enlargement | × | × | × |
| 3.9b: | Time pressure $\xrightarrow{\ominus}$ Job enrichment | × | × | × |

*Continued on next page*

Table 7.24 – *Continued from previous page*

| Hypothesis | | CS | VS | OA |
|---|---|---|---|---|
| 3.10a: | Time pressure $\xrightarrow{\ominus}$ Social interaction | NA | NA | NA |
| 3.10b: | Time pressure $\xrightarrow{\ominus}$ Codified information | × | × | × |
| 3.11: | Time pressure $\xrightarrow{\ominus}$ Inst. learning activities | × | × | × |
| 3.12: | Time pressure $\xrightarrow{\ominus}$ Constructive change | × | ✓ | × |
| *Moderator effects between organisational context factors and agentic actions* | | | | |
| 3.13a: | Work agency $\xrightarrow{\text{Job autonomy } \oplus}$ Job enlargement | × | × | × |
| 3.13b: | Work agency $\xrightarrow{\text{Job autonomy } \oplus}$ Job enrichment | × | × | × |
| 3.14a: | Work agency $\xrightarrow{\text{Job autonomy } \oplus}$ Social interaction | NA | NA | NA |
| 3.14b: | Work agency $\xrightarrow{\text{Job autonomy } \oplus}$ Codified information | × | × | × |
| 3.15: | Work agency $\xrightarrow{\text{Job autonomy } \oplus}$ Inst. learning activities | × | × | × |
| 3.16: | Work agency $\xrightarrow{\text{Job autonomy } \oplus}$ Constructive change | × | × | × |
| 3.17a: | Work agency $\xrightarrow{\text{Superv. support } \oplus}$ Job enlargement | × | × | × |
| 3.17b: | Work agency $\xrightarrow{\text{Superv. support } \oplus}$ Job enrichment | × | × | × |
| 3.17c: | Work agency $\xrightarrow{\text{Coworker support } \oplus}$ Job enlargement | × | × | × |
| 3.17d: | Work agency $\xrightarrow{\text{Coworker support } \oplus}$ Job enrichment | × | × | × |
| 3.18a: | Work agency $\xrightarrow{\text{Superv. support } \oplus}$ Social interaction | NA | NA | NA |
| 3.18b: | Work agency $\xrightarrow{\text{Superv. support } \oplus}$ Codified information | × | × | × |
| 3.18c: | Work agency $\xrightarrow{\text{Coworker support } \oplus}$ Social interaction | NA | NA | NA |
| 3.18d: | Work agency $\xrightarrow{\text{Coworker support } \oplus}$ Codified information | × | × | × |
| 3.19a: | Work agency $\xrightarrow{\text{Superv. support } \oplus}$ Inst. learn. activities | × | × | × |
| 3.19b: | Work agency $\xrightarrow{\text{Coworker support } \oplus}$ Inst. learn. activities | × | × | × |
| 3.20a: | Work agency $\xrightarrow{\text{Superv. support } \oplus}$ Constructive change | × | × | × |
| 3.20b: | Work agency $\xrightarrow{\text{Coworker support } \oplus}$ Constructive change | × | × | × |
| 3.21a: | Work agency $\xrightarrow{\text{Time pressure } \ominus}$ Job enlargement | × | × | × |
| 3.21b: | Work agency $\xrightarrow{\text{Time pressure } \ominus}$ Job enrichment | × | × | × |
| 3.22a: | Work agency $\xrightarrow{\text{Time pressure } \ominus}$ Social interaction | NA | NA | NA |

*Continued on next page*

Table 7.24 – *Continued from previous page*

| Hypothesis | | CS | VS | OA |
|---|---|---|---|---|
| 3.22b: | Work agency $\xrightarrow{\text{Time pressure } \ominus}$ Codified information | × | × | × |
| 3.23: | Work agency $\xrightarrow{\text{Time pressure } \ominus}$ Inst. learning activities | ✓ | × | × |
| 3.24: | Work agency $\xrightarrow{\text{Time pressure } \ominus}$ Constructive change | × | × | × |

*Note.* CS = Calibration sample; VS = Validation sample; OA = Overall; $\xrightarrow{\oplus}$ = Positive relationship assumed; $\xrightarrow{\ominus}$ = Negative relationship assumed; $x \xrightarrow{z\,\oplus} y$ = $z$ positively moderates the relationship between $x$ and $y$; $x \xrightarrow{z\,\ominus} y$ = $z$ negatively moderates the relationship between $x$ and $y$; ✓ = Hypothesis confirmed; × = Hypothesis rejected; NA = Not applicable because social interaction scale had to be removed for all further analyses because of psychometric reasons (see Section 7.2.1.1).

# 8 General Discussion and Conclusion

The main aim of this thesis was to empirically investigate the role of human agency in work-related learning and professional development processes by using hypothesis-testing methods. For this purpose, Chapter 2 reviewed discourses of human agency within the workplace learning literature (e. g., Billett, 2011b; Bryson et al., 2006; Eteläpelto et al., 2013; Vähäsantanen, 2013) as well as literature not yet integrated on social-cognitive psychology (e. g., Bandura, 1986, 2001, 2006b), life-course research (e. g., Clausen, 1991; Crockett, 2002; Hitlin & Elder, 2007b), and organisational behaviour (e. g., Bindl & Parker, 2011; Tornau & Frese, 2013; Wrzesniewski & Dutton, 2001). The aim of this review was twofold: First, the review aimed at clarifying how human agency is conceptualised and how the concept is used to explain work-related learning and professional development (Sub-goal 1; see Chapter 1). Second, the review intended to derive a definition of human agency that can be used to operationalise the concept (Sub-goal 2).

Within the literature on human agency two distinct perspectives of the concept emerged. The first perspective conceptualises agency as an individual feature that allows individuals to make choices and to engage in actions based on these choices. The second perspective is concerned with these choices and actions as such. This thesis does not consider both conceptualisations as mutually exclusive. Instead, both conceptual perspectives are integrated into a single framework: Actions and choices are the result of agency as an individual feature. In order to distinguish both conceptualisations, the first (agency as a feature) was referred to as human agency and the second (agency as something individuals do) as agentic actions.

Based on this distinction the following definition of human agency in work contexts (in short: work agency) was derived: Work agency describes the capacity and the tendency of human beings to make intentional choices, to initiate actions based on these choices, and to exercise control over their self and the environment in work-related contexts. This definition explicitly assumes that some individuals tend to be more capable and more inclined to take control over their working lives than others. The former are referred to as agentic and the latter as non-agentic. Manifestations of work agency are described as agentic actions in this thesis. Agentic actions are self-initiated and goal-directed behaviours that aim to take control over the work environment or the individual's work-related life course. Agentic individuals are expected to engage more often in such agentic actions than their non-agentic counterparts.

The presented definition of work agency treats the concept as a latent construct explaining differences between individuals' self-initiated and goal-directed behaviours. Based on the literature review presented in Chapter 2, three relevant facets of such a construct could be identified. First, agency competence describes the individual's ability to visualise desired states, to set goals, to translate these goals into actions, to engage in these actions, and to deal with potential problems that might occur. Second, agency beliefs describe the individual's perception of whether she has these abilities or not. Third, agency personality describes the individual's predisposition to make choices and to engage in actions based on these choices to take control over her life and her environment. These three facets are used to operationalise work agency as a second-order formative construct (see Sections 6.2.1 and 7.1.4.4). In other words, these three facets capture three different aspects of work agency by building a—so-called—composite agency index. Such an operationalisation of work agency did not previously exist.

In the next step, Chapter 3 set out to explain how individuals can exert control over their own professional learning and development processes in order to become experts in their respective work domains. A special focus was directed on the identification of self-initiated and goal-directed behaviours—that is, agentic actions—that are theoretically and empirically linked to the development of expertise at work. Three approaches could be identified: (a) crafting experiences at work, (b) information and feedback seeking, and (c) deliberate engagement in institutionalised learning activities. In combination with the results of the literature review presented in Chapter 2 it was also intended to single out potential organisational context factors that affect how and whether employees engage in these agentic actions. Three highly relevant factors were identified: job autonomy, social support, and time pressure.

Based on Chapters 2 and 3 it could be established that human agency has indeed been discussed as a key concept to explain learning and development in work contexts. At the same time, however, no empirical study existed that actually tests this presumed relationship. The overarching research question of this thesis therefore was as follows:

- How does human agency explain work-related learning and professional development?

Based on the theoretical insights of Chapters 2 and 3, this research question was then broken down into three separate—more manageable—research questions:

RQ1. How does agency as an individual-level feature explain employees' engagement in agentic actions?

RQ2. How does engagement in agentic actions relate to the development of work-related expertise?

RQ3. How do organisational context factors affect engagement in agentic actions?

Together, the findings of Chapters 2 and 3 helped to derive a set of testable hypotheses about the relationship of human agency at work and the development of professional expertise (Sub-goal 3). In addition, another set of hypotheses was derived that describe how organisational context factors should affect whether and how individuals exercise agency at work. A description of all hypotheses as well as the theoretical research model that was built upon these hypotheses was presented in Chapter 4. Within the literature on professional learning and development no such hypotheses have previously been derived.

To answer the research questions, three consequent empirical studies were conducted in the domain of geriatric care nursing (Chapters 5, 6, and 7; Subgoal 4). First, Study 1 aimed to get initial insights into geriatric care nurses' agency at work. In this study nine highly experienced staff nurses were interviewed (a) to make clear whether the theoretically derived research model of Chapter 4 could be used to empirically answer the research questions of this thesis in the domain of geriatric care nursing, and (b) to give further information on how to operationalise the concepts included in the model. All in all, this study found considerable evidence for the validity of the theoretically derived research model. However, based on the empirical insights the larger concept of crafting experiences at work was split into two more concrete concepts: (a) deliberate job enlargement, and (b) deliberate job enrichment. Similarly, the relatively abstract concept of information and feedback seeking was split into (a) deliberate interaction with other professional actors, and (b) deliberately seeking out codified information. Lastly, the organisational context factor social support was also split into two distinct facets: (a) supervisor support, and (b) coworker support. The research model was adjusted accordingly.

Second, based on the findings of Study 1 a research design as well as a quantitative survey instrument suited to answering the research questions in the domain of geriatric care nursing were developed in Chapter 6. The aim of Study 2 was then to pilot test both the general research design and the survey instrument (see Sections 6.3 to 6.5). The survey instrument was distributed to 94 geriatric care nurses working in a German nursing home. Unfortunately, only 21 completed questionnaires were returned. Moreover, certain parts of the questionnaire exhibited a high number of missing values and some of the items did not work out as expected. Based on these findings it was decided to adjust the research design and the survey instrument accordingly (e. g., introduction of an incentive system to increase participation rates, replacement of the peer-nomination approach of measuring expertise with self-reporting measures).

Third, Study 3 adapted the revised study design developed based on Study 2. The aim of Study 3 was to test the hypotheses underlying the advanced research model developed in Chapters 4 and 5. For this purpose, usable data of 879 geriatric care nurses working in 32 different German nursing homes were gathered. This dataset was then randomly split into a calibration and a validation sample. Both samples were used to cross validate all empirical findings. After the psychometric quality of the survey instrument was established a PLS-based structural equation modelling (PLS-SEM) approach was used to test the derived hypotheses. A detailed description of this study can be found in Chapter 7.

The findings of this study are now used to answer the overarching research questions of this thesis in Section 8.1. After this discussion, implications for further research (Section 8.2) as well as practical implications for the domain of geriatric care nursing (Section 8.3) are derived. This chapter closes with a final summary in Section 8.4.

## 8.1 Answering the Research Questions

### RQ1. How does agency as an individual-level feature explain employees' engagement in agentic actions?

Work agency was found to be a significant and positive predictor of all agentic actions included in the research model in both the calibration and the validation sample.[57] This finding provides considerable evidence that agentic nurses tend to engage more often in self-initiated and goal-directed behaviours (i. e., agentic actions) than their non-agentic counterparts.

Nurses are more likely to exercise agency by engaging in agentic actions as long as they (a) have the ability to visualise desired future states, to set goals, to translate these goals into action plans, to engage in these actions, and to deal with potential problems that might occur; (b) are convinced that they have these abilities; and (c) have a predisposition to make choices and to engage in actions in order to take control over their life and their environment. In other words, the stronger the capacity and the tendency of a nurse to make intentional choices, to initiate actions based on these choices, and to

57 Due to psychometric problems the deliberate social interaction scale was not included in the statistical structural equation model. Thus, no empirical findings concerning the relationship of work agency and deliberate efforts to interact with colleagues and other work-related stakeholders could be obtained.

exercise control over herself and the environment in work-related contexts, the more she actually exercises her agency by engaging in a range of different self-initiated and goal-directed behaviours.

These findings are in line with the conceptual framework developed in Chapter 2 and 3 and later advanced in Chapters 4 and 5. Work agency as an individual difference variable does indeed predict whether individuals engage in self-initiated and goal-directed behaviours that take control over their working lives (e. g., by engaging in activities that contribute to learning and development) and over their work environment (e. g., by questioning inefficient work procedures, by attempting to restructure non-functional work procedures or by advertising new equipment or information material).

Within this thesis, work agency has been conceptualised and operationalised as a situation-unspecific predictor of agentic actions. It is assumed that individuals who are agentically competent, who believe in their agency competences, and who feature a strong agency personality tend to—on average—more often take control over their working life and their work environment in a large range of situations. It is, nevertheless, important to understand that this conceptualisation—at the same time—explicitly acknowledges that situation-specific circumstances that affect more proximal motivational variables might indeed easily change an individual's a priori probability to exercise their human agency. This might be the reason why work agency alone[58] explained only between 7% and 20% (calibration sample) and 16% and 32% (validation sample) of the observed agentic actions' variance. In other words, other relevant determinants of these behaviours exist that were not accounted for by the research model tested in this thesis.[59] For instance, the model did not include any situational antecedents like feelings of responsibility, utility judgements or perceived costs associated with certain behaviours that might also explain why an individual actually engages in any of the included agentic actions in some situations but not in others (S. K. Parker et al., 2010; see also Section 2.2.3.2). In addition, the research model did not account

58 Controlled for job experience in years. However, the effect of job experience was found to be negligible.

59 They were not accounted for because they were not centrally related to one of the three guiding research questions of this thesis.

for any concrete or situation-specific motives except for a very general need to take control over events in one's own working life (i. e., desire for control, agency personality). For instance, some individuals might craft experiences at work because of boredom and monotony. Others, on the other hand, might deliberately seek out codified information because a particular situation demands it (e. g., a case of a rare illness in the domain of nursing).

Furthermore, the research model tested in this thesis did not include a range of other potential predictors of goal-directed and self-initiated behaviour. For instance, the degree to which an individual favours or disfavours some kind of behaviour might strongly determine whether she intends to engage in this behaviour or not (Ajzen, 1991). Some people might just not like participating in institutionalised learning activities because of past experiences within their school biography. These kinds of people might be agentic by nature but just choose not to participate in any kind of institutionalised learning activities. Another reason not to engage in particular agentic actions might be a lack of specific competences to do so. Agentic individuals who lack strong literacy skills might not agentically engage in seeking out codified information. In the same sense, individuals who do not feel competent interacting with computers might not do so irrespective of their tendency to act agentically. However, agentic nurses who either disfavour some kind of agentic actions or feel less competent to engage in others should channel their agentic tendency into goal-directed and self-initiated behaviours that they favour more strongly or with which they feel more competent.

The agentic actions included in the research model of this thesis can only be understood as a specific subset of a range of potential self-initiated and goal-directed behaviours. It is, however, unclear whether human agency as operationalised in this thesis also explains individuals' engagement in other agentic actions that were not part of the SEM analyses of Study 3. For instance, do agentic nurses more often attempt to take control over their career advancements (e. g., S. K. Parker & Collins, 2010; Tharenou & Terry, 1998) and do they also more often take on the role of multipliers at work (i. e., actively distribute information and knowledge gained from other sources to colleagues and other professional actors; see Section 5.3.2) than their less agentic counterparts? In addition, the hypothesised relationship between work agency and deliberate interaction with other professional actors could not be empirically investigated because of psychometric problems of the items measuring this specific agentic action. It is therefore unclear whether agentic individuals also more often initiate efforts to obtain work-related information from other individuals based on the findings of Study 3. Nevertheless, both Study 1 and Study 2 presented initial evidence that human agency is associated with such behaviour (see Sections 5.2.2 and 6.4.3).

Within this thesis, work agency was operationalised as a formative second-order construct. This operationalisation assumes that work agency is constituted by three theoretically derived agency facets: agency competence, agency beliefs, and agency personality. Empirically, these three facets constitute work agency as a weighted linear sum of the estimated factor scores of the three agency facets. It is however unclear whether such an additive model is the best possible predictor of agentic actions. It is also conceivable that a multiplicative model explains individuals' engagement in agentic actions much better. Such a model assumes that individuals only feature strong work agency when they do not have a factor score of zero in any of the three facets. However, presently no theoretical rationale exists for privileging the multiplicative model over the additive one. Furthermore, within a PLS framework the additive model can be used to measure work agency as a latent factor. This is not possible with the multiplicative model (see Section 6.2.1).

To sum up, this thesis presented considerable evidence that the chosen operationalisation of work agency as an individual-level feature predicts individuals' engagement in a range of agentic actions. At the same time, however, it has to be acknowledged that work agency can explain only some of the variance of individuals' behaviour. Other antecedents might be as important.

### RQ2. How does engagement in agentic actions relate to the development of work-related expertise?

Only two of the four development-related agentic actions included in the research model were positively and significantly related to the expertise measure in the calibration and the validation sample. Nurses who indicated more often initiating efforts to take over additional responsibilities from supervisors or other individuals on higher hierarchical levels (i. e., deliberate job enrichment) as well as deliberate efforts to participate in institutionalised learning activities (i. e., deliberate participation in institutionalised learning activities) exhibited a higher expertise level than nurses who indicated engaging less often in these activities. These findings are interpreted as initial evidence that deliberate job enrichment and deliberate participation in institutionalised learning activities contribute to development of work-related expertise.

However, the conclusiveness of these findings is limited since only a cross-sectional research design could be employed in Study 3 of this thesis (see Sections 6.1 and 7.1 for reasons that led to this decision). It follows that any causal interpretations of the findings of this thesis have to be made with care. Alternative interpretations cannot be ruled out based on the existing data. For instance, expertise could also cause nurses to engage more often in deliberate job enrichment and deliberate participation in institutionalised learning activities. However, based on the theoretical framework derived in Chapters 2, 3, and 4 such a reading of the findings is less reasonable. In addition, Study 1 revealed that staff nurses described both agentic actions as highly relevant prerequisites of the development of high performance at work. This also speaks in favour of the first interpretation just given for the findings of Study 3.

Deliberate efforts that increase the scope of a nurse's daily job by adding new tasks (deliberate job enlargement) as well as efforts to obtain information from impersonal information resources like books, journals or web pages (deliberate enquiry of codified information) were not found to be consistently related to expertise. This was surprising since evidence for the relevance of both agentic actions could be found in the literature (e. g., Berings et al., 2007; Bryson et al., 2006; Petrou et al., 2016) as well as in the empirical findings of Study 1 (see Section 5.2.2). Two plausible explanations for the missing relationship between these two variables and expertise have been presented (see Section 7.3.2). First, deliberate job enlargement might not have the assumed impact on expertise development as long as institutionalised job rotation programmes exist. Such job rotation programmes might automatically bring employees in touch with new tasks and problems. A deliberate approach towards the crafting of new work-related experience via deliberate job enlargement is just not necessary any more. Second, not all nurses are sufficiently trained to understand research literature and transfer complex information into new or improved working strategies (e. g., Estabrooks et al., 2005; Köpke et al., 2013). Under such circumstances, deliberate enquiry of codified information may only lead to the acquisition of inert knowledge that cannot be applied to tasks and problems emerging at work. Unfortunately, based on the data obtained in Study 3 these new hypotheses cannot be tested.

In total, 23% and 31% of the expertise measure's variance could be explained by four agentic actions (deliberate job enlargement, deliberate job enrichment, deliberate enquiry of codified information, and deliberate participation in institutionalised learning activities) as well as job experience as a control variable in the calibration and the validation sample, respectively. Put differently, about 70% to 80% of the observed variance of expertise could not be explained by the variables included in the model. This is not completely surprising, for three reasons.

First, the list of agentic actions that determine the development of expertise included in the statistical research model is not exhaustive (see also the discussion of RQ1). On the one hand, deliberate social interaction had to be excluded from the PLS-SEM analysis for psychometric reasons. There is much theoretical and empirical evidence that efforts to obtain feedback, to discuss unclear tasks and emerging problems, as well as to ask colleagues, supervisors, and/or other professional stakeholders for advice is indeed associated with professional learning and development (see Sections 3.2.2, 3.3.2, and the findings of Study 1 in Section 5.2.2). It is therefore highly plausible that deliberate efforts to obtain work-related information from other individuals explain—at least partially—how individuals learn and develop. On the other hand, still other agentic actions that influence the development of expertise might exist that have also not been included in the structural equation model of Study 3. For instance, Study 1 presented evidence that some agentic nurses tend to take their job more seriously and are willing to spend more time on job-related activities than their less agentic counterparts (see Section 5.3.2). Such behaviours could indeed contribute to the development of expertise if it causes the agentic nurses to make quantitatively and qualitatively more domain-related experiences during their career. In addition, it was also described that some nurses take on the role of multipliers after they participate in a training course. Similarly, such an approach might add to the development of expertise because nurses who tend to take on this role have to engage more deeply with the information presented within training courses in order to teach their colleagues afterwards.

Second, within the survey instrument it was only asked whether nurses tend to engage in the described agentic actions on a very general level. It was not asked how often participants are actually involved with a particular agentic action. Similarly, participants were not asked about the quality of the learning and development experience that resulted from the engagement in the agentic action of question. Both aspects might, however, strongly determine how individuals learn and develop. It was also not asked why participants engage in any agentic actions. Some individuals might decide to engage in deliberate job enrichment and enlargement because they want to learn more about their domain. Others might only do so to make a good impression with their peers and supervisors. Within the literature, such differences have been discussed under the broader topic of goal orientations—that is, different "dispositions toward developing or demonstrating ability in achievement situations" (Vandewalle, 1997, p. 996; see also Button et al., 1996; Dweck & Leggett, 1988). Individuals who adopt a performance goal tend to demonstrate their performance either to obtain positive judgements from their environment or to avoid negative ones. In comparison, individuals with a learning goal orientation strive to deeply understand new topics or to develop their level of expertise (Button et al., 1996; see Billett, 2006, for a similar argumentation within the workplace learning literature). Empirical research has shown that individuals adopting a learning-orientation approach perform and develop better than individuals adopting a performance-orientation approach (Payne, Youngcourt, & Beaubien, 2007; Van Yperen, Blaga, & Postmes, 2014). It is therefore possible that learning-oriented individuals who engage in agentic actions might actually learn more than their performance-oriented counterparts and might therefore be more prone to developing expertise in the long run.[60] This hypothesis could not be tested since

60 It is questionable whether individuals—at all—engage in certain work-related behaviours with concrete learning goals in mind. Section 3.1.4 presented empirical evidence that employees only very seldom engage in any work-related activities with an explicit aim to learn and develop. However, individuals with a learning goal orientation might not explicitly adapt learning goals when engaging with achievement situations. They might rather unconsciously attempt to deeply understand tasks and problem in order to perform well

no information about the goal orientation of the participants was obtained in the studies conducted as part of this thesis.

Third, no other study has yet attempted to investigate the relationship of work agency and professional learning and development with hypothesis-testing methods. The focus of this thesis was therefore mainly on empirically testing whether such a relationship exists at all. Because of the limited scope[61] of this thesis, it was not aimed to also show how much variance agency contributes above other factors that might explain how employees develop professionally. It has, however, still to be acknowledged that a range of other determinants might indeed exist. For instance, the research model did not include variables concerning the general learning potential of the participants' workplace. However, past research showed that variables like the level of challenges, the task interdependence, or the feedback afforded to an incumbent, just to name a few, are important predictors of what and how individuals learn and develop at work (e. g., Ketterl, 2014; Kyndt & Baert, 2013; Kyndt et al., 2009; Rausch, 2013). Moreover, neither the quantity nor the quality of past training offered to the participants was included in the PLS-SEM analysis.[62] Again, past research emphasised that both variables might indeed be relevant predictors of the development of expertise (e. g., Ericsson et al., 2007).

The missing empirical link between expertise and both variables, deliberate job enlargement and deliberate enquiry of codified information, as well as the high percentage of unexplained variance of expertise in Study 3 might also be explained with reference to how expertise was actually measured. Because of practical and psychometric reasons (see Sections 6.5 and 7.2.1.2) only a newly self-developed expertise scale including four self-reporting items could

instead of only to perform well without a deeper understanding of what exactly is happening in the situation in question. Such an approach might be chosen unknowingly and can therefore not be verbalised in interview settings or indicated when completing questionnaires.

61 This was largely because the length of the survey instrument used and therefore also the time required for participation in Studies 2 and 3 had to be limited in order to obtain a sample large that could be used to employ EFA, CFA, and PLS-SEM.

62 The survey instrument included questions about the number of further education courses participated in during the last year as well the further education certificates obtained. Unfortunately, because of a high number of missing values both variables had to be excluded from any further analyses.

be used. This measure has not been validated before. It is therefore unclear how well these items measure the real expertise degree of the participants who completed the survey instrument of Study 3. Other measures might have resulted in better and more valid expertise scores. It is, however, unclear how this would have changed the results presented in this thesis. Any interpretations concerning the relationship of individuals' engagement in agentic actions and their expertise development should therefore only be made with care.

Theoretically it has been argued that the exercise of human agency should be related to a range of desirable outcomes from the individual's perspective (see Section 2.3). A few studies including the ones in this thesis did indeed find empirical evidence for this hypothesis. However, at the same time, it can be questioned whether a strong tendency to exercise agency might not also sometimes lead to detrimental effects. For instance, employees who constantly ask for feedback and information at work might be perceived as insecure or even incompetent (e. g., Ashford & Cummings, 1983; Beenen et al., 2016; Cooper-Thomas & Burke, 2012). Such an attribution might cause supervisors to refuse the assignment of challenging tasks to them in the future. In a similar vein, individuals who try to constantly change the boundaries of their job may thereby strongly violate established practices at work (see Billett & Pavlova, 2005, for an empirical example of such a case). Such violations could be strongly disapproved by coworkers and supervisors and—in the worst case—lead to dismissal. In other words, too much agency can easily lead to a range of problems in work contexts that evoke reactions from colleagues or supervisors that could limit the potential for expertise development in the long run. However, it might not be the excessive exercise of agency as such that leads to detrimental outcomes. Problems might only occur if individuals exercise agency in an unreflective way that does not take situational constraints into account. This proposition, however, was not tested in this thesis.

To sum up, preliminary evidence was found that individuals' engagement in certain agentic actions might indeed contribute to their expertise development. However, only two of the hypothesised agentic actions (deliberate job enrichment and deliberate participation in institutionalised learning activities) proved to be significantly and robustly related to the expertise measure used in Study 3. Two other hypothesised agentic actions did not reach significance.

Moreover, especially because of the missing validation of this expertise measure as well as the employed cross-sectional design, other interpretations of the findings cannot be fully ruled out. Further studies are required to conclusively answer the second research question of this thesis.

**RQ3. How do organisational context factors affect engagement in agentic actions?**

Study 3 found almost no evidence that organisational context factors affect how and whether nurses engage in agentic actions or not. Job autonomy was the only context factor found to consistently predict the engagement in one of the agentic actions within both the calibration and validation sample: The more autonomy a nurse experiences at work, the more often she engages in deliberate efforts to take over additional responsibilities from supervisors or other individuals on a higher hierarchical level. In other words, if nurses perceive the opportunity to exercise discretion at work they are more likely to engage in deliberate job enrichment.

Apart from that, no consistent evidence was found that job autonomy, supervisor support, coworker support, or time pressure moderate the relationship between work agency and the agentic actions included in the research model. Taken together, these findings indicate that organisational context factors only negligibly affect whether and how nurses engage in agentic actions. Neither do work environments that are conducive to work agency automatically foster nurses' engagement in self-initiated behaviours nor do circumstances less conducive to agency at work inhibit agentic nurses from exercising their agency at work.

Again, these findings were surprising. Prior empirical studies (e. g., Beenen et al., 2016; Colquitt et al., 2000; Hökkä et al., 2012; Ohly et al., 2006; C. C. Rosen et al., 2013; Spenceley et al., 2008; Tornau & Frese, 2013; see Chapters 2 and 3 for a more detailed review of the relevant literature) as well as Study 1 (see Section 5.2.3) and Study 2 (see Section 6.4.3) found initial evidence for the relevance of organisational context factors. At the same time, these results show the importance of the capacity and the tendency to exercise agency to engage in self-initiated and goal-directed behaviour. Organisational context factors have much less of an effect on whether a nurse engages in agentic actions than the capacity and tendency to do so in the first place. Being agentic might therefore be more important for the development of expertise than situational characteristics. However, it has still to be acknowledged that environments that are conducive to learning might afford a range of development-related tasks and problem situations as well as opportunities to interact with other individuals that do not have to be self-initiated. In other words, workplaces might—to a certain extent—support professional learning and development irrespective of individuals' agency. Future studies should investigate the added value of exercising agency at work in comparison to situational characteristics that are already found to be strongly related to the development of expertise in work contexts.

Within this thesis only four theoretically and empirically derived organisational context factors could be included as potential antecedents of the identified agentic actions (see Section 5.3.4 for a description of the reasons behind this decision). It should, however, be noted that other relevant context factors might exist that affect how and whether individuals engage in agentic actions at work. Some of the participants of Study 1, for instance, mentioned the available budget of a nursing home as well as the general culture of appreciation as two other potential organisational context factors (see Sections 5.2.3 and 5.3.4). Knowledge about low budgets might prevent agentic individuals from asking for additional institutional learning opportunities from the outset. On the contrary, a culture of appreciation might motivate employees to go beyond the necessity of their daily job. However, at the same time, a devoid of appreciation easily signals to individuals that agency is not welcome. Agentic individuals could then invest their human agency into other life domains that are not related to work. Individuals might also face context factors outside their employment-related organisational contexts that somehow affect how they exercise agency at work. For instance, certain family situations (e. g., being a single mother without much support from other family members and/or the society; see also Section 2.2.2.3) can strongly constrain the agentic efforts an individual can put into institutionalised learning activities occurring outside working hours (see Goller & Harteis, 2014, for such findings in the context of PhD's agency in academic settings). Whether the context factors just described actually affect whether, how and why individuals engage in agentic actions at work, however, remains open for examination. Future studies should include more (organisational) context factors as antecedent of agentic actions in addition to job autonomy, coworker and supervisor support, and time pressure.

To sum up, only very limited evidence was found that organisational context factors affect individuals' engagement in a range of agentic actions. Organisational context factors neither directly predicted individuals' engagement in agentic actions nor moderated the relationship between work agency and such efforts. Based on the findings of Study 3, an individual's capacity and tendency to make intentional choices, to initiate actions based on these choices, and to exercise control over herself and the environment in work-related contexts explains her engagement in self-initiated and goal-directed behaviours much better than organisational context factors. However, future studies should investigate the effect of a larger set of relevant context factors than the ones studied in this thesis.

## 8.2 Implications for Further Research

Based on the interpretation of the empirical findings as well as the limitations of this thesis, a range of implications for further research can be derived:

1. Study 3 used a cross-sectional design where all relevant constructs were measured using self-reports. As previously discussed (see Section 7.3.3 and above), this research approach has certain disadvantages. First, cross-sectional studies do not allow for testing causal development hypotheses (i. e., engagement in certain agentic actions causes the development of expertise). Studies of this kind only indicate whether a statistical association between two variables exists. Statistical association is a requirement of causal relationships but does not indicate causality as such. Second, self-reports are prone to bias empirical findings because (a) participants tend to answer them in socially desirable ways, (b) they may lack validity, and (c) they might cause common method variance. Future studies should try to replicate the findings of this thesis by using research designs that can detect causal development relationships (e. g., longitudinal studies with several measurement points) as well as by using more objective measures of

the included constructs. For instance, the frequency of the engagement in agentic actions of a nurse could be measured with data obtained from supervisors or other coworkers. In addition, the expertise level of each employee could be measured using complex test-based diagnostic procedures (e. g., Achtenhagen & Winther, 2014). Such a longitudinal study design with multimethod elements and more objective measures would allow more rigorous insights to be gained into the relationship between work agency and the development of expertise in work contexts.

2. Studies 2 and 3 found some evidence that the operationalisation of human agency at work as a formative construct based on three theoretically derived agency facets (agency competence, agency beliefs, and agency personality) is a valid one. First, work agency positively predicts both agentic actions that aim to take control over the life course of the actor as well as her environment, as demonstrated in Study 3. Second, all three agency facets positively correlated with the proactive personality scale in Study 2 (a positive correlation was theoretically assumed because of the conceptual proximity of work agency and proactive personality). Unfortunately, because of psychometric problems the proactive personality scale could not be used in Study 3. It would therefore be helpful to investigate whether both scales correlate in other samples obtained by potential future studies. In addition, it would be interesting to test whether the formative operationalisation of work agency is suitable for detecting differences in groups that have—a priori—been identified as either highly agentic or less agentic. Again, such findings would provide further evidence about the validity of the work agency operationalisation employed in this thesis (known-groups validity; Davidson, 2014; Schnell et al., 2011).

3. Besides job autonomy, supervisor support, coworker support, and time pressure, another two potentially relevant organisational context factors were identified in Study 1: (a) the available budget of a nursing home, and (b) a culture of appreciation. Moreover, Study 1 also identified two additional agentic actions not yet discussed in the literature: (a) going beyond the necessity of their job by spending more time on job-related activities (e. g., by working overtime), and (b) taking on the role of a multiplier at work (e. g.,

by actively distributing information and knowledge gained from institutionalised learning activities). Since the research model already included a large number of concepts and the corresponding survey instrument already took 30 minutes to complete, it was decided not to include these concepts in Studies 2 and 3. However, it would be interesting to investigate whether and how these concepts have exploratory power to answer the research questions posed in this thesis. In addition, because of psychometric problems the scale measuring efforts to obtain work-related information from other individuals (deliberate social interaction) had to be removed from any further analysis in Study 3. Future studies should find better measures to operationalise this agentic action and investigate how it relates to the development of expertise.

4. Work agency, the four organisational context factors, and the control variable job experience were used as antecedents of the six agentic actions included in the research model. Future studies should include additional variables that potentially affect how and whether individuals engage in agentic actions. For instance, proximal antecedents like feelings of responsibility, utility judgements, and perceived costs associated with particular behaviours could be included in future studies to explain why individuals exercise agency in some situations but not in others. Furthermore, future studies should also include measures capturing individuals' attitudes towards the agentic actions of interest, their specific competence to actually engage in the agentic action in question, as well as their general goal orientation (i. e., learning vs. performance orientation). All together, these variables might give a clearer picture of whether, how, and why individuals engage in self-initiated and goal-directed behaviours in different work contexts.

5. No evidence could be found that deliberate job enlargement and deliberate enquiry of codified information leads to the development of expertise. Within the previous section it was hypothesised that some nursing homes might have installed institutionalised job rotation programmes and that some nurses might not be able to translate knowledge read in professional journals into practical problem-solving strategies. It would therefore be in-

teresting to include questions about the reading competence as well as the existence of such job rotation programmes in future studies. Both measures could then be modelled as moderators between the corresponding agentic action and expertise.

6. Almost no evidence was found that organisational context factors affect whether and how geriatric care nurses engage in agentic actions. Future studies should investigate (a) whether organisational context factors other than the ones included in the research model affect individuals' engagement in agentic actions, and (b) whether the investigated context factors have a lagged effect on individuals' inclination to exercise agency at work. First, only four organisational context factors were included in the statistical models analysed in this thesis. Other context factors like family support, the culture of appreciation within a nursing home or the available budget for training or other kinds of initiated measures of change might also either directly predict individuals' engagement in certain agentic actions or moderate the relationship between work agency and those agentic actions (see above). Second, the modelling approach used in this thesis in combination with the cross-sectional research design did not allow testing of whether the included organisational context factors have a lagged effect on nurses' capacity and tendency to exercise agency (in particular: agency beliefs and agency competence). Such a lagged effect, however, might explain how organisational context factors actually determine whether and how geriatric care nurses engage in agentic actions. Future studies should, therefore, investigate whether organisational context factors affect changes in employees' agency beliefs and/or agency competences in the long run.

7. Within this thesis, individuals' engagement in a set of theoretically derived agentic actions was—besides years of job experience as a control variable—used as a single predictor of expertise development. To this point, however, it is completely unclear how the engagement in those agentic actions explains differences in individuals' expertise development on top of already known determinants of professional learning and development. In other words, the question remains open as to what exactly is the added value of exercising agency at work in explaining learning and development pro-

cesses. Future studies including agency as something individuals do should control for a range of variables like the number of past training courses or the learning potential of individuals' workplaces in order to gather insights on such an added value.

8. This thesis investigated the role of agency in work-related learning and professional development processes in the domain of geriatric care nursing. At present it is still unclear whether the results of this thesis can be generalised to other professional domains. It would therefore be interesting to investigate whether the findings of Studies 1, 2, and 3 can be replicated by collecting data of participants working in other occupations. For this purpose, it might be necessary to slightly adapt the scales employed in Study 3 for the new domain in question.

9. This thesis successfully employed a cross-validation approach to test the robustness of the empirical findings of Study 3. Such an approach allows theoretically derived hypotheses to be tested more rigourously than studies that statistically analyse only on a single dataset. As long as the obtained sample is large enough, a cross-validation approach should also be used in future studies concerned with agency, expertise development, or workplace learning in general.

## 8.3 Practical Implications

Based on the empirical results of this study the following practical implications can be derived:

1. Individuals are more likely to engage in self-initiated behaviour if they (a) have the ability to visualise desired future states, to set goals, to translate these goals into action plans, to engage in these actions, and to deal with potential problems that might occur; (b) are convinced that they have these abilities; and (c) have a predisposition to make choices and to engage in actions in order to take control over their life and their environment. It therefore follows that employers who appreciate agentic employees should fill positions with individuals who feature profound agency competences,

strong agency beliefs, and a distinct agency personality. In addition, particularly since agency competences and agency beliefs are malleable (agency personality is conceptualised as a rather stable and immutable trait), employers can also seek to provide their employees with opportunities to develop these two agency facets. Such opportunities might range from designated trainings to boost abilities to engage in agentic actions as well as beliefs that one is capable of doing so (e. g., Eden & Aviram, 1993; Gist, 1989; Gist & Mitchell, 1992), to special work arrangements that allow or even require their employees to exercise agency. The latter have already been discussed as potentially favourable conditions that help individuals to strengthen their agency beliefs and to improve their agency competences (see Section 7.3.2).

2. A central finding of this thesis was that deliberate efforts to participate in institutionalised learning activities as well as deliberate efforts to take over additional responsibilities from supervisors or other individuals on a higher hierarchical level are positively related to the development of professional expertise. Employers should provide their employees with opportunities to do so. First, they should offer a diverse range of potential institutionalised learning activities (like training courses) from which their employees can choose. Another approach would be to encourage employees to choose training and seminars in which they would like to participate. Second, employers could use institutionalised job enrichment schemes where employees are motivated to take over additional responsibilities usually reserved for supervisors or other employees working on a higher hierarchical level. Such institutionalised schemes assist individuals to engage in deliberate participation in institutionalised learning activities and deliberate job enrichment by removing structural barriers.

3. Nurses are more likely to engage in deliberate efforts to take over additional responsibilities from supervisors or other individuals on a higher hierarchical level in relation to the more autonomy they experience at work. If deliberate job enrichment is appreciated, employers are advised to design workplaces in such a way that they offer a great extent of freedom, independence, and discretion. Employees should be given the opportunity to make

their own decisions on how to carry out their work. In addition, discretion should be provided concerning how to schedule the work. Obviously, this is only possible in regard to existing regulations and constraints like legally binding guidelines.

4. Deliberate enquiry of codified information was not found to be a consistent predictor of expertise in Study 2 and 3. However, both theoretical accounts as well as Study 1 emphasised how efforts to read professional literature are important for learning and development. It was therefore hypothesised that nurses might not always have the abilities to transfer information described in scientific literature into task- and problem-solving strategies. It would therefore be sensible to offer nurses training in how to read such literature and how to use new information obtained from these sources within their daily work practice.

## 8.4 Chapter Summary

To sum up, this thesis found preliminary evidence that human agency is indeed relevant for the development of professional expertise. Individuals who frequently engage in actions that are aimed at taking control over their life and their environment tend to develop expertise more quickly and effectively than individuals who do not frequently engage in such actions. Whether individuals engage in such agentic actions mainly depends on their disposition and general tendency to do so. Individuals who (a) have the ability to visualise desired states, to set goals, to translate these goals into actions, to engage in these actions, and to deal with potential problems that might occur; (b) are convinced that they have these abilities; and (c) have predispositions to take control over their life and their environment are more likely to exercise agency at work than individuals who do not have these abilities, beliefs, and predispositions. These abilities, beliefs, and predispositions are even more important than work environments that are more or less conducive to exercising work agency to explain whether individuals engage in agentic actions or not.

These empirical results were obtained using hypothesis-testing methods on two samples of more than 400 geriatric care nurses. Earlier empirical studies about the role of human agency in work-related learning and development have only been achieved using qualitative methods with much smaller samples. This thesis has therefore contributed to the literature by showing that human agency—both as an individual feature and as something individuals do—is indeed related to work-related learning and professional development, using more rigorous methods than have been employed before. Similar empirical evidence has not yet been presented. It is hoped that future studies find the theoretical framework as well as the operationalisation of work agency proposed in this thesis useful and that they manage to go beyond the limitations of the empirical research presented and discussed here.

# Bibliography


Abele, A. E., & Spurk, D. (2009). The longitudinal impact of self-efficacy and career goals on objective and subjective career success. *Journal of Vocational Behavior, 74*(1), 53–62

Achtenhagen, F., & Winther, E. (2014). Workplace-based competence measurement: Developing innovative assessment systems for tomorrow's VET programmes. *Journal of Vocational Education & Training, 66*(3), 281–295

Afentakis, A., & Maier, T. (2010). Projektionen des Personalbedarfs und -angebots in Pflegeberufen bis 2025 [Projections of the supply and demand of personnel working in care professions till 2025]. *Wirtschaft und Statistik, 11*, 990–1002.

Ajzen, I. (1991). The theory of planned behavior. *Organizational Behavior and Human Decision Processes, 50*(2), 179–211

Anderson, J. C., & Gerbing, D. W. (1988). Structural equation modeling in practice: A review and recommended two-step approach. *Psychological Bulletin, 103*(3), 411–423

Anderson, J. R. (1982). Acquisition of cognitive skill. *Psychological Review, 89*(4), 369–406

Anderson, J. R. (1987). Skill acquisition: Compilation of weak-method problem situations. *Psychological Review, 94*(2), 192–210

Anderson, J. R. (1993). Problem solving and learning. *American Psychologist, 48*(1), 35–44

Anseel, F., Beatty, A. S., Shen, W., Lievens, F., & Sackett, P. R. (2015). How are we doing after 30 years? A meta-analytic review of the antecedents and outcomes of feedback-seeking behavior. *Journal of Management, 41*(1), 318–348

Archer, M. S. (2000). *Being human: The problem of agency*. Cambridge: Cambridge University Press.

Ashford, S. J., & Black, J. S. (1996). Proactivity during organizational entry: The role of desire for control. *Journal of Applied Psychology, 81*(2), 199–214

Ashford, S. J., Blatt, R., & VandeWalle, D. (2003). Reflections on the looking glass: A review of research on feedback-seeking behavior in organizations. *Journal of Management, 29*(6), 773–799

Ashford, S. J., & Cummings, L. L. (1983). Feedback as an individual resource: Personal strategies of creating information. *Organizational Behavior and Human Performance, 32*(3), 370–398

Ashford, S. J., & Tsui, A. S. (1991). Self-regulation for managerial effectiveness: The role of active feedback seeking. *Academy of Management Journal, 34*(2), 251–280

Bagozzi, R. P., & Yi, Y. (1988). On the evaluation of structural equation models. *Journal of the Academy of Marketing Science, 16*(1), 74–94

Bahn, D. (2007). Orientation of nurses towards formal and informal learning: Motives and perceptions. *Nurse Education Today, 27*(7), 723–730

Bandura, A. (1977). Self-efficacy: Toward a unifying theory of behavioral change. *Psychological Review, 84*(2), 191–215

Bandura, A. (1978). The self system in reciprocal determinism. *American Psychologist, 33*(4), 344–358

Bandura, A. (1982). The self and mechanisms of agency. In J. Suls (Ed.), *Psychological perspectives on the self* (Vol. 1, pp. 3–39). Hillsdale, NJ: Erlbaum.

Bandura, A. (1986). *Social foundations of thought and action: A social cognitive theory.* Upper Saddle River: Prentice-Hall.

Bandura, A. (1989). Human agency in social cognitive theory. *American Psychologist, 44*(9), 1175–1184

Bandura, A. (1997). *Self-efficacy: The exercise of control.* New York: W.H. Freeman.

Bandura, A. (2001). Social cognitive theory: An agentic perspective. *Annual Review of Psychology, 52*(1), 1–26

Bandura, A. (2006a). Guide for constructing self-efficacy scales. In F. Pajares, & T. C. Urdan (Eds.), *Self-efficacy beliefs of adolescents* (pp. 307–337). Greenwich: Information Age Pub.

Bandura, A. (2006b). Toward a psychology of human agency. *Perspectives on Psychological Science, 1*(2), 164–180

Bandura, A. (2012). Social cognitive theory. In P. Van Lange, A. Kruglanski, & E. Higgins (Eds.), *Handbook of theories of social psychology* (Vol. 1, pp. 349–374). London: SAGE Publications.

Barcikowski, R. S. (1981). Statistical power with group mean as the unit of analysis. *Journal of Educational and Behavioral Statistics, 6*(3), 267–285

Barney, J. (1991). Firm resources and sustained competitive advantage. *Journal of Management, 17*(1), 99–120

Baruch, Y., & Holtom, B. C. (2008). Survey response rate levels and trends in organizational research. *Human Relations, 61*(8), 1139–1160

Bateman, T. S., & Crant, J. M. (1993). The proactive component of organizational behavior: A measure and correlates. *Journal of Organizational Behavior, 14*(2), 103–118

Bateman, T. S., & Crant, J. M. (1999). Proactive behavior: Meaning, impact, recommendations. *Business Horizons, 42*(3), 63–70

Bauer, J. (2008). *Learning from errors at work. Studies on nurses' engagement in error related learning activities.* (Doctoral dissertation, University of Regensburg, Regensburg). Retrieved from http://www.opus-bayern.de/uni-%20regensburg/volltexte/2008/990

Bauer, J., & Harteis, C. (Eds.). (2012). *Human fallibility: The ambiguity of errors for work and learning.* Dordrecht: Springer.

Bauer, T. N., Bodner, T., Erdogan, B., Truxillo, D. M., & Tucker, J. S. (2007). Newcomer adjustment during organizational socialization: A meta-analytic review of antecedents, outcomes, and methods. *Journal of Applied Psychology, 92*(3), 707–721

Baumeister, R. F., & Vohs, K. D. (2012). Self-regulation and the executive function of the self. In M. R. Leary, & J. P. Tangney (Eds.), *Handbook of self and identity* (2nd ed., pp. 180–197). New York: Guilford.

Beauducel, A., & Wittmann, W. W. (2005). Simulation study on fit indexes in CFA based on data with slightly distorted simple structure. *Structural Equation Modeling: A Multidisciplinary Journal, 12*(1), 41–75

Becker, J.-M., Klein, K., & Wetzels, M. (2012). Hierarchical latent variable models in PLS-SEM: Guidelines for using reflective-formative type models. *Long Range Planning, 45*(5), 359–394

Beenen, G., Pichler, S., & Levy, P. E. (2016). Self-determined feedback seeking: The role of perceived supervisor autonomy support. *Human Resource Management, Advance online publication.*

Belschak, F. D., & Den Hartog, D. N. (2010). Pro-self, prosocial, and pro-organizational foci of proactive behaviour: Differential antecedents and consequences. *Journal of Occupational and Organizational Psychology, 83*(2), 475–498

Bender, S.-F. (2010). Age-Diversity: Wertschätzung statt Abwertung älterer Arbeitnehmerinnen und Arbeitnehmer? [Age-Diversity: Appreciation instead of depreciation of older workers?] In K. Brauer, & W. Clemens (Eds.), *Zu alt? "Ageism" und Altersdiskriminierung auf Arbeitsmärkten* (pp. 171–186). Wiesbaden: VS Verlag für Sozialwissenschaften.

Benner, P. (1984). *From novice to expert: Excellence and power in clinical nursing practice.* Reading: Addison-Wesley.

Benner, P. (2004). Using the Dreyfus model of skill acquisition to describe and interpret skill acquisition and clinical judgment in nursing practice and education. *Bulletin of Science, Technology and Society, 24*(3), 188–199

Bereiter, C., & Scardamalia, M. (1993). *Surpassing ourselves: An inquiry into the nature and implications of expertise.* Chicago: Open Court.

Berg, J. M., Grant, A. M., & Johnson, V. (2010). When callings are calling: Crafting work and leisure in pursuit of unanswered occupational callings. *Organization Science, 21*(5), 973–994

Berg, J. M., Wrzesniewski, A., & Dutton, J. E. (2010). Perceiving and responding to challenges in job crafting at different ranks: When proactivity requires adaptivity. *Journal of Organizational Behavior, 31*(2), 158–186

Berings, M. G., Poell, R. F., & Simons, P. R.-J. (2005). Conceptualizing on-the-job learning styles. *Human Resource Development Review, 4*(4), 373–400

Berings, M. G., Poell, R. F., Simons, P. R.-J., & van Veldhoven, M. J. (2007). The development and validation of the on-the-job learning styles questionnaire for the nursing profession. *Journal of Advanced Nursing, 58*(5), 480–492

Berings, M. G., Poell, R., & Gelissen, J. (2008). On-the-job learning in the nursing profession: Developing and validating a classification of learning activities and learning themes. *Personnel Review, 37*(4), 442–459

Berk, R. A. (1983). An introduction to sample selection bias in sociological data. *American Sociological Review, 48*(3), 386–398.

Berliner, D. C. (2001). Learning about and learning from expert teachers. *International Journal of Educational Research, 35*(5), 463–482

Berryman, S. E. (1993). Learning for the workplace. *Review of Research in Education, 19*(1), 343–401

Betz, N. E., & Hackett, G. (1983). The relationship of mathematics self-efficacy expectations to the selection of science-based college majors. *Journal of Vocational Behavior, 23*(3), 329–345

Biesta, G., & Tedder, M. (2007). Agency and learning in the lifecourse: Towards an ecological perspective. *Studies in the Education of Adults, 39*(2), 132–149.

Billett, S. (1995). Workplace learning: Its potential and limitations. *Education + Training, 37*(5), 20–27

Billett, S. (1996). Towards a model of workplace learning: The learning curriculum. *Studies in Continuing Education, 18*(1), 43–58

Billett, S. (2000). Guided learning at work. *Journal of Workplace Learning, 12*(7), 272–285

Billett, S. (2001a). Knowing in practice: Re-conceptualising vocational expertise. *Learning and Instruction, 11*(6), 431–452

Billett, S. (2001b). *Learning in the workplace: Strategies for effective practice.* Crows Nest: Allen & Unwin.

Billett, S. (2001c). Learning through work: Workplace affordances and individual engagement. *Journal of Workplace Learning, 13*(5), 209–214

Billett, S. (2002). Workplace pedagogic practices: Co-participation and learning. *British Journal of Educational Studies, 50*(4), 457–481

Billett, S. (2004a). Learning through work: Workplace participatory practices. In H. Rainbird, A. Fuller, & A. Munro (Eds.), *Workplace learning in context* (pp. 109–125). London: Routledge.

Billett, S. (2004b). Workplace participatory practices: Conceptualising workplaces as learning environments. *Journal of Workplace Learning, 16*(6), 312–324

Billett, S. (2006). Relational interdependence between social and individual agency in work and working life. *Mind, Culture, and Activity, 13*(1), 53–69

Billett, S. (2008a). Learning through work: Exploring instances of relational interdependencies. *International Journal of Educational Research, 47*(4), 232–240

Billett, S. (2008b). Learning throughout working life: A relational interdependence between personal and social agency. *British Journal of Educational Studies, 56*(1), 39–58

Billett, S. (2011a). Subjectivity, self and personal agency in learning through and for work. In M. Malloch, L. Cairns, K. Evans, & B. O'Conner (Eds.), *The SAGE handbook of workplace learning* (pp. 60–72). London: Sage.

Billett, S. (2011b). Workplace curriculum: Practice and propositions. In F. Dochy, D. Gijbels, M. Segers, & P. Van den Bossche (Eds.), *Theories of learning for the workplace: Building blocks for training and professional development programmes* (pp. 17–36). London: Routledge.

Billett, S. (2014). *Mimetic learning at work.* New York: Springer.

Billett, S., Barker, M., & Hernon-Tinning, B. (2004). Participatory practices at work. *Pedagogy, Culture & Society, 12*(2), 233–258

Billett, S., & Pavlova, M. (2005). Learning through working life: Self and individuals' agentic action. *International Journal of Lifelong Education, 24*(3), 195–211

Billett, S., & Smith, R. (2006). Personal agency and epistemology at work. In S. Billett, T. Fenwick, & M. Somerville (Eds.), *Work, subjectivity and learning* (pp. 141–156). Dordrecht: Springer.

Billett, S., & Somerville, M. (2004). Transformations at work: Identity and learning. *Studies in Continuing Education, 26*(2), 309–326

Bindl, U. K., & Parker, S. K. (2011). Proactive work behavior: Forward-thinking and change-oriented action in organizations. In S. Zedeck (Ed.), *APA handbook of industrial and organizational psychology, Vol. 2: Selecting and developing members for the organization* (pp. 567–598). Washington: American Psychological Association.

Bliese, P. (2013). *Multilevel: Multilevel functions.* R package version 2.5. Retrieved from https://CRAN.R-project.org/package=multilevel

Blinkert, B., & Klie, T. (2004). Gesellschaftlicher Wandel und demographische Veränderungen als Herausforderungen für die Sicherstellung der Versorgung von pflegebedürftigen Menschen [Societal and demographic changes as a challenge for securing the treatment and provision of people in need of care]. *Sozialer Fortschritt, 43*(11), 319–325.

Boero, R., & Novarese, M. (2012). Feedback and learning. In N. M. Seel (Ed.), *Encyclopedia of the sciences of learning* (pp. 1282–1285). Boston: Springer.

Bollen, K., & Lennox, R. (1991). Conventional wisdom on measurement: A structural equation perspective. *Psychological Bulletin, 110*(2), 305–314

Bonacich, P., & Lloyd, P. (2001). Eigenvector-like measures of centrality for asymmetric relations. *Social Networks, 23*(3), 191–201

Borgatti, S. P., & Cross, R. (2003). A relational view of information seeking and learning in social networks. *Management Science, 49*(4), 432–445

Bortz, J., & Döring, N. (2006). *Forschungsmethoden und Evaluation für Human- und Sozialwissenschaftler [Research methods and evaluation techniques for researches in human and social sciences]* (4th ed.). Heidelberg: Springer.

Bortz, J., & Schuster, C. (2010). *Statistik für Human- und Sozialwissenschaftler [Statistics for researchers working in human and social sciences]* (7th ed.). Berlin: Springer.

Boshuizen, H. P. A., & Schmidt, H. G. (1992). On the role of biomedical knowledge in clinical reasoning by experts, intermediates and novices. *Cognitive Science, 16*(2), 153–184

Boshuizen, H. P. A., & Schmidt, H. G. (2008). The development of clinical reasoning expertise. In J. Higgs (Ed.), *Clinical reasoning in the health professions* (pp. 113–121). Amsterdam: Elsevier.

Boshuizen, H. P. A., & van de Wiel, M. W. J. (2014). Expertise development through schooling and work. In A. Littlejohn, & A. Margaryan (Eds.), *Technology-enhanced professional learning: Processes, practices, and tools* (pp. 71–84). New York: Routledge.

Boud, D., Keogh, R., & Walker, D. (1999a). Promoting reflection in learning: A model. In D. Boud, R. Keogh, & D. Walker (Eds.), *Reflection: Turning experience into learning* (pp. 18–40). London: Kogan Page.

Boud, D., Keogh, R., & Walker, D. (1999b). What is reflection in learning? In D. Boud, R. Keogh, & D. Walker (Eds.), *Reflection: Turning experience into learning* (pp. 7–17). London: Kogan Page.

Bowen, N. K., & Guo, S. (2012). *Structural equation modeling.* Oxford: Oxford University Press.

Brandtstädter, J., & Rothermund, K. (2002). Intentional self-development: Exploring the interfaces between development, intentionality, and the self. In L. J. Crockett (Ed.), *Agency, motivation, and the life course: Volume 48 of the Nebraska symposium on motivation* (pp. 31–75). Lincoln: University of Nebraska Press.

Bratton, J., & Gold, J. (2007). *Human resource management: Theory and practice* (4th ed.). Basingstoke: Palgrave Macmillan.

Bromme, R. (2014). *Der Lehrer als Experte: Zur Psychologie des professionellen Wissens [The teacher as an expert: About the psychology of professional knowledge]* (Reprint). Münster: Waxmann.

Brown, S. D., Lent, R. W., Telander, K., & Tramayne, S. (2011). Social cognitive career theory, conscientiousness, and work performance: A meta-analytic path analysis. *Journal of Vocational Behavior, 79*(1), 81–90

Bryson, J., Pajo, K., Ward, R., & Mallon, M. (2006). Learning at work: Organisational affordances and individual engagement. *Journal of Workplace Learning, 18*(5), 279–297

Bühner, M. (2011). *Einführung in die Test- und Fragebogenkonstruktion [Introduction into test and questionnaire construction]* (3rd ed.). München: Pearson Studium.

Bund-Länder-Arbeitsgruppe Weiterentwicklung der Pflege. (2012). *Eckpunkte zur Vorbereitung des Entwurfs eines neuen Pflegeberufegesetzes [Key points of the preparation of a draft of a new law for care professions]*. Berlin. Retrieved from http://www.bmfsfj.de/BMFSFJ/aeltere-menschen,did=194274.html

Bunnin, N., & Yu, J. (2004). *The Blackwell dictionary of Western philosophy*. Malden, MA: Blackwell Pub.

Burger, J. M., & Cooper, H. M. (1979). The desirability of control. *Motivation and Emotion, 3*(4), 381–393

Butler, D. L., & Winne, P. H. (1995). Feedback and self-regulated learning: A theoretical synthesis. *Review of Educational Research, 65*(3), 245–281

Button, S. B., Mathieu, J. E., & Zajac, D. M. (1996). Goal orientation in organizational research: A conceptual and empirical foundation. *Organizational Behavior and Human Decision Processes, 67*(1), 26–48

Cabrera-Nguyen, P. (2010). Author guidelines for reporting scales development and validation results in the journal of the society for social work and research. *Journal of the Society for Social Work and Research, 1*(2), 99–103.

Campbell, D. J. (2000). The proactive employee: Managing workplace initiative. *Academy of Management Perspectives, 14*(3), 52–66

Campbell, D. T., & Fiske, D. W. (1959). Convergent and discriminant validation by the multitrait-multimethod matrix. *Psychological Bulletin, 56*(2), 81–105

Campbell, J. (1990). Modeling the performance prediction problem in industrial and organizational psychology. In M. Dunnette, & L. Hough (Eds.), *Handbook of industrial and organizational psychology* (Vol. 1, pp. 687–732). Palo Alto: Consulting Psychologists Press.

Caplan, R. D., Vinokur, A. D., Price, R. H., & Van Ryn, M. (1989). Job seeking, reemployment, and mental health: A randomized field experiment in coping with job loss. *Journal of Applied Psychology, 74*(5), 759–769

Caprara, G. V., Vecchione, M., Alessandri, G., Gerbino, M., & Barbaranelli, C. (2011). The contribution of personality traits and self-efficacy beliefs to academic achievement: A longitudinal study. *British Journal of Educational Psychology, 81*(1), 78–96

Carver, C. S., & Scheier, M. F. (2005). On the structure of behavioral self-regulation. In M. Boekaerts, P. R. Pintrich, & M. Zeidner (Eds.), *Handbook of self-regulation* (pp. 41–84). San Diego: Academic Press.

Carver, C. S., & Scheier, M. F. (2014). Dispositional optimism. *Trends in Cognitive Sciences, 18*(6), 293–299

Cattell, R. B. (1966). The scree test for the number of factors. *Multivariate Behavioral Research, 1*(2), 245–276

Champely, S. (2015). *Pwr: Basic functions for power analysis.* R package version 1.1-3. Retrieved from https://CRAN.R-project.org/package=pwr

Chase, W. G., & Simon, H. A. (1973). Perception in chess. *Cognitive Psychology, 4*(1), 55–81

Check, J. W., & Schutt, R. K. (2012). *Research methods in education.* Thousand Oaks: Sage Publications.

Chen, G., Gully, S. M., & Eden, D. (2001). Validation of a new general self-efficacy scale. *Organizational Research Methods, 4*(1), 62–83

Chesnut, S. R., & Burley, H. (2015). Self-efficacy as a predictor of commitment to the teaching profession: A meta-analysis. *Educational Research Review, 15,* 1–16

Chi, M. T. H. (2006). Two approaches to study of experts' characteristics. In K. A. Ericsson, N. Charness, P. J. Feltovich, & R. R. Hoffmann (Eds.), *The Cambridge handbook of expertise and expert performance* (pp. 21–30). Cambridge: Cambridge University Press.

Chi, M. T. H., Feltovich, P. J., & Glaser, R. (1981). Categorization and representation of physics problems by experts and novices. *Cognitive Science, 5*(2), 121–152

Chin, W. W. (1998a). Commentary: Issues and opinion on structural equation modeling. *MIS quarterly, 22*(1), vii–xvi.

Chin, W. W. (1998b). The partial least squares approach for structural equation modelling. In G. A. Marcoulides (Ed.), *Modern methods for business research* (pp. 295–336). Mahwah: Erlbaum.

Chin, W. W. (2010). How to write up and report PLS analyses. In V. Esposito Vinzi, W. W. Chin, J. Henseler, & H. Wang (Eds.), *Handbook of partial least squares* (pp. 655–690). Berlin: Springer.

Clausen, J. S. (1991). Adolescent competence and the shaping of the life course. *American Journal of Sociology, 96*(4), 805–842.

Cohen, J. (1988). *Statistical power analysis for the behavioral sciences* (2nd ed.). Hillsdale: Lawrence Erlbaum Associates.

Cohen, J. (1992). A power primer. *Psychological Bulletin, 112*(1), 155–159

Cole, M. (1995). The zone of proximal development where culture and cognition create each other. In J. V. Wertsch (Ed.), *Culture, communication and cognition: Vygotskian perspective* (pp. 146–161). Cambridge: Cambridge University Press.

Collier, D., & Mahoney, J. (1996). Insights and pitfalls: Selection bias in qualitative research. *World Politics, 49*(1), 56–91

Collin, K. (2002). Development engineers' conceptions of learning at work. *Studies in Continuing Education, 24*(2), 133–152

Collin, K. (2004). The role of experience in work and learning among design engineers. *International Journal of Training and Development, 8*(2), 111–127

Colquitt, J. A., LePine, J. A., & Noe, R. A. (2000). Toward an integrative theory of training motivation: A meta-analytic path analysis of 20 years of research. *The Journal of Applied Psychology, 85*(5), 678–707.

Conway, J. M., & Huffcutt, A. I. (2003). A review and evaluation of exploratory factor analysis practices in organizational research. *Organizational Research Methods, 6*(2), 147–168

Cooper-Thomas, H., & Burke, S. E. (2012). Newcomer proactive behavior: Can there be too much of a good thing? In C. R. Wanberg (Ed.), *The Oxford handbook of organizational socialization* (pp. 56–77). New York: Oxford University Press.

Costenbader, E., & Valente, T. W. (2003). The stability of centrality measures when networks are sampled. *Social Networks, 25*(4), 283–307

Crant, J. M. (1995). The proactive personality scale and objective job performance among real estate agents. *Journal of Applied Psychology, 80*(4), 532–537

Crant, J. M. (2000). Proactive behavior in organizations. *Journal of Management, 26*(3), 435–462

Crockett, L. J. (2002). Agency in the life course: Concepts and processes. In L. J. Crockett (Ed.), *Agency, motivation, and the life course: Volume 48 of the Nebraska symposium on motivation* (pp. 1–29). Lincoln: University of Nebraska Press.

Cross, S., & Markus, H. (1991). Possible selves across the life span. *Human Development, 34*(4), 230–255

Curran, P. J., West, S. G., & Finch, J. F. (1996). The robustness of test statistics to nonnormality and specification error in confirmatory factor analysis. *Psychological Methods, 1*(1), 16–29

Custers, E. J. F. M., Boshuizen, H. P. A., & Schmidt, H. G. (1996). The influence of medical expertise, case typicality, and illness script component on case processing and disease probability estimates. *Memory & Cognition, 24*(3), 384–399

Daley, B. J. (1999). Novice to expert: An exploration of how professionals learn. *Adult Education Quarterly, 49*(4), 133–147

Davidson, M. (2014). Known-groups validity. In A. C. Michalos (Ed.), *Encyclopedia of quality of life and well-being research* (pp. 3481–3482). Dordrecht: Springer.

De Charms, R. (1970). *Personal causation: The internal affective determinants of behavior.* New York: Academic Press.

De Vaus, D. A. (2002). *Surveys in social research.* London: Routledge.

Deci, E. L., & Ryan, R. M. (1993). Die Selbstbestimmungstheorie der Motivation und ihre Bedeutung für die Pädagogik [Self-determination theory of motivation and its relevance for pedagogy]. *Zeitschrift für Pädagogik, 39*(2), 223–238.

Deci, E. L., & Ryan, R. M. (2000). The "what" and "why" of goal pursuits: Human needs and the self-determination of behavior. *Psychological Inquiry, 11*(4), 227–268

Deci, E. L., Ryan, R. M., & Williams, G. C. (1996). Need satisfaction and the self-regulation of learning. *Learning and Individual Differences, 8*(3), 165–183

Diamantopoulos, A., & Winklhofer, H. M. (2001). Index construction with formative indicators: An alternative to scale development. *Journal of Marketing Research, 38*(2), 269–277

Dobischat, R., Fischell, M., & Rosendahl, A. (2015). *Einführung in das Recht der Weiterbildung [Introduction into legal aspects of further education].* Wiesbaden: Springer VS.

Dokko, G., Wilk, S. L., & Rothbard, N. P. (2009). Unpacking prior experience: How career history affects job performance. *Organization Science, 20*(1), 51–68

Donaldson, S. I., & Grant-Vallone, E. J. (2002). Understanding self-report bias in organizational behavior research. *Journal of Business and Psychology, 17*(2), 245–260.

Doornbos, A. J., Bolhuis, S., & Denessen, E. (2004). Exploring the relation between work domains and work-related learning: The case of the dutch police force. *International Journal of Training and Development, 8*(3), 174–190

Doty, D. H., & Glick, W. H. (1998). Common methods bias: Does common methods variance really bias results? *Organizational Research Methods, 1*(4), 374–406

Dreyfus, H. L., & Dreyfus, S. E. (1988). *Mind over machine: The power of human intuition and expertise in the era of the computer.* New York: Free Press.

Dreyfus, H. L., & Dreyfus, S. E. (2005). Peripheral vision: Expertise in real world contexts. *Organization Studies, 26*(5), 779–792

Dunn, T. G., & Shriner, C. (1999). Deliberate practice in teaching: What teachers do for self-improvement. *Teaching and Teacher Education, 15*(6), 631–51.

Dutton, J. E., & Ashford, S. J. (1993). Selling issues to top management. *Academy of Management Review, 18*(3), 397–428

Dweck, C. S., & Leggett, E. L. (1988). A social-cognitive approach to motivation and personality. *Psychological Review, 95*(2), 256–273

Eccles, J. S., & Wigfield, A. (2002). Motivational beliefs, values, and goals. *Annual Review of Psychology, 53*(1), 109–132

Ecclestone, K. (2007). An identity crisis? Using concepts of 'identity', 'agency' and 'structure' in the education of adults. *Studies in the Education of Adults, 39*(2), 121–131.

Eden, D., & Aviram, A. (1993). Self-efficacy training to speed reemployment: Helping people to help themselves. *Journal of Applied Psychology, 78*(3), 352–360

Edwards, A. (2005). Relational agency: Learning to be a resourceful practitioner. *International Journal of Educational Research, 43*(3), 168–182

Edwards, A. (2009). Relational agency in collaborations for the well-being of children and young people. *Journal of Children's Services, 4*(1), 33–43

Edwards, A. (2010). *Being an expert professional practitioner: The relational turn in expertise.* Dordrecht: Springer.

Edwards, A., & Mackenzie, L. (2005). Steps towards participation: The social support of learning trajectories. *International Journal of Lifelong Education, 24*(4), 287–302

Eichorn, D. H. (1981). Samples and procedures. In D. H. Eichorn, J. S. Clausen, N. Haan, M. P. Honzik, & P. H. Mussen (Eds.), *Present and past in middle life* (pp. 33–51). New York: Academic Press.

Eisenhardt, K. M. (1989). Agency theory: An assessment and review. *Academy of Management Review, 14*(1), 57–74

Elder, G. H. (1998). The life course and the human development. In W. Damon, & R. M. Lerner (Eds.), *Theoretical models of human development* (5th ed., Vol. 1, pp. 939–991). New York: Wiley.

Elder, G. H. (2000). The life course. In E. F. Borgatta, & R. J. V. Montgomery (Eds.), *Encyclopedia of sociology* (2nd ed., pp. 1614–1622). New York: Macmillan Reference.

Elder, G. H. (2003). The emergence and development of life course theory. In J. T. Mortimer, & M. J. Shanahan (Eds.), *Handbook of the life course* (pp. 3–19). New York: Springer.

Elder, G. H., & Shanahan, M. J. (2007). The life course and human development. In W. Damon, & R. M. Lerner (Eds.), *Handbook of child psychology.* Hoboken: John Wiley & Sons, Inc.

Ellinger, A. D. (2005). Contextual factors influencing informal learning in a workplace setting: The case of 'reinventing itself company'. *Human Resource Development Quarterly, 16*(3), 389–415

Elliot, A. J., McGregor, H. A., & Thrash, T. M. (2002). The need for competence. In E. L. Deci, & R. M. Ryan (Eds.), *Handbook of self-determination research* (pp. 361–387). Rochester: The University of Rochester Press.

Ellström, P.-E. (2006). The meaning and role of reflection in informal learning at work. In D. Boud, P. Cressey, & P. Docherty (Eds.), *Productive reflection at work* (pp. 43–53). London: Routledge.

Emirbayer, M., & Mische, A. (1998). What is agency? *American Journal of Sociology, 103*(4), 962–1023

Eraut, M. (2000). Non-formal learning and tacit knowledge in professional work. *British Journal of Educational Psychology, 70*(1), 113–136

Eraut, M. (2004). Informal learning in the workplace. *Studies in Continuing Education, 26*(2), 247–273

Eraut, M. (2007). Learning from other people in the workplace. *Oxford Review of Education, 33*(4), 403–422

Eraut, M. (2010a). Knowledge, working practices, and learning. In S. Billett (Ed.), *Learning through practice: Models, traditions, orientations and approaches* (pp. 37–58). Dordrecht: Springer.

Eraut, M. (2010b). The balance between communities and personal agency: Transferring and integrating knowledge and know-how between different communities and contexts. In N. Jackson (Ed.), *Learning to be professional through a higher education e-book* (pp. 1–20). Guildford: Surrey Centre for Excellence in Professional Training and Education. Retrieved from http://lifewidelearningconference.pbworks.com/w/page/24285296/E%20proceedings

Eraut, M. (2012). Developing a broader approach to professional learning. In A. Mc Kee, & M. Eraut (Eds.), *Learning trajectories, innovation and identity for professional development* (pp. 21–45). Dordrecht: Springer.

Eraut, M., Alderton, J., Cole, G., & Senker, P. (2002). Learning from other people at work. In R. Harrison, F. Reeve, A. Hanson, & J. Clarke (Eds.), *Supporting lifelong learning* (Vol. 1, pp. 90–108). London: Routledge/Falmer.

Eraut, M., & Hirsh, W. (2007). *The significance of workplace learning for individuals, groups and organisations.* Oxford: University of Oxford.

Ericsson, K. A. (2006a). An introduction to Cambridge handbook of expertise and expert performance: Its development, organization, and content. In K. A. Ericsson, N. Charness, P. J. Feltovich, & R. R. Hoffmann (Eds.), *The Cambridge handbook of expertise and expert performance* (pp. 3–19). Cambridge: Cambridge University Press.

Ericsson, K. A. (2006b). The influence of experience and deliberate practice on the development of superior expert performance. In K. A. Ericsson, N. Charness, P. J. Feltovich, & R. R. Hoffmann (Eds.), *The Cambridge handbook of expertise and expert performance* (pp. 683–703). Cambridge: Cambridge University Press.

Ericsson, K. A., & Crutcher, R. J. (1990). The nature of exceptional performance. *Lifespan development and behaviour, 10*, 187–217.

Ericsson, K. A., Krampe, R. T., & Tesch-Römer, C. (1993). The role of deliberate practice in the acquisition of expert performance. *Psychological Review, 100*(3), 363–406

Ericsson, K. A., & Lehmann, A. C. (1996). Expert and exceptional performance: Evidence of maximal adaptation to task constraints. *Annual Review of Psychology, 47*(1), 273–305

Ericsson, K. A., & Smith, J. (Eds.). (1991). *Toward a general theory of expertise: Prospects and limits.* Cambridge: Cambridge Univ. Press.

Ericsson, K. A., & Towne, T. J. (2010). Expertise. *Wiley Interdisciplinary Reviews: Cognitive Science, 1*(3), 404–416

Ericsson, K. A., Whyte, J., & Ward, P. (2007). Expert performance in nursing: Reviewing research on expertise in nursing within the framework of the expert-performance approach. *Advances in Nursing Science, 30*(1), 58–71.

Esposito Vinzi, V., Chin, W. W., Henseler, J., & Wang, H. (Eds.). (2010). *Handbook of partial least squares: Concepts, methods and applications.* Berlin: Springer.

Est, V. (2010). Personalentwicklung [Personnel development]. In P. Bechtel, D. Friedrich, & A. Kerres (Eds.), *Mitarbeitermotivation ist lernbar: Mitarbeiter in Gesundheitseinrichtungen motivieren, führen, coachen* (pp. 143–158). Berlin: Springer.

Estabrooks, C. A., Rutakumwa, W., O'Leary, K. A., Profetto-McGrath, J., Milner, M., Levers, M. J., & Scott-Findlay, S. (2005). Sources of practice knowledge among nurses. *Qualitative Health Research, 15*(4), 460–476

Eteläpelto, A. (1994). Work experience and the development of expertise. In W. Nijhof, & J. Streumer (Eds.), *Flexibility in training and vocational education* (pp. 319–341). Utrecht: Lemma.

Eteläpelto, A., Hökkä, P., Vähäsantanen, K., & Collin, K. (2010). *Recent notions of agency: Towards reconceptualising professional agency at work.* Presentation held at SIG-14 Conference., Munich.

Eteläpelto, A., & Saarinen, J. (2006). Developing subjective identities through collective participation. In S. Billett, T. Fenwick, & M. Somerville (Eds.), *Work, subjectivity and learning* (Vol. 6, pp. 157–177). Dordrecht: Springer.

Eteläpelto, A., Vähäsantanen, K., Hökkä, P., & Paloniemi, S. (2013). What is agency? Conceptualizing professional agency at work. *Educational Research Review, 10,* 45–65.

Eteläpelto, A., Vähäsantanen, K., Hökkä, P., & Paloniemi, S. (2014). Identity and agency in professional learning. In S. Billett, C. Harteis, & H. Gruber (Eds.), *International handbook of research in professional and practice-based learning* (pp. 645–672). Dordrecht: Springer.

Eurostat. (2011). *Demography report 2010. Older, more numerous and diverse Europeans.* Luxembourg: Publications Office of the European Union.

Evans, K. (2002). Taking control of their lives? Agency in young adult transitions in England and the new Germany. *Journal of Youth Studies, 5*(3), 245–269

Evans, K. (2007). Concepts of bounded agency in education, work, and the personal lives of young adults. *International Journal of Psychology, 42*(2), 85–93

Evans, K., & Kersh, N. (2006). Learner biographies, workplace practices, and learning. In K. Evans, P. Hodkinson, H. Rainbird, & L. Unwin (Eds.), *Improving workplace learning* (pp. 68–94). London: Routledge.

Evans, K., Kersh, N., & Sakamoto, A. (2004). Learner biographies: Exploring tacit dimensions of knowledge and skill. In H. Rainbird, A. Fuller, & A. Munro (Eds.), *Workplace learning in context* (pp. 126–144). London: Routledge.

Fabrigar, L. R., Wegener, D. T., MacCallum, R. C., & Strahan, E. J. (1999). Evaluating the use of exploratory factor analysis in psychological research. *Psychological Methods, 4*(3), 272–299

Facteau, J. D., Dobbins, G. H., Russell, J. E., Ladd, R. T., & Kudisch, J. D. (1995). The influence of general perceptions of the training environment on pretraining motivation and perceived training transfer. *Journal of Management, 21*(1), 1–25

Fay, D., & Frese, M. (2001). The concept of personal initiative: An overview of validity studies. *Human Performance, 14*(1), 97–124
Fay, D., & Sonnentag, S. (2002). Rethinking the effects of stressors: A longitudinal study on personal initiative. *Journal of Occupational Health Psychology, 7*(3), 221–234
Federal Employment Agency. (2014). *Der Arbeitsmarkt in Deutschland: Altenpflege [The job market in Germany: Geriatric care]*. Bundesagentur für Arbeit. Nürnberg. Retrieved from http://doku.iab.de/externe/2014/k140709r07.pdf
Feltovich, P. J., Johnson, P. E., Moller, J. H., & Swanson, D. B. (1984). LCS: The role and development of medical knowledge in diagnostic expertise. In W. Clancey, & E. Shortliff (Eds.), *Readings in medical artificial intelligence* (pp. 275–319). Reading: Addison-Wesley.
Feltovich, P. J., Prietula, M. J., & Ericsson, K. A. (2006). Studies of expertise from psychological perspectives. In K. A. Ericsson, N. Charness, P. J. Feltovich, & R. R. Hoffmann (Eds.), *The Cambridge handbook of expertise and expert performance* (pp. 41–67). Cambridge: Cambridge University Press.
Finney, S. J., & DiStefano, C. (2006). Non-normal and categorical data in structural equation modeling. In G. R. Hancock, & R. O. Mueller (Eds.), *Structural equation modeling: A second course* (pp. 269–314). Greenwich: Information Age Publishing.
Fischer, C., & O'Connor, B. N. (2014). Informal learning in workplaces: Understanding learning culture as a challenge for organizational and individual development. In C. Harteis, A. Rausch, & J. Seifried (Eds.), *Discourses on professional learning* (pp. 11–24). Dordrecht: Springer.
Fornell, C., & Larcker, D. F. (1981). Evaluating structural equation models with unobservable variables and measurement error. *Journal of Marketing Research, 18*(1), 39
Forsman, P., Collin, K., & Eteläpelto, A. (2014). The practice of professional agency and the emergence of collaborative creativity in developmental staff meetings. In C. Harteis, A. Rausch, & J. Seifried (Eds.), *Discourses on professional learning: On the boundary between learning and working* (pp. 45–74). Dordrecht: Springer.
Fox, A., Deaney, R., & Wilson, E. (2010). Examining beginning teachers' perceptions of workplace support. *Journal of Workplace Learning, 22*(4), 212–227
Fox, A., & Wilson, E. G. (2015). Networking and the development of professionals: Beginning teachers building social capital. *Teaching and Teacher Education, 47*, 93–107
Fox, A., Wilson, E., & Deaney, R. (2011). Beginning teachers' workplace experiences: Perceptions of and use of support. *Vocations and Learning, 4*(1), 1–24
Freeman, L. C. (1978). Centrality in social networks conceptual clarification. *Social Networks, 1*(3), 215–239
French, J. R., & Raven, B. (1959). The bases of social power. In D. P. Cartwright (Ed.), *Studies of social power* (pp. 150–167). Ann Arbor: University of Michigan.
Frese, M., & Fay, D. (2001). Personal initiative: An active performance concept for work in the 21st century. *Research in Organizational Behavior, 23*, 133–187
Frese, M., Fay, D., Hilburger, T., Leng, K., & Tag, A. (1997). The concept of personal initiative: Operationalization, reliability and validity in two German samples. *Journal of Occupational and Organizational Psychology, 70*(2), 139–161
Frese, M., Garst, H., & Fay, D. (2007). Making things happen: Reciprocal relationships between work characteristics and personal initiative in a four-wave longitudinal structural equation model. *Journal of Applied Psychology, 92*(4), 1084–1102

Frese, M., van Gelderen, M., & Ombach, M. (2000). How to plan as a small scale business owner: Psychological process characteristics of action strategies and success. *Journal of Small Business Management, 38*(2), 1–18.

Friesacher, H. (2009). Professionalisierung der Pflege – vom Hilfsberuf zur evidenzbasierten Heilkunde? [Professionalisation of care–from unskilled work towards evidence-based medical science?]. *intensiv, 17*(4), 177–181

Fritz, C., & Sonnentag, S. (2009). Antecedents of day-level proactive behavior: A look at job stressors and positive affect during the workday. *Journal of Management, 35*(1), 94–111

Fuchs, S. (2001). Beyond agency. *Sociological Theory, 19*(1), 24–40

Fuller, A., & Unwin, L. (2004). Expansive learning environments: Integrating organizational and personal development. In H. Rainbird, A. Fuller, & A. Munro (Eds.), *Workplace learning in context* (pp. 126–144). London: Routledge.

Fuller, A., & Unwin, L. (2005). Older and wiser? Workplace learning from the perspective of experienced employees. *International Journal of Lifelong Education, 24*(1), 21–39.

Fuller, B., & Marler, L. E. (2009). Change driven by nature: A meta-analytic review of the proactive personality literature. *Journal of Vocational Behavior, 75*(3), 329–345

Fuller, J. B., Marler, L. E., & Hester, K. (2012). Bridge building within the province of proactivity. *Journal of Organizational Behavior, 33*(8), 1053–1070

Furnham, A., & Steele, H. (1993). Measuring locus of control: A critique of general, children's, health- and work-related locus of control questionnaires. *British Journal of Psychology, 84*(4), 443–479

Gartmeier, M., & Schüttelkopf, E. M. (2012). Tracing outcomes of learning from errors on the level of knowledge. In J. Bauer, & C. Harteis (Eds.), *Human fallibility: The ambiguity of errors for work and learning* (pp. 33–51). Dordrecht: Springer.

Gecas, V. (2003). Self-agency and the life course. In J. T. Mortimer, & M. J. Shanahan (Eds.), *Handbook of the life course* (pp. 369–388). New York: Springer.

Gegenfurtner, A. (2011). Motivation and transfer in professional training: A meta-analysis of the moderating effects of knowledge type, instruction, and assessment conditions. *Educational Research Review, 6*(3), 153–168

Gegenfurtner, A., Veermans, K., Festner, D., & Gruber, H. (2009). Motivation to transfer training: An integrative literature review. *Human Resource Development Review, 8*(3), 403–423

George, L. K. (2003). Life course research. In J. T. Mortimer, & M. J. Shanahan (Eds.), *Handbook of the life course* (pp. 671–680). New York: Springer.

Gerber, R. (1998). How do workers learn in their work? *The Learning Organization, 5*(4), 168–175

Gerber, R., Lankshear, C., Larsson, S., & Svensson, L. (1995). Selfdirected learning in a work context. *Education + Training, 37*(8), 26–32

Ghitulescu, B. E. (2007). *Shaping tasks and relationships at work: Examining the antecedents and consequences of employee job crafting* (Doctoral dissertation, University of Pittsburgh, Pittsburgh). Retrieved from http://d-scholarship.pitt.edu/10312/

Giddens, A. (1984). *The constitution of society: Outline of the theory of structuration.* Cambridge: Polity Press.

Girbig, M., & Bauer, A. (2011). Kompetenzerfassung in der stationären Krankenpflege – Übersetzung, Modifizierung und kulturelle Adaption der Nurse Competence Scale (NCS)

[Competence measurement in the domain of stationary nursing—Translation, modification and cultural adaption of the nurse competence scale (NCS)]. *Pflegewissenschaft, 13*(12), 655–663.

Gist, M. E. (1989). The influence of training method on self-efficacy and idea generation among managers. *Personnel Psychology, 42*(4), 787–805

Gist, M. E., & Mitchell, T. B. (1992). Self-efficacy: A theoretical analysis of its determinants and malleability. *Academy of Management Review, 17*(2), 183–211

Gläser, J., & Laudel, G. (2008). *Experteninterviews und qualitative Inhaltsanalyse als Instrumente rekonstruierender Untersuchungen [Expert interviews and qualitative content analysis as an instrument for reconstructing investigations].* Wiesbaden: VS Verlag für Sozialwissenschaften.

Glaser, R., & Chi, M. T. H. (1988). Overview. In M. T. H. Chi, R. Glaser, & M. Farr (Eds.), *The nature of expertise* (pp. xv–xxviii). Hillsdale: Lawrence Erlbaum.

Goller, M., & Billett, S. (2014). Agentic behaviour at work: Crafting learning experiences. In C. Harteis, A. Rausch, & J. Seifried (Eds.), *Discourses on professional learning: On the boundary between learning and working* (pp. 25–44). Dordrecht: Springer.

Goller, M., & Harteis, C. (2014). Employing agency in academic settings: Doctoral students shaping their own experiences. In C. Harteis, A. Rausch, & J. Seifried (Eds.), *Discourses on professional learning: On the boundary between learning and working* (pp. 189–210). Dordrecht: Springer.

Götz, O., Liehr-Gobbers, K., & Krafft, M. (2010). Evaluation of structural equation models using the partial least squares (PLS) approach. In V. Esposito Vinzi (Ed.), *Handbook of partial least squares: Concepts, methods and applications* (pp. 691–711). Berlin: Springer.

Grant, A. M., & Ashford, S. J. (2008). The dynamics of proactivity at work. *Research in Organizational Behavior, 28*, 3–34

Griffin, M. A., Neal, A., & Parker, S. K. (2007). A new model of work role performance: Positive behavior in uncertain and interdependent contexts. *Academy of Management Journal, 50*(2), 327–347

Groeben, N. (Ed.). (1988). *Das Forschungsprogramm Subjektive Theorien: Eine Einführung in die Psychologie des reflexiven Subjekts [Research programme subjective theories: An introduction into the psychology of reflexive subjects].* Tübingen: Francke.

Gruber, H. (1994). *Expertise: Modelle und empirische Untersuchungen [Expertise: Models and empirical studies].* Opladen: Westdeutscher Verlag.

Gruber, H. (1999a). *Erfahrung als Grundlage kompetenten Handelns [Experience as foundation of competent action].* Bern: Huber.

Gruber, H. (1999b). Wissen [Knowledge]. In Perleth, & A. Ziegler (Eds.), *Pädagogische Psychologie: Grundlagen und Anwendungsfelder* (pp. 94–112). Bern: Huber.

Gruber, H., & Degner, S. (2016). Expertise und Kompetenz [Expertise and competence]. In M. Dick, W. Marotzki, & H. A. Mieg (Eds.), *Handbuch Professionsentwicklung* (pp. 173–180). Bad Heilbrunn: Verlag Julius Klinkhardt.

Gruber, H., & Mandl, H. (1996). Expertise und Erfahrung [Expertise and experience]. In H. Gruber, & A. Ziegler (Eds.), *Expertiseforschung: Theoretische und methodische Grundlagen* (pp. 18–34). Wiesbaden: Springer.

Gruber, H., & Ziegler, A. (1996). Expertise als Domäne psychologischer Forschung [Expertise as domain of pedagogical research]. In H. Gruber, & A. Ziegler (Eds.), *Expertiseforschung: Theoretische und methodische Grundlagen* (pp. 7–16). Wiesbaden: Springer.

Gustavsson, M. (2007). The potential for learning in industrial work. *Journal of Workplace Learning, 19*(7), 453–463

Hacker, W. (1992). *Expertenkönnen: Erkennen und Vermitteln [Expert competence: Identification and instruction].* Göttingen: Verlag für Angewandte Psychologie.

Hackman, J. R., & Oldham, G. R. (1975). Development of the job diagnostic survey. *Journal of Applied Psychology, 60*(2), 159–170

Hager, P. (2011). Theories of workplace learning. In M. Malloch, L. Cairns, K. Evans, & B. O'Conner (Eds.), *The SAGE handbook of workplace learning* (pp. 17–31). London: Sage.

Hair, J. F., Black, W. C., Babin, B. J., & Anderson, R. E. (2014). *Multivariate data analysis* (7th ed.). Harlow: Pearson.

Hair, J. F., Hult, G. T. M., Ringle, C. M., & Sarstedt, M. (2014). *A primer on partial least squares structural equations modeling (PLS-SEM).* Los Angeles: SAGE.

Hair, J. F., Ringle, C. M., & Sarstedt, M. (2011). PLS-SEM: Indeed a silver bullet. *The Journal of Marketing Theory and Practice, 19*(2), 139–152

Hänninen, S., & Eteläpelto, A. (2008). Promoting professional subjectivities and personal agency at work. In S. Billett, C. Harteis, & A. Eteläpelto (Eds.), *Emerging perspectives of workplace learning* (pp. 94–112). Rotterdam: Sense.

Harteis, C., & Bauer, J. (2014). Learning from errors at work. In S. Billett, C. Harteis, & H. Gruber (Eds.), *International handbook of research in professional and practice-based learning* (pp. 699–732). Dordrecht: Springer.

Harteis, C., & Billett, S. (2013). Intuitive expertise: Theories and empirical evidence. *Educational Research Review, 9*, 145–157

Harteis, C., & Goller, M. (2014). New skills for new jobs: Work agency as a necessary condition for successful lifelong learning. In T. Halttunen, M. Koivisto, & S. Billett (Eds.), *Promoting, assessing, recognizing and certifying lifelong learning: International perspectives and practices* (pp. 37–56). Dordrecht: Springer.

Harteis, C., Koch, T., & Morgenthaler, B. (2008). How intuition contributes to high performance: An educational perspective. *US-China Education Review, 5*(1), 68–80.

Harteis, C., Morgenthaler, B., Kugler, C., Ittner, K.-P., Roth, G., & Graf, B. (2012). Professional competence and intuitive decision making. A simulation study in the domain of emergency medicine. *Vocations and Learning, 5*(3), 119–136.

Hattie, J. (2009). *Visible learning: A synthesis of over 800 meta-analyses relating to achievement.* London: Routledge.

Haywood, H., Pain, H., Ryan, S., & Adams, J. (2013). Continuing professional development: Issues raised by nurses and allied health professionals working in musculoskeletal settings. *Musculoskeletal Care, 11*(3), 136–144

Heise, M. (2007). Professionelles Lernen jenseits von Fortbildungsmaßnahmen: Was tun Lehrkräfte im Vergleich zu anderen akademischen Berufsgruppen? [Professional learning beyond formal trainings: What are teachers doing in comparison to other academic professions?] *Zeitschrift für Erziehungswissenschaft, 10*(4), 513–531

Hendrickson, A. E., & White, P. O. (1964). PROMAX: A quick method for rotation to oblique simple structure. *British Journal of Statistical Psychology, 17*(1), 65–70

Henseler, J., & Chin, W. W. (2010). A comparison of approaches for the analysis of interaction effects between latent variables using partial least squares path modeling. *Structural Equation Modeling, 17*(1), 82–109

Henseler, J., & Fassott, G. (2010). Testing moderating effects in PLS path models: An illustration of available procedures. In V. Esposito Vinzi (Ed.), *Handbook of partial least squares: Concepts, methods and applications* (pp. 713–735). Berlin: Springer.

Henseler, J., & Sarstedt, M. (2013). Goodness-of-fit indices for partial least squares path modeling. *Computational Statistics, 28*(2), 565–580

Henson, R. K. (2006). Use of exploratory factor analysis in published research: Common errors and some comment on improved practice. *Educational and Psychological Measurement, 66*(3), 393–416

Herzberg, F. (1968). One more time: How do you motivate employees? *Harvard Business Review, 46*(1), 53–62.

Hetzner, S., Heid, H., & Gruber, H. (2015). Using workplace changes as learning opportunities: Antecedents to reflection in professional work. *Journal of Workplace Learning, 27*(1), 34–50

Hewitt-Taylor, J. (2002). Evidence-based practice. *Nursing Standard, 17*(14), 47–52

Hielscher, V., Nock, L., & Kirchen-Peters, S. (2015). *Technikeinsatz in der Altenpflege: Potenziale und Probleme in empirischer Perspektive [Usage of technology in geriatric care: Potentials and problems from an empirical perspective].* Baden-Baden: Nomos.

Hinkin, T. R. (1998). A brief tutorial on the development of measures for use in survey questionnaires. *Organizational Research Methods, 1*(1), 104–121

Hirschi, A., Freund, P. A., & Herrmann, A. (2014). The career engagement scale: Development and validation of a measure of proactive career behaviors. *Journal of Career Assessment, 22*(4), 575–594

Hitlin, S., & Elder, G. H. (2007a). Agency: An empirical model of an abstract concept. *Advances in Life Course Research, 11*, 33–67

Hitlin, S., & Elder, G. H. (2007b). Time, self, and the curiously abstract concept of agency. *Sociological Theory, 25*(2), 170–191

Hitlin, S., & Kirkpatrick Johnson, M. (2015). Reconceptualizing agency within the life course: The power of looking ahead. *American Journal of Sociology, 120*(5), 1429–1472

Hitlin, S., & Long, C. (2009). Agency as a sociological variable: A preliminary model of individuals, situations, and the life course. *Sociology Compass, 3*(1), 137–160

Hobfoll, S. E. (2001). The influence of culture, community, and the nested-self in the stress process: Advancing conservation of resources theory. *Applied Psychology, 50*(3), 337–421

Hodkinson, P., & Hodkinson, H. (2004). The significance of individuals' dispositions in workplace learning: A case study of two teachers. *Journal of Education and Work, 17*(2), 167–182

Hoekstra, A., Korthagen, F., Brekelmans, M., Beijaard, D., & Imants, J. (2009). Experienced teachers' informal workplace learning and perceptions of workplace conditions. *Journal of Workplace Learning, 21*(4), 276–298

Hökkä, P., Eteläpelto, A., & Rasku-Puttonen, H. (2012). The professional agency of teacher educators amid academic discourses. *Journal of Education for Teaching: International Research and Pedagogy, 38*(1), 83–102.

Holland, D., Lachicotte, W., Skinner, D., & Cain, C. (2003). *Identity and agency in cultural worlds.* Cambridge: Harvard Univ. Press.

Holtgraves, T. (2004). Social desirability and self-reports: Testing models of socially desirable responding. *Personality and Social Psychology Bulletin, 30*(2), 161–172

Holzberger, D., Philipp, A., & Kunter, M. (2013). How teachers' self-efficacy is related to instructional quality: A longitudinal analysis. *Journal of Educational Psychology, 105*(3), 774–786

Honaker, J., King, G., & Blackwell, M. (2011). Amelia II: A program for missing data. *Journal of Statistical Software, 45*(7), 1–47.

Hornsby, J. (1995). Agent. In T. Honderich (Ed.), *The Oxford companion to philosophy* (pp. 98–99). Oxford: Oxford University Press.

Hornung, S., Rousseau, D. M., & Glaser, J. (2008). Creating flexible work arrangements through idiosyncratic deals. *Journal of Applied Psychology, 93*(3), 655–664

Hornung, S., Rousseau, D. M., Glaser, J., Angerer, P., & Weigl, M. (2010). Beyond top-down and bottom-up work redesign: Customizing job content through idiosyncratic deals. *Journal of Organizational Behavior, 31*(2), 187–215

Høyrup, S. (2004). Reflection as a core process in organisational learning. *Journal of Workplace Learning, 16*(8), 442–454

Hu, L.-t., Bentler, P. M., & Kano, Y. (1992). Can test statistics in covariance structure analysis be trusted? *Psychological Bulletin, 112*(2), 351–362

Huber, G. P. (2001). Transfer of knowledge in knowledge management systems: Unexplored issues and suggested studies. *European Journal of Information Systems, 10*(2), 72–79

Hulin, C. L., & Blood, M. R. (1968). Job enlargement, individual differences, and worker responses. *Psychological Bulletin, 69*(1), 41–55

Hunt, E. (2006). Expertise, talent, and social encouragement. In K. A. Ericsson, N. Charness, P. J. Feltovich, & R. R. Hoffmann (Eds.), *The Cambridge handbook of expertise and expert performance* (pp. 31–38). Cambridge: Cambridge University Press.

Hussein, S., & Manthorpe, J. (2005). An international review of the long-term care workforce. *Journal of Aging & Social Policy, 17*(4), 75–94

Illeris, K. (2007). What do we actually mean by experiential learning? *Human Resource Development Review, 6*(1), 84–95

Ivancevich, J. M., & Matteson, M. T. (1993). *Organizational behavior and management* (3rd ed.). Homewood, IL: Irwin.

Jaccard, J., & Jacoby, J. (2010). *Theory construction and model-building skills: A practical guide for social scientists.* New York: Guilford Press.

Jacobi, C., Brand-Jacobi, J., Westenhöfer, J., & Weddige-Diedrichs, A. (1986). Zur Erfassung von Selbstkontrolle. Entwicklung einer deutschsprachigen Form des Self-Control-Schedule und der Desirability of Control Scale [The measurement of self control. Development of a German form of the self-control schedule and the desirability of control scale]. *Diagnostica, 32*(3), 229–247.

Jarek, S. (2012). *Mvnormtest: Normality test for multivariate variables.* R package version 0.1-9. Retrieved from https://CRAN.R-project.org/package=mvnormtest

Jarvis, C. B., MacKenzie, S. B., & Podsakoff, P. M. (2003). A critical review of construct indicators and measurement model misspecification in marketing and consumer research. *Journal of Consumer Research, 30*(2), 199–218

Jensen, K. (2007). The desire to learn: An analysis of knowledge-seeking practices among professionals. *Oxford Review of Education, 33*(4), 489–502

Jessor, R., Donovan, J. E., & Costa, F. M. (1988). *Denver health behaviour questionnaire.* Institute of Behavioral Science, University of Colorado. Boulder.

Jöreskog, K. G. (1999). *How large can a standardized coefficient be?* LISREL Technical Documents. Chicago. Retrieved from http://www.ssicentral.com/lisrel/techdocs/HowLargeCanaStandardizedCoefficientbe.pdf

Judge, T. A., & Bono, J. E. (2001). Relationship of core self-evaluations traits–self-esteem, generalized self-efficacy, locus of control, and emotional stability–with job satisfaction and job performance: A meta-analysis. *Journal of Applied Psychology, 86*(1), 80–92

Judge, T. A., Erez, A., Bono, J. E., & Thoresen, C. J. (2002). Are measures of self-esteem, neuroticism, locus of control, and generalized self-efficacy indicators of a common core construct? *Journal of Personality and Social Psychology, 83*(3), 693–710

Judge, T. A., Jackson, C. L., Shaw, J. C., Scott, B. A., & Rich, B. L. (2007). Self-efficacy and work-related performance: The integral role of individual differences. *Journal of Applied Psychology, 92*(1), 107–127

Judge, T. A., Locke, E. A., Durham, C. C., & Kluger, A. N. (1998). Dispositional effects on job and life satisfaction: The role of core evaluations. *Journal of Applied Psychology, 83*(1), 17–34

Judge, T. A., Thoresen, C. J., Bono, J. E., & Patton, G. K. (2001). The job satisfaction-job performance relationship: A qualitative and quantitative review. *Psychological Bulletin, 127*(3), 376–407

Kaiser, H. F. (1974). An index of factorial simplicity. *Psychometrika, 39*(1), 31–36

Kanfer, R., Wanberg, C. R., & Kantrowitz, T. M. (2001). Job search and employment: A personality-motivational analysis and meta-analytic review. *Journal of Applied Psychology, 86*(5), 837–855

Karsten, R., Mitra, A., & Schmidt, D. (2012). Computer self-efficacy: A meta-analysis. *Journal of Organizational and End User Computing, 24*(4), 54–80

Kaschube, J. (2003). *Eigenverantwortliches Handeln in Organisationen [Autonomous acting in organisations]* (Habilitationsschrift, Ludwig-Maximilians-Universität, München).

Ketterl, K. (2014). *Informelles Lernen im Arbeitsprozess: Eine Untersuchung kontextueller Einflussfaktoren auf Lernaktivitäten von Softwareentwicklern [Informal learning at work: An investigation of contextual determinants of learning activities of software developers].* Hamburg: Kovač.

Kirwan, C., & Birchall, D. (2006). Transfer of learning from management development programmes: Testing the Holton model. *International Journal of Training and Development, 10*(4), 252–268

Kishton, J. M., & Widaman, K. F. (1994). Unidimensional versus domain representative parceling of questionnaire items: An empirical example. *Educational and Psychological Measurement, 54*(3), 757–765

Klette, K., & Smeby, J.-C. (2012). Professional training and knowledge sources. In K. Jensen, L. C. Lahn, & M. Nerland (Eds.), *Professional learning in the knowledge society* (pp. 143–162). Rotterdam: SensePublishers.

Kline, R. B. (2011). *Principles and practice of structural equation modeling* (3rd ed.). New York: Guilford Press.

Kolb, A. Y., & Kolb, D. A. (2012). Experiential learning theory. In N. M. Seel (Ed.), *Encyclopedia of the sciences of learning* (pp. 1215–1219). Boston: Springer US.

Kolb, D. A. (1984). *Experiential learning: Experience as the source of learning and development.* Englewood Cliffs: Prentice-Hall.

Kolodner, J. L. (1983). Towards an understanding of the role of experience in the evaluation from novice to expert. *International Journal of Man-Machine Studies, 19*(5), 497–518.

Kolodner, J. L. (1993). *Case-based reasoning.* San Mateo: Morgan Kaufmann Publishers.

Koop, S., de Reu, T., & Frese, M. (2000). Sociodemographic factors, entrepreneurial orientation, personal initiative and environmental problems in Uganda. In M. Frese (Ed.), *Success and failure of microbusiness owners in Africa. A psychological approach* (pp. 55–76). Westport: Quorum.

Köpke, S., Koch, F., Behncke, A., & Balzer, K. (2013). Einstellungen Pflegender in deutschen Krankenhäusern zu einer evidenzbasierten Pflegepraxis [Attitudes about evidence-based care of nurses in German hospitals]. *Pflege, 26*(3), 163–175

Korečić, J. (2012). *Pflegestandards Altenpflege [Standards of care in geriatric care professions]* (5th ed.). Berlin: Springer Medizin.

Kossinets, G. (2006). Effects of missing data in social networks. *Social Networks, 28*(3), 247–268

Kreft, I. G. (1996). *Are multilevel techniques necessary? An overview including simulation studies* (Doctoral dissertation, California State University, Los Angeles).

Krippendorff, K. (2004). Reliability in content analysis: Some common misconceptions and recommendations. *Human Communication Research, 30*(3), 411–433

Kristiansen, M. H. (2014). *Agency as an empirical concept. An assessment of theory and operationalization* (No. 2014/9). NIDI. The Hague.

Kruger, J., & Dunning, D. (1999). Unskilled and unaware of it: How difficulties in recognizing one's own incompetence lead to inflated self-assessments. *Journal of Personality and Social Psychology, 77*(6), 1121–1134

Kwakman, K. (2003). Factors affecting teachers' participation in professional learning activities. *Teaching and Teacher Education, 19*(2), 149–170

Kyndt, E., & Baert, H. (2013). Antecedents of employees' involvement in work-related learning: A systematic review. *Review of Educational Research, 83*(2), 273–313

Kyndt, E., Dochy, F., & Nijs, H. (2009). Learning conditions for non-formal and informal workplace learning. *Journal of Workplace Learning, 21*(5), 369–383

Kyndt, E., Dochy, F., Onghena, P., & Baert, H. (2012). The learning intentions of low-qualified employees: A multilevel approach. *Adult Education Quarterly, 63*(2), 165–189

Kyndt, E., Govaerts, N., Claes, T., De La Marche, J., & Dochy, F. (2013). What motivates low-qualified employees to participate in training and development? A mixed-method study on their learning intentions. *Studies in Continuing Education, 35*(3), 315–336

Kyndt, E., Govaerts, N., Dochy, F., & Baert, H. (2011). The learning intention of low-qualified employees: A key for participation in lifelong learning and continuous training. *Vocations and Learning, 4*(3), 211–229

Lämsä, A.-M., & Sintonen, T. (2006). A narrative approach for organizational learning in a diverse organisation. *Journal of Workplace Learning, 18*(2), 106–120

Lang-von Wins, T., & Triebel, C. (2005). Die Kompetenzenbilanz – ein Verfahren zur Förderung eigenverantwortlichen Handelns? [The competence balance—a procedure to foster proactive action?] *Zeitschrift für angewandte Sozialpsychologie, 36*(2), 173–188.

Lave, J. (1993). The practice of learning. In S. Chaiklin, & J. Lave (Eds.), *Understanding practice* (pp. 3–32). New York: Cambridge University Press.

Lave, J., & Wenger, E. (1991). *Situated learning: Legitimate peripheral participation.* Cambridge: Cambridge University Press.

Lee, V. E. (2000). Using hierarchical linear modeling to study social contexts: The case of school effects. *Educational Psychologist, 35*(2), 125–141

Lee, Y.-J., & Roth, W.-M. (2005). The (unlikely) trajectory of learning in a salmon hatchery. *Journal of Workplace Learning, 17*(4), 243–254

Leinhardt, G., McCarthy Young, K., & Merriman, J. (1995). Integrating professional knowledge: The theory of practice and the practice of theory. *Learning and Instruction, 5*(4), 401–408

Leitl, J., & Zempel-Dohmen, J. (2006). Die Bedeutung des Arbeitsumfelds für die Veränderung der Transfermotivation [About the relevance of work contexts for changing transfer motivation]. *Zeitschrift für Arbeits- und Organisationspsychologie A&O, 50*(2), 92–102

Lent, R. W., & Hackett, G. (1987). Career self-efficacy: Empirical status and future directions. *Journal of Vocational Behavior, 30*(3), 347–382

Linde, C. (2001). Narrative and social tacit knowledge. *Journal of Knowledge Management, 5*(2), 160–171

Lipponen, L., & Kumpulainen, K. (2011). Acting as accountable authors: Creating interactional spaces for agency work in teacher education. *Teaching and Teacher Education, 27*(5), 812–819

Little, T. D., Cunningham, W. A., Shahar, G., & Widaman, K. F. (2002). To parcel or not to parcel: Exploring the question, weighing the merits. *Structural Equation Modeling: A Multidisciplinary Journal, 9*(2), 151–173

Lohman, M. C. (2005). A survey of factors influencing the engagement of two professional groups in informal workplace learning activities. *Human Resource Development Quarterly, 16*(4), 501–527

Lohmöller, J.-B. (1989). *Latent variable path modeling with partial least squares.* Heidelberg: Physica-Verlag HD.

Lombard, M., Snyder-Duch, J., & Bracken, C. C. (2002). Content analysis in mass communication: Assessment and reporting of intercoder reliability. *Human Communication Research, 28*(4), 587–604

Lukic, D., Littlejohn, A., & Margaryan, A. (2012). A framework for learning from incidents in the workplace. *Safety Science, 50*(4), 950–957

Lyons, P. (2008). The crafting of jobs and individual differences. *Journal of Business and Psychology, 23*(1), 25–36

Mackenzie, C. S., & Peragrine, G. (2003). Measuring and enhancing self-efficacy among professional caregivers of individuals with dementia. *American Journal of Alzheimer's Disease and Other Dementias, 18*(5), 291–299

Major, D. A., Turner, J. E., & Fletcher, T. D. (2006). Linking proactive personality and the big five to motivation to learn and development activity. *Journal of Applied Psychology, 91*(4), 927–935

Malcolm, J., Hodkinson, P., & Colley, H. (2003). The interrelationships between informal and formal learning. *Journal of Workplace Learning, 15*(7), 313–318

Marinova, S. V., Peng, C., Lorinkova, N., Van Dyne, L., & Chiaburu, D. (2015). Change-oriented behavior: A meta-analysis of individual and job design predictors. *Journal of Vocational Behavior, 88*, 104–120

Markus, H. (1983). Self-knowledge: An expanded view. *Journal of Personality, 51*(3), 543–565

Marsh, H. W. (1987). The big-fish-little-pond effect on academic self-concept. *Journal of Educational Psychology, 79*(3), 280–295

Marsh, H. W., Balla, J. R., & Hau, K.-T. (1996). An evaluation of incremental fit indices: A clarification of mathematical properties. In G. A. Marcoulides, & R. E. Schumacker (Eds.), *Advanced structural equation modeling issues and techniques* (pp. 315–353). Mahwah: Lawrence Erlbaum.

Marsh, H. W., Balla, J. R., & McDonald, R. P. (1988). Goodness-of-fit indexes in confirmatory factor analysis: The effect of sample size. *Psychological Bulletin, 103*(3), 391–410

Marsh, H. W., Hau, K.-T., Balla, J. R., & Grayson, D. (1998). Is more ever too much? The number of indicators per factor in confirmatory factor analysis. *Multivariate Behavioral Research, 33*(2), 181–220

Marsh, H. W., & Parker, J. W. (1984). Determinants of student self-concept: Is it better to be a relatively large fish in a small pond even if you don't learn to swim as well? *Journal of Personality and Social Psychology, 47*(1), 213–231

Marsick, V. J., & Volpe, M. (1999). The nature and need for informal learning. *Advances in Developing Human Resources, 1*(3), 1–9

Marsick, V. J., & Watkins, K. E. (1990). *Informal and incidental learning in the workplace.* London: Routledge.

Martin, J. (2004). Self-regulated learning, social cognitive theory, and agency. *Educational Psychologist, 39*(2), 135–145

Martin, J., Sugarman, J., & Hickinbottom, S. (2010). *Persons: Understanding psychological selfhood and agency.* New York: Springer.

Maurer, T. J., Lippstreu, M., & Judge, T. A. (2008). Structural model of employee involvement in skill development activity: The role of individual differences. *Journal of Vocational Behavior, 72*(3), 336–350

Maurer, T. J., & Tarulli, B. A. (1994). Investigation of perceived environment, perceived outcome, and person variables in relationship to voluntary development activity by employees. *Journal of Applied Psychology, 79*(1), 3–14

Maurer, T. J., Weiss, E. M., & Barbeite, F. G. (2003). A model of involvement in work-related learning and development activity: The effects of individual, situational, motivational, and age variables. *Journal of Applied Psychology, 88*(4), 707–724

Mayer, K. U. (2009). New directions in life course research. *Annual Review of Sociology, 35*(1), 413–433

Mayring, P. (2002). *Einführung in die qualitative Sozialforschung. Eine Anleitung zu qualitativem Denken [Introduction into qualitative research in social science: An intruction for qualitative thinking]* (5th ed.). Weinheim: Beltz.

Mayring, P. (2004). Qualitative content analysis. In U. Flick, E. von Kardoff, & I. Steinke (Eds.), *A companion to qualitative research* (pp. 266–269). London: Sage.

Mayring, P. (2015). *Qualitative Inhaltsanalyse: Grundlagen und Techniken [Qualitative content analysis: Foundations and techniques]* (12th ed.). Weinheim: Beltz.

McCauley, C. D. (2006). *Developmental assignments: Creating learning experiences without changing jobs.* Greensboro: Center for Creative Leadership Press.

McCauley, C. D., & Hezlett, S. A. (2005). Individual development in the workplace. In N. Anderson, D. S. Ones, H. K. Sinangil, & C. Viswesvaran (Eds.), *Handbook of industrial, work and organizational psychology. Vol. 1* (pp. 313–335). London: SAGE.

Meretoja, R., Isoaho, H., & Leino-Kilpi, H. (2004). Nurse competence scale: Development and psychometric testing. *Journal of Advanced Nursing, 47*(2), 124–133

Merkens, H. (2004). Selection procedures, sampling, case construction. In U. Flick, E. v. Kardorff, & I. Steinke (Eds.), *A companion to qualitative research* (pp. 165–171). London: Sage.

Meyer, G., Balzer, K., & Köpke, S. (2013). Evidenzbasierte Pflegepraxis—Diskussionsbeitrag zum Status quo [Evidence-based care—Discussion about the status quo]. *Zeitschrift für Evidenz, Fortbildung und Qualität im Gesundheitswesen, 107*(1), 30–35

Mieg, H. A. (2006). Studies of expertise from psychological perspectives. In K. A. Ericsson, N. Charness, P. J. Feltovich, & R. R. Hoffmann (Eds.), *The Cambridge handbook of expertise and expert performance* (pp. 743–760). Cambridge: Cambridge University Press.

Miller, V. D., & Jablin, F. M. (1991). Information seeking during organizational entry: Influences, tactics, and a model of the process. *The Academy of Management Review, 16*(1), 92

Mirowsky, J., & Ross, C. E. (1991). Eliminating defense and agreement bias from measure of the sense of control: A 2 x 2 index. *Social Psychology Quarterly, 54*(2), 127–145.

Mirowsky, J., & Ross, C. E. (1998). Education, personal control, lifestyle and health: A human capital hypothesis. *Research on Aging, 20*(4), 415–449

Morgeson, F. P., & Humphrey, S. E. (2006). The work design questionnaire (WDQ): Developing and validating a comprehensive measure for assessing job design and the nature of work. *Journal of Applied Psychology, 91*(6), 1321–1339

Moritz, S. E., Feltz, D. L., Fahrbach, K. R., & Mack, D. E. (2000). The relation of self-efficacy measures to sport performance: A meta-analytic review. *Research Quarterly for Exercise and Sport, 71*(3), 280–294

Morrison, E. W. (1993a). Longitudinal study of the effects of information seeking on newcomer socialization. *Journal of Applied Psychology, 78*(2), 173–183

Morrison, E. W. (1993b). Newcomer information seeking: Exploring types, modes, sources, and outcomes. *Academy of Management Journal, 36*(3), 557–589

Morrison, E. W. (2002). Information seeking within organizations. *Human Communication Research, 28*(2), 229–242

Morrison, E. W., & Phelps, C. C. (1999). Taking charge at work: Extrarole efforts to initiate workplace change. *Academy of Management Journal, 42*(4), 403–419

Müller, M. (2013). Nursing competence: Psychometric evaluation using Rasch modelling. *Journal of Advanced Nursing, 69*(6), 1410–1417

Multon, K. D., Brown, S. D., & Lent, R. W. (1991). Relation of self-efficacy beliefs to academic outcomes: A meta-analytic investigation. *Journal of Counseling Psychology, 38*(1), 30–38

Nash, J. E., & Calonico, J. M. (1996). *The meanings of social interaction an introduction to social psychology.* Dix Hills: General Hall.

Neuendorf, K. A. (2002). *The content analysis guidebook.* Thousand Oaks: Sage Publications.

Ng, T. W. H., Eby, L. T., Sorensen, K. L., & Feldman, D. C. (2005). Predictors of objective and subjective career success: A meta-analysis. *Personnel Psychology, 58*(2), 367–408

Ng, T. W. H., Sorensen, K. L., & Eby, L. T. (2006). Locus of control at work: A meta-analysis. *Journal of Organizational Behavior, 27*(8), 1057–1087

Norman, G., Eva, K., Brooks, L., & Hamstra. (2006). Studies of expertise from psychological perspectives. In K. A. Ericsson, N. Charness, P. J. Feltovich, & R. R. Hoffmann (Eds.), *The Cambridge handbook of expertise and expert performance* (pp. 339–353). Cambridge: Cambridge University Press.

O'connor, B. P. (2000). SPSS and SAS programs for determining the number of components using parallel analysis and velicer's MAP test. *Behavior Research Methods, Instruments, & Computers, 32*(3), 396–402

Ohly, S., & Fritz, C. (2010). Work characteristics, challenge appraisal, creativity, and proactive behavior: A multi-level study. *Journal of Organizational Behavior, 31*(4), 543–565

Ohly, S., Sonnentag, S., & Pluntke, F. (2006). Routinization, work characteristics and their relationships with creative and proactive behaviors. *Journal of Organizational Behavior, 27*(3), 257–279

O*NET. (2016). *Personal care aides (SOC code: 39-9021.00)*. National Center for O*NET Development. Retrieved July 22, 2016, from http://www.onetonline.org/link/summary/39-9021.00

Organ, D. W. (1988). *Organizational citizenship behavior: The good soldier syndrome*. Lexington: Lexington Books.

Orr, J. E. (1996). *Talking about machines: An ethnography of a modern job*. Ithaca: ILR Press.

Oser, F., Näpflin, C., Hofer, C., & Aerni, P. (2012). Towards a theory of negative knowledge (NK): Almost-mistakes as drivers of episodic memory amplification. In J. Bauer, & C. Harteis (Eds.), *Human fallibility: The ambiguity of errors* (pp. 53–70). Dordrecht: Springer.

Oser, F., & Spychiger, M. (2005). *Lernen ist schmerzhaft: Zur Theorie des negativen Wissens und zur Praxis der Fehlerkultur [Learning is painful: About the theory of negative knowledge and about the practice of error culture]*. Weinheim: Beltz.

Oude Groote Beverborg, A., Sleegers, P. J., & van Veen, K. (2015). Promoting VET teachers' individual and social learning activities: The empowering and purposeful role of transformational leadership, interdependence, and self-efficacy. *Empirical Research in Vocational Education and Training, 7*(1)

Pajares, F., & Schunk, D. H. (2002). Self and self-belief in psychology and education. In J. Aronson (Ed.), *Improving academic achievement* (pp. 3–21). New York: Academic Press.

Palmeri, T. J. (2006). Automaticity. In L. Nadel (Ed.), *Encyclopedia of cognitive science*. Chichester: John Wiley & Sons.

Paloniemi, S. (2006). Experience, competence and workplace learning. *Journal of Workplace Learning, 18*(7), 439–450

Parker, S. K., Bindl, U. K., & Strauss, K. (2010). Making things happen: A model of proactive motivation. *Journal of Management, 36*(4), 827–856

Parker, S. K., & Collins, C. G. (2010). Taking stock: Integrating and differentiating multiple proactive behaviors. *Journal of Management, 36*(3), 633–662

Parker, S. K., & Turner, N. (2002). Work design and individual work performance: Research findings and an agenda for future inquiry. In S. Sonnentag (Ed.), *Psychological management of individual performance* (pp. 69–94). Chichester: John Wiley & Sons.

Parker, S. K., Williams, H. M., & Turner, N. (2006). Modeling the antecedents of proactive behavior at work. *Journal of Applied Psychology, 91*(3), 636–652

Payne, S. C., Youngcourt, S. S., & Beaubien, J. M. (2007). A meta-analytic examination of the goal orientation nomological net. *Journal of Applied Psychology, 92*(1), 128–150

Pearlin, L. I., Nguyen, K. B., Schieman, S., & Milkie, M. A. (2007). The life-course origins of mastery among older people. *Journal of Health and Social Behavior, 48*(2), 164–179

Pearlin, L. I., & Schooler, C. (1978). The structure of coping. *Journal of Health and Social Behavior, 19*(1), 2–21.

Peterson, C. (2000). The future of optimism. *American Psychologist, 55*(1), 44–55

Petrou, P., Demerouti, E., & Schaufeli, W. B. (2016). Crafting the change: The role of employee job crafting behaviors for successful organizational change. *Journal of Management, Advance online publication.*

Piedmont, R. L. (2014). Inter-item correlations. In A. C. Michalos (Ed.), *Encyclopedia of quality of life and well-being research* (pp. 3303–3304). Dordrecht: Springer.

Pintrich, P. R. (2005). The role of goal orientation in self-regulated learning. In M. Boekaerts, P. R. Pintrich, & M. Zeidner (Eds.), *Handbook of self-regulation* (pp. 452–502). San Diego: Academic Press.

Podsakoff, P. M. (1986). Self-reports in organizational research: Problems and prospects. *Journal of Management, 12*(4), 531–544

Podsakoff, P. M., MacKenzie, S. B., Lee, J.-Y., & Podsakoff, N. P. (2003). Common method biases in behavioral research: A critical review of the literature and recommended remedies. *Journal of Applied Psychology, 88*(5), 879–903

Polanyi, M. (1969). The logic of tacit inference. In M. Grene (Ed.), *Knowing and being: Essays by Michael Polanyi* (pp. 138–158). Chicago: The University of Chicago Press.

Pool, I. A., Poell, R. F., Berings, M. G., & ten Cate, O. (2016). Motives and activities for continuing professional development: An exploration of their relationships by integrating literature and interview data. *Nurse Education Today, 38*, 22–28

Posner, M. I. (1988). Introduction: What is it to be an expert? In M. T. H. Chi, R. Glaser, & M. Farr (Eds.), *The nature of expertise* (pp. xxix–xxxvi). Hillsdale: Lawrence Erlbaum.

Pudrovska, T., Schieman, S., Paerlin, L. I., & Nguyen, K. B. (2005). The sense of mastery as a mediator and moderator in the association between economic hardship and health in late life. *Journal of Aging and Health, 17*(5), 634–660

Putz, D., Schilling, J., & Kluge, A. (2012). Measuring organizational climate for learning from errors at work. In J. Bauer, & C. Harteis (Eds.), *Human fallibility* (pp. 107–123). Dordrecht: Springer.

Quiñones, M. A., Ford, J. K., & Teachout, M. S. (1995). The relationship between work experience and job performance: A conceptual and meta-analytical review. *Personnel Psychology, 48*(4), 887–910

R Core Team. (2016). R: A language and environment for statistical computing. Vienna: R Foundation for Statistical Computing. Retrieved from https://www.R-project.org/

Raelin, J. A. (1997). A model of work-based learning. *Organization Science, 8*(6), 563–578

Rank, J., Carsten, J. M., Unger, J. M., & Spector, P. E. (2007). Proactive customer service performance: Relationships with individual, task, and leadership variables. *Human Performance, 20*(4), 363–390.

Rank, J., Nelson, N. E., Allen, T. D., & Xu, X. (2009). Leadership predictors of innovation and task performance: Subordinates' self-esteem and self-presentation as moderators. *Journal of Occupational and Organizational Psychology, 82*(3), 465–489

Raubenheimer, J. (2004). An item selection procedure to maximise scale reliability and validity. *SA Journal of Industrial Psychology, 30*(4), 59–64.

Rausch, A. (2011). *Erleben und Lernen am Arbeitsplatz in der betrieblichen Ausbildung [Emotions and learning in the workplace within in-firm vocational education and training].* Wiesbaden: VS Verlag für Sozialwissenschaften.

Rausch, A. (2013). Task characteristics and learning potentials—empirical results of three diary studies on workplace learning. *Vocations and Learning, 6*(1), 55–79

Raykov, T. (2001). Estimation of congeneric scale reliability using covariance structure analysis with nonlinear constraints. *British Journal of Mathematical and Statistical Psychology, 54*(2), 315–323

Rees, R. (1985a). The theory of principal and agent: Part 1. *Bulletin of Economic Research, 37*(1), 3–26

Rees, R. (1985b). The theory of principal and agent: Part 2. *Bulletin of Economic Research, 37*(2), 75–97

Reinartz, W., Haenlein, M., & Henseler, J. (2009). An empirical comparison of the efficacy of covariance-based and variance-based SEM. *International Journal of Research in Marketing, 26*(4), 332–344

Renkema, A. (2006). Individual learning accounts: A strategy for lifelong learning? *Journal of Workplace Learning, 18*(6), 384–394

Renkl, A. (2015). Wissenserwerb. In E. Wild, & J. Möller (Eds.), *Pädagogische Psychologie* (pp. 3–24). Berlin, Heidelberg: Springer Berlin Heidelberg.

Renkl, A., Mandl, H., & Gruber, H. (1996a). Inert knowledge: Analyses and remedies. *Educational Psychologist, 31*(2), 115–121

Renkl, A., Mandl, H., & Gruber, H. (1996b). Inert knowledge: Analyses and remedies. *Educational Psychologist, 31*(2), 115–121

Renn, R. W., & Fedor, D. B. (2001). Development and field test of a feedback seeking, self-efficacy, and goal setting model of work performance. *Journal of Management, 27*(5), 563–583

Revelle, W. (2015). Psych: Procedures for psychological, psychometric, and personality research. Evanston: Northwestern University. Retrieved from http://CRAN.R-project.org/package=psych

Richard, P. J., Devinney, T. M., Yip, G. S., & Johnson, G. (2009). Measuring organizational performance: Towards methodological best practice. *Journal of Management, 35*(3), 718–804

Richardson, H. A., Simmering, M. J., & Sturman, M. C. (2009). A tale of three perspectives: Examining post hoc statistical techniques for detection and correction of common method variance. *Organizational Research Methods, 12*(4), 762–800

Rigotti, T., Schyns, B., & Mohr, G. (2008). A short version of the occupational self-efficacy scale: Structural and construct validity across five countries. *Journal of Career Assessment, 16*(2), 238–255

Robra, B.-P. (2016). Evidenz [Evidence]. In M. Dick, W. Marotzki, & H. Mieg (Eds.), *Handbuch Professionsentwicklung* (pp. 193–202). Bad Heilbrunn: Klinkhardt.

Rogoff, B. (1991). *Apprenticeship in thinking: Cognitive development in social context.* New York: Oxford Univ. Press.

Rogoff, B. (1995). Observing sociocultural activity on three planes: Participatory appropriation, guided participation, and apprenticeship. In J. V. Wertsch, P. del Rio, & A. Alvarez (Eds.), *Sociocultural studies of mind* (pp. 139–164). Cambridge: Cambridge University Press.

Rollinson, D., & Broadfield, A. (2002). *Organisational behaviour and analysis: An integrated approach* (2nd ed.). New York: Prentice Hall.

Ropo, E. (2004). Teaching expertise. Empirical finding on expert teachers and teacher development. In H. P. A. Boshuizen, R. Bromme, & H. Gruber (Eds.), *Professional learning: Gaps and transitions on the way from novice to expert* (pp. 159–179). Drodrecht: Kluwer Academic Publishers.

Rosen, C. C., Slater, D. J., Chang, C.-H., & Johnson, R. E. (2013). Let's make a deal: Development and validation of the ex post i-deals scale. *Journal of Management, 39*(3), 709–742

Ross, C. E., & Mirowsky, J. (2013). The sense of personal control: Social structural causes and emotional consequences. In C. S. Aneshensel, J. C. Phelan, & A. Bierman (Eds.), *Handbook of the sociology of mental health* (pp. 379–402). Dordrecht: Springer.

Rosseel, Y. (2012). Lavaan: An R package for structural equation modeling. *Journal of Statistical Software, 48*(2), 1–36.

Rost, D. H., & Schilling, S. R. (2006). Leseverständnis [Reading ability]. In D. H. Rost (Ed.), *Handwörterbuch Pädagogische Psychologie* (3rd ed., pp. 450–460). Weinheim: Beltz.

Rotter, J. B. (1966). Generalized expectancies for internal versus external control of reinforcement. *Psychological Monographs, 80*(1), 1–28.

Rottinghaus, P. J., Larson, L. M., & Borgen, F. H. (2003). The relation of self-efficacy and interests: A meta-analysis of 60 samples. *Journal of Vocational Behavior, 62*(2), 221–236

Rousseau, D. M., Ho, V. T., & Greenberg, J. (2006). I-deals: Idiosyncratic terms in employment relationships. *Academy of Management Review, 31*(4), 977–994

Ryan, R. M., & Deci, E. L. (2000a). Intrinsic and extrinsic motivations: Classic definitions and new directions. *Contemporary Educational Psychology, 25*(1), 54–67

Ryan, R. M., & Deci, E. L. (2000b). Self-determination theory and the facilitation of intrinsic motivation, social development, and well-being. *American Psychologist, 55*(1), 68–78

Rynne, S. B., Mallett, C. J., & Tinning, R. (2010). Workplace learning of high performance sports coaches. *Sport, Education and Society, 15*(3), 315–330

Sackett, D. L., Rosenberg, W. M. C., Gray, J. A. M., Haynes, R. B., & Richardson, W. S. (1996). Evidence based medicine: What it is and what it isn't. *BMJ, 312*(7023), 71–72

Sackett, D. L., & Rosenberg, W. M. C. (1995). The need for evidence-based medicine. *Journal of the Royal Society of Medicine, 88*(11), 620–624.

Sadri, G., & Robertson, I. T. (1993). Self-efficacy and work-related behaviour: A review and meta-analysis. *Applied Psychology, 42*(2), 139–152

Saks, A. M., Gruman, J. A., & Cooper-Thomas, H. (2011). The neglected role of proactive behavior and outcomes in newcomer socialization. *Journal of Vocational Behavior, 79*(1), 36–46

Salas, E., & Rosen, M. A. (2012). Experts at work: Principles for developing expertise in organizations. In S. W. J. Kozlowski, & E. Salas (Eds.), *Learning, training, and development in organizations* (pp. 99–302). New York: Routledge.

Sanchez, G. (2013). *PLS path modeling with R.* Berkeley. Retrieved from http://gastonsanchez.com/PLS_Path_Modeling_with_R.pdf

Sanchez, G., Trinchera, L., & Russolillo, G. (2015). *Plspm: Tools for partial least squares path modeling (PLS-PM).* R package version 0.4.7. Retrieved from https://CRAN.R-project.org/package=plspm

Satorra, A., & Bentler, P. M. (1994). Corrections to test statistics and standard errors in covariance structure analysis. In A. von Eye, & C. C. Clogg (Eds.), *Latent variables analysis: Applications to development research* (pp. 399–419). Thousand Oaks: SAGE Publications.

Savolainen, R. (2006). Time as a context of information seeking. *Library & Information Science Research, 28*(1), 110–127

Schaeffer, D., Moers, M., & Rosenbrock, R. (2012). Zur Entwicklung von Pflege und Pflegewissenschaft [About the development of nursing and nursing science]. In F. W. Schwartz, U. Walter, J. Siegrist, P. Kolip, R. Liedl, M.-L. Dierks, … & N. Schneider (Eds.), (3rd ed., pp. 308–310). München: Urban & Fischer.

Schank, R. C., & Abelson, R. P. (1977). Scripts, plans, and knowledge. In P. N. Johnson-Laird, & P. C. Wason (Eds.), *Thinking: readings in cognitive science* (pp. 421–435). Cambridge: Cambridge University Press.

Scheier, M. F., Carver, C. S., & Bridges, M. W. (1994). Distinguishing optimism from neuroticism (and trait anxiety, self-mastery, and self-esteem): A reevaluation of the life orientation test. *Journal of Personality and Social Psychology, 67*(6), 1063–1078

Schendera, C. F. G. (2007). *Datenqualität mit SPSS [Data quality with SPSS].* München: Oldenbourg.

Schermerhorn, J. R., Osborn, R. N., Uhl-Bien, M., & Hunt, J. G. (2000). *Organizational behavior* (7th ed.). Hoboken: John Wiley & Sons.

Schley, T., & van Woerkom, M. (2014). Reflection and reflective behaviour in work teams. In C. Harteis, A. Rausch, & J. Seifried (Eds.), *Discourses on professional learning* (pp. 113–139). Dordrecht: Springer.

Schlosser, M. (2015). Agency. In E. N. Zalta (Ed.), *The Stanford encyclopedia of philosophy* (Vol. Fall 2015). Stanford: Stanford University. Retrieved from http://plato.stanford.edu/archives/fall2015/entries/agency/

Schmidt, H. G., & Boshuizen, H. P. A. (1993). On acquiring expertise in medicine. *Educational Psychology Review, 5*(3), 205–221

Schmidt, H. G., & Rikers, R. M. J. P. (2007). How expertise develops in medicine: Knowledge encapsulation and illness script formation. *Medical Education, 41*(12), 1133–1139

Schmitt, T. A. (2011). Current methodological considerations in exploratory and confirmatory factor analysis. *Journal of Psychoeducational Assessment, 29*(4), 304–321

Schnell, R., Hill, P. B., & Esser, E. (2011). *Methoden der empirischen Sozialforschung [Empirical methods in social science]* (9th ed.). München: Oldenbourg.

Schön, D. A. (2000). *The reflective practicitioner. How professionals think in action.* Aldershot: Ashgate Arena.

Schreier, M. (2012). *Qualitative content analysis in practice.* London: SAGE.

Schunk, D. H. (1981). Modeling and attributional effects on children's achievement: A self-efficacy analysis. *Journal of Educational Psychology, 73*(1), 93–105

Schwarzer, R., Bäßler, J., Kwiatek, P., Schröder, K., & Zhang, J. X. (1997). The assessment of optimistic self-beliefs: Comparison of the German, Spanish, and Chinese versions of the general self-efficacy scale. *Applied Psychology, 46*(1), 69–88

Schwarzer, R., & Jerusalem, M. (1995). Generalized self-efficacy scale. In J. Weinman, S. Wright, & M. Johnston (Eds.), *Measures in health psychology: A user's portfolio. Causal and control beliefs* (pp. 35–37). Windsor: Nfer-Nelson.

Schwarzer, R., & Schmitz, G. S. (1999). Proaktive Einstellung von Lehrern: Konstruktbeschreibung und psychometrische Analysen [Proactive attitude of teachers: Construct description and psychometric analyses]. *Zeitschrift für Empirische Pädagogik, 13*(1), 3–27.

Scribner, S., & Sachs, P. (1991). Knowledge acquisition at work. *IEE Brief, 2*, 1–4.

Segers, M., & van der Haar, S. (2011). The experiential learning theory: D. Kolb and d. Boud. In F. Dochy, D. Gijbels, M. Segers, & P. Van den Bossche (Eds.), *Theories of learning for the workplace: Building blocks for training and professional development programmes* (pp. 52–35). London: Routledge.

Seibert, S. E., Crant, J. M., & Kraimer, M. L. (1999). Proactive personality and career success. *Journal of Applied Psychology, 84*(3), 416–427

Seibert, S. E., Kraimer, M. L., & Crant, J. M. (2001). What do proactive people do? A longitudinal model linking proactive personality and career success. *Personnel Psychology, 54*(4), 845–874

Seligman, M. E. P. (1972). Learned helplessness. *Annual Review of Medicine, 23*(1), 407–412

Seligman, M. E. P. (1992). *Helplessness: On depression, development, and death.* New York: W. H. Freeman.

Semmer, N., Zapf, D., & Dunckel, H. (1999). Instrument zur stressbezogenen Tätigkeitsanalyse (ISTA) [Inventory to analyse activities in terms of stressful conditions]. In H. Dunckel (Ed.), *Handbuch psychologischer Arbeitsanalyseverfahren* (pp. 179–204). Zürich: vdf Hochschulverlag.

semTools Contributors. (2016). *semTools: Useful tools for structural equation modeling.* R package version 0.4-11. Retrieved from http://cran.r-project.org/package=semTools

Sen, A. (2001). *Development as freedom.* Oxford: Oxford University Press.

Sfard, A. (1998). On two metaphors for learning and the dangers of choosing just one. *Educational Researcher, 27*(2), 4–13

Shanahan, M. J., & Elder, G. H. (2002). History, agency, and the life course. In L. J. Crockett (Ed.), *Agency, motivation, and the life course: Volume 48 of the Nebraska symposium on motivation* (pp. 145–186). Lincoln: University of Nebraska Press.

Shanahan, M. J., & Hood, K. E. (2000). Adolescents in changing social structures: Bounded agency in life course perspective. In L. J. Crockett, & R. K. Silbereisen (Eds.), *Negotiating adolescence in times of social change* (pp. 123–134). Cambridge: Cambridge University Press.

Sheets, D. J. (2012). Gerontological nursing: Developing the art and science. *The Gerontologist, 52*(6), 876–879

Shoji, K., Cieslak, R., Smoktunowicz, E., Rogala, A., Benight, C. C., & Luszczynska, A. (2015). Associations between job burnout and self-efficacy: A meta-analysis. *Anxiety, Stress, & Coping*, 1–20

Singer, E., & Ye, C. (2013). The use and effects of incentives in surveys. *The ANNALS of the American Academy of Political and Social Science, 645*(1), 112–141

Sitzmann, T., & Yeo, G. (2013). A meta-analytic investigation of the within-person self-efficacy domain: Is self-efficacy a product of past performance or a driver of future performance? *Personnel Psychology, 66*(3), 531–568

Skår, R. (2010). How nurses experience their work as a learning environment. *Vocations and Learning, 3*(1), 1–18

Skinner, E. A. (1995). *Perceived control, motivation, & coping*. Thousand Oaks: Sage Publications.

Skinner, E. A. (1996). A guide to constructs of control. *Journal of Personality and Social Psychology, 71*(3), 549–570

Skinner, E. A., Chapman, M., & Baltes, P. B. (1988). Control, means-ends, and agency beliefs: A new conceptualization and its measurement during childhood. *Journal of Personality and Social Psychology, 54*(1), 117–133

Skule, S. (2004). Learning conditions at work: A framework to understand and assess informal learning in the workplace. *International Journal of Training and Development, 8*(1), 8–20

Slotte, V., Tynjälä, P., & Hytönen, T. (2004). How do HRD practitioners describe learning at work? *Human Resource Development International, 7*(4), 481–499

Smith, R. (2006). Epistemological agency in the workplace. *Journal of Workplace Learning, 18*(3), 157–170

Sonnentag, S. (1995). Excellent software professionals: Experience, work activities, and perception by peers. *Behaviour & Information Technology, 14*(5), 289–299

Sonnentag, S. (1998a). Expertise in professional software design: A process study. *Journal of Applied Psychology, 83*(5), 703–715

Sonnentag, S. (1998b). Identifying high performers: Do peer nominations suffer from a likeability bias? *European Journal of Work and Organizational Psychology, 7*(4), 501–515

Sonnentag, S. (2000). Excellent performance: The role of communication and cooperation processes. *Applied Psychology, 49*(3), 483–497

Sonnentag, S., & Frese, M. (2002). Performance concepts and performance theory. In S. Sonnentag (Ed.), *Psychological management of individual performance* (pp. 1–25). Chichester: John Wiley & Sons.

Sonnentag, S., & Kleine, B. M. (2000). Deliberate practice at work: A study with insurance agents. *Journal of Occupational and Organizational Psychology, 73*(1), 87–102

Sonnentag, S., Niessen, C., & Ohly, S. (2004). Learning at work: Training and development. In C. L. Cooper, & I. T. Robertson (Eds.), *International review of industrial and organizational psychology 2004* (pp. 249–289). Chichester, UK: John Wiley & Sons, Ltd.

Sonnentag, S., Niessen, C., & Volmer, J. (2006). Expertise in software design. In K. A. Ericsson, N. Charness, P. J. Feltovich, & R. R. Hoffmann (Eds.), *The Cambridge handbook of expertise and expert performance* (pp. 373–387). Cambridge: Cambridge University Press.

Spagnoli, P., Caetano, A., Tanucci, G., & Lourenço de Sousa, V. (2012). Information-seeking behaviour: Implicit and explicit strategies during the organizational entry process. *Management Research: Journal of the Iberoamerican Academy of Management, 10*(1), 6–28

Sparrowe, R. T., Liden, R. C., Wayne, S. J., & Kraimer, M. L. (2001). Social networks and the performance of individuals and groups. *Academy of Management Journal, 44*(2), 316–325

Spector, P. E., & Fox, S. (2010). Counterproductive work behavior and organisational citizenship behavior: Are they opposite forms of active behavior? *Applied Psychology, 59*(1), 21–39

Spenceley, S. M., O'Leary, K., Chizawsky, L. L., Ross, A. J., & Estabrooks, C. A. (2008). Sources of information used by nurses to inform practice: An integrative review. *International Journal of Nursing Studies, 45*(6), 954–970

Stadtmüller, S., & Porst, R. (2005). Zum Einsatz von Incentives bei postalischen Befragungen [About the usage of incentives in postal surveys]. *ZUMA How-to-Reihe,* (14), 1–13.

Stajkovic, A. D., & Luthans, F. (1998). Self-efficacy and work-related performance: A meta-analysis. *Psychological Bulletin, 124*(2), 240–261

Stark, R., Graf, M., Renkl, A., Gruber, H., & Mandl, H. (1995). Förderung von Handlungskompetenz durch geleitetes Problemlösen und multiple Lernkontexte [Promotion of skills and abilities through instructed problem solving and multiple learning contexts]. *Zeitschrift für Entwicklungspsychologie und pädagogische Psychologie, 27*(4), 289–312.

Steca, P., & Monzani, D. (2014). Locus of control. In A. C. Michalos (Ed.), *Encyclopedia of quality of life and well-being research* (pp. 3678–3680). Dordrecht: Springer.

Stegmann, S., Dick, R. v., Ullrich, J., Charalambous, J., Menzel, B., Egold, N., & Wu, T. T.-C. (2010). Der Work Design Questionnaire: Vorstellung und erste Validierung einer deutschen Version [The work design questionnaire: Introduction and first validation of a German version]. *Zeitschrift für Arbeits- und Organisationspsychologie A&O, 54*(1), 1–28

Sternberg, R. J., Forsythe, G. B., Hedlund, J., Horvath, J. A., Wagner, R. K., Williams, W. M., ... & Grigorenko, E. L. (2000). *Practical intelligence in everyday life.* Cambridge: Cambridge University Press.

Stoker, J. I., & Van der Heijden, B. I. J. M. (2001). Competence development and appraisal in organizations. *Journal of Career Development, 28*(2), 97–113

Stork, D., & Richards, W. D. (1992). Nonrespondents in communication network studies: Problems and possibilities. *Group & Organization Management, 17*(2), 193–209

Strasser, J., & Gruber, H. (2004). The role of experience in professional training and development of psychological counselors. In H. P. A. Boshuizen, R. Bromme, & H. Gruber (Eds.), *Professional learning: Gaps and transitions on the way from novice to expert* (pp. 11–27). Dordrecht: Kluwer Academic Publishers.

Szulanski, G. (1996). Exploring internal stickiness: Impediments to the transfer of best practice within the firm. *Strategic Management Journal, 17,* 27–43

Tabachnick, B. G., & Fidell, L. S. (2007). *Using multivariate statistics* (5th ed.). Boston: Pearson.

Taylor, M., Locke, E. A., Lee, C., & Gist, M. E. (1984). Type A behavior and faculty research productivity: What are the mechanisms? *Organizational Behavior and Human Performance, 34*(3), 402–418

Tenenhaus, M., Amato, S., & Vinzi, V. E. (2004). A global goodness-of-fit index for PLS structural equation modeling. In *Proceedings of the XLII SIS scientific meeting* (pp. 739–742). Padova, Italy: CLEUP.

Tenenhaus, M., Vinzi, V. E., Chatelin, Y.-M., & Lauro, C. (2005). PLS path modeling. *Computational Statistics & Data Analysis, 48*(1), 159–205

Terman, L., & Oden, M. (1959). *Genetic studies of genius. IV. The gifted group at midlife: Thirty five years' follow-up of the superior child.* Stanford: Stanford University Press.

Tharenou, P., & Terry, D. J. (1998). Reliability and validity of scores on scales to measure managerlal aspirations. *Educational and Psychological Measurement, 58*(3), 475–492

Thomas, J. P., Whitman, D. S., & Viswesvaran, C. (2010). Employee proactivity in organizations: A comparative meta-analysis of emergent proactive constructs. *Journal of Occupational and Organizational Psychology, 83*(2), 275–300

Thompson, J. A. (2005). Proactive personality and job performance: A social capital perspective. *Journal of Applied Psychology, 90*(5), 1011–1017

Tiger, L. (1979). *The biology of hope.* New York: Simon & Schuster.

Tikkanen, T. (2002). Learning at work in technology intensive environments. *Journal of Workplace Learning, 14*(3), 89–97

Tillé, Y., & Matei, A. (2013). *Sampling: Survey sampling.* R package version 2.6. Retrieved from https://CRAN.R-project.org/package=sampling

Tims, M., & Bakker, A. B. (2010). Job crafting: Towards a new model of individual job redesign. *SA Journal of Industrial Psychology, 36*(2)

Tims, M., Bakker, A. B., & Derks, D. (2012). Development and validation of the job crafting scale. *Journal of Vocational Behavior, 80*(1), 173–186

Tims, M., Bakker, A. B., & Derks, D. (2014). Daily job crafting and the self-efficacy – performance relationship. *Journal of Managerial Psychology, 29*(5), 490–507

Tomaskovic-Devey, D., Leiter, J., & Thompson, S. (1994). Organizational survey nonresponse. *Administrative Science Quarterly, 39*(3), 439–457.

Tornau, K., & Frese, M. (2013). Construct clean-up in proactivity research: A meta-analysis on the nomological net of work-related proactivity concepts and their incremental validities. *Applied Psychology, 62*(1), 44–96

Tschannen-Moran, M., & Hoy Woolfolk, A. (2001). Teacher efficacy: Capturing an elusive construct. *Teaching and Teacher Education, 17*(7), 783–805

Tulving, E. (1972). Episodic and semantic memory. In E. Tulving, & W. Donaldson (Eds.), *Organization of memory* (pp. 381–404). New York: Academic Press.

Tynjälä, P. (2008). Perspectives into learning at the workplace. *Educational Research Review, 3*(2), 130–154

Tynjälä, P. (2013). Toward a 3-P model of workplace learning: A literature review. *Vocations and Learning, 6*(1), 11–36

Tynjälä, P., Nuutinen, A., Eteläpelto, A., Kirjonen, J., & Remes, P. (1997). The acquisition of professional expertise—a challenge for educational research. *Scandinavian Journal of Educational Research, 41*(3), 475–494

Vähäsantanen, K. (2013). *Vocational teachers' professional agency in the stream of change.* Jyväskylä: Jyväskylä University Printing House.

Vähäsantanen, K., & Billett, S. (2008). Negotiating professional identity: Vocational teachers' personal strategies in a reform context. In S. Billett, C. Harteis, & A. Eteläpelto (Eds.), *Emerging perspectives of workplace learning* (pp. 35–49). Rotterdam: Sense Publishers.

Vähäsantanen, K., Hökkä, P., Eteläpelto, A., Rasku-Puttonen, H., & Littleton, K. (2008). Teachers' professional identity negotiations in two different work organisations. *Vocations and Learning, 1*(2), 131–148

Vähäsantanen, K., Paloniemi, S., Hökkä, P., Eteläpelto, A., & Räikkönen, E. (2016). *Professional agency and learning at work: developing a practical assessment tool.* Presentation held at SIG-14 Conference., Regensburg.

Vähäsantanen, K., Saarinen, J., & Eteläpelto, A. (2009). Between school and working life: Vocational teachers' agency in boundary-crossing settings. *International Journal of Educational Research, 48*(6), 395–404

Valecha, G. K., & Ostrom, T. M. (1974). An abbreviated measure of internal-external locus of control. *Journal of Personality Assessment, 38*(4), 369–376

Valentine, J. C., DuBois, D. L., & Cooper, H. (2004). The relation between self-beliefs and academic achievement: A meta-analytic review. *Educational Psychologist, 39*(2), 111–133

Valsiner, J. (1998). *The guided mind: A sociogenetic approach to personality.* Cambridge: Harvard University Press.

van de Wiel, M. W. J., Szegedi, K. H. P., & Weggeman, M. C. D. P. (2004). Professional learning: Deliberate attempts at developing expertise. In H. P. A. Boshuizen, R. Bromme, & H. Gruber (Eds.), *Professional learning: Gaps and transitions on the way from novice to expert* (pp. 181–206). Dordrecht: Kluwer Academic Publishers.

van de Wiel, M. W. J., & Van den Bossche, P. (2013). Deliberate practice in medicine: The motivation to engage in work-related learning and its contribution to expertise. *Vocations and Learning, 6*(1), 135–158

van de Wiel, M. W. J., Van den Bossche, P., Janssen, S., & Jossberger, H. (2011). Exploring deliberate practice in medicine: How do physicians learn in the workplace? *Advances in Health Sciences Education, 16*(1), 81–95

van der Heijden, B., Boon, J., van der Klink, M., & Meijs, E. (2009). Employability enhancement through formal and informal learning: An empirical study among dutch non-academic university staff members. *International Journal of Training and Development, 13*(1), 19–37

van der Rijt, J., van de Wiel, M. W. J., Van den Bossche, P., Segers, M. S. R., & Gijselaers, W. H. (2012). Contextual antecedents of informal feedback in the workplace. *Human Resource Development Quarterly, 23*(2), 233–257

Van Dyne, L., & LePine, J. A. (1998). Helping and voice extra-role behaviors: Evidence of construct and predictive validity. *Academy of Management Journal, 41*(1), 108–119

Van Yperen, N. W., Blaga, M., & Postmes, T. (2014). A meta-analysis of self-reported achievement goals and nonself-report performance across three achievement domains (work, sports, and education). *PLoS ONE, 9*(4), e93594

van Daal, T., Donche, V., & De Maeyer, S. (2014). The impact of personality, goal orientation and self-efficacy on participation of high school teachers in learning activities in the workplace. *Vocations and Learning, 7*(1), 21–40

van Gelderen, M., Frese, M., & Thurik, R. (2000). Strategies, uncertainty and performance of small business startups. *Small Business Economics, 15*(3), 165–181.

van Veldhuizen, B. G. (2011). *Werkend Leren, Lerend Werken Professionele Ontwikkeling van Docenten in Persoonlijk en Organisatieperspectief [Learning while working, working while learning: Professional development of teachers in personal and organizational perspective]* (Doctoral dissertation, Universiteit Utrecht, Utrecht).

van Veldhuizen, B. G., Simons, P. R.-J., & Ritzen, H. (2012). Agency and affordances for work related learning of teachers in middle vocational education. (pp. 1–30). Conference of Deutsche Gesellschaft für Erziehungswissenschaft. Osnabrück.

van Woerkom, M. (2003). *Critical reflection at work: Bridging individual and organisational learning*. Enschede: Twente University Press.

Vandewalle, D. (1997). Development and validation of a work domain goal orientation instrument. *Educational and Psychological Measurement, 57*(6), 995–1015

Velicer, W. F. (1976). Determining the number of components from the matrix of partial correlations. *Psychometrika, 41*(3), 321–327

Vennekel, M. (2000). *Redefinitionsbreite der Arbeitsrolle: Mediator und Moderatoreffekte von Umgebungs- und Personenvariablen. [Breadth of work role: Mediator and moderator effects of person variables and the environment.]* (Doctoral dissertation, University of Giessen, Giessen).

VERBI. (2012). MAXQDA: Software for qualitative data analysis. Berlin: VERBI Software – Consult – Sozialforschung GmbH.

Vessey, I. (1986). Expertise in debugging computer programs: An analysis of the content of verbal protocols. *IEEE Transactions on Systems, Man, and Cybernetics, 16*(5), 621–637

Vinchur, A. J., & Koppes, L. L. (2011). A historical survey of research and practice in industrial and organizational psychology. In S. Zedeck (Ed.), *APA handbook of industrial and organizational psychology, Vol. 1: Building and developing the organization.* (pp. 3–36). Washington: American Psychological Association.

Vygotsky, L. S. (1978). *Mind in society: The development of higher psychological processes* (Reprint) (M. Cole, Ed.). Cambridge: Harvard University Press.

Watkins, D. (2011). Motivation and expectations of German and British nurses embarking on a masters programme. *Nurse Education Today, 31*(1), 31–35

Wehmeyer, M. L. (2004). Beyond self-determination: Causal agency theory. *Journal of Developmental and Physical Disabilities, 16*(4), 337–359

Werner, C. A. (2011). *The older population: 2010. 2010 census briefs.* Washington: US Census Bureau.

Westland, J. C. (2010). Lower bounds on sample size in structural equation modeling. *Electronic Commerce Research and Applications, 9*(6), 476–487

Wetzels, M., Odekerken-Schröder, G., & van Oppen, C. (2009). Using PLS path modeling for assessing hierarchical construct models: Guidelines and empirical illustration. *MIS quarterly, 33*(1), 177–195.

White, R. W. (1959). Motivation reconsidered: The concept of competence. *Psychological Review, 66*(5), 297–333

Widaman, K. F. (1985). Hierarchically nested covariance structure models for multitrait-multimethod data. *Applied Psychological Measurement, 9*(1), 1–26

Williams, L. J., & Brown, B. K. (1994). Method variance in organizational behavior and human resources research: Effects on correlations, path coefficients, and hypothesis testing. *Organizational Behavior and Human Decision Processes, 57*(2), 185–209

Williams, L. J., Cote, J. A., & Buckley, M. R. (1989). Lack of method variance in self-reported affect and perceptions at work: Reality or artifact? *Journal of Applied Psychology, 74*(3), 462–468

Wilson, T. D. (2009). Know thyself. *Perspectives on Psychological Science, 4*(4), 384–389

Winship, C., & Mare, R. D. (1992). Models for sample selection bias. *Annual Review of Sociology, 18*(1), 327–350

Wisnewski, J. (2008). *The politics of agency: Towards a pragmatic approach to philosophical anthropology.* Aldershot: Ashgate Pub. Ltd.

Wood, R., & Bandura, A. (1989). Social cognitive theory of organizational management. *Academy of Management Review, 14*(3), 361–384

Worthington, R. L., & Whittaker, T. A. (2006). Scale development research: A content analysis and recommendations for best practices. *The Counseling Psychologist, 34*(6), 806–838

Wrzesniewski, A., & Dutton, J. E. (2001). Crafting a job: Revisioning employees as active crafters of their work. *Academy of Management Review, 26*(2), 179–201

Yielder, J. (2004). An integrated model of professional expertise and its implications for higher education. *International Journal of Lifelong Education, 23*(1), 60–80

Zagorski, L. (2013). Dispositional optimism. In M. D. Gellman, & J. R. Turner (Eds.), *Encyclopedia of behavioral medicine* (pp. 607–607). New York: Springer.

Zempel, J. (1999). Selbständigkeit in den neuen Bundesländern: Prädiktoren, Erfolgsfaktoren und Folgen – Ergebnisse einer Längsschnittsuntersuchung [Self-dependence in East Germany: Predictors, factors for success, and consequences – Results of a longitudinal study]. In K. Moser, J. Batinic, & J. Zempel (Eds.), *Unternehmerisch erfolgreiches Handeln* (pp. 69–91). Göttingen: Verlag für Angewandte Psychologie.

Zucchermaglio, C., & Alby, F. (2016). Theorizing about practice: Story telling and practical knowledge in cancer diagnoses. *Journal of Workplace Learning, 28*(4), 174–187

# Appendix



The appendix is not included in the printed version of this book. Please visit www.springer.com and search for "Michael Goller" to access the book's appendix under OnlinePlus.

MIX
Papier aus verantwortungsvollen Quellen
Paper from responsible sources
FSC® C105338

If you have any concerns about our products,
you can contact us on
**ProductSafety@springernature.com**

In case Publisher is established outside the EU,
the EU authorized representative is:
**Springer Nature Customer Service Center GmbH**
**Europaplatz 3, 69115 Heidelberg, Germany**

Printed by Libri Plureos GmbH
in Hamburg, Germany